OXFORD HISTORICAL MONOGRAPHS

Religion
in Industrial Society

Oldham and Saddleworth
1740–1865

MARK SMITH

CLARENDON PRESS · OXFORD

1994

Oxford University Press, Walton Street, Oxford OX2 6DP

Oxford New York Toronto
Delhi Bombay Calcutta Madras Karachi
Kuala Lumpur Singapore Hong Kong Tokyo
Nairobi Dar es Salaam Cape Town
Melbourne Auckland Madrid
and associated companies in
Berlin Ibadan

Oxford is a trade mark of Oxford University Press

Published in the United States
by Oxford University Press Inc., New York

British Library Cataloguing in Publication Data
Data available

Library of Congress Cataloging in Publication Data
Smith, Mark (Mark A.)
Religion in industrial society : Oldham and Saddleworth, 1740–1865
/ Mark Smith.
p. cm. — (Oxford historical monographs)
Includes bibliographical references and index.
1. Greater Manchester (England)—Church history—18th century.
2. Greater Manchester (England)—Church history—19th century.
3. Church work with the working class—England—Greater Manchester—History.
4. City churches—England—Greater Manchester—History.
I. Title. II. Series.
BR765.M35S55 1994 274.27'393081—dc20 94–4545

ISBN 0–19–820451–5

1 3 5 7 9 10 8 6 4 2

Typeset by Graphicraft Typesetters, Hong Kong

Printed in Great Britain
on acid-free paper by
Bookcraft Ltd.
Midsomer Norton, Avon

For my parents
and
for Jane

Acknowledgements

I SHOULD like to thank the owners of the manuscript collections listed in the bibliography for permission to use their material, and the archivists, librarians, ministers, and church members who kindly provided me with access. Particular thanks are due to the Baptist Church, Glodwick; the Baptist Church, King Street, Oldham; Cheshire County Council Archives and Local Studies; the Governors of Chetham's Library, Manchester; the Church of England Record Centre; the Congregational Church, Greenacres; the Congregational Church, Middleton; the Vicar, Holy Trinity Church, Waterhead; the Independent Methodist Church, Oldham; the John Rylands Library; the Lancashire Congregational Union Inc.; the County Archivist, Lancashire Record Office; the Librarian, Lambeth Palace Library; the City of Manchester Arts and Leisure Committee, and Jean Ayton and her staff for access to material held in Manchester Public Library (Central), the Moravian Church, Westwood; the Vicar, St Mary with St Peter's Church, Oldham; Oldham Metropolitan Borough Council. The assistance and hospitality provided by Mr Julian Hunt and his staff at Oldham's Local Interest Centre went well beyond the call of duty.

This book grew out of an Oxford D.Phil. thesis, and special thanks are due to my supervisor, John Prest, and my examiners, Geoffrey Rowell and Hugh McLeod, who made many helpful suggestions for revisions. It is a particular pleasure to record my thanks to John Walsh, who first kindled my interest in this field and who has provided much valuable advice during the course of my research. Warm thanks are also due to Anne Gelling and her colleagues at OUP and to the friends who encouraged my endeavours: Arthur Burns, who shared with John Prest the burden of commenting on the penultimate version of my manuscript and who shared with me the fruits of his own research into diocesan reform, Rosemary Chadwick, Martin Davie, Jim Garrard, Grant Gillett, Michael Green, Peter Nockles, and John Wolffe. The completion of this work would have been impossible without the generous support and assistance of my parents, for which I am profoundly grateful. To Jane, who cheerfully accepted the risk of taking on a husband with an unfinished manuscript, I owe most of all.

Mark Smith

Oxford
June 1993

Contents

Abbreviations

ACS	Additional Curates Society	IMGS	Independent Methodist Church, George Street
AM	*Arminian Magazine*		
BFBS	British and Foreign Bible Society	*IMM*	*Independent Methodist Magazine*
BSHS	*Bulletin of the Saddleworth Historical Society*	IMSS	Independent Methodist Church, Smith Street
CBC	Church Building Commissioners	JRL	John Rylands Library, Manchester
CC	Church Commissioners	KSBC	King Street Baptist Church
CCLM	Chetham's College Library, Manchester	LCBA	Lancashire and Cheshire Baptist Association
CDA	Church Defence Association	LCU	Lancashire Congregational Union
CERC	Church of England Record Centre	LPL	Lambeth Palace Library
CPAS	Church Pastoral Aid Society	LRO	Lancashire Record Office
CRO	Chester Record Office	MARC	Methodist Archives and Research Centre
CVR	Chester Visitation Returns	MCC	Middleton Congregational Church
EA	Evangelical Alliance		
EC	Ecclesiastical Commissioners	MHBC	Mills Hill Baptist Church
GCC	Greenacres Congregational Church	*MM*	*Methodist Magazine*
		MNC	Methodist New Connexion
ICBS	Incorporated Church Building Society	*MNCM*	*Methodist New Connexion Conference Minutes*
IMCM	*Independent Methodist Conference Minutes*		

MNM	*Methodist New Connexion Magazine*	UPL	Uppermill Public Library
MPL	Manchester Public Library	USLMM	Union Street, Methodist New Connexion Leaders' Meeting Minutes
NS	National Society		
OLIC	Oldham Local Interest Centre (Now Oldham Local Studies Library)	USMH	Union Street, Methodist New Connexion Church, MS History
PMCM	*Primitive Methodist Conference Minutes*	*WACM*	*Wesleyan Methodist Association Conference Minutes*
PMM	*Primitive Methodist Magazine*	*WAM*	*Wesleyan Methodist Association Magazine*
PMQ	Primitive Methodist Quarter Day Board Minutes	WDM	Wesleyan Manchester District Meeting Minutes
PP	Parliamentary Papers		
RTS	Religious Tract Society	WLMM	Werneth Methodist New Connexion Church Leaders' Meeting Minutes
RVR	Rushton Visitation Returns		
SMC	Salem Moravian Church	*WMCM*	*Wesleyan Methodist Conference Minutes*
SMO	St Mary's, Oldham		
SPCK	Society for the Promotion of Christian Knowledge	WMCSA	Wesleyan Methodist Circuit Steward's Accounts
SPG	Society for the Propagation of the Gospel	*WMM*	*Wesleyan Methodist Magazine*
UMFCCM	*United Methodist Free Church Conference Minutes*	YMCA	Young Men's Christian Association

Introduction

This is a book about churches. It is also about the people who joined and attended churches and what they did there. Its focus, therefore, is different from many accounts of religion and society in industrializing Britain, which have tended to place considerable emphasis on the people who did *not* participate in the activities of organized religion, and have consequently represented the churches as institutions at the outset of a long decline. The notion that the 'modernization' of society is associated with (irreversible) decline in the social significance of religious ideas and institutions has been a sociological commonplace since the early days of the discipline.[1] The notion that the industrialization and urbanization of Britain from the later eighteenth century was associated with an acceleration of this decline has been a commonplace among historians for more than a century. The origins of this historiographical tradition can be traced back to expressions of concern by nineteenth-century churchmen faced with what they feared was a vast growth of irreligion in British towns and cities. This concern seemed amply justified when, in 1851, a census of church attendance appeared to reveal that more than five million people in England and Wales (mainly the urban working classes) habitually neglected public worship. Contemporaries were shocked. Historians were quick to draw conclusions and, as early as 1874, W. N. Molesworth's *History of England* noted that, in the first half of the nineteenth century, 'great masses of the working classes, especially in the large manufacturing towns, were already lost to Christianity'.[2] The tradition of Anglican concern about urban

[1] For an account of the theory of secularization and an application of it to the case of Britain very much in the Weberian tradition, see A. D. Gilbert, *The Making of Post-Christian Britain* (1980). This line of argument has been taken up and refined by a number of sociologists: see especially the work of B. R. Wilson, where secularization is linked with the decline of the face-to-face relationships characteristic of 'community' and the rise of a more impersonal 'society': B. R. Wilson, 'Aspects of Secularization in the West', *Japanese Journal of Religious Studies*, 3/4 (1976), 259–81; *Religion in Sociological Perspective* (Oxford, 1982). A number of sociologists have challenged the usefulness of the theory of secularization, and in particular the notion of its inevitability and irreversibility; see e.g. D. Martin, *The Religious and the Secular* (1969); *A General Theory of Secularization* (Oxford, 1978); also the general discussion in J. Cox, *The English Churches in a Secular Society: Lambeth, 1870–1930* (Oxford, 1982), 8–18.

[2] Quoted in W. O. Chadwick, *The Secularization of the European Mind in the Nineteenth Century* (Cambridge, 1975), 89.

irreligion continued to flourish and in 1957 produced perhaps its most important historical account of the failure of the churches in E. R. Wickham's study of Sheffield, published as *Church and People in an Industrial City*. Wickham's views have been influential both in the theology of industrial mission and in the historiography of eighteenth- and nineteenth-century England. Echoes of his approach can be detected in the Church of England's report on *Faith in the City* (1985), and his conclusions have been taken up and elaborated in a number of widely read accounts of the progress of religion in England.[3]

Subsequent work has differed in emphasis from Wickham's and occasionally modified his conclusions, but when considered as a whole it reveals a common view of the historical fortunes of the churches—recently characterized by Callum Brown as the pessimistic thesis. From the mid-eighteenth century, it is contended, a sustained population rise, particularly in the Midlands and the north of England, began seriously to embarrass an Established Church whose resources had for centuries been concentrated in the south of the country to match the rather different population distributions of the Middle Ages. The Church's position had already been seriously weakened by the Toleration Act of 1689, which removed its legal monopoly, and its problems became particularly acute as industrialization and urbanization freed people from the bonds of traditional society and brought them together in numbers which overwhelmed the existing facilities for public worship and religious supervision. Hampered by a combination of legal restrictions and its own corruption and complacency, the Church adapted only slowly to the new conditions. By the 1820s and 1830s, when its institutional regeneration was stimulated by state aid and a series of centrally directed reforms imposed by the authority of Parliament, Anglicanism had already forfeited its traditional position as 'the church of the people'. Into the resulting vacuum rushed a variety of nonconformist churches which developed a special appeal to the new urban middle class, the more respectable artisans, and, for a brief period, a wider range of working people who found in the chapels a substitute for organic communities disintegrated by the process of urbanization. The majority of the working classes, however, escaped the lure of both the nonconformists and the revived Anglican

---

[3] On the general influence of Wickham, see J. Morris, 'Church and People Thirty-Three Years On: A Historical Critique', *Theology*, 94 (1991), 92–10; K. S. Inglis, *Churches and the Working Classes in Victorian England* (1963); A. D. Gilbert, *Religion and Society in Industrial England: Church, Chapel and Social Change 1740–1914* (1976).

Church to form that vast multitude of the 'spiritually destitute' which so concerned Victorian observers.[4]

Although the 'pessimistic thesis' continues to be reproduced in general works on the nineteenth century,[5] it has recently come under vigorous challenge. Jeffrey Cox, examining churches in Lambeth, Hugh McLeod, summarizing oral evidence relating to the turn of the century, and Callum Brown, describing the experience of the Scottish churches, have all pointed to the vitality of religious life in the late nineteenth century and the enormous social influence exercised by religious organizations. They have consequently suggested that the notion of significant secularization of English society should be relocated from the end of the eighteenth century to the end of the nineteenth or even the beginning of the twentieth.[6]

Most of this revisionist work has concentrated on the late Victorian period. The present study seeks to re-evaluate the 'pessimistic thesis' during the period to which it has primarily been applied—the second half of the eighteenth century and the first half of the nineteenth century. It operates through the medium of a local study of the industrial town of Oldham in south-east Lancashire and the industrial villages of the neighbouring district of Saddleworth in south-west Yorkshire. The study opens with a brief sketch of the economic and social context within which the churches had to operate. This is based in part on the pioneering work of John Foster, whose controversial interpretation of society and politics in Oldham has sparked a lively debate on the development of the town.[7] The next four chapters are devoted to a discussion of the fortunes of the churches. Chapter 2 looks at the Established Church in its 'unreformed' period prior to 1830 and questions the notion that it failed to adapt successfully to the new conditions. Chapter 3 examines the same Church

---

[4] Significant contributions to this view include: O. J. Brose, *Church and Parliament: The Reshaping of the Church of England 1828–1860* (London, 1959); K. A. Thompson, *Bureaucracy and Church Reform: The Organizational Response of the Church of England to Social Change 1800–1965* (Oxford, 1970); Gilbert, *Religion and Society*. It also underlies more general accounts, including: G. I. T. Machin, *Politics and the Churches in Great Britain 1832–1868* (Oxford, 1977); W. O. Chadwick, *The Victorian Church*, 3rd edn. (1971), i.

[5] H. Perkin, *The Origins of Modern English Society, 1780–1880* (1969); N. Gash, *Aristocracy and People: Britain 1815–1865* (1979); E. Royle, *Modern Britain: A Social History 1750–1985* (1987); R. Brown, *Church and State in Modern Britain 1700–1850* (1991).

[6] Cox, *English Churches*; H. McLeod, 'New Perspectives on Victorian Working-Class Religion: The Oral Evidence', *Oral History Journal*, 14 (1986), 31–49; C. G. Brown, *The Social History of Religion in Scotland since 1730* (1987). Brown has recently extended his work in a wide ranging article: 'Did Urbanization Secularize Britain?', *Urban History Yearbook* (1988), 1–14.

[7] J. O. Foster, *Class Struggle and the Industrial Revolution: Early Industrial Capitalism in Three English Towns* (1974).

in the period of 'institutional renewal' from 1830 to 1865, discussing the advantages and disadvantages of the central reforms and the growth of Evangelical influence among the clergy. The fourth chapter is concerned with the development of the Dissenting churches, which first began to make a significant impact in Oldham and Saddleworth at the beginning of the nineteenth century, and Chapter 5 examines the growth of the most vigorous and the most fissiparous of the nonconformist churches—the various branches of Methodism. This structure makes it possible to trace in detail the pattern of development of each group of churches in Oldham and Saddleworth, examining the different problems they faced, the distinctive approaches they adopted, and their degree of success in the new industrial environment. It also reveals, in a cumulative fashion, the extent to which all the local churches faced the same problems, found the same solutions, and participated in a common evangelical culture. The sixth chapter discusses the way in which the churches related to each other, challenging the traditional view that a pattern of interdenominational conflict predominated, and suggesting instead that the churches coexisted in a mixture of co-operation and competition contained within a broad evangelical consensus. A final chapter considers the impact of the various churches on the society of Oldham and Saddleworth and concludes that they were more successful as institutions and also more generally influential than is suggested by the proponents of the 'pessimistic thesis'.

Clearly, no local study can provide conclusive evidence about the general success of the churches during the industrial revolution. It is bound, in particular, to fail to do justice to the spiritual experience of ordinary church members and adherents, concerning which clear evidence is difficult to come by. Similarly, the reasons for church growth most commonly given by participants—a combination of their own labours in the Gospel and divine grace mediated through 'special providences' and outpourings of the Holy Spirit—tend from the external perspective available to their historian to be seen at best 'as through a glass darkly'. There is a tendency, therefore, to undervalue those elements in the situation which contemporaries felt were the most important, not out of any conscious reductionism, but because of the nature of the evidence; because, as Owen Chadwick has noted in another context, 'measuring tithe is easier for the historian than measuring the inside of John Stuart Mill'.[8] Thus it is well at the outset to acknowledge that this account of the social history of the churches does not pretend to provide an exhaustive account

---

[8] Chadwick, *Secularization*, 14.

of their internal dynamics. Neither, in a country with so many diverse regional religious cultures, can any local study genuinely claim to be typical. It can, however, represent what was possible to the churches, and, even in the rather difficult circumstances of Oldham and Saddleworth between 1740 and 1865, this turns out to have been a very great deal.

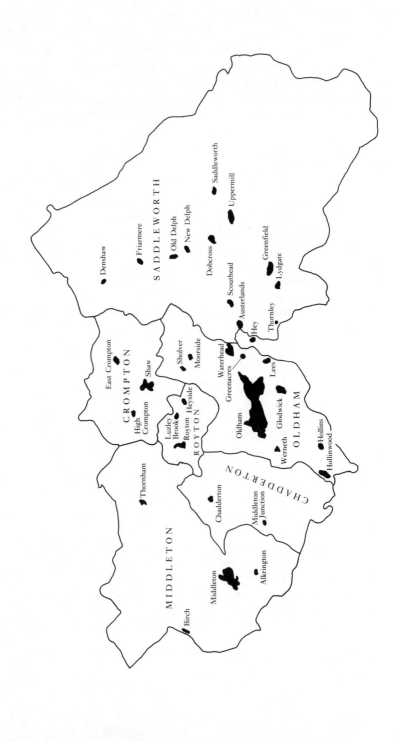

1. *An Industrial Society*

In the early eighteenth century the township of Oldham, situated on a bleak ridge emerging from the western slopes of the Pennines, was the market centre for a scatter of small villages and farmsteads spreading north and south over the adjacent moorland, and west towards the lower ground of the Lancashire plain. To the east, straggling along the course of the upper reaches of the River Tame and nestling in the moorland valleys of its tributaries, lay a galaxy of small hamlets, known collectively as Saddleworth. Each of these settlements had its own name, local character, and a burgeoning communal identity, reflected in the rhythms of what was still partly an agricultural economy. It is with the people of these communities, amalgamated into the Poor Law Unions of Oldham and Saddleworth under the legislation of 1834, that this study is concerned.

People and Communities

In 1725 a combination of farming and domestic industry supported a population of at most 5,000 in the future Oldham Union, and perhaps 1,500 in that of Saddleworth. This population seems to have increased steadily until the third quarter of the eighteenth century, and at an increased rate thereafter in the wake of the mechanization of the local textile industry. The population of the Oldham Union reached over 26,000 in 1801, and had risen dramatically to around 120,000 in 1865. The demographic change in Saddleworth, while less spectacular, was still substantial, the total population rising from over 10,000 in 1801 to almost 19,000 in 1865.[1] In the early stages at least, this growth in population did not lead to any significant increase in its nucleation. As Wadsworth and Mann pointed out, 'the increase in the population of Lancashire was not so much an urban increase as a thickening of the population over the countryside, particularly in the manufacturing districts'.[2] However, from the third decade of the nineteenth century onwards, a shift in the

---

[1] Table 1.1; A. P. Wadsworth and J. L. Mann, *The Cotton Trade and Industrial Lancashire 1600–1780* (Manchester, 1937), 315.

[2] Ibid. 311.

TABLE 1.1. *The population of Oldham and Saddleworth 1714–1871*

Date	Oldham central township	Oldham out-townships	Oldham Poor Law Union	Saddleworth Poor Law Union	Oldham and Saddleworth Poor Law Unions
1714			3,615		
1726				1,500	
1778			9,850		
1782				6,918	
1789			14,026		
1792			15,776		
1801	12,024	14,662	26,646	10,665	37,311
1811	16,690	19,784	36,474	12,579	49,053
1821	21,662	25,477	47,139	13,902	61,041
1831	32,381	28,657	61,038	15,986	77,024
1841	42,595	29,813	72,408	16,829	89,237
1851	52,820	33,968	86,788	17,799	104,587
1861	72,333	38,943	111,276	18,631	129,927
1871	82,629	44,353	126,982	19,923	146,905

Sources: E. Baines, *History, Directory and Gazetteer of the County Palatine of Lancaster*, ii (Liverpool, 1825); M. Brierley, *Outlines of the History of Saddleworth* (Manchester, 1883); C. E. Halbert (ed.), *The Jubilee Celebration of the Charter of Incorporation* (Oldham, 1899); E. Butterworth, *Historical Notices of the Town and Parish of Middleton* (Middleton, 1840), 36–8; Published Census Returns: PP 1852–3, lxxxvi pts. 1 and 2 [1632], Census of Great Britain; PP 1863, liii pts. 1 and 2 [3221], Census of England and Wales (1861); PP 1872, lxvi pt 2 [*c*.676–I], Census of England and Wales, 1871.

distribution of population between the central township of Oldham and its surrounding out-townships became increasingly visible.

Until the late 1820s, at least half of the population of the Oldham Poor Law Union lived in the four out-townships of Middleton, Chadderton, Royton, and Crompton, but thereafter the twin divisions of 'Oldham above town' and 'Oldham below town', which together took in the central built-up area, assumed a greater importance. At the 1831 census they accounted for a majority of the population for the first time, and by 1865 the proportion had risen to almost two-thirds. There is, however, little evidence of any significant depopulation in the out-townships. Their rate of growth slowed, and there were individual fluctuations, but the total for the four showed an increase at each census, and a general recovery was underway by the 1840s.[3] Moreover, the divisions of Oldham above and below town included not only the central built-up area, but also a ring of smaller settlements separated by stretches of open moorland like the villages of Lees, Waterhead, and Greenacres to the east of the town, and the mining settlement of Glodwick to the south. It was, therefore, not until the late 1850s at the earliest that a clear majority of the population lived in the more truly urban environment of the town centre.[4] In Saddleworth the population increase did produce a heightened level of nucleation, as the settlements nearer the valley bottom—like Delph and Uppermill—and those nearer to Oldham—like Springhead—expanded faster than their less-favourably placed neighbours. However, no settlement achieved a dominant position in the district, which retained its traditional ecology as a collection of distinct industrial villages.[5]

Demographic change produced a considerable increase in the size of the central township, but did not destroy the ring of communities in its vicinity. Oldham grew, not by a simple advance of its borders, submerging the adjacent villages, but by a process of agglomeration as those settlements themselves expanded to meet the encroaching central township. Only in the second half of the nineteenth century were they completely absorbed, by a gradual process of infill, into the central mass, and even then they retained much of their own identity. This process of geographical development suggests that, even as far as the central township was concerned, Oldham developed less as a monolithic whole than as a patchwork of residential neighbourhood communities.[6] A high level of 'residential persistence' is usually regarded as essential to the viability of community life, and certainly there is little sign of any massive influx of long-distance migrants which might have disrupted the stability of Oldham's neighbourhoods. Foster's sample of heads of household from the 1851-census enumerators' books yielded a total of 61 per cent born within three miles of their current residence, and only 12 per cent who had migrated from a distance of more than twenty miles, including 2 per cent born in Ireland. Long-distance migrants never formed a large proportion of the local population, and even after the large-scale migrations of the 1840s and 1850s the Irish made up only about 7 per cent of the total in Oldham and 2 per cent of the total in Saddleworth.[7] It is difficult to be certain

---

[3] Table 1.1.   [4] Table 1.1. See also Foster, *Class Struggle*, 79, 84.
[5] D. Newton, 'Aspects of Historical Geography in the Saddleworth Area', BA thesis (Durham, 1971), 55–60.
[6] R. Dennis, *English Industrial Cities of the Nineteenth Century: A Social Geography* (Cambridge, 1984), 250–69.
[7] Foster, *Class Struggle*, 77, 244, 333; PP 1863, liii pt. 2 [3221], Census of England and Wales (1861), 731.

about the extent to which this stability was reflected in terms of residential persistence, though it seems unlikely that, in a town where private-rented housing predominated, many families remained at the same address for any length of time. Nevertheless, there is no reason to believe that Oldham was not characterized by the pattern of short-distance moves within a fairly small area, traced in other nineteenth-century towns, and consequently low rates of persistence at the same address need not have disrupted residential communities based on a neighbourhood. It is, moreover, open to question whether a high rate of persistence for the general population was necessary for the maintenance of a communal identity, so long as a central core of people remained rooted in the neighbourhood.[8]

Neighbourhood identity in Oldham and Saddleworth was manifested in a number of ways. Some neighbourhoods were differentiated by their physical appearance, others were defined by a range of features including streams, main roads, and belts of land given up exclusively to industrial use. Given the small size of the town, these must have served primarily as psychological rather than physical barriers and boundaries.[9] Many social organizations were based firmly on the neighbourhood, and friendly societies in particular tended to recruit on a community rather than on a trade basis. Radical politics, too, was sheltered by local communal solidarities, and some villages, like Lees and Royton, became notorious for their political activity.[10] However, perhaps the clearest indicator of the persistence of strong neighbourhood identities in Oldham was the vitality of the local wakes tradition. The annual wakes was the chief public holiday in south-east Lancashire, at the centre of which stood the rush-cart ceremony, originating in the need to cover church floors with fresh rushes each year. The rushes were brought on carts from each neighbourhood—symbols of local pride and identity, guarded by the local youth—and fights over precedence frequently broke out between rival parties moving towards the church.[11] Local employers bowed before the

---

[8] C. G. Pooley, 'Residential Mobility in the Victorian City', *Transactions of the Institute of British Geographers*, NS 4 (1979), 258–77; Dennis, 'Intercensal Mobility in a Victorian City', *Transactions of the Institute of British Geographers*, NS 2 (1977), 349–63; M. Anderson, *Family Structure in Nineteenth Century Lancashire* (Cambridge, 1971), 101–6. For an example of the persistence of community life under similar conditions in later nineteenth century New York see H. McLeod, 'The "Golden Age" of New York City Catholicism', in J. Garnett and C. Matthew (eds.), *Revival and Religion since 1700* (1993), 251–3.

[9] The role of such barriers in defining areas within towns is discussed in H. Carter, *The Study of Urban Geography*, 3rd edn. (1981), ch. 14.

[10] Foster, *Class Struggle*, 142, 217; D. S. Gadian, 'Class Formation and Class Action in North-West Industrial Towns, 1830–50', in R. J. Morris (ed.), *Class, Power and Social Structure in British Nineteenth-Century Towns* (Leicester, 1986), 51–2.

[11] e.g. Oldham Local Interest Centre (OLIC), Rowbottom Diary, Aug. 1810.

power of this communal tradition, closing their mills and legitimizing the wakes as formal holidays.[12] Oldham Wakes itself was the highlight of the summer, receiving rush-carts from the out-townships and from some two dozen hamlets and villages throughout the district. Robert Poole has noted that Northmoor and Greenacres Moor—localities completely absorbed within the central built-up area—were particularly consistent in sending carts during the early nineteenth century. Perhaps they felt all the more need to advertise their neighbourhood identities when no longer separated from the rest of the town by open ground. Although the local wakes began to decline with the coming of the cheap day rail trip to Blackpool in the 1850s, this seems to have affected the smaller district fairs more than the central Oldham one, which actually continued to expand, and was still receiving rush-carts in the early 1860s, while the day trips themselves became occasions for communal and familial celebration.[13]

If the settlements of the central township were characterized by a prominent sense of neighbourhood identity, this was even more true of the out-townships. The village of Middleton had a particularly strong local identity—well chronicled by its most famous inhabitant, Samuel Bamford—and possessed a powerful wakes tradition of its own which, according to Walton and Poole, 'expressed family, village and parish identity through conviviality and ceremony', providing 'a legitimate outlet for conflicts between individuals and groups and an opportunity for the display of skills, hospitality, and possessions'.[14] The other out-townships also displayed strong local identities, particularly Crompton, whose annual wakes regularly attracted up to nine rush-carts from outlying hamlets. Much the same pattern could be found in Saddleworth, whose villages were federated in four districts or 'meres', and subject to intense rivalries, which occasionally issued in pitched battles.[15]

Although neighbourhood loyalties seem to have been particularly strong within Oldham, there is also clear evidence of a more general identification with a wider residential community based on the town as a whole. This continued to be expressed in the traditional rhythms of riot and festival,

[12] J. K. Walton and R. Poole, 'The Lancashire Wakes in the Nineteenth Century', in R. Storch (ed.), *Popular Culture and Custom in Nineteenth Century England* (1982), 115; J. Rule, *The Labouring Classes in Early Industrial England 1750–1850* (1986), 137.

[13] R. Poole, 'Oldham Wakes', in J. K. Walton and J. Walvin (eds.), *Leisure in Great Britain 1780–1939* (Manchester, 1983), 73, 81–93.

[14] S. Bamford, *Passages in the Life of a Radical* (Heywood, 1842), and *Early Days* (1849), *passim*; Walton and Poole, 'Lancashire Wakes', 101.

[15] G. Allen, *Notes on Shaw Church in Byegone Days* (York, 1907), 13–14; *Manchester Mercury*, 29 Apr. 1826. For similarly persistent solidarities in the out-townships of Leeds, described as 'communities within a community', see R. J. Morris, *Class, Sect and Party: The Making of the British Middle Class: Leeds, 1820–50* (Manchester, 1990), 51–3.

and, though neighbourhood identity had, by its very nature, to be expressed in contradistinction to the rest of the town, some occasions, such as the local wakes, managed to affirm the identity of both simultaneously.[16] At the opposite end of the scale it is probable that there was a sense of common identity based on the street or the court in the built-up areas, and the group of farmsteads or isolated fold of houses in the hinterland beyond the central township. It is arguable that these communities, based on the everyday interactions of people who shared the same facilities for drawing and disposing of water, who met at the same corner shop, and who were available as neighbours to lend an additional cooking pot, mend a broken shuttle, or to bicker with about the activities of their respective children, may have been the most significant social groups of all, especially for mothers, children, and domestic outworkers. This sort of community was celebrated in much of the local dialect literature of the nineteenth century, perhaps most notably in the poetry of Sam Laycock.[17]

The strength of residential communities in the mid-nineteenth century has led James Walvin to suggest that 'in the factory towns . . . the nature and quality of community life was much more that of a village than of a city'.[18] This analysis seems to fit the development of Oldham much better than Koditschek's picture of Bradford, where, it is suggested, early nineteenth-century urbanization destroyed the infrastructure of community, creating in its place an anomic environment which reified the 'antagonistic impersonality' of the new industrial relations of production.[19] In Oldham and Saddleworth, by contrast, the dramatic social and economic changes of the century after 1760 were played out against a background of continuity and growth in local neighbourhood identities. Local workers, therefore, did not face the associated problems in enforced anomic isolation. The persistence of communal solidarities provided both a secure base for protest at social and economic change and, especially as local neighbourhoods became more socially homogeneous, a framework round which new class-based identities began gradually to cohere.

Economic Change

At the beginning of the eighteenth century, the majority of the local population supported themselves by a combination of domestic manufacture

[16] Rowbottom Diary, 1787–1830.
[17] e.g. S. Laycock, 'Bowton's Yard', in J. Bennett (ed.), *Lancashire Miscellany* (Oldham, 1980), 93–6.
[18] J. Walvin, *English Urban Life 1776–1851* (1984), 45.
[19] T. Koditschek, *Class Formation and Urban–Industrial Society: Bradford 1750–1850* (Cambridge, 1990), 65, 79–85, 429.

and subsistence agriculture. The production of woollen textiles had been the mainstay of this economy for well over a century before 1700, and it was to retain its pre-eminent position until about 1740. Then, first in Oldham and later in the western half of Saddleworth, it was overtaken by a variety of other activities. Fustians and other cotton–linen mixes intended for the expanding Manchester markets provided the first significant alternative to wool, and then, in their turn, they were displaced by the production of pure cotton textiles. The cotton and cotton–linen manufacture, which was organized on a putting-out basis both by resident clothiers and by Manchester merchants, grew steadily in the middle years of the eighteenth century, assisted by the widespread adoption of the fly-shuttle and other technological developments which increased the productive capacity of the weavers. The same period also saw a diversification of the local economy with the development of hat-making, conducted in small workshops, and the first serious attempts to exploit the area's more accessible coal deposits. The rapid population growth of the final quarter of the century was associated with a quickening of the pace of industrial development. For textile producers, the position was transformed by the mechanization of cotton-spinning on Hargreaves's jenny. According to Butterworth, the jenny was adopted enthusiastically in Oldham, cotton 'became the almost universal material for employment', and consequently woollen textile production had disappeared almost completely by 1790. Led by the new cotton textiles, the economy as a whole began to grow. Coal-mining, organized by some of the largest local landowners, became much more extensive, the number of pits increasing from fourteen in 1771 to around thirty-seven in 1832, and the same period also saw the development of Oldham's first giant capitalist enterprise—the Clegg and Henshaw hatting concern.[20]

Perhaps the most significant change at the turn of the century was the development of new varieties of industrial organization. In the mid-eighteenth century, woollen textile manufacture had been carried out almost exclusively in the homes of domestic outworkers, together with a handful of small-scale loom shops, and perhaps a dozen mills specializing in preparatory and finishing processes. The introduction of the jenny was associated with a proliferation of workshops for cotton and cotton–linen production and the introduction of mills applying horse or water power to spin cotton on the larger jennies or Arkwright water frames. In

[20] E. Butterworth, *Historical Sketches of Oldham* (Oldham, 1856), 93–123; K. McPhillips, *Oldham, the Formative Years* (Swinton, 1981), 16.

Saddleworth, too, where woollen manufacture still retained much of its old importance, patterns of industrial organization may have changed as the owners of fulling and scribbling mills began to develop a more widespread putting-out system at the expense of the semi-independent small clothiers. The first decades of the nineteenth century saw the handicraft economy reach its zenith in Oldham and Saddleworth. The introduction of Crompton's mule and the application of steam power from the late 1790s onwards led to a proliferation of small factories producing cotton yarn. In 1811 there were some forty-two mills of both the Crompton and Arkwright varieties, and by 1820, according to Foster's estimate, there were approximately 500 adult men working in the mills, together with perhaps 2,000 women and children. However, the plentiful supply of cotton yarn also provoked a dramatic increase in the number of handloom weavers, with the result that they continued to outnumber the factory workers by as much as eight to one.[21]

Although hand-working remained strong in some of the traditional craft-based trades like shoemaking and metal-working, which continued to be organized on a workshop basis, the gradual mechanization of weaving in the 1820s and 1830s produced, with the eclipse of the domestic system, a fundamental change in the nature of the local textile industry. Cotton handloom weaving, at its peak only twenty years before had virtually disappeared by the end of the 1830s, and Foster has calculated that by 1841 Oldham's cotton mills were employing some 14,000 out of a total labour force of 26,000. The mid-1840s also saw the decline of the other great source of local handicraft work—the hatting industry. In the first decade of the nineteenth century, the partnership of Henshaw, Barker, and Hadfield had employed some 300 hatters in its town-centre works, easily the largest single production unit in the area, as well as promoting an extensive putting-out system. However, the new popularity of silk hats caused a severe reduction in the demand for the local fur-based product. A. B. Reach, the correspondent of the *Morning Chronicle*, found 'a vast number' of unemployed hatters when he visited the town in 1849, and by 1861 the work-force had fallen from its peak of around 3,000 to less than 500.[22] To some extent the expansion of coal-mining in response to the

[21] Butterworth, *Oldham*, 98–148; B. Barnes, 'Early Woollen Mills in a Pennine Parish: Saddleworth and the Upper Tame Valley', *Bulletin of the Saddleworth Historical Society*, 13 (1983), 30; M. T. Wild, 'The Saddleworth Parish Registers', *Textile History*, 1 (1969), 223; Foster, *Class Struggle*, 9, 79; M. Berg, *The Age of Manufactures* (1985), 207–33.

[22] Foster, *Class Struggle*, 80; Butterworth, *Oldham*, 154; E. Butterworth, *A Statistical Sketch of the County Palatine of Lancaster* (1841), 99; H. Bateson, *A History of Oldham* (Oldham, 1949), 88; J. Ginswick (ed.), *Labour and the Poor in England and Wales 1849–1851* (1983), 93; PP 1863, liii pt. 2 [3221], Census of England and Wales (1861), tables 13–16.

demand created by the new steam engines compensated for the decline in handicraft-working in textiles and hatting. However, the exhaustion of the most accessible seams meant that it became necessary to sink deeper pits, giving greater prominence to the firms with large capitals like the great Evans, Lees, and Jones combine. If Foster's estimate of a colliery work-force of 1,600 men in the early 1840s is correct, then almost 53 per cent of the total must have been employed by the combine, which succeeded in maintaining its dominant position in local coal production until after the end of the period.[23]

The most important economic development of the 1840s was the growth, from a flourishing base of small subcontracting firms mainly occupied in servicing the machinery operated by the surrounding mills, of a new machine-making industry dominated by a few very large enterprises. Located in the Soho region at the eastern end of the central township, the three largest firms were together employing some 1,150 workers by the early 1840s. In 1844 one of these firms, the Hibbert and Platt partnership, established a new factory on a site adjacent to the recently constructed railway and assumed a leading role, first in the machine-making sector, and then in the local economy as a whole.[24] According to D. A. Farnie:

No other firm approached it in its range of machines, including power looms from 1857 or in its speed of expansion of production . . . During the 1840s Platt's became the largest employer of labour in Oldham: during the 1850s it became the largest machine making firm in the world as well as 'the largest manufacturing establishment in Great Britain'. Its hands increased in number from 400 in 1837 to 6,000 in 1870.[25]

From the mid-nineteenth century Platt's became the linchpin of Oldham's economic development, and the close integration of machine-making with the town's textile-manufacturing industry added greatly to the stability of the local economy.

The period after 1840, therefore, saw the rise of the large enterprise in engineering and to a lesser extent in coal-mining. However, this pattern was not replicated in the textile sector, in which Oldham became the major centre for the subsidiary processes of yarn-doubling and the spinning of cotton waste. Many of the firms operating these processes were very small, and the average work-force even of the mainline cotton firms was

[23] Foster, *Class Struggle*, 294–5; PP 1842, xvii [382], Appendix to the First Report of Commissioners (Mines), 819–60.

[24] Foster, *Class Struggle*, 225; Butterworth, *Oldham*, 184–5.

[25] D. A. Farnie, 'The Emergence of Victorian Oldham as the Centre of the Cotton Spinning Industry', *Bulletin of the Saddleworth Historical Society*, 12 (1982), 48.

smaller than in most other comparable towns.[26] The majority of Oldhams's textile employers remained petty capitalists, and Reach noted in 1846 that 'In Oldham there are a great number of small capitalists renting floors or small portions of factories. These employers have generally risen from the mule or the loom, and maintain in a great degree their operative appearance, thought and habits.'[27] Although most of Oldham's textile employers belonged to this class, the majority of textile workers were employed neither by these men, nor by the owners of the town's handful of large combined spinning and weaving firms, but by small- to medium-sized firms employing between 50 and 250 workers each. These already employed a clear majority of cotton workers in 1841 and, after the depression of 1846–8, played a major role in a further rapid expansion of the industry, which saw an increase in productive capacity from one million to three million spindles by 1866. As a consequence, in 1863 Oldham ranked fourth in a list of eighteen towns produced by the factory inspectorate in terms of the size of its textile work-force, but only twelfth in terms of the average size of work-force per firm.[28] The average size of production units in Saddleworth's textile industry was even smaller. By 1838 there were fifty-seven woollen mills employing a total of 1,288 workers, and thirty-nine cotton mills employing together a work-force of 2,201, giving an average of twenty-three workers a mill in wool, fifty-six in cotton, and thirty-six overall.[29] Oldham and Saddleworth, therefore, clearly illustrate Farnie's conclusion that 'The representative unit of enterprise in the cotton industry was the small rather than the large firm and the representative employer was a yeoman of industry rather than a captain of industry.'[30]

Despite the rapid growth in textile-manufacturing after mechanization, perhaps the most salient feature of its development was its relative decline as a source of employment compared to other sectors of the economy. In Saddleworth during the last quarter of the eighteenth century about 85

---

[26] R. A. Sykes, 'Some Aspects of Working-Class Consciousness in Oldham 1830–1842', *Historical Journal*, 23 (1980), 168–9; D. S. Gadian, 'Class Consciousness in Oldham and other North-West Industrial Towns 1830–1850', *Historical Journal*, 21 (1978), 168–70.

[27] Ginswick, *Labour and the Poor*, 93.

[28] Foster, *Class Struggle*, 81; Farnie, 'Victorian Oldham' 42; PP 1864, xxii [3309], Reports of the Inspectors of Factories to Her Majesty's Principal Secretary of State for the Home Department for the half-year ending 31 October 1863, 16–35.

[29] B. Barnes, 'The Upper Tame Valley', BA thesis (Manchester, 1957), 17; PP 1842, xxii [31], Reports of the Inspectors of Factories for the half-year ending 31 December 1841, 66–80.

[30] D. A. Farnie, *The English Cotton Industry and the World Market 1815–1896* (Oxford, 1979), 209.

TABLE 1.2. *Employment of adult males in Oldham and Saddleworth, by Industry, 1861*

Industry	Oldham (%)	Saddleworth (%)
Textiles	37.0	54.6
Retail	5.6	4.5
Metal and engineering	13.0	0.5
Transport	3.5	1.4
Coal	6.8	1.9
Hatting	1.2	0.0
Craft	16.2	13.8
Farm	5.4	7.4
Professional	3.4	3.2
Domestic service	0.6	0.4
Other	7.3	12.3
TOTAL	100.0	100.0

Source: PP 1863, liii pt. 2 [3221].

per cent of the adult male population considered their primary occupation to be textile production. In Oldham, already a more diverse economy, the corresponding figure was 55.5 per cent. By 1861 these figures had fallen to 54.6 and 37 per cent respectively, reflecting not just the rise of coal and engineering, but also the continuing vitality of older, craft-based trades like shoemaking.[31] This development tends to reinforce D. S. Gadian's view that one must beware of an overemphasis on the role of the factory proletariat during the 1840s in an Oldham in which small-scale units of production were prevalent and in which a significant proportion of adult males were still engaged in workshop-based trades.[32] This position persisted into the 1860s in a local economy which continued to exhibit what Patrick Joyce had described as archaism: 'the persistence of small scale unmechanised sectors, and the primitive organisation of the supposedly "modern" large scale, increasingly mechanised sectors.'[33]

[31] Calculated from the estimates based on Parish Registers made in Wild, 'Saddleworth Parish Registers', 221, and in Wadsworth and Mann, *Cotton Trade*, 315; Table 1.2.

[32] Gadian, 'Class Consciousness', 169.

[33] P. Joyce, 'Labour Capital and Compromise: A Response to Richard Price', *Social History*, 9 (1984), 68.

The impact of mechanization and industrial growth on local communities was complex. At first, reliance on water power and the expansion of handloom weaving favoured growth in the outlying areas of Oldham and its out-townships, and the early nineteenth century saw not only continued population growth in these areas, but also the development of a degree of industrial specialization in some villages. The populations of Hollins and Glodwick, for example, were employed mainly in local collieries, while the Middleton out-township became a centre of silk textile production, in which handloom weaving continued to flourish until after the middle of the nineteenth century.[34] However, as already noted, the more thorough-going mechanization of the period after 1830 was associated with the greater relative growth of larger, valley-bottom settlements in Saddleworth, and of Oldham's central township, which was transformed from a small market town (which in 1824 still contained patches of cultivated ground within its boundaries) into a more densely packed industrial settlement surrounded by a ring of suburbs straggling across the newly enclosed moorland.[35]

While it is important not to underestimate the difficult physical conditions in which much domestic industry was carried on, it is probable that this new industrialization was accompanied by a deterioration in both the living and the working conditions of the mass of the population. This deterioration seems to have been particularly severe in the central township, with its concentration of new enterprises supported by small capitals which left little to spare for workplace improvements. Reach commented on what appeared to be a 'chronic system of dirt and neglect' and described one of Oldham's candlewick mills as, 'out of all sight, the most repulsive working place I have seen in Lancashire'. He also remarked on the unhealthy appearance of many of the millworkers and on the prevalence of respiratory disease.[36] The provision of a relatively clean water supply probably helped to spare Oldham from the cholera epidemics which ravaged other industrial towns in the mid-nineteenth century, but deaths from tuberculosis in the early 1850s were twice the national average, infant mortality was high, and life expectancy at birth was only thirty-three years for boys and thirty-five for girls compared with averages for England and Wales of forty-one and forty-three respectively.[37] The prevalence of disease was a product not just of poor working conditions,

---

[34] OLIC, Microfilm, St Margaret's, Hollinwood, Baptism Register; Ginswick, *Labour and the Poor*, 102–12.

[35] Butterworth, *Oldham*, 189–90.

[36] Ginswick, *Labour and the Poor*, 93–101.   [37] Foster, *Class Struggle*, 92–3.

but also of the general character of the urban environment. Samuel Bamford described the Oldham of the early 1840s as 'a multitude of human dwellings crowded round huge factories, whose high taper funnels vomit clouds of darkening smoke',[38] while 'the general appearance of the operatives' housing', noted Reach in his report to the *Morning Chronicle*, 'is filthy and smouldering. Airless little back streets and close nasty courts are common.' The cellar-dwellings and lodging houses in which many of the poorest members of the population lived were potentially even worse.[39]

However, while Oldham shared with the Bradford described by Koditschek an experience of environmental deterioration, this strained rather than destroyed the cohesion of neighbourhood communities. Even the decline in handicraft production, which meant that a greater propor-tion of the population had to work away from home, does not seem to have produced any general loosening of communal ties. Most people probably continued to live close to their place of work and, as Joyce has demonstrated, the new factories played an important part in reinforcing neighbourhood identities.[40] The persistence of these solidarities in Oldham and Saddleworth played a part in easing the impact of the poverty ex-perienced by much of the local population in the first half of the nineteenth century. Reach noticed that this poverty afflicted handloom weavers, unemployed hatters, and Irish labourers with particular severity. Foster has drawn attention to more widespread if less intense economic difficul-ties that led commonly, even in good years, to the formation of combined households with relatives, in order to ease the passage of the family through the vulnerable period when the children were themselves too young to work and child-bearing kept their mother out of the mill.[41] This practice may in itself have reinforced communal feeling, as the ties of kinship helped to turn mere neighbouring into neighbourliness.[42] Never-theless, poverty and environmental deterioration were such that Oldham proved no exception to the rule that, as 'ever more English people found themselves living in towns or cities, life continued to be both as nasty and brutish—if not quite as short—as it always had been'.[43]

[38] S. Bamford, *Walks in South Lancashire* (1844; ed. J. D. Marshall, Hassocks, Sussex, 1972), 62.
[39] Ginswick, *Labour and the Poor*, 93.
[40] P. Joyce, *Work, Society and Politics* (Hassocks, Sussex, 1980), 103–26.
[41] Ginswick, *Labour and the Poor*, 97–101; Foster, *Class Struggle*, 91–9. On the crucial role of the life-cycle in determining the economic position of working-class families, see Rule, *Labouring Classes*, 41; Koditschek, *Class Formation*, 371.
[42] Walvin, *Urban Life*, 45.   [43] Ibid. 41.

Individual responses to these problems varied markedly. Bamford commented during the depression of the early 1840s on the regular practice of crowding two or three families into one house, but he also observed that the dwellings of the workers were generally kept very clean and that there had been a perceptible improvement in this regard since the 1820s. 'It was evident that the poor people, though sorely pressed, were struggling nobly with their adverse circumstances—that they were fighting with a stout heart and would not descend to rags and squalor, however they might suffer from toil and hunger.'[44] Similarly, while Reach met with appalling conditions in some cellar-dwellings, others 'though miserably poor were kept beautifully clean, and the little ornaments and paltry pictures ranged around the walls often showed a touching struggle between pinching poverty and a decent desire to keep up appearances'.[45] In helping to sustain this sense of dignity in the face of poor conditions, the churches were to play a crucial role.

Although poverty was widespread and the associated formation of combined households not uncommon, conditions in the less-crowded environment of the out-townships and the Saddleworth villages seem to have been rather easier than those in the central township. Bamford found a mixture of well-kept and partially dilapidated houses in Thornham near Middleton, while at High Crompton he was able to visit a row of 'beautifully clean' tenements with small gardens, occupied by millworkers.[46] Middleton weavers' houses were, according to Reach, 'commonplace' and 'mean', but 'wanting the grime and smoke dried air, and the close hot smell of the town operatives' lodging' and 'by no means uncomfortable, inspiring neither the idea of privation nor unwholesomeness'. In Saddleworth he found working conditions dependent on whether the wool required extensive dyeing before it was processed—in which case 'the aspect of the mill and the workpeople is grimy and filthy in the extreme'; if instead the product was lighter and coarser cloth, the mills were 'clean looking and agreeable to all the senses'. Living conditions seem to have been similar to those in Middleton, and Reach described the cottages close to Whiteheads' mill as 'without a single exception . . . neat, warm, comfortable and clean'. However, he also encountered poor, uncared-for cottages on the hillsides above Delph. Thus, in Saddleworth and the out-townships too, living conditions had much to do with individual responses as well as with the state of trade.[47]

---

[44] Bamford, *Walks*, 68–9.
[46] Bamford, *Walks*, 30–3.
[45] Ginswick, *Labour and the Poor*, 88–9.
[47] Ginswick, *Labour and the Poor*, 104–14, 142–53.

Social Structure and Social Relationships

The structure of Saddleworth's economy, and the distribution of its population in a collection of industrial villages, would suggest a social structure like that of Oldham's out-townships, the most important changes over time being a consequence of the gradual decline in handloom weaving and the rise in the importance of the mills as employers of labour. A local pamphlet of 1795 identified four main social groupings in the area: 'the yeomen or land-owners, the Master clothiers, the Shopkeepers, Innkeepers and all persons of other Public Professions, and the Industrious who work at the woollen business for wages'. Allowing for a gradual amalgamation of the first two categories as mill-building increased, and also the development of a small craft-workshop sector, the local trade directory for the mid-1860s, together with the 1861 census, gives a rather similar picture. The bulk of the population remained textile operatives, with the directory listing only 173 retailers, 49 professionals, 195 workshop operators, 10 farmers, and 165 manufacturers. The majority of the latter were the owners of small woollen mills, or were independent clothiers, and this left most of the wealth of the locality concentrated in the hands of a few rich manufacturers.[48]

The most comprehensive contemporary analysis of Oldham's social structure is contained in A. C. Oliver's *An Appeal to the Christians of Oldham*, a missionary tract published in 1852. It identified three main social groupings: an upper class comprising 200 families, a middle class of 2,100 families, and a lower class of 11,567 families. Foster suggests that these three groupings had a more-or-less continuous existence from the previous century—the upper-class merchant manufacturers of the late eighteenth century, for example, having, by the 1840s, transformed themselves into millowners, engineers, and coal owners, a close-knit group of under 200 households, which expanded only slightly in subsequent decades. Foster has traced a complex internal structure within this upper class, and his identification of three major friendship groups—the 'Traditional', 'County', and 'Manchester' sets—each with its own network of marriage and business partnerships, appears to be well founded. Nevertheless, these networks do not seem entirely to have followed the geographical, economic, and cultural patterns described by Foster, and we should be cautious about any suggestion that they represented discrete cultural

---

[48] D. Nield, *Addresses to the Different Classes of Men in the Parish of Saddleworth* (1795; repr. Saddleworth, 1983).

blocs.[49] As in Saddleworth, most of the wealth of the locality was concentrated in the hands of these upper-class families, and their economic
power was, through much of the period, translated successfully into
social influence. Members of this group took key leadership positions in
many important local institutions, developing a rich associational culture
in a variety of voluntary bodies, including churches and religious societies,
educational institutions like the Oldham Lyceum, and organizations with
a more straightforwardly social emphasis like the 'Oldham Floral and
Agricultural Society'.[50] They naturally played a key role in the course
of industrial relations in the town, in its local politics, and, after 1832, in
its parliamentary representation. However, their political action never
took the form of a united intervention by a monolithic class-based group.
Denominational loyalties, particularly prominent in 1834 and 1843, cut
across both the Traditional and Manchester sets, and differing political
loyalties cut across all three networks. A series of political divisions along
both party and religious lines fragmented the bourgeois front in parliamentary elections throughout the 1830s and 1840s, and, though the upper
class occasionally may have united in the face of a common threat, it was
more often characterized by a variety of different alignments according to
changes in political circumstances. In 1835, for example, only a year after
a week-long general strike had indicated the potential strength of the
radical challenge, prominent liberal members of the Manchester group
could be found, in a parliamentary by-election, voting for a radical candidate against the Tories' County group candidate, Major John Lees.
Similarly, in the late 1840s, the upper class split over whether the town
should seek incorporation, with the Tories lining up alongside the
Cobbettite radicals in a losing battle against a liberal initiative to petition
for a charter.[51]

[49] Foster, *Class Struggle*, 8–34, 177–186; M. A. Smith, 'Religion in Industrial Society:
The Case of Oldham and Saddleworth 1780–1865', D.Phil. thesis (Oxford, 1987), 16–17.
The value of the concepts of class and class consciousness as analytical categories has come
under vigorous challenge in recent years. However, class as a descriptive term identifying
groups who shared a similar position in the local economy clearly had a resonance for some
contemporaries. It is primarily in this sense that the term is used here. For an analysis and
critique of recent thinking in the social history of the 'working class' in particular, see e.g.
N. Kirk, 'Traditional Working-Class Culture and the Rise of Labour: Some Preliminary
Questions and Observations', *Social History*, 16 (1991), 203–16; D. Mayfield and S. Thorne,
'Social History and its Discontents: Gareth Stedman Jones and the Politics of Language',
Social History, 17 (1992), 165–88.
[50] Foster, *Class Struggle*, 177–86; for the importance of voluntary societies in the
development of middle-class culture, see Koditschek, *Class Formation*, 252–319; Morris, *Class,
Sect and Party*, 167–98.
[51] Anon., *Oldham Poll Book* (Oldham, 1835); Sykes, 'Working-Class Consciousness', 176;
Foster, *Class Struggle*, 208–9; Morris, *Class, Sect and Party*, 127, 157–8, 265–77.

If anything united the upper class beyond the logic of its economic position, it was probably a common evangelical culture, which was also the rationale behind much employer paternalism.[52] However, while evangelicalism provided an important avenue of contact between the upper class and the rest of the town, sometimes transcending class barriers in local communities, it never entirely removed them. Some sections of the upper class became particularly socially exclusive—a characteristic reflected not only in the pattern of its marriages, but also, after the early nineteenth century, in an increasing degree of residential segregation. The more traditional bourgeoisie may have resisted this trend, continuing to reside in the industrial villages of Saddleworth and the out-townships, and maintaining face-to-face relationships with the workers in their industrial enterprises. In the central township, however, many of the members of the County and Manchester groups moved out of the residential communities inhabited by their employees and into small upper-class enclaves or parkland estates on the edge of town. The social exclusiveness of these families, together with the alternative attractions presented by the wider world of the county aristocracy, the Manchester merchants, and national politics, seems to have led, particularly after the middle of the nineteenth century, to a partial disengagement from local life. Some families did maintain an interest in local politics, especially in the town council established after incorporation, and competition for the borough's parliamentary seats also remained strong. John Platt, for example, head of the great engineering firm, became chairman of the Oldham Liberal Party in 1847, mayor of the borough from 1854 to 1856, and Member of Parliament from 1865 until his death in 1872. However, Platt acquired an estate at Llanfairfechan in 1857, and succumbed to the attractions of county society. He accepted appointment as High Sheriff of Caernarvon in 1863, and later served as Deputy-Lieutenant of Lancashire.[53] The trend towards disengagement, which for many of the richest local families culminated in a move out of the town altogether, made Oldham's upper class among the most exclusive in Lancashire.[54] This was to have important consequences for the churches. It also meant that only a few of the richest local families, mainly in Saddleworth and the out-townships, developed the sort of hegemony over their localities traced by Joyce in

[52] See Ch. 6; B. Hilton, *The Age of Atonement* (Oxford, 1988), *passim*; Morris, *Class, Sect and Party*, 216, 321.
[53] Foster, *Class Struggle*, 182, 268; V. O. Williams, 'The Platts of Oldham: A Chapter in the History of a Caernarvonshire Parish', *Transactions of the Caernarvonshire Historical Society*, 18 (1957), 75–88; D. J. Jeremy (ed.), *Dictionary of Business Biography*, iv (London, 1985), 725–8.
[54] Joyce, *Work*, 26.

other factory towns.[55] This disengagement, together with the growing local economic importance of the small firm, left a wide field of action open to the various sections of the 'middle class'.

In the eighteenth century, these middling families ran the shops and provided the professional services required by a small market town. They also organized networks of domestic textile producers, sometimes acting as agents for the merchants of Manchester and the Yorkshire cloth towns, and in 1818, along with the owners of small hat-making and cotton-spinning concerns, they made up the bulk of the 800 or so entries in the commercial directory of Oldham and its out-townships.[56] By the 1830s, according to Foster's analysis, there were four subgroups within the middle class, though the boundaries between these subgroups were unclear, as were the boundaries between the middle class as a whole and the upper and lower classes of the town. The smallest of the four subgroups was that of the 'professionals'—around 100 families, mainly lawyers, doctors, and clergymen, together with a few schoolteachers and the providers of financial services.[57] The next two groups, 150 or so 'tradesmen' and 350 'little masters', were together classified by Foster as the 'petty bourgeoisie'. The economic basis for the distinction between the two subgroups was the possession by the tradesmen of substantial blocks of working capital, invested mainly in retailing or small-scale manufacturing; the little masters, who did not possess this advantage, operated only the smallest type of cotton or craft-based subcontracting enterprise. It has been suggested that these groups inhabited separate cultural worlds: the world of the tradesmen was exclusive and focused on the chapels of Oldham's town centre, while the little masters 'had no use for the exclusiveness (or religion) of the tradesmen . . . They shared the general working-class allegiance to the neighbourhood, and the communities within which they lived were those of street, beerhouse and trade.'[58] However, although there may have been two cultures within the petty bourgeoisie, it is not clear that they were coterminous with the division between those who did and those who did not possess a substantial block of working capital. It would be equally plausible to suggest that any culture of 'respectability' would have been likely to include not only the tradesmen but also, in some contexts, many of the little masters, together with some of the

---

[55] Ibid. *passim.*

[56] *Leigh's Directory* (1818; repr. in McPhillips, *Oldham*, 27–32).

[57] Foster, *Class Struggle*, 163–5, 182, 197; J. Pigot and Son, *General, Classified and Street Directory of Manchester and Salford* (Manchester, 1838), 102–18.

[58] Foster, *Class Struggle*, 166–77.

working-class families they employed and with whom they tended to live and intermarry.[59] It would also have included members of the fourth subgroup, which comprised the shopkeepers, clerical workers, and owners of small dairy farms in the out-townships, who made up the bulk of families identified as middle class in the 1852 survey. These men have not loomed large in earlier analyses of the town, but Winstanley has recently drawn attention to the vitality of their social world and, together with the professionals, tradesmen, and little masters, the shopkeepers seem to have occupied many of the key positions of influence in local communities left vacant by the small size and growing disengagement of the upper class.

From the first decades of the nineteenth century, middle-class men became increasingly prominent in most of the religious, educational, and cultural organizations partronized by the upper class and, as the century progressed, they began to develop institutions more exclusively their own. In 1838 a bank was opened by local tradesmen which provided business support during periods of economic depression; in 1850 a Shopkeepers' Association was formed 'for the purpose of protecting the general interests of the trade'; small employers also dominated the membership of the cotton masters' association when it was refounded in 1866. In the later 1850s, just as the prospects of their small- and medium-sized firms were beginning to improve, professionals and tradesmen became increasingly prominent in local politics. Abraham Leach, a surgeon from Waterhead, became mayor of Oldham in 1859 and was followed by a tradesman, John Riley in 1862, and William Knott, a draper and small hat-manufacturer, in 1865. Foster has argued that some elements of the middle class, especially the tradesmen and professionals, tended to behave as a social tail of the upper class.[60] However, a number of the professionals were rich enough to merit a place in the upper class in their own right: Kay Clegg, for example, a lawyer and secretary to the cotton masters' association, was also a substantial local landowner. Although the professionals were by no means so powerful as their contemporaries in Leeds, they did not always behave simply as a 'social tail', and the clergymen, at least, were quite prepared to stand in judgement on upper-class behaviour when they thought that it clashed with the interests of the

---

[59] Smith, 'Oldham', 21–4; N. Kirk, *The Growth of Working-Class Reformism in Mid-Victorian England* (1985), 176–231. On the ambiguous nature of 'Respectability', see Koditschek, *Class Formation*, 452.

[60] Foster, *Class Struggle*, 166–70; M. J. Winstanley, *The Shopkeeper's World 1830–1914* (Manchester, 1983), *passim*; Halbert, *Jubilee Celebration*, 32–4.

Church.[61] Middle-class leaders were conscious that their own interests did not necessarily coincide with those of the upper class, and in both local and parliamentary politics they seem often to have pursued an independent line. However, the families comprising this group were too diverse for a sense of class to play a decisive role in the formation of their political identity and, like the big bourgeoisie, they were divided by a number of denominational and party political loyalties. Some, like the little masters, whom Foster has identified as the main proponents of the Cobbett tradition in local politics, or the liberal tradesmen who supported the move to incorporation in the 1840s, could often be found in temporary alliance with sections of the upper class. However, these partnerships remained perennially unstable. Some of the little masters could be found lining up with more thoroughgoing radicals in defiance of the big employers over issues such as the limitation of factory hours, and Foster has also found evidence of a significant split, in 1861, between the tradesman and upper-class portions of the Oldham Liberal Party.

As possessors of the majority of votes in the new parliamentary borough, created in 1832, the tradesmen, shopkeepers, and small farmers naturally played a significant role in local politics. Foster has suggested that they were unable to make use of this preponderance of votes in any autonomous fashion because the shopkeepers and tradesmen were constrained to support radical candidates by a campaign of intimidation orchestrated by a radical working-class vanguard, whose principal tactic was the threat of exclusive dealing. However, both D. S. Gadian and R. A. Sykes have shown that violence and exclusive dealing played very little part in the initial radical victory at the 1832 general election, when Fielden and Cobbett easily topped the poll against weak Whig and Tory candidates tainted by involvement with the West Indian slavery interest. Even in defeat at the 1847 election, when a split in local radical ranks made exclusive dealing impossible, Fielden managed to poll over 600 votes despite the suspicions aroused by his choice of the conservative J. M. Cobbett as his running-mate. As an expression of local opinion mobilized against those who broke the norms of the neighbourhood community, exclusive dealing, like the bread riots of the previous century, could be extremely powerful. However, it seems that such tactics were used mainly against a

---

[61] Foster, *Class Struggle*, 197; Morris, *Class, Sect and Party*, 25, 220–1, 236; Chester Record Office (CRO), Chester Diocesan Visitation Returns (CVR), 1811, 183; D. M. Alexander, *Lay Co-operation in Oldham* (Oldham, 1863), 10–15.

minority of shopkeepers and tradesmen who did not vote for radical candidates out of personal preference.[62]

Although some middle-class families seem to have sought a degree of exclusiveness analogous to that achieved by the big bourgeoisie, most, either from choice or from economic necessity, remained rooted within local residential communities, living among and mixing with the working-class families who formed the bulk of the population.[63] They were, therefore, much better placed than the upper class to take a leading role in the social and political life of those communities, whether as publicans, as leaders of organizations for mutual self-improvement, or as radical politicians. Winstanley and Gadian have demonstrated that tradesmen actively sought and filled many key leadership positions within Oldham's radical movement, especially during its period of maximum strength in the 1830s and 1840s. Alexander Taylor, for example, secretary of the radical Oldham Political Association, was a prosperous flour-dealer who left over £6,000 at his death. Some radical leaders were recruited directly from the ranks of the small employers, and some working-class radicals themselves became small employers, in a gradual process of embourgeoise-ment during the 1830s. To the extent that the exceptional strength of the Oldham radical movement was due to the determination and consistency of its leadership, the middle-class contribution was crucial.[64]

The vast majority of Oldham's population, comprising more than 11,000 families, were described by the 1852 survey as working class. Economically the most marginalized of the town's social groups, these families had borne the brunt of the hardships associated with industrial change and poor living conditions, especially in those neighbourhoods which merged to form the central built-up area. There was a wide variety of economic experience within the working class, with journeymen cotton-spinners, handloom weavers, and the higher-paid engineering workers at various periods and stages of the life-cycle all being significantly better off than the majority of unskilled workers and poor labourers among whom

[62] Foster, *Class Struggle*, 53–6, 166–77, 246–9; Gadian, 'Class Consciousness'; Sykes, 'Working-Class Consciousness'; Winstanley, *Shopkeeper's World*, 21–6; S. A. Weaver, *John Fielden and the Politics of Popular Radicalism 1832–1847* (Oxford, 1987), 268–74; A. Howe, *The Cotton Masters 1830–1860* (Oxford, 1984), 139–40.

[63] Foster, *Class Struggle*, 166–77.

[64] Winstanley, *Shopkeeper's World*, 21–6; Gadian, 'Class Formation', 28–31. For the vital role played by the petty bourgeoisie in the radical politics of Leeds, see Morris, *Class, Sect and Party*, 124, 258–9.

they lived. Despite the wide variation in wage rates and working experience, however, local communities were characterized by a high degree of social integration between craft and labouring, locally born and immigrant families. This communal solidarity provided a firm foundation for a strong radical movement in which skilled craft-workers played a key role. In the 1830s and 1840s local trades unions were able to mount a powerful series of strikes and radicals were able to capitalize on divisions among the opposing forces to gain control of the borough's parliamentary representation, together with a number of more local institutions.[65]

The question of class has dominated the historiography of Oldham since the publication of Foster's work and it does seem that there is much to be said for the notion of the gradual development of a sense of identity among the generality of local labourers in contradistinction to their employers. There is some evidence for the existence of such feeling in the later eighteenth century among textile workers over and against the merchants who ran the putting-out system. Daniel Nield, for example, in his 1795 pamphlet, *Addresses to the Different Classes of Men in the Parish of Saddleworth*, employed a version of the labour theory of value derived from Adam Smith to advance the claims of the 'working class' against the 'master clothiers'. It is difficult to be certain that these ideas achieved widespread acceptance in Oldham and Saddleworth during the 1790s, but attitudes may well have hardened in the early nineteenth century, especially in the sphere of industrial relations. The result was a long period of intermittent industrial militancy and also, according to Foster, a powerful class-based radical challenge in the 1830s and 1840s. Foster has suggested that this position was transformed in the later 1840s by the rise of sectional differences among the operative population. Within the workplace, it is argued, profound shifts in the structure of authority changed the nature of relationships between employer and employee as the skilled men who previously had exercised control over their craft were transformed into 'Labour Aristocrats' imposing a new work-discipline on other workers on behalf of the employers. The men who had formed the old radical vanguard were thus 'bought off' and isolated from the bulk of the workers both by their changed role at work and by their insulation in a maze of cultural and religious institutions which enshrined their sectional consciousness.[66]

[65] Foster, *Class Struggle*, 47–160; Gadian, 'Class Formation', 51.
[66] Foster, *Class Struggle*, 203–46.

There has been an extensive debate about the nature and role of the Labour Aristocracy in mid-nineteenth-century Britain, and it now seems clear that Foster's original interpretation requires substantial revision. Labour Aristocrats, especially in textiles, may sometimes have been occupied in the supervision of members of their own families, and this makes it difficult to talk about a renewed fragmentation of the working class along status lines in the workplace. Moreover, in the sphere of politics, the working class was no more successful in producing a consistently united response to the problems it faced than were the upper and middle classes, and Foster has probably overemphasized the degree of political control exercised by class-based radical groups in Oldham during the 1830s and 1840s. Thus a major problem with Foster's notion of Labour Aristocracy is that it explains too much. The instability of radical control in Oldham before 1847 and the continuing poor industrial relations thereafter make it inappropriate to build an analysis of social relationships in the locality on a hypothesis of rapid change around mid-century.[67]

More fundamentally, recent writing has challenged both Foster's emphasis on class interest as the basis of politics in Oldham and his interpretation of the radical agenda. Neville Kirk has questioned the notion that Labour Aristocrats were culturally isolated—demonstrating that many organizations in which they played important roles also had a much wider membership among the working class as a whole. Michael Winstanley has demonstrated that those same institutions were, in fact, central to mainstream radicalism in Oldham. Its agenda was dominated not by the ideology of class conflict but by a culture of rational recreation, moral and spiritual self-improvement, and opposition to fiscal mismanagement by an unrepresentative national government. Based in the nonconformist chapels of Oldham's urban core, this form of radicalism had a broad appeal among all classes in the town and its proponents actively sought cooperation with more moderate reformers. From the later 1830s it was probably the dominant political force in the locality—more significant than the populist tory radicalism of William Cobbett and his successors with which it was perennially in tension—and its leaders were prominent both in the

---

[67] G. Stedman Jones, 'Class Struggle and the Industrial Revolution', *New Left Review*, 90 (1975), 35–69; H. F. Moorhouse, 'The Marxist Theory of the Labour Aristocracy', *Social History*, 3 (1978), 61–82; A. E. Musson, 'Class Struggle and the Labour Aristrocracy 1830–1860', *Social History*, 1 (1976), 335–66; Joyce, *Work*, 51–8; R. J. Morris, *Class and Class Consciousness in the Industrial Revolution 1780–1850* (1979); Sykes, 'Working-Class Consciousness'; Gadian, 'Class Consciousness'; Gadian, 'Class Formation', 29–30, 45; Koditschek, *Class Formation*, 517–77; Kirk, *Working Class Reformism, passim.*

Chartist agitation of the 1840s and in the promotion of liberal causes like local government reform and the repeal of the corn laws. If there was a lowering of the political temperature around the middle of the century, this was probably due partly to the final eclipse of Cobbettism. It must also have owed much to the new fiscal policies adopted by Peel and Gladstone, which seemed to accommodate national policy to the radical agenda, and to the gradual stabilization of the local economy after 1850, which would have had a particularly significant effect on the vital small-firm sector.[68]

In the neighbourhoods of Oldham and Saddleworth, where they took concrete form, the eventuality of some kind of class identity and the gradual liberalization of class relations seem clearly established. However, the prevalence of divisions within classes and of alliances between them— the warp and weft of the process of 'class bargaining'—seems equally clear. At the same time, alternative solidarities—sometimes based on local residential communities, more often on communities of common interest like religious denominations and political associations—competed for the allegiance of people for whom an unstable sense of class interest was only one loyalty among the many which combined to shape their social relations.[69] In Oldham and Saddleworth the texture of life was complex. Even at the residential level there developed over the period a hierarchy of different identities, its components at times mutually antagonistic, at times mutually affirming. These in turn were undermined or reinforced by the interplay of identities based on class or other interests. Although, with the gradual withdrawal of the upper class, most local communities probably became more socially homogeneous, their social meaning must have comprised a complex matrix of different perceptions, varying with the character and priorities of, and the opportunities available to, the individuals comprising them. Clearly the middle-class tradesman with servants and business contacts in Manchester would view the life of the neighbourhood in which he lived through very different eyes from those of a juvenile factory worker, whose life orbited around the twin poles of the mill and a cellar-dwelling in the same street. There must, however, have been many more subtle shades of individual perception, lending thousands of different colours even to the monotony of life under the new

[68] Ibid. *passim*. For a full account of radical politics in Oldham see M. Winstanley, 'Oldham Radicalism and the Origins of Popular Liberalism', *Historical Journal*, 36 (1993), 619–43.

[69] Gadian, 'Class Formation', 51–7; Sykes, 'Working-Class Consciousness'; Kirk, *Working Class Reformism*, 176–352; Morris, *Class, Sect and Party*, 108–9, 157.

capitalist work discipline. It is with the attempts made by the churches to present their gospel to, and integrate within their life the aspirations of, all of these individuals—to build congregations within communities and communities within churches—that the following chapters are concerned.

2. The 'Unreformed' Establishment

New Problems

The rapid social and demographic transformation of the years between 1730 and 1830 certainly posed major problems for the Established Church. It is often suggested that the processes of industrialization and urbanization combined to produce a rootless proletariat, disorientated by the breakdown of traditional community in an unfamiliar urban environment, alienated by the new capitalist relations of production, and plunged into a state of 'anomie'—'a generalised feeling of insecurity, rootlessness, and social fragmentation reflecting a dearth of familiar institutions, associations and unifying social activities'.[1] In such an atmosphere, it is argued, traditional religious ties were rapidly abandoned, along with the rest of the culture of pre-industrial society; and this, together with the inertia of the Anglican Church, left a vacuum which was quickly filled by various nonconformist groups, who provided, for many of the new proletarians, 'the only community group they knew in the Industrial Wilderness'.[2]

Clearly the development of Oldham and Saddleworth between 1730 and 1830 will not bear this sort of interpretation. Locally at least, neighbourhood identities were created rather than destroyed by the progress of urbanization, the chief feature of which was not the breakdown of community, but the proliferation of communities. In part, therefore, the challenge to the Established Church took the form of an intensification of problems with which it had long been familiar. The parochial system had always been under strain in large 'open' parishes like those of Oldham and Saddleworth, where long distances between the homes of a scattered population, and the highly fragmented nature of local landownership, made it impossible to duplicate the easier conditions of the 'closed' parishes found in parts of the south and east of England.[3] However, there

---

[1] Gilbert, *Post-Christian Britain*, 82.
[2] H. McLeod, *Religion and the People of Western Europe* (Oxford, 1981), 67; Chadwick, *Victorian Church*, i. 325; E. P. Thompson, *The Making of the English Working Class*, 2nd edn. (1968), 400.
[3] J. Obelkevich, *Religion and Rural Society: South Lindsey 1825–1875* (Oxford, 1976), 8–14.

were also new elements in the situation. The proliferating communities of Oldham and Saddleworth were not traditional communities: they were industrial and—as the upper and middle classes began to segregate themselves—very largely working-class communities. They created, perhaps for the first time, the social space in which a class-segregated, dechristianized culture might develop, claiming the allegiance of the mass of an unchurched population. The real task facing the Established Church— the penetration of growing communities within Oldham and Saddleworth —was perhaps an even greater challenge than would have been that of ministering to a population suffering from anomie. Local clergymen were quick to detect the arrival of new conditions, often signalled by increasing absenteeism from public worship, which many blamed on the process of industrialization itself, though this absenteeism was generally put down to indifference rather than unbelief. Some ministers also expressed concern about excessive drinking, perhaps indicating an increasing tension between the Church and the alehouse—the traditional resort of working-class nonattenders.[4] Urgent action was certainly required, for, if the Church failed to participate in the formation of the new working-class culture, it risked losing what remained of its traditional position by default.

The Hanoverian Church, with its unenviable reputation for combining inefficiency and corruption with inert complacency, is commonly regarded as a body singularly ill-equipped to cope with the new conditions, especially in the north of England. The general historiographical view of the Establishment remains dominated by the interpretation offered by Norman Sykes, who portrayed, albeit sympathetically, a comfortable Church, resting in years of plenty 'wherein all its ways were pleasantness and all its paths were peace'.[5] Such an institution could hardly be expected to respond energetically to changes in its circumstances, and A. D. Gilbert, writing some forty years after Sykes, was clear about the consequences:

Little was done between the reign of Queen Anne and the second quarter of the nineteenth century to enlarge the Church of England as a religious service organisation. Historians have argued about its pastoral and administrative effectiveness, but by virtual consensus they have recognised the eighteenth century Church as a static institution, characterised by inertia if not always by complacency.[6]

The Church, it is argued, was so enmeshed, both organizationally and psychologically, with the rural society of the south of England that it was

---

[4] CVR 1789, 151; 1811; 183; 1778, Middleton.
[5] N. Sykes, *Church and State in England in the Eighteenth Century* (Cambridge, 1934), 405.
[6] Gilbert, *Religion and Society*, 27–8.

unable to respond to the growing needs of the industrial north. Too many of its clergy were comfortable in the enjoyment of their pluralities and of their easy non-residence for the Church to generate any significant pastoral improvement; 'the clerical horse needed to be whipped before it would move', and those few Anglican leaders who were determined enough to provide the required stimulus were frustrated by a series of legal obstacles to reform. This view is called into question by the experience of the Church in Oldham and Saddleworth, which, while still displaying many of the irrationalities of the 'unreformed' Establishment, neverthe-less combined a high degree of engagement at most levels of local society with a good deal of faithful pastoral activity in the parishes, and succeeded in rising to the challenge of its new circumstances with surprising vigour and imagination.[7]

New Accommodation

In 1730 Oldham and Saddleworth were served by four Anglican churches: the ancient parish church of Middleton (in the village of that name), two medieval parochial chapels in Oldham and Saddleworth, dependent on the rectories of Prestwich and Rochdale respectively; and a small chapel of ease at Shaw (the chief settlement of the Crompton out-township), recovered late in the previous century after a dispute over possession with a local Presbyterian congregation. As the population increased, it soon became apparent that the existing accommodation was inadequate, and efforts were made, first, to expand the seating capacity of existing churches, and then, from 1742, to build new 'chapels of ease' in Saddleworth and the out-townships of Oldham. By 1788 five chapels had been built or rebuilt in Oldham and district: one to provide additional accommodation in the town centre; three to serve the out-townships of Royton, Crompton, and Chadderton; and the fifth at Hey, where it could serve a growing cluster of settlements to the east of the town, on both sides of the border with Saddleworth. Three chapels were also built in outlying areas of Saddleworth: in Quickmere and Friarmere, and in the newly industrialized village of Dobcross on Lordsmere, a few miles from the parochial chapel.

---

[7] P. Virgin, *The Church in an Age of Negligence* (Cambridge, 1989), 207. Other recent restatements of the pessimistic view of the Hanoverian church can be found in: S. Gilley, 'Official Religion', in T. Thomas (ed.), *The British: Their Religious Beliefs and Practices, 1800–1986* (1988), 20; H. D. Rack, *Reasonable Enthusiast* (1989), 17. This view requires modification in the light of a number of local studies, in particular: A. Warne, *Church and Society in Eighteenth Century Devon* (Newton Abbot, 1969); P. Rycroft, 'Church, Chapel, and Community in Craven 1764–1851', D.Phil. thesis (Oxford, 1988).

The chapels varied in size, from St Paul's, Royton, which seated 493 when it was built in 1768, to the much larger Holy Trinity, Dobcross, constructed in 1786 to hold approximately 840. In aggregate, the building of new churches had added just under 5,000 new sittings by 1788. The extension of existing buildings also continued apace, and, as the population pressure increased, additional sittings were introduced into the new buildings too. St John's, Hey, for example, added over 200 new seats in 1772, twenty-one years after its consecration, while Holy Trinity, Shaw, which was completely rebuilt in 1739, added around 300 more seats in 1797.

The overall effects of this vigorous activity are displayed in Table 2.1. In what may be termed the first phase of new church-building in the area, between 1739 and 1800, the seating capacity of Anglican churches in Oldham almost trebled from 2,300 to 6,255, and in Saddleworth it increased almost five times from 517 to 2,517. There was an increase for the area as a whole of 5,995 sittings, 4,958 from fresh building and 997 by the extension of existing structures—a considerable achievement in a period before church-building societies and the Ecclesiastical Commission. Moreover, when the seating is expressed as a percentage of the population, producing a figure for its 'density', it becomes apparent that church accommodation in Oldham actually increased faster than did the population in the middle decades of the eighteenth century, reaching a peak of 57.8 per cent in 1770. Given the universal practice of opening churches at least twice a Sunday, this meant that, in theory, every parishioner could be accommodated once on a Sunday throughout the 1760s and 1770s—an achievement never equalled in the following century, despite the best efforts of the 'reformed' Establishment. Church extension began later in Saddleworth, rising to a climax in the 1780s, and the density of accommodation reached 31.5 per cent in 1790. This again represented a rate of increase marginally greater than that of the population, even when the attendance of some Saddleworth people at the new chapels in Hey and Mossley, a few yards beyond its borders, is disregarded.[8] Moreover, local churches seem often to have been able to accommodate greater numbers than might be suggested by their estimated seating capacity. In 1821 it was reported that St Peter's, Oldham, could contain 1,500 people, and St Chad's, Saddleworth, 1,000, although they seated only 853 and 517 respectively. Even these estimates may have been on the conservative side. Saddleworth church certainly accommodated congregations of over 1,000 more than once. On one occasion, at least 2,000 crowded into the

[8] See Table 2.1; E. Ballard, *A Chronicle of Crompton* (Crompton, 1967), 48–55.

TABLE 2.1. *The density of church accommodation in Oldham and Saddleworth 1730-1830*

Date	Oldham			Saddleworth			Oldham and Saddleworth		
	Seating	Population	Density (%)	Seating	Population	Density (%)	Seating	Population	Density (%)
1730	2,300	6,000	38.3	517	1,700	30.4	2,817	7,700	37.6
1740	3,000	6,700	44.8	517	2,500	20.7	3,517	9,200	39.1
1750	3,505	7,750	45.2	517	3,400	15.2	4,022	11,150	36.9
1760	3,998	8,350	47.9	517	4,200	12.3	4,515	12,550	36.7
1770	5,258	9,100	57.8	1,017	5,000	20.3	6,275	14,100	45.5
1780	5,485	11,200	49.0	1,017	5,800	17.5	6,502	17,000	39.9
1790	5,485	18,600	29.5	2,517	8,000	31.5	8,002	26,600	32.0
1800	6,255	29,200	21.4	2,517	10,300	24.4	8,772	39,500	24.2
1810	6,348	35,600	17.8	2,517	12,400	20.3	8,865	48,000	18.5
1820	6,348	46,100	13.8	2,517	13,500	18.6	8,865	59,600	14.9
1830	9,464	60,000	15.8	2,517	15,900	15.8	11,981	75,000	15.8

Note: The table assumes steady population growth between known points.

Sources: CVR 1821; RMV ii; PRO HO 129.475, 496, Religious Census MS Returns; Shaw MSS 17, St Leonard's, Middleton, Papers; Shaw MSS 103, Holy Trinity, Shaw, Vestry Minutes; Holy Trinity, Shaw, Faculty, 1797, Gallery Accounts, 1800; ICBS files, 0 box 1, 5 box 1, 3330; CC, files 5,841, 15,839, 17,647, 20,536, 20,836; *Manchester Diocesan Directory* (Manchester, 1860); C. E. Higson, 'Lees Chapel, otherwise Hey Chapel in Lees', *Transactions of the Lancashire and Cheshire Antiquarian Society*, 34 (1916), 179–200; A. J. Howcroft, *The Chapelry and Church of Saddleworth and Quick* (Oldham, 1915); Howcroft, *Supplement to the History of the Chapelry and Church of Saddleworth* (Oldham, 1933); W. J. Smith, *A Brief History and Description of the Parish Church of St Leonard's, Middleton* (Gloucester, 1970).

church so that 'the aisles, baptistery and even the vestry were filled and many stood for want of room'.[9] If this experience was repeated elsewhere, it is even conceivable that the whole of Oldham's population could have been accommodated simultaneously in 1770.

The vast majority of these new seats were 'appropriated', and this may have limited their accessibility in districts where many members of the community could not afford to rent a sitting or family pew. This would have been a problem particularly in the new churches built by subscription, like St Peter's, which contained only a handful of free seats until it was extended in 1794. An analysis by occupation of the thirty-one purchasers of sittings in a new gallery added to St Leonard's, Middleton, in 1794 yields the following results:

3 gentlemen
7 manufacturers
4 farmers
3 timber merchants
1 corn factor
1 clerk
1 clockmaker
1 glazier
2 coopers
2 joiners
5 weavers
1 indeterminate Occupation

The handloom weavers, who made up the bulk of the local population, were clearly under-represented, and this is hardly surprising since the option to rent even the cheapest pew cost £6. Nevertheless, working people were not entirely excluded. Five weavers, three of them unable to sign their own names, were able to buy seats in the gallery, which also provided some free sittings for the Sunday school.[10] In fact, historians seem to have exaggerated the problems caused by appropriated seats. Sometimes, appropriation presented no barrier to the poor at all: at St Chad's, the Saddleworth parochial chapel, there were no free seats until after 1836, but few of the seats carried a rent, and they were 'appropriated'

[9] CVR 1821, St Peter's, St Chad's; F. R. Raines, 'Diary' (extracts published in the *Oldham Chronicle*, 23 Jan.–27 Feb. 1926), 20, 27 July 1826.

[10] W. A. Westley, 'The Position occupied by St Peter's Schools in the History of Education in Oldham' (cuttings from the *Oldham Chronicle*, 1936); Manchester Public Library (MPL), Rushton Visitation Returns (RVR) 52, p. 197; MPL, Giles Shaw MSS 17.

only in the sense that each was attached to a particular house in the villages surrounding the church. In the chapels of ease, seats were allocated in proportion to the amount subscribed to their erection. However, arrangements were usually made to ensure that any seats surplus to the requirements of their 'owners' would be relet at the standard rent—thus avoiding the potential problem of a large number of unoccupied seats. Moreover, seats were commonly given in exchange for contributions of materials or labour; the system of appropriation, therefore, did not necessarily exclude even the poorest members of the community.[11] Early nineteenth-century records suggest that absent pew-owners were often willing to open their seats to the poor. In 1821 the Minister of Holy Trinity, Dobcross, recorded that he had no accommodation set aside for the poor, but that, nevertheless, all were admitted—a pattern which was repeated in other local churches without 'free seats'.[12] Much of the eighteenth-century effort to expand church accommodation has been discounted, even in the most recent literature, on the ground that it effectively excluded the poor; but in Oldham and Saddleworth the poor seem to have found little difficulty in securing entry to the new chapels, at least so long as the overall provision of seating remained relatively generous.[13]

The costs of building operations were considerable, especially for developing communities in an uncertain economic environment. The reconstruction of Holy Trinity, Shaw, for example, cost £1,100 in 1739. New buildings and enlargements were financed in a variety of ways. The £300 required for alterations at Middleton in the 1790s was raised by a combination of a Church rate, donations, the sale of seats in the gallery, and a loan from the church's patron, Lord Suffield. Holy Trinity, Shaw, was built partly by sending out church briefs, which allowed the mobilization of funds from outside the immediate area, and one collection of £7 10s. for Shaw has been traced from as far afield as Hampshire. Queen Anne's Bounty was also mobilized in the cause of Church extension, since it was used to provide part of the endowment of the new churches.[14] By far the most important source of finance, however, was the local subscription, donations usually being made in return for the right to occupy seats

---

[11] MPL, St Chad's, Vestry Minutes, 1839; Chetham's College Library, Manchester (CCLM), Raines MSS xxxiv. 109, Wray to Speed, 24 Mar. 1768; S. Andrew, *A History of Hey* (Oldham, 1905), 9.

[12] CVR 1821, 341, 390, 392.

[13] e.g. T. V. Parry, 'The Incorporated Church Building Society 1818–1851', M. Litt. thesis (Oxford, 1984), 13–15; Rack, *Reasonable Enthusiast*, 18.

[14] John Rylands Library, Manchester (JRL), Rushton MSS ix. 121; Shaw MSS 17; anon., *The Churches of Oldham and District* (book of cuttings in OLIC); RVR 52, p. 197; 53, pp. 36, 69, 101, 103.

in the new chapels. Most of the major donations necessarily came from local men of substance and, especially when they took the form of the gift of sites for new churches, they probably represented the last significant intervention of the old gentry of the area in local affairs.[15] However, the subscriptions demonstrated that the local Established Church was also able to tap the newly accumulated wealth of the rising manufacturing and trading classes. The town-centre chapel of St Peter's, for example, was built, according to Foster, by men who 'were largely the grandfathers of the big industrialists of the early nineteenth century'.[16] This generosity was not limited to the particular neighbourhood in which a manufacturer or his work-force resided, but seems to have been exercised in support of Church extension throughout the locality. Thus, at least two of the subscribers to St Peter's also made donations to St Margaret's, Hollinwood, on the edge of the Chadderton out-township. Similarly, while, according to its historian, St John's, Hey, benefited from the 'purse and presence' of several local families, 'nearly all the leading people in Oldham were [also] concerned in its promotion'.[17]

It would be a mistake to deduce from the heavy involvement of local élites that the new chapels were, in any way, imposed on an indifferent working class. Consecration deeds recorded a strong local demand for additional accommodation, in language unlikely to reflect merely middle-class interests. St Peter's, Oldham, was built in 1768 in response to a request from those who 'for want of room at the ancient chapel are destitute of seats *for whom* this chapel was erected by the voluntary con-tributions of several pious and well disposed persons'.[18] Similar formulae appeared in most local consecration deeds and faculties for extensions to churches, and other evidence indicates that these statements were not merely pious fictions.[19] Philip Rycroft has pointed out that the ability of Anglicans to persuade vestry meetings to build and enlarge churches in Craven presupposed a good deal of popular support for the Establishment, and in Oldham and Saddleworth, too, there seems to have been little dif-ficulty in persuading open vestries to authorize building operations, even

---

[15] Shaw MSS 7, St Peter's Consecration Deed 1768; Butterworth, *Oldham*, 94; Andrew, *Hey*, 10.

[16] Foster, *Class Struggle*, 26.

[17] Ibid. 26; RVR 53, p. 39; Andrew, *Hey*, 9. For support for church building at all levels of society in Lancashire, see J. M. Albers, 'Seeds of Contention: Society, Politics and the Church of England in Lancashire 1689–1790', Ph.D. thesis (Yale, 1988).

[18] Shaw MSS 7, St Peter's Consecration Deed.

[19] e.g. 'St Margaret's, Hollinwood, Consecration Deed 1766', in G. P. Gore, *The Story of the Ancient Parochial Chapelry of St Mary's, Oldham* (Oldham, 1906); Holy Trinity, Shaw, Faculty for Extension, 1797; 'St John's, Hey, Consecration Deed 1743', in Andrew, *Hey*, 9.

when the expense was to be borne by a general rate on all inhabitants. Thus extensions to St Leonard's, Middleton, were approved in a series of open vestry meetings between 1790 and 1799, 'The Rector and a large number of the inhabitants being present'.[20] Subscriptions for the erection of new churches could also evoke a positive response from the community as a whole, as at Friarmere in 1788, where those who could not afford to subscribe money did so in kind, or with their own labour, and received appropriated seats in return. The building of St John's, Hey, in 1742–4, presents a similar picture: 'Those who had neither material nor money to give helped with their labour. It was the boast of an old member of the congregation that his great-grandfather had trodden with his clogs all the mortar required to build the first chapel.'[21] Apparently, in Saddleworth and the out-townships at least, the Anglican Church, throughout the eighteenth century, could still count on that strange mixture of affectionate indifference and occasional enthusiasm known as 'Church feeling'.

The construction of a chapel in each of the out-townships clearly served both a religious and a social function. It may have symbolized the viability of each village as an independent settlement distinct from the central township, a sort of rite of passage confirming the maturity of each new community. Certainly, the chapels quickly became centres of communal activity in the out-townships—especially of the activities in which the community participated as a whole, like the annual rush-cart ceremony. As in Craven, the chapels also provided the focus for a more regular round of social life, not only through church attendance itself, but also through popular church music and bell-ringing societies. Bell-ringing seems to have been the object of considerable enthusiasm: great interest was maintained in the prowess of the various teams of ringers, and ringing competitions were extensively reported in the Manchester press. It was contended that the ringers of St Mary's, Oldham, were the best in east Lancashire, and they maintained a long-standing rivalry with their neighbours in Ashton.[22] Educational institutions centred on the chapels also provided an amenity for the community at large. Sunday schools spread rapidly in the area, and village day schools were built in Royton in 1785, and in Chadderton, attached to St Margaret's, Hollinwood, in 1786. At Hey, communal attachments were strong enough to bridge even the widening division between Church and alehouse, and a new village

[20] Shaw MSS 17; Rycroft, 'Craven', 134.

[21] Anon., *Friarmere Parish 1768–1968* (Uppermill, 1968), 2; Andrew, *Hey*, 9.

[22] *Manchester Mercury*, 20 Aug., 8 Oct. 1782, 12 Sept. 1784; Rycroft, 'Craven', 132.

pub was built next door to the chapel, specifically for the convenience of the congregation, some members of which came from a considerable distance away.[23] The widespread support for the erection of chapels of ease and the wider communal function they served makes it clear that the 'orthodox' view—that eighteenth-century chapels were almost invariably upper- and middle-class concerns[24]—is wide of the mark, at least in the case of Oldham and Saddleworth.

There remains, however, a further criticism of eighteenth-century Church extension: that the construction of church buildings was diminished in value by the failure to undertake a complementary overhaul of the parochial map. Geoffrey Best has described parochial subdivision as 'the only kind of Church extension that was really adequate to the situation', and Peter Virgin has concluded that the failure to subdivide parishes in the new industrial towns was 'catastrophic'. It has also been suggested that the dependence of the ministers of parochial chapels on the subscriptions of their hearers, and their lack of any legally recognized ecclesiastical jurisdiction over the population of their localities, lent to new eighteenth-century churches a character that smacked less of parochial Anglicanism than of congregationalism.[25] However, while the failure to subdivide may have caused difficulties in the largest conurbations, like Leeds and Manchester, in the smaller towns and industrial villages, in which much of the population was concentrated, it had many compensatory advantages. It may have helped to create a culture of Church extension, with the existence of a large number of chapelries at the start of the century setting a precedent for the building of new chapels of ease when population growth began to gather pace. It certainly allowed the local Church to evade the legal difficulties which would have hampered any attempt to pursue Church extension by means of parochial subdivision, and it encouraged the mobilization of finance for church building from across the whole locality, rather than solely from within the district in which a new chapel was being built—a situation which at least one mid-nineteenth-century observer recalled with nostalgia. The multiplication of chapels of ease also helped to create local clerical communities, with senior clergymen sometimes exercising quasi-ruridecanal powers—an important development for a Church lacking in structures of intermediate

---

[23] L. J. Beswick, *History of the Village School Royton* (Royton, 1922), 1–10; RVR 53, p. 53; Andrew, *Hey*, 13.

[24] Parry, 'Church Building Society', 16.

[25] G. F. A. Best, *Temporal Pillars: Queen Anne's Bounty, the Ecclesiastical Commissioners, and the Church of England* (Cambridge, 1964), 193–6; Virgin, *Age of Negligence*, 34.

ecclesiastical authority.[26] It is, moreover, easy to underestimate the degree to which the provision of a church represented a move, at least from the point of view of the laity, to relative ecclesiastical autonomy, as the curates of the new chapels began taking over the important tasks of administering baptism and communion in their localities. Ecclesiastical issues often provided the occasion for expressions of local feeling against the claims of the central township. At Shaw, the reconsecration of Holy Trinity in 1739 sparked a dispute over the inhabitants' liability for the Oldham Church rate which dragged on for twenty years, and a further series of church-rate disputes developed in all the out-townships in the 1820s.[27] Similarly, a requirement placed on the curates of the chapels of ease to do occasional duty at the mother church seems to have been generally neglected because of its unpopularity, as the vicar of St Mary's, the parochial chapel, noted, in 1804: 'the curates of the chapels of St Peter's and Hollinwood are required by their consecration deeds to attend those festivals [Christmas and Easter], their congregations are displeased with my insisting on it, which has induced me to leave it to the option of their curates.'[28] The clergy of the chapels visited regularly in their localities despite their lack of formal jurisdiction, and when, in 1859, St John's, Hey, was finally assigned an enlarged district, carved out of the parishes of Oldham, Saddleworth, and Ashton its curate reported: 'I have been virtually and practically the incumbent of the proposed district for nearly 21 years, having more or less worked it during that time.'[29] Clearly, their position in the local community did give a parochial dimension to the role of the chapels, *de facto*, if not *de jure*— the product of local feeling rather than any pastoral theory.

In the last decade of the eighteenth century, the local economy was plunged into crisis by a combination of changes in the textile industry and the state of uncertainty created by the war with France. In Saddleworth the situation had deteriorated so far by 1800 that the vestry was forced to appeal for help to the local Member of Parliament, William Wilberforce, who organized charitable relief, both from elsewhere in Yorkshire and

[26] A. J. B. Beresford-Hope, quoted in B. F. L. Clarke, *The Building of the Eighteenth Century Church* (1963), 193; M. A. Smith, 'The Reception of Richard Podmore', in J. D. Walsh, C. Haydon, and S. Taylor (eds.), *The Church of England c.1689–c.1833* (Cambridge, 1993), 116–17; W. B. Maynard, 'The Response of the Church of England to Economic and Demographic Change: The Archdeaconry of Durham, 1800–1851', *Journal of Ecclesiastical History*, 42 (1991), 445; Albers, 'Seeds of Contention', 30, 64–5.

[27] Butterworth, *Oldham*, 65–6; G. Shaw, *Local Notes and Gleanings*, ii (Oldham, 1888), 246.

[28] CVR 1804, 371.

[29] Church of England Record Centre (CERC), Church Commissioners (CC), file 21, 197, Grundy to Ecclesiastical Commissioners (EC) 31 Nov. 1859.

from the capital. Even so, the area seems to have continued to experience severe problems, at least until the early 1820s. A similar situation developed in Oldham, and Foster has traced a series of local crises between 1792 and 1808. Only for a brief period following the Peace of Amiens did local wages begin to approach pre-war levels. Economic difficulties had a general dampening effect on local communal activity and seem to have squeezed severely the finance available for Church extension in many parts of the country.[30] Together with the relatively comfortable position achieved as a result of the strenuous church-building effort of the preceding decades, this probably explains a lull, at the beginning of the nineteenth century, in efforts to expand church room. There was no corresponding cessation in demographic change, however, and much of the achievement of the eighteenth century was submerged beneath a rising tide of population.[31] By the early 1820s, the need for renewed effort was obvious and the Anglicans responded with a further energetic bout of church-building.

The second phase of church-building in the locality concentrated on three main objects: the rebuilding, on an enlarged scale, of Oldham's parochial chapel; and the construction of two large new churches, at Birch in the parish of Middleton, and at Greenacres at the eastern end of the Oldham township. A third new church was contemplated at Tonge in Chadderton, but no suitable site could be found, and the plans were shelved until 1834, when a site finally became available.[32] The second phase was differentiated from the first by the availability, for the first time, of large-scale financial aid from outside the locality, in the form of government grants, administered by the Church Building Commissioners, and assistance from the newly established Church Building Society.[33] Local Anglicans were quick to take advantage of these new opportunities. In November 1818 John Fallowfield, the new perpetual curate of St Mary's, Oldham, made an application to the Church Building Society for aid, explaining that 'The Church is in a very serious state, and the parishioners feel anxious to rebuild it upon an enlarged site and erect galleries,

---

[30] MPL 09, Saddleworth Vestry Minutes, 1794–1820; Foster, *Class Struggle*, 34–41; Rowbottom Diary, 31 Aug. 1793; C. W. Chalkin, 'The Financing of Church Building in the Provincial Towns of Eighteenth-Century England', in P. Clark (ed.), *The Transformation of English Towns 1600–1800* (1984), 295.

[31] See Table 2.1. For a brief account of the general incidence of this lull in south Lancashire, see Smith, 'Richard Podmore', 115–16.

[32] CC, file 20, 833, Petition to Church Building Commissioners (CBC), 23 May 1824, Rector of Middleton to CBC, 16 July 1834.

[33] M. H. Port, *Six Hundred New Churches: The Church Building Commissioners, 1818–1856* (1961), 1–5.

if means can be found to meet the expense.'[34] However, local differences over the extent of building required, and the competing ecclesiatical needs of other parts of the town, delayed the decision to rebuild, which was not confirmed in vestry until December 1822. It was then decided to apply for an act of parliament, to rebuild the nave of the church. The money required, estimated at £8,000–9,000, was to be raised locally on the understanding that a second church would be built in the town by parliamentary grant. Fallowfield had applied for aid for the additional church in 1820, stressing the need to build in the new suburb, which had grown up to the east of the central township and had begun to develop the characteristics of a separate district.[35]

The needs of new communities were also emphasized, together with a stress on the value of supporting attachment to Anglicanism while it still continued to flourish, in the grant applications made on behalf of the new church at Birch in 1824.[36] This application was strongly supported by C. J. Blomfield, the bishop of Chester, who described Birch as a village with a population of 3,000 'mostly in very moderate circumstances', and commented on their desire for a church:

They are extremely anxious to obtain one for themselves and by subscriptions amongst themselves can raise about £600. In addition to this, one person will give a site, and many others have offered to carry the materials with their own teams, while some labourers have offered to work on lower terms than usual. A very great anxiety prevails amongst them generally, to have a church and to be spared the necessity of going to dissenting places of worship which they say must be the case, if they can have no accommodation in church. It is so pleasing an example of sincere attachment to the Establishment in a large body of men placed in a humble sphere of life that it well deserves encouragement from the Commissioners.[37]

With the active support of Blomfield, and his equally vigorous successor, J. B. Sumner, the building of the church seems to have proceeded fairly smoothly. At its consecration in 1829, the completed structure could seat 1,000 people, just over half in free sittings, at a total cost of £4,101 or £4 2s. per seat. A sum of £50 had been contributed by the landowner in the form of a site, £220 4s. 0d. by local subscribers, and the remainder by the Commissioners.[38]

---

[34] Lambeth Palace Library (LPL), Incorporated Church Building Society (ICBS) ICBS, 0 box 1, Fallowfield to 3 Nov. 1818.

[35] Ibid., Fallowfield to ICBS, 7 Dec. 1822; *Manchester Guardian*, 28 Dec. 1822; CC, file 20,536, Fallowfield to CBC, 19 June 1820.

[36] CC, file 17,647, Houghton to CBC, 7 July 1825.

[37] Ibid., Blomfield to CBC, 23 Sept. 1825.　　　　[38] Ibid., Summary, 9 Nov. 1869.

The new churches in Oldham had a much more difficult passage, as their promoters became enmeshed both in a mass of bureaucratic detail and in disputes with government representatives, who seemed not to appreciate local conditions. The Church Building Commissioners' favoured architect, Charles Barry, submitted plans for both St Mary's and St James's. These plans were found unsuitable by the local committees, and had to be abandoned after causing considerable delay. In the case of St Mary's, the trustees had to resist pressure both from the Commissioners and from their bishop, who supported the Barry plan despite the fact that the alternative design was cheaper and promised to seat 500 more people. The extra seating, the trustees pointed out, 'was in itself considered as no trifling advantage, owing to the greatly increasing population of this township'. The trustees finally won their point after much correspondence, a deputation to Chester, and a year's delay.[39] However, no sooner was this problem nearing resolution than the Commissioners began to complain that the act obtained for rebuilding the church infringed their own powers. While this wrangle proceeded, matters took a turn for the worse, when part of the north-east corner of the building gave way, scattering slates on to a packed evening congregation and causing several injuries. Proposals were then put forward for a complete demolition of the old church and its reconstruction, at a cost considerably in excess of the original scheme, to be financed by Church rate. These proposals met with opposition from the out-townships, but the ratepayers of Oldham were overwhelmingly in favour, and they carried the vote at a crucial meeting in March 1828. An amended act, extending the powers of the Trustees to cover the chancel, and altered to the satisfaction of the Commissioners, was obtained in June 1828.[40] The work began later the

[39] CC, file 20,536, Barlow to Goodwin, 23 Sept. 1824; St Mary's, Oldham (SMO), Acts, Orders, and Proceedings of the Trustees for Rebuilding Oldham Church 1824–41, Dec. 1825; ibid., Trustees to Bishop of Chester, Aug. 1825.

[40] RVR 52, pp. 48–111; *Manchester Mercury*, 12 July 1825. Vote on the rebuilding of Oldham's parochial chapel:

Township	For	Against
Oldham	2,275	192
Chadderton	112	35
Royton	5	570
Crompton	0	1,007[a]
TOTAL	2,392	1,804

Majority in favour 588.

[a] 1,007 was the total number of rate-payers in Crompton: *Manchester Courier*, 22 Mar. 1828.

same year, and was completed in 1830, at a cost of just over £30,000. Some £25,000 was raised by Church rate and the remainder by the sale of various items, including the old church bell.[41] St James's, in the new suburb of Greenacres Moor, had a fairly smooth run in comparison. It was begun in August 1827 and completed in 1829 for £9,651 15s. 7d., the site value of £300 being raised by local subscription and the rest of the cost being met by the Commissioners. The church was the largest in Oldham, seating, at the lowest estimate, 1,837, including more than 1,200 in free seats; and its construction attracted considerable popular interest.[42]

The second phase of Church extension in Oldham was, therefore, reasonably successful. After a period of enforced inactivity, the local Establishment had responded well to the new circumstances. Over 3,000 seats were added in the second half of the decade; for the first time, a high proportion of the new seats were unappropriated, and these additions restored, to some extent, the density of accommodation in the locality. Moreover, it is clear that the Anglicans could still count on considerable popular support, demonstrated both by the manifest demand for new churches, and by the popular vote in favour of large-scale expenditure on the rebuilding of St Mary's. However, along with new financial resources came the problem of dealing with remote metropolitan bodies, like the Church Building Commissioners, which made external aid a decidedly mixed blessing. The resultant delays and complications did much to hamper local initiatives, and were to bedevil Church extension after 1830. Nevertheless, in the provision of additional accommodation, the achievements of the 'unreformed' Establishment were considerable. If the Church had lost ground over the period as a whole, this was clearly not due to corruption or complacency; nor, in a period of unprecedented demographic change, was it particularly surprising.

Clerical Standards and Religious Services

Although the Hanoverian Church in Oldham and Saddleworth was successful in the provision of functional buildings, its record with regard to the provision of decent accommodation for its clergy, and of the resources to improve their standard of living, was rather poor. Even as late as 1825, only three of the eleven local churches and chapels could provide parsonages, and a number of clergymen, while resident in the locality,

---

[41] Anon., *Oldham Church Rebuilding Accounts* (Oldham, 1834).
[42] CC, file 20,536; *Manchester Courier*, 8 Sept. 1827; CC, file 20,836, Walker to CBC, 26 Mar. 1832; RVR 53, pp. 4–9, 21–2.

TABLE 2.2. *Estimated values of Benefices in Oldham and Saddleworth*

Benefice	Value in	
	1814 ($£$)	1832 ($£$)
St Mary's, Oldham	106	191
St Leonard's, Middleton[a]	—	705
St Chad's, Saddleworth	108	143
Holy Trinity, Shaw	93	220
St John's, Hey	100	130
St Paul's, Royton	108	146
St Thomas's, Friarmere	97	90
St Peter's, Oldham	60	126
St Margaret's, Hollinwood	85	136
Holy Trinity, Dobcross	85	124
St Anne's, Lydgate	88	130
St James's, Oldham	—	72
St Mary's, Birch	—	48

[a] In 1814 estimates were made only for benefices worth less than $£150$.

Sources: PP HOL 1818, xciii CP, Account of Benefices and Population, Churches, Chapels, and their capacity; Number and Condition of Glebe Houses; and Income of All Benefices not exceeding $£150$ per annum, 42–9; PP 1835, xxii (54), Report of the Commissioners appointed by His Majesty to Inquire into the Ecclesiastical Revenues of England and Wales, table iv.

could not find a suitable house close to the church.[43] Clerical incomes seem to have increased during the eighteenth century, but these too were far from lavish, as is apparent from the estimates collected in the course of parliamentary inquiries in 1814 and 1832, which are displayed in Table 2.2. Most local benefices had been augmented by Queen Anne's Bounty before 1832, and some had received quite considerable capital sums, which were usually invested in land. St Margaret's, Hollinwood, for example, received six grants between 1756 and 1829, making a total of $£2,200$.[44] Nevertheless, with the exception of the rectory of Middleton, the only local living to receive tithe, none of the benefices in Oldham and Saddleworth were of great value. The increase in income between the two inquiries appears significant, especially given the deflationary conditions

[43] CVR 1825.   [44] RVR 53, p. 36.

of the time, but in part it simply represented the instability of stipends based largely on pew rents: 1814 was a bad year for local textiles, while the years before 1832 were mostly good ones. In fact, clergymen without private means or additional employment were not too far removed from the position of the skilled cotton workers, whose wages could have formed the basis of a family income in excess of £80 per annum in 1832.[45]

The quality of the Hanoverian clergy, of their pastoral activity, and of the services at which they presided, has been subjected to severe censure. Criticism has focused, in particular, on the prevalence of pluralism and non-residence among the clergy, and Peter Virgin, for example, has concluded that the whole of Georgian church reform was a failure, because it did not secure 'the provision of a resident beneficed clergyman in every parish throughout the land'.[46] Low incomes and inadequate accommodation might have been expected to make Oldham and Saddleworth particularly prone to these vices, but in practice pluralism and non-residence were relatively rare in Oldham, where the bishop of Chester's 1778 visitation found all seven incumbents resident either on or adjacent to their cures.[47] The Saddleworth churches seem to have done rather less well in this respect. Several perpetual curates of St Anne's, Lydgate, were non-resident for at least part of their incumbencies, and the cure was twice sequestered during the incumbency of Bowness Cleasby (1807–29), the most disreputable of the Lydgate parsons. St Chad's, the parochial chapel, also had two successive incumbents who were unable or unwilling to reside in the locality. However, it would be a mistake to draw premature conclusions from the mere fact of non-residence. The vast majority of non-residents made arrangements for their benefices to be served and, as Paul Langford has noted, 'The impoverished curate was not bound to be [a] less effective pastor than a well-fed parson.' In fact, the Church may often have been at its most effective in parishes served by its humbler clergy, in a more proximate economic relation to the bulk of their parishioners. Neither Lydgate nor Saddleworth seems to have suffered unduly in the absence of its incumbent. Both were well served by a series of competent and dedicated stipendiary curates and thus exhibited, in characteristic eighteenth-century style, a paradoxical combination of formal corruption and pastoral excellence.[48] The one notable example of local

---

[45] Foster, *Class Struggle*, 295; Rycroft, 'Craven', 91; Albers, 'Seeds of Contention', 71–6.

[46] Virgin, *Age of Negligence*, 163.   [47] CVR 1778.

[48] Raines MSS xv. 17–18, 57–8; C. C. W. Airne, *St Anne's Lydgate: The Story of a Pennine Parish 1788–1988* (Saddleworth, 1988), 11–8. P. Langford, *A Polite and Commercial People:*

pluralism was similarly anomalous. William Winter, the Evangelical curate of St Peter's from 1797, also held the cure of St John's, Hey, from 1810 until his death in 1838. However, Winter employed a curate, permanently resident at Hey, at the generous salary of £90 per annum plus fees (probably more than the previous incumbent had earned from the living) as well as doing occasional duty there himself. It could, therefore, be regarded as a beneficial arrangement, whereby a richer benefice subsidized a poorer one, rather than as an example of corruption.[49]

In the early eighteenth century, many of the clergy had supplemented their income by farming, but towards the end of the century schoolmastering seems increasingly to have become the most popular secondary occupation. Some had official posts, like John Darby, who held the position of second master at Manchester Grammar School together with the perpetual curacy of St Margaret's, Hollinwood, throughout his incumbency from 1769 to 1801. The more usual practice, however, seems to have been teaching in the village school, or the coaching of a few private pupils. The curate of Royton, for example, informed his bishop in 1825 that he taught five pupils for two hours at the end of each day.[50] There is little evidence that these subsidiary occupations absorbed an undue proportion of the time and energy of local clergy, and, by broadening the base of contact with their parishioners, they may actually have enhanced their pastoral work.[51] It is clear, from the evidence of the visitation returns, that the clergy of Oldham and Saddleworth maintained a high standard of 'Sunday duty'. Already by 1778, in line with the standard practice throughout south Lancashire and west Yorkshire, all the local clergymen were providing two services, each with a sermon, every Sunday. By the beginning of the nineteenth century, some local churches had even begun to experiment with three services and sermons each Sunday, especially during the summer, when the longer hours of daylight made evening journeys easier. However, weekday services were, in most local churches, confined to major festivals and holidays, or to other special occasions, like friendly-society anniversaries, when large congregations could be expected. Although the parish church in Middleton and St Mary's, the parochial chapel in Oldham,

England 1727–1783 (Oxford, 1989), 260; W. B. Maynard, 'Pluralism and Non-Residence in the Archdeaconry of Durham 1774–1856: The Bishop and Chapter as Patrons', *Northern History*, 26 (1990), 122–3; Rycroft, 'Craven', 116; Warne, *Church and Society*, 42; M. Cragoe, 'The Tory and Anglican Gap in Welsh Historiographical Perceptions: The Case of Carmarthenshire 1832–1886', D.Phil. thesis (Oxford, 1990), 285.

[49] RVR 52, p. 200; Andrew, *Hey*, 25; CVR 1825, St Peter's, Oldham, St John's, Hey.
[50] Anon., *St Margaret's Church, Hollinwood, 1769–1969* (n.p., 1969), 2; CVR 1825, 409.
[51] e.g. Raines MSS i. 270–8.

persisted with Wednesday and Friday prayers into the first half of the
nineteenth century, these seem to have met with a poor response, partly,
no doubt, because of the difficulty of combining weekday attendance with
work, but also because they omitted the most popular element in the
Anglican service—the sermon.[52]

The provision of two and sometimes three sermons every Sunday was
comfortably in advance of the canonical minimum, and necessarily so,
since local people seem to have regarded preaching, rather than sacraments or liturgy, as central to their church experience. This emphasis was
reflected in the architecture of the new chapels, which was often designed
to concentrate attention on the pulpit, and incorporated a rather perfunc-
tory chancel at most. Moreover, space around the altar was frequently
sacrificed in the face of the need for increased accommodation, both in
the new chapels and in the older medieval churches, as their chancels
were filled with galleries and additional seating.[53] A number of local
clergymen in the earlier eighteenth century established reputations as
memorable preachers, and surviving correspondence from the end of the
century indicates that some of their successors devoted considerable
attention to the cultivation of an attractive pulpit style.[54] The bishops of
Chester placed considerable emphasis on the quality of preaching in their
diocese, particularly Bishop Sumner, who warned specifically against 'the
legal style' as opposed to the 'Evangelical Spirit', arguing that mere moral
instruction was useless, and that only Gospel preaching was effective.[55]
Certainly, the most popular preachers seem to have been Evangelicals,
and the standard of preaching probably rose as their influence grew in the
locality from the later eighteenth century. High standards were urgently
required, because the popular preference for the sermon, over the more
distinctively Anglican parts of the service, exposed the Church to direct

[52] CVR 1778–1825; Rowbottom Diary, Oct. 1792. This level of service compares favourably with rural areas in the south and south-west of England and with the industrial villages
of Craven, but seems to have been fairly typical of south Lancashire: Warne, *Church and
Society*, 44–5; M. Ransome (ed.), *Wiltshire Returns to the Bishop's Visitation Queries 1783*
(Devizes, 1972); Rycroft, 'Craven', 129; F. C. Mather, 'Georgian Churchmanship Reconsidered: Some Variations in Anglican Public Worship 1714–1830', *Journal of Ecclesiastical
History*, 36 (1985), 267.

[53] E. Owen, *A Brief History of the Church and Parish of St Peter's Oldham* (Oldham, 1868),
8; C. E. Higson, 'Lees Chapel' otherwise Hey Chapel in Lees', *Transactions of the Lancashire
and Cheshire Antiquarian Society*, 34 (1916), 179–200; T. E. Clerworth, *A Sketch of the
History of the Parish Church of St Leonard Middleton* (1898), 12; N. Yates, *Buildings, Faith
and Worship* (Oxford, 1991), 75–90.

[54] Raines, 'Diary', 1 Feb. 1829; Raines MSS v. 204, H. Zouch to C. Zouch, 8 July 1792.

[55] J. B. Sumner, *A Charge Delivered to the Clergy of the Diocese of Chester at the Primary
Visitation* (London, 1829).

competition from the nonconformists, who began increasingly to make their presence felt during the second half of the century. Local people, like the Wiltshire villagers studied by Donald Spaeth, 'wanted not just a sermon but a good sermon', and they seem to have been quite prepared to move between denominations in order to find it. Poor preachers might see their hearers drifting away to the Dissenting chapel; conversely, a good preacher could expect very large congregations—like the hundreds who flocked to Saddleworth church to hear F. R. Raines—and might win back many who had drifted into Dissent.[56]

Of the two sacraments celebrated in Anglican churches, baptism was by far the more popular. The rite seems to have remained firmly in the public realm in Oldham and Saddleworth, private baptisms being exceptional, and almost invariably followed by a public reception of the child in church.[57] Mass participation in Holy Communion, on the other hand, seems, in general to have been limited to great festivals, and even then concerned a relatively small proportion of the adult population. In 1778, for example, the various chapelries of Oldham and Saddleworth produced for the Easter celebration one communicant for every 2.5 households at best, and one communicant for every 5 households at worst, the proportions varying between 1 to 3 and 1 to 6 at the other celebrations—figures which seem to have been entirely typical of south-east Lancashire.[58] This low level of popular involvement certainly did not stem from any lack of preparation. The large-scale confirmation services of the period were popular events, and a high proportion of the local youth must have been confirmed; there were, for example, over 2,500 candidates at Sumner's first confirmation in Oldham in 1829. Neither was the low level of popular participation a product of failure to celebrate with canonical frequency. According to the evidence of the visitation returns, even among the chapels of ease, although much depended on the enthusiasm of individual curates, nowhere did the annual number of celebrations fall below four, and returns of between five and nine celebrations per annum were common. Moreover, in both the Oldham parochial chapel and Middleton

---

[56] G. F. Grundy, 'A Sketch of the Life of the late Revd G. D. Grundy', in Andrew, *Hey*, ch. 3; Raines, 'Diary', 27 July 1828; D. A. Spaeth, 'Common Prayer? Popular Observance of the Anglican Liturgy in Restoration Wiltshire', in S. J. Wright (ed.), *Parish, Church and People: Local Studies in Lay Religion 1350–1750* (1988). 143. On the widespread incidence of this sort of 'occasional nonconformity' in Bristol, see J. Barry, 'The Parish in Civic Life: Bristol and its Churches 1640–1750', in ibid.

[57] CVR 1804, 371; MPL MSS. 922/3/N21, Diary of Henry Newcome, Rector of Middleton, 1701–14, 8 Feb. 1706.

[58] CVR 1778; Albers, 'Seeds of Contention', 145–51.

parish church, a pattern of one celebration a month, already established in 1778, was maintained throughout the remainder of the period. Although this represented a good performance by contemporary national standards, it was nevertheless entirely typical of clerical practice in the Chester diocese—a region characterized by F. C. Mather as possessing a conservative religious culture.[59] Some ministers made considerable efforts to build up a body of communicants, and did experience a measure of success. James Hordern, the curate of Holy Trinity, Shaw, reported in 1825 that he had increased average participation from ten to between forty and fifty in eighteen months, but even so, the reception of communion remained a minority practice in a congregation which was estimated at between 400 and 500 strong. The notion of a conservative religious culture in north-west England clearly requires some modification. Placed as they were on the periphery of the old south-east Lancastrian Presbyterian redoubt, attitudes to the sacraments in Oldham and Saddleworth are likely to have been similar to those of the old southern protestant areas also described by Mather. Widespread absence from communion, therefore, rather than simply reflecting 'the torpor that commonly gripped the Georgian Church of England', probably indicated a popular belief that communion was only for the very religious and for people in the upper ranks of society.[60]

Evangelicals were in the forefront of attempts to increase participation in communion, and, where large numbers of regular communicants are recorded, a combination of Evangelical activity and Methodist enthusiasm often seems to have been involved in breaking down popular reluctance. The clearest example of this process was at St Peter's, where the perpetual curate William Winter had, by 1811, raised the number of his regular communicants to 350, a figure greater than that returned in the same year for the parochial chapel on great festivals.[61] Other Evangelicals seem to have accepted that communion would remain a minority practice, and attempted to make a virtue of the necessity. W. F. Walker, the Evangelical incumbent of St James's, Oldham, explained his own policy to Raines in 1833:

[59] Rowbottom Diary, 19 Sept. 1829; CVR 1778–1825; Mather, 'Georgian Churchmanship', 269–75; Rycroft, 'Craven', 129; Warne, *Church and Society*, 44–5; S. J. Wright, 'Confirmation, Catechism and Communion: The Role of the Young in the Post-Reformation Church', in Wright (ed.), *Parish, Church and People*, 203–27.

[60] CVR 1825, 433; Mather, 'Georgian Churchmanship', 272–3, R. B. Walker, 'Religious Changes in Cheshire, 1750–1850', *Journal of Ecclesiastical History*, 17 (1966), 77–94; Spaeth, 'Common Prayer?', 130–9.

[61] CVR 1811, 183, 189.

I am disposed to think it is better in every way to begin with a small body of communicants—as they increase you know the characters of such as are added to the church: whereas, if you find a large number, you may, as you become better acquainted with the flock, discover that many are outward partakers of the Lord's table, whom you cannot think worthy recipients.[62]

This seems to represent a determination that, if communicants were to be an élite group within the congregation, rather like nonconformist 'members', then the Church should at least reap the corresponding benefit of an improved discipline.

The bishops of Chester were also concerned about proper performance of the liturgical elements of the Anglican service, and Bishop Law, for example, noted in 1817 that a lifeless delivery was likely to produce a lifeless congregation. According to the visitation returns, the rubrics in the Prayer Book seem generally to have been observed in Oldham and Saddleworth, and some local clergymen took great pains to ensure that the liturgy was clearly and attractively rendered. Raines, for instance, paid careful attention to the precise modulation of his voice.[63] There is little direct evidence, however, concerning popular responses to the liturgy. Intercessory prayer was certainly highly valued, and a book of persons 'To be Remembered in Prayer' from St Peter's, in the 1790s, records a number of public offerings of thanksgiving for prayers answered. However, the services in which the liturgy played the most prominent part—the weekday evening prayer at St Mary's and St Leonard's—always attracted very small congregations. Some bishops became concerned about the intelligibility of the liturgy to local congregations,[64] and even as late as 1853 illiteracy was causing problems in Oldham, as one incumbent noted:

Our Sunday Service is above the masses of the people. The prayer book supposes a population capable of reading, and of taking part in an intelligent and devotional manner, in solemn worship. But how many are deterred from going to church because they cannot find the Prayers and because they are insensible to the excellencies and beauties of the liturgy . . . When the sermon alone is regarded as the great object of attendance at church: when the responses are left to the Clerk or are very listlessly performed by the scattered few, then the simple grandeur of our reformed worship is lost, and it becomes in the view of many, even professed churchmen, a matter of supreme indifference whether the sermon be taken at the church or at the meeting house.[65]

[62] CCLM Mun ES7, Box 5, Raines Letter Collection, Walker to Raines, 1 Jan. 1833.

[63] *Manchester Mercury*, 26 Aug. 1817; Raines, 'Diary', 1 Feb. 1829; CVR 1778–1825.

[64] C. J. Blomfield, *A Charge Delivered to the Clergy of the Diocese of Chester at the Primary Visitation in August and September 1825* (1825).

[65] J. Bumstead, *Church Matters Past and Present in Oldham* (Oldham, 1853), 7.

It seems unlikely that the experience of his Hanoverian predecessors was significantly different.

However, though the spoken elements of the Anglican liturgy may have been unpopular, there is no doubt that the musical elements of the service combined high technical standards with a broad popular appeal. In the second half of the eighteenth century, Oldham and Saddleworth already possessed a long and flourishing musical tradition. The musical society at St Mary's was founded as early as 1696, and none of the new churches seems to have had any difficulty in raising choirs and groups of instrumentalists to provide music at its services. The early music societies were predominantly male in composition and popular in character. At St John's, Hey, for example, so many men were anxious to join the society that a system of 'vice-members' was created, and fines and expulsions for non-attendance at meetings imposed. Some of these groups achieved a high level of technical proficiency; thus the Lees singers were said to be 'superior to any previously known' at a great northern music festival held in Liverpool in 1766. Leading local performers were frequently called upon to assist other musical groups throughout the country, and the Shaw Singers, on their foundation in 1740, employed a professional singing master and began to accumulate a considerable library of scores and parts. An examination of churchwardens' accounts also reveals a continuous expenditure on musical instruments and commissions for anthems and psalm settings.[66]

One upshot of this professional approach was that the pattern of conflict between musicians and clergy over musical standards, detected by Obelkevich in south Lindsey, was absent from Oldham and Saddleworth.[67] Locally, the initiative for the substitution of organists for string and pipe bands seems to have come largely from the musical groups themselves, as they sought a more congenial accompaniment for their choral performances. As early as the mid-eighteenth century, the possession of an organ had been accepted as a norm in local churches, and the only objection to their introduction seems to have been the expense. At Hollinwood, for example, the Consecration Deed of 1769 specifically set aside the west gallery for an organ, but it was occupied by an instrumental band until

---

[66] Andrew, *Hey*, 10, 15; Holy Trinity, Shaw, Deed of Formation of Society of Singers, 1740, Singers' Society Book, 1800–1826; Shaw MSS 88, St Peter's, Oldham, Churchwarden's Accounts; St Thomas's, Friarmere, Vestry Minutes, 1805–12; Elias Hall MSS, repr. in G. P. Gore, *St Mary's*, 43–4. For similar developments in Devon during this period, see Warne, *Church and Society*, 47–8.

[67] Obelkevich, *Religion and Rural Society*, 146–50.

the church could afford its first organ in 1810. Some organs were extremely expensive, that installed in St James's, Oldham, in 1830 costing around £700. In practice, the introduction of an organ did not always lead to the exclusion of the instrumentalists. At St Paul's, Royton, for example, the old strings and woodwind seem to have coexisted amicably with an organ for at least ten years. There is no evidence that local people felt in any way alienated by the arrival of the organ. The 'opening' of a new instrument was often a great public occasion, and in 1825 St Leonard's, Middleton, was 'crowded almost to suffocation' for one such event.[68]

As semi-autonomous popular institutions which performed their own concerts as well as being intimately involved with the running of church services, the musical societies provided a bridge between the Church and the community at large. The Shaw Society was certainly an important focus of social activity, and included among its members such notable local characters as 'Tim Bobbin', the dialect poet; it was also a powerful attraction to attendance at church, especially at special musical services, providing an important exception to the 'comparatively dull, plain and unceremonious' Anglican worship described by Gerald Parsons.[69] The societies pioneered a local tradition of popular oratorio performance, participating in the first full 'Messiah' performed in the north of England, at Manchester in 1765. Sacred music concerts were frequently held in local churches too, and seem to have had a wide popular appeal, while services at which collections were to be made in support of the singers would fill the churches to capacity. At Hey Chapel, devotion to music went so far that the congregation seems to have provided a house for their organist before a parsonage was built for the minister.[70]

The elements of the Anglican church service which seem to have undergone the most significant change in the Hanoverian period were congregational hymn-singing and the rehearsal of the catechism. The former, judging by the sums paid for the printing of hymns from the late eighteenth century onwards, seems to have increased in importance, owing

---

[68] Andrew, *Hey*, 16; Shaw MSS 116, St Margaret's, Hollinwood, Consecration Deed 1769; anon., *Notes on the History of St Margaret's Church and Parish* (Oldham, 1950); RVR 53, p. 4; Shaw MSS 11, St Paul's, Royton, Chapelwarden's Accounts; *Manchester Mercury*, 19 July 1825; Yates, *Buildings, Faith and Worship*, 64–5.

[69] G. Parsons, 'Reform, Revival and Realignment: The Experience of Victorian Anglicanism', in Parsons (ed.), *Religion in Victorian Britain*, i (Manchester, 1988), 47.

[70] R. Elbourne, *Music and Tradition in Early Industrial Lancashire 1780–1840* (Woodbridge, 1980); Allen, *Shaw Church*, 21; Shaw MSS 82; *Manchester Chronicle*, 1 Aug. 1828; *Manchester Mercury*, 12 July 1825; J. Obelkevich, 'Music and Religion in the Nineteenth Century', in J. Obelkevich, L. Roper, and R. Samuel (eds.), *Disciplines of Faith* (1987), 550–65.

partly to the growing influence of Sunday schools. These nurtured the literacy that made the widespread use of hymns easier, and also adopted a common practice of teaching hymns to the children especially for use at Sunday-school anniversary services.[71] Catechism, on the other hand, which seems increasingly to have been regarded simply as a preparation for confirmation, probably declined as a feature of the regular round of church services in the locality. Already, by 1778, catechism in church was confined to part of the year only, often during Lent or in the summer, and in the succeeding decades, perhaps because it was felt to disrupt the balance of the service, some clergymen began to experiment with catechizing on a regular basis in local schools or in their own homes, and limiting its use in the chapel to two or three Sundays a year. This sort of arrangement depended less on the willingness of parents to send their children along to church, but it did place clergymen at the mercy of schoolmasters, not all of whom were prepared to co-operate. An alternative approach, adopted in some local chapels, was to present the catechism in a series of sermons or lectures, either as part of the general preaching round or as a special event. Some catechetical lectures proved a considerable success, and in 1804 Winter reported that he lectured in St Peter's for six months in each year, to an audience of around 1,000.[72]

Notwithstanding the reputation of the eighteenth-century Church for neglect, the standard of the general pastoral work undertaken by the local clergy appears to have been high. Henry Newcome, rector of Middleton from 1701 to 1713, visited his sick parishioners on a regular basis, administering the sacrament and encouraging them to attend public worship when they had recovered. His other pastoral activities ranged from admonishing parishioners whose behaviour he regarded as scandalous to reconciling a man and wife who were on the verge of separation, and intervening on behalf of a local man who had been pressed into the army. Similarly, in 1751, John Heginbottom, the curate of Saddleworth, reminded his parishioners that:

When I first became your lawful Pastor, such gross ignorance I met with in some persons in this Chapelry, and such indecency and un-uniformity I observed in the behaviour of others in the Public Worship of God, that I dearly lamented the same, and made it my business in a familiar and gentle manner often to instruct the former and to reduce the latter to decency, uniformity and good order in the Service of God, which most of this Congregation is now remarkable for . . . Have

---

[71] MPL 09/2/3, St Chad's, Saddleworth, Church Warden's Accounts; Shaw MSS 88; CVR 1825.

[72] CVR 1778–1825.

I not duly visited many that have been sick among you which I might lawfully have refused by reason of their Distemper being infectious.[73]

Heginbottom was a popular figure, not only because of his conscientious performance of his pastoral duties, but also because of his willingness to play his fiddle for Sunday evening parish dances and his custom of providing a barrel of beer for those parishioners who helped him gather in the harvest on his glebe. His predilection for drinking occasionally provoked episcopal censure, but this sort of easy familiarity between a clergyman and his parishioners must have enriched the more regular ministrations of Heginbottom and his colleagues.[74] Other local clergy were also indefatigable visitors of their parishioners, especially of the sick. Winter at St Peter's, for example, remarked that he was 'daily engaged in visiting the sick', and John Buckley of St Thomas's, Friarmere, explained that he always visited the sick when sent for and made visits at other times too.[75] From the appointment, in the mid-1770s, of Mortimer Grimshaw as perpetual curate of St Peter's, Evangelical influence began gradually to increase in Oldham and Saddleworth until, by 1829, five or six local benefices were served by Evangelical curates.[76] Several studies have pointed to the role of Evangelicalism in improving clerical standards, and there is some local evidence of a quickening of the pace, especially at St Peter's under William Winter, and at St Chad's, Saddleworth, under Francis Raines, whose diary describes a regular round of pastoral visits which must have cost him considerable effort. There is also some evidence that the more 'old-fashioned' clergymen had begun to feel under pressure when confronted with more exacting Evangelical standards. Raines recorded an encounter with one such, who 'made some ill tempered remarks on Low Churchmen, or the "tight laced gentlemen" and "Saints" as he termed them, I clearly saw it was all directed at me'.[77] Certainly, men like Raines had a clear idea of the sort of behaviour now to be expected of a serious clergyman and his family, and he noted in July 1828, following a visit to one of his clerical neighbours in Saddleworth: 'Called with Mr Alkin (the curate of Lydgate) at the Revd Mr Mills's. The magistrate was from home; his lady very polite, though very fashionable and aping the modern fine lady. Routs, cards and dancing, for a Churchman's wife with a church income of not more than £150 per annum is inconsistent and

---

[73] Newcome Diary, *passim.*; Raines MSS i. 280.
[74] Ibid. xxxviia. 22.   [75] CVR 1825.   [76] See Appendix 1.
[77] B. Heeney, *A Different Kind of Gentleman* (Hamden, Conn., 1976), ch. 2; A. Russell, *The Clerical Profession* (1980), ch. 4; A. Haig, *The Victorian Clergy* (1984), 13; Raines, 'Diary', 29 Aug. 1829.

reprehensible.' Raines's Evangelicalism was moderate in its theology and non-partisan in its approach; he consciously rejected the term 'low Churchman' with its erastian connotations and was on occasion (though perhaps only as a debating-point) willing to describe himself as a 'high Churchman'. The conflict between men like Raines and their more old-fashioned neighbours was a matter not so much of party as of style.[78] Evangelicals were not the only local clergy conscientiously performing their duty, and what clergymen like Heginbottom may have lost in the respect of their parishioners they probably gained in their affection. It would, in any case, be anachronistic to judge the performance of such men by the professional standards of a later age.

New Departures

Local Anglicans responded not only vigorously but imaginatively to their new environment. Not content with promoting the development of church music and experimenting with different approaches to the catechism, local ministers also introduced special services as a deliberate attempt to draw in those who were deterred from attending their usual 'Sabbath Ministrations'. Newcome in Middleton invited his congregation into his own home for prayers, and the minister of St Margaret's, Hollinwood, explained in 1804 that, because the poor had informed him 'that they have not decent clothing and are on this account ashamed to attend the public service', he had established a less formal, evening lecture at 7 p.m. each Sunday. The same formula of evening prayer with an informal lecture was also in use at St Peter's, the town-centre Evangelical stronghold, from 1789 at the latest.[79] Perhaps the most enduring of the eighteenth-century innovations in local Church life, however, was the Sunday school. On 3 November 1783 Robert Raikes's famous letter publicizing Sunday schools appeared in the *Gloucester Journal*, and, later that same month, the first Sunday school was opened in Oldham. It was a joint venture financed by two local hat-manufacturers, Thomas Henshaw (Anglican) and John Clegg (Methodist), and was held on the premises of the Oldham Grammar School, with the co-operation of Thomas Fawcett, the incumbent of the parochial chapel. Writing formed part of the curriculum, and the school quickly became a popular institution, with 200–300 scholars, all of whom attended morning service in St Mary's chapel. The idea spread

---

[78] Ibid. 29 July 1828, 29 Aug. 1829.
[79] Newcome Diary, 6 Jan. 1705; CVR 1804, 243; 1789, 56.

rapidly around the neighbourhood, and two more schools were opened by Henshaw and Clegg at Glodwick and Greenacres Moor. In August 1784 St Margaret's, Hollinwood, opened a school, and in March 1785 the Wesleyan Methodists opened a Sunday school whose pupils attended St Peter's chapel of ease for Divine Service. This school may have been the first in the country to which the teachers gave their services gratuitously— the teachers in question being volunteers from local Methodist classes. William Winter opened a Sunday school in more direct connection with St Peter's in 1798, and by 1818 he was superintending a federation of between eight and fifteen schools run by members of his congregation in locations all over the town. John Beckett of St John's had adopted a similar plan some ten years earlier, and by March 1786 his church stood at the centre of a network of seven Sunday schools in the villages around Hey.

The Sunday schools rapidly built up a large working-class clientele, and by 1822 there were about 1,770 scholars connected with St Peter's schools alone.[80] It was hoped that the children might help to reform their own parents, Bishop Beilby Porteus recommending that they be given tracts to take home for this purpose; the schools themselves may also have contained working-class adults anxious to acquire the skills of reading and writing. It was not only in the number of their pupils that the influence of the Sunday schools must be measured. They represented a mobilization of the laity for active participation in the pastoral work of the Church, as Sunday-school teachers and visitors—an important development for a Church, the demands on which were beginning to outstrip even the most energetic clerical efforts. Bishop Sumner both recognized and welcomed this new lay involvement in his charge of 1829.[81] The schools also functioned as an important additional point of contact between the Church and the population at large. Their hugely popular anniversary services in some places approached the level of festivals embracing the whole community, and must have brought many into the ambit of the churches who would not otherwise have been drawn in.[82]

Joint Sunday-school activity was only one aspect of a long and fruitful

---

[80] C. A. O'Neil, *An Account of the Origin of Sunday Schools in Oldham and its Vicinity* (Oldham, 1848), 4–22; *Manchester Mercury*, 7 Mar. 1786.

[81] Ibid.; Sumner, *Charge* (1829); R. J. Dell, 'Social and Economic Theories and Pastoral Concerns of a Victorian Archbishop', *Journal of Ecclesiastical History*, 16 (1965), 196–208; B. Porteus, *A Letter to the Clergy of the Diocese of Chester, Concerning Sunday Schools* (1786); T. W. Laqueur, *Religion and Respectability: Sunday Schools and Working-Class Culture 1780– 1850* (New Haven, Conn., 1976), 89–90.

[82] e.g. *Manchester Mercury*, 6 Sept. 1785, 4 Nov. 1785.

relationship between the Methodists and some representatives of the 'unreformed' Establishment. Once they had become rooted in the locality, the Methodists were quickly integrated into a number of local churches, notably St Chad's, Saddleworth, St John's, Hey, and St Peter's, Oldham. Good relationships continued well after the Methodists and Anglicans officially drifted apart after Wesley's death, so that Wesleyanism continued in many respects to preserve its character as simply a particularly enthusiastic form of Anglicanism, especially during the crucial period of industrial change between 1780 and 1815. The Methodists made a valuable contribution to many aspects of the churches' work. The Clegg family, local Methodist hat-manufacturers, for example, provided financial support for a regular Thursday evening lecture at St Peter's, and, as already noted, the exceptionally high numbers of communicants in Winter's congregation may, in part, have been a consequence of a high level of Methodist participation. According to one observer, the Methodists soon became 'some of the most valuable members of the congregation. They introduced class and band meetings, prayer meetings also, and were useful in a considerable degree in promoting the work of God.'[83] Like the Sunday schools, these informal gatherings also represented a manifestation of vigorous lay activity in support of the Church, at a period when the increase in population threatened completely to overload the local clergy. William Winter, in particular, seems to have given 'his' Methodists considerable freedom of action, and most of their activities were carried out under lay rather than clerical supervision. The Methodists were thus free to bring to the aid of the Church their flexibility of structure based on small cottage or class meetings. This enabled them to penetrate the proliferating residential communities of Oldham and Saddleworth at the lowest level—small neighbourhoods within the built-up area, and remote folds of houses in the countryside beyond—and thus to develop to a high degree that 'proximity' which has been identified as an important factor in Church growth. The addition of Methodist informality to the renewed institutional infrastructure provided by the Established Church produced a formidable pastoral combination.[84] Some local ministers themselves adopted a Methodist methodology. Samuel

---

[83] *Wesleyan Methodist Magazine (WMM)*, 76 (1853), 786; CVR 1789, 156; Methodist Archives and Research Centre (MARC), Notes on the Early Days of Methodism in Oldham and District Compiled by Revd John McOwan, Minister in the Oldham Circuit, 1825–6; a transcript of this source is also available in OLIC.

[84] Anon., *Centenary Souvenir of the Establishment of Independent Methodism in Oldham, 1816–1916* (Oldham, 1916), 1–2; R. Currie, A. Gilbert, and L. Horsley, *Churches and Church-Goers* (Oxford, 1977), 59–60.

Stones, for example, assistant curate to Heginbottom at the Saddleworth parochial chapel, led a miniature revival in the district:

> The Gospel of Christ, thus made to him 'the power of God unto Salvation', he began to proclaim it in its simplicity, and with marked success. An extensive religious awakening followed; meetings for prayer and supplication were convened in the houses of his parishioners; and many, by the force of truth, were 'turned from darkness unto light and from the power of Satan unto God'.[85]

So popular was Stones's Methodistical ministry that, when the patron selected an alternative candidate to succeed Heginbottom in the living of Saddleworth, the local population turned out, *en masse*, to oppose his institution and to express their support for Stones. This demonstration proved so formidable that the erstwhile incumbent felt constrained to leave the locality immediately after reading himself into the living—never to return. Stones continued for some time afterwards as *de facto* minister of the district, being provided with a measure of financial support by his parishioners.[86]

The 'unreformed' Establishment was thrust by industrial change into a strange new environment, often indifferent, and sometimes potentially hostile. The ultimate impact the Church made on the area and on its population in these new circumstances is hard to evaluate. There are some rather sketchy church-attendance figures, provided for the 1825 visitation, most of which give indications of undeniable prosperity, with full churches and growing congregations. It would be wrong to attempt to draw firm conclusions from this limited evidence, but it is clear that the Establishment did at least maintain a strong subculture of regular attendance at church, together with a wider penumbra of support, expressed in terms of participation in Sunday-school anniversaries and local festivals, as well as other religious observances, such as fast days.[87] The total influence of the 'unreformed' Establishment was very wide, and, despite the problems of indifference, the Church found, fostered, and capitalized upon a good deal of popular attachment to its cause. The vigorous programme of church-building did enable it to penetrate many of the new communities growing up in the area and, finding a measure of acceptance by the population as a whole, the Church was able to participate in the development of community life. This was exemplified in the role of the popular musical societies, in the development of Sunday schools, and in the legitimation sought by friendly societies which used Anglican churches

---

[85] *WMM* 76 (1853), 786.   [86] Raines MSS i. 278.
[87] CVR 1825; Rowbottom Diary, 10 Mar. 1813.

for their anniversary services.[88] The partnership with Methodism and the local clergy's vigorous pastoral activity had begun to weave the influence of the Church closely into the textures of everyday life; and the great schism between Anglican and Methodist, after Wesley's death, may therefore have been far more damaging to the Church in general than is often realized.

Judged by almost any standards, the 'unreformed' Establishment of Oldham and Saddleworth was an impressive institution. Its clergy were dedicated and creative, and, where standards had not improved by the end of the period, it is usually because they were so high at its outset. Local Anglicans worked hard to extend the influence of their Church, and succeeded in laying a firm foundation for the future. If some of the Church's efforts were overwhelmed, this was a consequence of the sheer magnitude of the changes with which it had to contend, not of its own complacency or corruption. To suggest otherwise, is to underestimate both the vitality of local Anglicanism, and the scale of industrial and demographic change. The derogatory view of the Hanoverian Church has largely been shaped by a historiographical concentration on its bishops and on its rural parishes. Moreover, much of the writing has, in the past, been anecdotal rather than systematic in form, and eccentricity, flagrant abuse, and the accusations of later generations have all tended to attract greater notice than has conscientious work in the parishes.[89] Systematic research where it has been brought to bear suggests that standards were higher than previously thought, and perhaps particularly so in what have traditionally been regarded as areas of Anglican weakness, including the north and the industrial towns.[90] The Church, therefore, may have been responding energetically just where the need was greatest, and of this response, the vigour of the Establishment in Oldham and Saddleworth may well be a fair reflection.

[88] Ibid., Oct. 1791, 22 Oct. 1794. The important part played by the church in legitimating emergent working-class organizations in Lancashire is described in Albers, 'Seeds of Contention', 192–6.

[89] Sykes, *Church and State*; S. C. Carpenter, *Eighteenth Century Church and People* (1959); R. W. Malcolmson, *Life and Labour in England 1700–1780* (1981), 83–5.

[90] Mather, 'Georgian Churchmanship'; Rycroft, 'Craven'; Cragoe, 'Tory and Anglican Gap'; Warne, *Church and Society*; Albers, 'Seeds of Contention'.

3. The 'Reformed' Establishment

The period between 1831 and 1865 saw a series of dramatic changes in the position of the Established Church in Oldham and Saddleworth. Church accommodation expanded at an unprecedented rate, the number of clergy increased, and the parochial structure changed almost beyond recognition. However, as had been the case in the eighteenth century, these changes depended on local initiative and at the outset they marked the consolidation of earlier achievements rather than any radical new departure.

Parish Reformation

In 1832 W. F. Walker, the energetic incumbent of St James's, Oldham, wrote to the Church Building Commissioners stressing the existence of strong local identities within the Oldham townships and suggesting the separation of the chapelry of Oldham from the parish of Prestwich, and the assignment of an independent ecclesiastical district to each of the chapels of ease. A few months later Walker's petition received the support of Bishop Sumner and in March 1835 an Order in Council provided for the creation of districts for all six churches in the former chapelry. This set a precedent which was followed with the assignment of a district to a new church at Tonge in 1842 and the subdivision of the chapelry of Saddleworth in 1843.[1] The reorganization of Oldham's parochial chapelry seems to have been a concession to local feeling articulated by the clergy[2] and represented an institutional recognition of the role already being played by the chapels within the residential communities of Oldham and its out-townships. More importantly it served to confirm the strategy the Establishment was to follow in the future development of its mission to Oldham: a persistent attempt to colonize local communities rather than to build gathered churches. It also set a precedent for the Establishment's

---

[1] CC, file 20,836, Walker to CBC, 26 Mar. 1832, Sumner to CBC, 3 Nov. 1832; CC, file 20,833, Lawler to CBC, 11 Jan. 1842, 7 Feb. 1842, CBC to Bourchier, 28 Apr. 1842; CC, file 5,879, Molesworth to Whitelock, 12 Oct. 1843, Whitelock to Commissioners, 20 Jan. 1845.

[2] Butterworth Diary, July–Aug. 1836.

chief tactic—that of parochial subdivision. As already noted, it has become a historiographical commonplace that a failure to pursue the subdivision of large parishes lay at the root of Anglican difficulties in the industrial north. It is also assumed that the whole process of subdivision became relatively easy once nineteenth-century zeal had replaced clerical lethargy, and Peel's District Church Act had swept away many of the legal impediments. Those who questioned the value of subdivision in the nineteenth century and those who did not seek to prosecute it in the eighteenth century are thus by implication condemned as obscurantist defenders of vested interest out of tune with the age of reform. However, both these notions are called into question by the experience of Oldham and Saddleworth, where, although parochial subdivision was pursued with unusual energy and thoroughness, enormous complications were introduced by this particular approach to Church extension.

Shortly after his appointment to the incumbency of Oldham in 1842, Thomas Lowe carried out a thorough survey of his chapelry and presented the results, early in the following year, as the background to a remarkable plan for the ecclesiastical reorganization of the area. The key to the scheme, as Lowe explained to the Commissioners, lay in its comprehensive nature: 'For the removing of the evils of my parish—I propose the sowing of the good seed of truth—not the placing of one or two labourers—for then their influence would almost be destroyed but to take the whole and in dependence on the divine blessing render the work irresistible.'[3] He proposed a division of the old parochial chapelry into fifteen independent districts, each with a population of approximately 4,000 and a resident clergyman with a room licensed for worship where there was no existing chapel. The rooms were to be replaced as soon as possible by nine new churches, each with its own Sunday school, and a system of National and infant schools was to follow. Lowe's scheme found favour with an Ecclesiastical Commission newly armed with the powers of Peel's district church measure. In February 1844 the first five of the new districts were approved, and by August, following consultation with the incumbents of the existing chapels, all the districts had been established.[4] The whole undertaking seems to have proceeded very smoothly, and by late March the *Manchester Guardian* could announce that 'What the Revd Dr Hook is endeavouring to effect by a division of the extensive parish of Leeds . . . has already been effected at Oldham by the

---

[3] CC, file 1,443, Lowe, Application . . . to Divide the Parish of Oldham.
[4] CC, file 1,443, Note.

active exertions of the Revd Thomas Lowe.'[5] The organizational changes of the early 1840s effectively fixed the area's ecclesiastical structure for the remainder of the period, the only subsequent alterations being the creation of a new district at Moorside, mainly out of the parish of St James's in Oldham, the assignment of districts to new churches at Friezland and Denshaw in Saddleworth, and the enlargement of the parish of St John's, Hey, which took in territory from both Poor Law Unions. A series of local initiatives thus gradually created what might be regarded as a rational ecclesiastical structure for Oldham and Saddleworth: most of the new parishes served a residential community at district level in Oldham, though some, especially as the central built-up area continued to expand and the population rose in the out-townships, took in several. In Saddleworth, the districts tended to follow the boundaries of the ancient 'meres', each of which, after 1848, had its own ecclesiastical district containing several villages.

In most recent historiography the work of pastoral reorganization undertaken by the Church Building Commissioners in the 1830s has received a rather less favourable assessment than that undertaken by the Ecclesiastical Commissioners beginning in the 1840s. According to K. A. Thompson, the Church Building Commissioners' potential for innovation was vitiated by their conservatism and their dependence on voluntary local enterprise, whereas the Ecclesiastical Commission was both more bureaucratically rational and more free to take radical initiatives of its own. A concentration on the more controversial aspects of the work of the Ecclesiastical Commission, moreover, has tended to reinforce the impression that reform was imposed on a rather unwilling Church in a series of initiatives generated by the new central bureaucracy.[6] In Oldham, however, the impetus for change came entirely from the locality itself, and reform was at most facilitated rather than initiated by the Ecclesiastical Commissioners. The obvious need of their parishioners evoked in local Churchmen a spirit that transcended preoccupations with property rights: only one incumbent raised objections to the subdivision of his district, and these were quickly settled through the arbitration of Archdeacon Rushton.[7] The spirit of the early 1840s is epitomized by a letter

---

[5] *Manchester Guardian*, 23 Mar. 1844.

[6] Thompson, *Bureaucracy and Church Reform*, 10, 48; Chadwick, *Victorian Church*, i. 126, 141; Parsons, 'Reform, Revival and Realignment', 20–2; Virgin, *Age of Negligence*, 143; Maynard, 'Pluralism and Non-Residence', *passim*.

[7] CC, file 1,443, Holme to EC, 31 Aug. 1844, 16 Sept. 1844, 1 Oct. 1844, Rushton to EC, 1 Oct. 1844.

from Lowe to the Ecclesiastical Commissioners. 'I look to the day when you will pass my districts as the most blessed of my life—it will take away almost my whole income but while it makes me poor it will enrich thousands, sheltering them from sorrow here and misery forever hereafter.'[8] In this sort of atmosphere, reliance on local enterprise was a strength rather than a weakness, while attempts to manage reorganization in the manner suggested by bureaucratic rationality would tend to hinder, not promote, ecclesiastical reform.

Notwithstanding the commitment of the local Establishment to parochial subdivision, the incumbents of the new districts of the 1840s faced severe difficulties in bringing Lowe's scheme to fruition. Unlike the districts created by the Church Building Commissioners, which in some cases represented the culmination of almost a century of pastoral activity on the part of the incumbents of the chapels of ease, the new 'Peel parishes'—even though they might be closely related to new residential communities—necessarily cut across the grain of existing local ecclesiastical organization. The new clergymen, therefore, had not only to battle with relatively recently established patterns of non-church-going among some sections of the population, but also to cope with deeply rooted loyalties among the minority of committed church-going Anglicans to the parochial chapels or the chapels of ease which they had habitually attended prior to the establishment of the new districts. Thus, while Patrick Reynolds, the first incumbent of the new district of Waterhead, was soon able to gather the nucleus of a church, including some Waterhead residents who had previously attended St James's, Oldham, he was reliant for Sunday-school teachers on the generosity of G. D. Grundy, the minister of Hey, and, despite Grundy's willingness to co-operate, he was unable to persuade many of the Waterhead attenders at Hey to join his new congregation.[9] The problem for the incumbents of 'Peel parishes' was not simply that many of the most useful prospective members of their congregations were to be found worshipping at—and expending their energies and financial resources in the service of—churches outside the new districts in which they now lived; but also that the clergymen of the older chapels were drawn by the pastoral needs of these same people to disregard, in the course of their ministry, the boundaries of the new districts, thus violating their ecclesiastical independence.

In Saddleworth, this difficulty was thought to apply even to the independent districts created for the eighteenth-century chapels of ease, as

---

[8] Ibid., Lowe to EC, 8 June 1844.   [9] Shaw, *Local Notes*, 213.

the incumbent of St Chad's explained in 1843: 'I hold it impossible for the incumbent of Saddleworth Church to confine himself within the limits of an appointed district within his own chapelry as the congregation is formed from all parts however remote—in a great measure owing to a feeling of attachment to the Parochial Chapel and partly owing to the whole of the seats being free of payment.'[10] However, the problem was both more severe and more prolonged in Oldham, as the incumbent of the Peel district of Glodwick pointed out as late as 1853:

the Clergy of the elder churches by continuing to solemnize marriages, to visit pastorally, and to discharge ecclesiastical duties over the old area of their parishes . . . cherish the opinion among the people at large that they are quite justified in their present total neglect of ecclesiastical boundaries, and encourage a course of conduct which not only prevents the prosperity of the Church, but throws contempt upon her authority and discipline.[11]

The new Peel churches inevitably tended to suffer most from the negative effects of parochial subdivision—a factor which goes some way towards explaining their relatively poor performance in the 1851 Religious Census. Nevertheless, the process could also pose problems for the older churches. In Oldham, attempts by successive incumbents of St Mary's to supplement their depleted income by maintaining the right to perform marriages for the residents of the whole of the former chapelry provoked a series of squabbles over jurisdiction. This culminated in 1863 in a legal dispute which finally established the exclusive right of the ministers of the new churches to solemnize Anglican marriages in their districts. In Saddleworth, the creation of a new church at Friezland caused severe problems for the old chapel of ease at Lydgate, when a series of disputes with their incumbent provoked the majority of the congregation to move to the new church, which offered a more thoroughgoing Evangelical ministry. The situation at Lydgate became so serious that the church was closed for a time in 1851, ostensibly because the departure of the congregation had depleted its income below the level required to carry out vital repairs.[12] When problems of this nature are considered, the reservations of men who wished to preserve the parochial status quo begin to seem rather less unreasonable.

---

[10] CC, file 20,826, Whitelock to EC, 2 Feb. 1843.
[11] Bumstead, *Church Matters*, 11.
[12] RVR 52, p. 184; SMO, Marriage Question Correspondence; Airne, *Lydgate*, 29–34.

Church-Building

The tensions between local and central approaches to reform and the difficulties inherent in parish reorganization became particularly evident when local Anglicans turned to the task of providing church buildings as a focus for the devotional life of their new districts. The first new church to be built in the area after 1830 was St Michael's at Tonge, a village on the border between the Chadderton and Middleton out-townships, consecrated in 1839 with sittings for 536. St Michael's was financed with the aid of a large grant from the Church Building Commissioners, amounting to £1,000 out of a total cost of £1,731 7s. 6d. The ICBS made a smaller grant of £230 and the remainder was raised by local subscription.[13] The 'third phase' of church-building in Oldham and Saddleworth, however, began more properly in 1844 with the laying of the foundation stone for the first of the 'Peel churches', Christ Church, Glodwick, consecrated by the Bishop of Chester in November of the same year with seating for 800 people.[14] It was followed by St John's, Chadderton, in 1845; St James's, East Crompton, and Holy Trinity, Waterhead, in 1846; St Thomas's, Leesfield, and Holy Trinity, Coldhurst in 1848; St Thomas's, Werneth, in 1855; and, finally, by St Matthew's Chadderton, consecrated in 1857. The new churches varied considerably in size from St Matthew's, which seated only 400 on its completion, to St Thomas's, Leesfield, over twice as large, with 1,001 seats. Nevertheless, in aggregate, the new churches represented a considerable increase in the amount of accommodation provided by the Establishment—some 6,222 seats in all. In Saddleworth, church-building got off to a rather later start, and only two new churches were completed between 1831 and 1865: Christ Church, Friezland, consecrated in 1850, and Christ Church, Denshaw, built in 1863, with a total of 900 seats between them.

As in the period before 1830, local Churchmen were also active in enlarging existing structures. St Chad's, Saddleworth, was significantly enlarged during 1833–6, and its accommodation more than doubled to a new total of approximately 1,147 seats. Less ambitious alterations were carried out in several of the eighteenth-century chapels and even, as the population of their districts continued to grow, in some of the new churches of the 1840s and 1850s. In all, the thirty-five years after 1830 saw the addition of about 1,277 seats through the extension of existing

[13] RVR 54, pp. 196–7, 201, 203; CC, file 20,833, Note, 24 Apr. 1869.
[14] RVR 56, p. 173.

buildings.[15] A new departure in this period was the use of licensed rooms with regular Sunday services to supplement existing church accommodation. The first such experiment was probably 'Burn Chapel', acquired by the incumbent of Holy Trinity, Shaw, around 1830 and used as a mission station among the scattered communities of the northern portion of his chapelry. As a means of Church extension, such licensed rooms stood in lineal succession to the branch day and Sunday schools of the eighteenth century, allowing the Establishment to take its regular ministrations directly into new communities with no church-building of their own. Most of the new churches of the 1840s and 1850s began in some such building, or in converted cottages, hired rooms, and, in one case, that of St Matthew's, Chadderton, in a purpose-built wooden church with seating for 150.[16] As the Church began to expand its educational infrastructure, it became standard practice to license schoolrooms for regular Sunday worship. This approach could prove doubly advantageous, as the incumbent of St Paul's, Royton, explained: 'these used as National Schools on weekdays and as churches on Sundays, would be likely to bring parents and children to the latter from motives of gratitude for the good done to the scholars during the week.'[17] The irregular use of some of these rooms makes it difficult to assess their aggregate contribution to Anglican accommodation, but it could have been substantial; certainly in 1860 there were three licensed rooms each with a resident curate and two services on a Sunday, providing together some 1,400 additional sittings.[18]

The third phase of church-building in Oldham was crowned with considerable success. A total of at least 7,499 new seats was provided in local churches between 1830 and 1865, together with at least 1,700 in licensed rooms. In terms of the density of Anglican accommodation, however, success was rather less marked. In Oldham, the provision of accommodation gained on the rising tide of population only during the 1840s, even then never approached late eighteenth-century levels, and had fallen back to only 15.4 per cent by 1865. In Saddleworth, the slower rate of population growth gave greater opportunities for advance, and density increased in both the 1830s and 1840s and again in the 1860s,

[15] CC and ICBS files; RVR 1–62; PRO HO 129 1851 Religious Census MS Returns 475, 496, *Manchester Diocesan Directory* (1860–5).

[16] Allen, *Shaw Church*, 73; S. Deem, *St Thomas' Church and Parish of Werneth 1844–1937* (Oldham, 1938), 6; RVR 56, pp. 57, 73–4, Godson to Rushton, Apr. 1846, Circular, May 1853.

[17] CERC, National Society (NS) file, St Paul's, Royton, Dobie to NS, 5 Sept. 1843.

[18] *Manchester Diocesan Directory* (1860), 120.

though its peak in 1865 of 21.4 per cent was well below the 1791 level. The population of Oldham almost doubled between 1830 and 1865 and these figures, therefore, are no disgrace to the Church, but this was no dramatic recovery from eighteenth-century decline. The Church was sprinting, as it had sprinted before, largely in order to stand still.

Table 3.1 indicates the degree to which the density of accommodation varied from parish to parish. In Oldham both the size of ecclesiastical districts and the level of accommodation varied considerably, so it was not always the case that the largest districts had the lowest density of seating. In fact no clear pattern emerges, and, although as a rule the central districts seem to have done badly, the worst provided of all was the out-township parish of St Paul's, Royton. In Saddleworth the main problem clearly lay in the district of Lydgate, though here the situation was partially relieved by the licensing of two schools which, because they were not used every Sunday, have been excluded from the estimate of seating.[19] It should also be noted that the figures in the table represent a conservative estimate of the capacity of local churches. It is probable that, as in the previous century, many of the local churches could hold greater numbers than their returns for seating might suggest.[20]

In every one of the new churches built in Oldham after 1840 at least half the seats were free, and in some cases the proportion was considerably greater than half. Nevertheless, even when the free seats of the licensed rooms are taken into account, appropriated sittings in 1865 still accounted for 58.2 per cent of the total in Oldham and no less than 81 per cent in Saddleworth. The provision of free seats became the object of a crusade by later generations of Tractarian Churchmen both locally and nationally, and this seems to have coloured the prevailing historiographical view of the system. G. P. Gore, for example, the Tractarian historian of St Mary's, Oldham, claimed that, as a result of the increase in appropriation consequent on the rebuilding operations of the 1820s, 'The poor were practically excluded, and the church became for all intents and purposes a proprietary chapel of the wealthy and well-to-do middle classes.'[21] There is, however, no evidence to support this contention, and Lowe informed the Additional Curates' Society (ACS) in the early 1850s that 'the

---

[19] Ibid. (1869), 121; St Mary's, Oldham, and Christ Church, Friezland, also had such a school, and by 1865 St Paul's, Royton, may have been using one at Heyside.

[20] CC, file 2,093, Questions to be Answered by Incumbents, 19 Jan. 1861, Holy Trinity, Dobcross.

[21] W. R. Ward, 'The Cost of Establishment: Some Reflections on Church Building in Manchester', *Studies in Church History*, 3 (1966), 286–9; K. S. Inglis, *Churches and the Working Classes in Victorian England* (1963), 48–57; Gore, *St Mary's*, 48.

Ecclesiastical district	Population	Number of buildings	Seats			Density (%)
			Free	Appropriated	Total	
St Leonard's, Middleton[a]	10,028	2	350	1,334	1,684	16.8
St Mary's, Birch	3,773	1	504	496	1,000	26.5
St Mary's, Oldham[a]	16,576	1	438	1,041	1,479	8.9
St Peter's, Oldham	7,094	1	100	753	853	12.0
St James's, Oldham[a]	17,520	2	1,396	941	2,337	13.3
Christ Church, Glodwick[b]	7,200	1	520	300	820	11.4
Holy Trinity, Coldhurst	3,046	1	301	200	501	16.4
St Thomas's, Werneth	5,888	1	348	250	598	10.2
Holy Trinity, Waterhead	3,941	1	500	300	800	20.3
St John's, Hey	3,132	1	338	720	1,058	33.8
St Thomas's, Leesfield	5,358	1	526	475	1,001	18.7
St Margaret's, Hollinwood[b]	6,298	1	140	560	700	11.1
St John's, Chadderton	6,081	1	560	440	1,000	16.4
St Matthew's, Chadderton[b]	4,273	2	900	200	1,100	25.7
St Michael's, Tonge[b]	5,029	1	156	380	536	10.7
St Paul's, Royton	7,493	1	94	493	587	7.8
Holy Trinity, Shaw[b]	3,618	2	569	757	1,326	36.7
St James's, East Crompton	3,414	1	340	246	586	17.2
St Chad's, Saddleworth	2,954	1	413	716	1,147	38.8
St Thomas's, Friarmere	2,229	1	—	500	500	22.4
Holy Trinity, Dobcross	1,972	1	100	740	840	42.6
Christ Church, Friezland[b]	2,191	1	200	450	650	29.7
St Anne's, Lydgate	6,124	1	—	660	660	10.8
Christ Church, Denshaw	750	1	84	316	400	53.3

[a] Three clergymen serving in the parish.
[b] Two clergymen serving in the parish.

Sources: CC and ICBS Files; PRO HO 129 475, 496; *Manchester Diocesan Directory* (1860–65), RVR 1–62.

congregation of the Parish Church consists mainly of Mill Hands'.[22] In some cases the preponderance of appropriated pews did cause difficulties, the worst affected church being St Paul's, Royton, where, as its incumbent explained in 1843, 'The chapel is not filled by those who hold pews nor will they permit strangers or native residents to use them, and the difficulties on this subject . . . have been so great, that I have for some time been obliged to give over inviting them to church as there is no church for them.'[23]

The extent of this problem should not be exaggerated. There were many mitigating factors, especially in the older churches, where the relatively easygoing eighteenth-century attitude to appropriation seems to have persisted. Even where pew-owners did prove recalcitrant, some incumbents were prepared to ride roughshod over the feelings of their wealthier hearers in order to admit the poor.[24] In Saddleworth, where most of the appropriated pews were concentrated, many carried only a nominal rent. At Dobcross many were let for the quarterly rent of a farthing, and the appropriated free seats in Saddleworth Church were redistributed after the enlargements of the mid-1830s to secure a more rational provision for the changing needs of the area.[25] There was, moreover, a certain ambivalence in the general reaction to the widespread introduction of free sittings. When the promoters of Christ Church, Denshaw, expressed a desire to build it as a free and open church, they encountered popular resistance; they were forced to abandon the proposal and instead to make provision for a large number of appropriated seats.[26] Free sittings, even in a completely free church, may have seemed a symbol of condescending charity to the poor, who wanted to feel they actually owned a stake in their own parish church, with as much right to sit there as their wealthier neighbours. The incumbent of St Matthew's, Chadderton, for example, noted that 'The people of Chadderton though poor prefer paying a shilling per half year for their sitting in church to the uncertainty of a free sitting. As far as I am personally concerned I should not object to make the whole free but I know such an arrangement would not meet with the

[22] SMO ACS Enquiry Form.

[23] NS file, St Paul's, Royton, Dobie to NS, 5 Sept. 1843.

[24] R. Whittaker, *Sermon Preached at St Thomas' Leesfield* (Oldham, 1867). See also Questions to be Answered by Incumbents: CC, file 2,093, Holy Trinity, Dobcross, 30 Nov. 1843, and CC, file 1,886, St John's, Chadderton, 23 Mar. 1853; SMO, Hardman to Littler, 1 Mar. 1860.

[25] CC, file 2,093, Questions to Incumbents, 9 Jan. 1861; A. J. Howcroft, *The Chapelry and Church of Saddleworth and Quick* (Oldham, 1915), 43.

[26] CC, file 26,611, Bishop of Manchester to EC.

approbation of my parishioners.' Certainly the poor seem to have been just as tenacious as the wealthy of rights to their family pews, and the incumbent of Royton related many of his problems to the existence of 'some superstition attached to the possession of this kind of property'.[27]

Although the building of new churches ultimately represented a considerable success, construction in this third phase proved to be an expensive, slow, and often painful process. More than £22,000 was expended on building the eight new churches in Oldham between 1844 and 1856, a period in which the town experienced considerable economic turmoil. The costs were met from a variety of sources, but among the most important of these, and almost invariably the most difficult to deal with, were three London-based bodies: the Church Building Commissioners, the Ecclesiastical Commissioners, and the Incorporated Church Building Society. Working closely together, these bodies contributed some £7,555, or just over 28 per cent of the total costs of construction, and also provided most of the endowment of the new churches.[28] Together they stood at the organizational peak of Anglican ecclesiastical redevelopment, and without their aid many local initiatives would probably have failed. At the same time, however, the correspondence between the metropolitan bodies and the committees responsible for the local church-building effort reveals a level of friction that itself threatened to bring all progress to a halt.

Major problems began with the provision of suitable sites for the new churches. At Werneth, for example, the gift of a site on the Lees estate was finally secured in 1852, with the twin provisos that the new owners should accept responsibility for the coal road which ran beneath the land, and that there should be no interments. However, the Church Building Commissioners stuck firmly to their policy of accepting only unconditional conveyances, despite an offer by the owners to abandon their first condition, and a visit to London made by the incumbent, Thomas Ireland, to press his case in person.[29] A few months later, Ireland wrote to Sumner, by then Archbishop of Canterbury, asking for his support and revealing the extent of his own anxiety, 'if they do not [accept the site] it will amount almost to saying that no church shall be built in the district: for

[27] ICBS, file 3,663, Dunne to ICBS, 20 Mar. 1853; NS file, St Paul's, Royton, Dobie to NS, 5 Sept. 1843.

[28] Subscription lists: RVR 56, Christ Church, Glodwick, St Matthew's, Chadderton, St John's, Chadderton, Holy Trinity, Coldhurst; RVR 53, Holy Trinity, Waterhead, St Thomas's, Werneth; RVR 2, St Thomas's, Leesfield.

[29] CC, file 17,466, Summerscales to Ireland, 22 May 1852; CBC to Greenwood, 11 June 1852, Ireland to Commissioners, 17 Nov. 1852.

the parties who are now again offering me a site own more than half the land which is eligible for a site in the whole district.' However, even Sumner's intervention proved insufficient to move the Commissioners and only the providential sale of the Lees estate in the following year enabled the building of the church to go ahead.[30]

Similar delays hampered the building of Holy Trinity, Waterhead, and St Thomas's, Leesfield, where the sites stood over profitable coal measures, which the donors attempted to reserve the right to mine. At Leesfield, the Church Building Commissioners compounded the problem by querying the donor's title to the proposed site. The local custom of holding land by 'chief rent' made it a difficult and expensive process to prove good title to land even when there was no effective doubt, and the donor expressed his considerable irritation to the Commissioners early in 1848. With similar problems at Waterhead in the background,[31] the Commissioners' ultimate decision to reject the site must have seemed the final straw, and Robert Whittaker, the incumbent, wrote to convey the frustration felt by his committee. He pointed out that 'all the buildings in the neighbourhood including chapels and cotton mills are built on top of mines'. Moreover, he concluded:

I am very sorry on many accounts that so much of what people here regard as unnecessary difficulty should be experienced in getting a church site accepted. I am sorry because it is annoying and discouraging to the members of the church building committees who, as in this instance, come forward in the noblest and most self-sacrificing spirit to supply the want of churches. I am sorry on account of the proprietor of the land who in addition to being a member of the committee and so necessarily a large subscriber is willing to give a costly site . . . I am sorry on account of the interests of the Church in these districts because I know that from the difficulties we have incurred in this and similar cases, an impression is abroad which will render it almost impossible to find either parties to give sites when they are required or committees to erect churches upon them.

The Commissioners remained intransigent, however, and the problem was solved only when the owner agreed to sell his mineral rights, so that the policy of accepting only unconditional conveyances in effect cost the local committee an additional £250.[32]

Although the problems over church sites were serious, they were neither so frustrating nor so frequent as disputes over the buildings themselves,

---

[30] CC, file 17,466, Ireland to Sumner, 11 Nov. 1852, Ireland to CBC, 7 Apr. 1853.

[31] CC, file 16,537, Gill to Commissioners, 14 Jan. 1848; CC, file 20,825, Rushton to CBC, 7 Aug. 1846.

[32] CC, file 16,537, Whittaker to CBC, 3 Mar. 1848, Summary, 14 June 1869.

where the inflexibility and insensitivity even of the Church Building Commissioners was sometimes exceeded by that of the Incorporated Church Building Society. These disputes had three main focuses: the size of grants offered by the metropolitan bodies, the conditions they imposed on local projects, and the dates on which the grants were paid over. The size of grants made by the Commissioners varied considerably, from the £1,000 given to St John's, Chadderton, in 1845, to the rather less munificent £100 given to the neighbouring parish of St Matthew's in 1857. The Commissioners were handicapped by the declining value of their funds, but given this sort of variation it is perhaps not surprising that some of the incumbents of Oldham's new industrial parishes felt hard done by. From St James's, East Crompton, the Commissioners received an urgent request that their grant of £250 be doubled, Littler, the incumbent, explaining that the grant offer was so small that he had not yet dared to announce its value to his local church-building committee.[33] Only three days earlier he had been moved to pen a powerful appeal for an increase in the ICBS grant which had been fixed at £200:

I should do wrong to hide from the committee the deep regret and disappointment I feel at the smallness of the amount, which I fear will defeat their kind and noble intentions by rendering their grant of no avail for its purposes. [Unless the grant is increased] I cannot see the possibility of the church being erected, and fear that after all we have done, or can do, the project will have to be *at last* abandoned, the local contributions lost, and *a poor people who cannot help themselves* still left without the opportunity of worshipping God in the Church of their fathers which they claim as their own Church also.[34]

The ICBS provided an additional £100 a few months later, and another £50 in 1846, but despite three appeals, one made on the strength of news that their funds had been augmented and pointing out the inequality in the grants made to local churches, no further support was forthcoming from the Church Building Commissioners.[35]

Perhaps more frustrating even than the inadequate size of the grants were the conditions imposed on their provision. The ICBS was particularly concerned to exercise control over the design of the churches it supported. Sometimes this merely caused delay and annoyance, as when one incumbent, caustically quoting its architects' report, informed the

---

[33] CC, files 1,443 and 13,299; CC, file 17,466, Ireland to CBC, 21 May 1852, 23 Mar. 1855; Best, *Temporal Pillars*, 351–2; CC, file 17,789, Littler to CBC, 24 Nov. 1845.

[34] ICBS, file 3,672, Littler to ICBS, 21 Nov. 1845.

[35] Ibid., Littler to ICBS, 18 Dec. 1845, 23 May 1846; CC, file 17,789, Littler to CBC, 24 Nov. 1845, 6 June 1846, 29 Oct. 1846.

society that he would rather have a church with its 'Elevations very much below the average of the Ecclesiastical designs of the present day' than suffer the disaster threatened by a delay in starting the building. More serious was the society's preoccupation with the question of chancels. Local incumbents, whose prime concern was to build a shelter and central focus for their growing congregations, do not always seem to have placed much emphasis on giving their churches a distinctive 'Anglican' shape by adding a chancel which contributed little to the accommodation of their hearers. At Holy Trinity, Coldhurst, for example, the ICBS made a grant of £200 on condition that a chancel be added to the original design, and the incumbent was forced to apply for further funds—since the cost of the proposed alteration was likely to be at least as much as the proffered grant. No further money was forthcoming, however, and only a depression in local construction costs enabled the building to proceed and the grant to be accepted.[36] A final difficulty created by the metropolitan bodies was their refusal to pay over any of the money granted to local projects until certificates of satisfactory completion were received from their own inspecting architect and the buildings had been consecrated by the bishop. The delays consequent on payment at completion caused severe cash-flow problems for local committees who had to meet continuous building costs, and they were a matter for complaint by almost every local incumbent. At St James's, East Crompton, the interest on the 'bridging loan' threatened seriously to embarrass the local committee, and Sumner was persuaded to consecrate early so that the incumbent could claim the grant. Elsewhere delays led to problems with contractors, and it is not surprising that Godson of Coldhurst, writing in an attempt to speed up the payment of his grant, reported that 'Church building has been in such disrepute in this town that it was with great difficulty that I could get anyone to undertake this building . . . I believe it was entirely on account of the builder having had an opportunity of witnessing my proceedings in the district for nearly two years and giving me credit for sincerity that he undertook the work.'[37]

It is easy, though perhaps a little unjust, to criticize the Church Building Commissioners and the ICBS for their inflexibility. What in the

[36] ICBS, file 4,274, Ireland to ICBS, 9 May 1853; ICBS, file 3,672, Littler to ICBS, 2 Mar. 1846; ICBS, file 3,795, Godson to ICBS, 17 July 1846, 15 Sept. 1846, 8 May 1847. The problem was repeated at St Matthew's, Chadderton, ICBS, file 3,663, Dunne to ICBS, 26 Apr. 1853; Yates, *Buildings*, 116–19.

[37] CC, file 1,886, Rushton to CBC, 7 July 1847; CC, file 16,537, Whittaker to CBC, 13 July 1848; CC, file 15,685, Lowe to CBC, 1 Jan. 1846; CC, file 17,236, Godson to CBC, 8 Jan. 1848.

locality appeared to be insensitive interference and unnecessary delay must have seemed to the Commissioners to be the degree of caution and regulatory control appropriate to the custodians of large amounts of public money. Nevertheless the distance between the two groups did cause severe friction, a distance measured not so much in miles as in the different priorities of hard-pressed incumbents in the parishes and well-intentioned bureaucrats in London. Far from being vitiated by their reliance on local enterprise, the problem with the Church Building Commissioners seems to have been their unwillingness to give it their full support.[38]

These metropolitan attitudes do not compare well with those of the more local institutional subscribers: the Chester and Manchester Diocesan Church Building Societies. The Chester Society, which was the most important single subscriber to local projects, made grants to all eight of the new churches built after 1840, and distributed them much more evenly than did the metropolitan bodies, in blocks of £400, £450, or £500. The Manchester Society made two grants to churches not yet completed on its foundation in 1848: £200 to St Matthew's, Chadderton and £285 to St Thomas's, Werneth, and a small grant of £11 towards additional expenses incurred at Holy Trinity, Coldhurst. These diocesan societies, products of an alternative tradition of church reform, were local bodies formed to meet local needs, and they displayed the responsiveness so lacking in the Commissioners and ICBS. They did not impose conditions on their grants, and they were prepared to pay the money before completion in order to cover accumulating building costs—an attitude which in at least one case made it possible to proceed with a project which would otherwise have failed because of cash-flow problems. The local societies were also willing to intervene to compensate for the deficiencies of the metropolitan bodies. At Coldhurst, for example, the Chester Society made a special award of an additional £100 because of the architectural conditions with which the ICBS had 'saddled their grant'.[39]

[38] On the bureaucratic difficulties created by the Commissioners, see also: Koditschek, *Class Formation*, 254; Brose, *Church and Parliament*, 202; R. O'Day, 'The Clerical Renaissance in Victorian England and Wales', in Parsons (ed.), *Religion in Victorian Britain*, i. 193. The importance of the Church's own efforts at reform and the vitality of local ecclesiastical approaches in contrast to the 'modernizing' approach of rational, bureaucratic central reform have also been revealed in an important new study of the church at diocesan level: R. A. Burns, 'The Diocesan Revival in the Church of England *c*.1825–1865', D. Phil. thesis (Oxford, 1990).

[39] ICBS, file 3,795, Godson to ICBS, 12 Jan. 1848; RVR 56, p. 80, Chester Diocesan Church Building Society, Minute, 30 Sept. 1846. For diocesan reform see Burns, 'Diocesan Revival' *passim*.

When to these grants are added five small grants from the Derby Co-operative Society, two special awards from Sir Robert Peel's private fund which was administered by the Commissioners, and one from the Evangelical 'Church Extension Fund', the total institutional subscriptions to new church-building in the area between 1844 and 1856 amounted to £11,202 or just under half the total expenditure. For the remainder the promoters of local churches were dependent (with the exception of the small amounts of tax on building materials which could be reclaimed from the government) entirely upon private subscriptions. Faced with the need to build a number of new churches simultaneously, local Churchmen took a deliberate decision early in 1844 to rely not on town-wide appeals, but on the community sense of the new districts, and great exertions were made to persuade residents of all classes to subscribe. There seems to have been considerable popular support for the construction of new parish churches, especially in the districts where a clergyman had been operating for some time, and Littler, for example, describing his experiences among the working-class inhabitants of the new district of East Crompton, noted:

I have visited amongst them for the last five months. They receive me very kindly and manifest no hostility to the Established Church, but on the contrary great numbers of them say that they are Church-people if anything but they will add 'if anything'. They also feel their want and express themselves as very desirous of a church of their own to which they can go without intrusion.[40]

Such favourable attitudes provided a good basis for fund-raising. In Waterhead, 'collecting cards were distributed throughout the parish for subscriptions and most people paid small sums weekly' and from Leesfield it was reported that: 'We have to raise £1,100 which is a great sum for so poor a district, the poor people are subscribing to our help in good earnest—we have collecting books in every mill in the village—and the hands pay 2d or more each pay day . . . This is a good feeling not before known towards the Church in these parts.'[41]

However ready the poor might be to subscribe, it was always clear that the main burden would have to rest on the 'upper' and 'middle' classes of the town. Local Churchmen displayed little reticence about emphasizing the responsibilities of the rich; thus, for example, Lowe, in a circular

---

[40] CC, file, 15,685, Lowe to CBC, 31 May 1844; ICBS, file 3,421, Lowe to ICBS, 18 Apr. 1844; ICBS, file 3,663, Littler to ICBS, 14 Apr. 1847, 17 Apr. 1847.
[41] Holy Trinity, Waterhead, MS History, ch. 2; ICBS, file 3,500, Lowe to ICBS, 18 Oct. 1844. Rycroft found a similarly positive reaction to church extension in 'Craven', 300.

letter promoting Christ Church, Glodwick, declared that 'all those who derive an income, in whatever manner, from the labours of artisans . . . are bound in duty to their Maker and their fellow creatures, to contribute after their power to the multiplication of temples of the living God'.[42] Despite the incomplete nature of most local subscription lists, it is clear that some of the employers were quite generous: James and John Platt, for example, gave both the site and £500 towards St Thomas's, Werneth, and the Milne family of High Crompton gave £525 towards the building of St James's, East Crompton. However, the combination of parochial subdivision and developing residential segregation may have caused problems in the distribution of such subscriptions analogous to those experienced by Hook at Leeds. Most large local subscribers limited themselves to a single donation: out of a total of 139 subscribers of sums of £1 or more, only two made donations valued at £50 or over to more than one project and only thirteen made multiple donations of any sort. In part, this was the result of the policy of the local clergy, who encouraged subscribers to give to their own districts; in part it reflected general reluctance to give generously on a wide scale. The pressures of so many local projects being promoted simultaneously and continuing economic instability were particularly significant,[43] but it was often a calculation about the future development of the parish that provoked local employers to husband their resources. Thus, according to Archdeacon Rushton reviewing East Crompton, 'the men of wealth in the district are sharp enough to foresee that a church soon leads to schools, parsonage and charities which they will be expected to promote. Considering what is doing and done there his local subscriptions are astonishingly handsome.'[44]

Such attitudes left some districts much worse off than others. While St James's, East Crompton, had eight resident subscribers both rich and generous enough to donate £50 or more, Holy Trinity, Coldhurst, had only one—since, according to its incumbent, there could be found among the residents 'only *one individual* who is not a working person'.[45] These problems might have been compounded by the religious pluralism of the area, but there is little evidence of Dissenting hostility to the Establishment proving an obstacle to Anglican Church extension, and in 1844 the promoters of Christ Church, Glodwick, could report: 'The committee

---

[42] RVR 52, p. 21.
[43] S. Meacham, 'The Church in the Victorian City', *Victorian Studies*, 11 (1967–8), 368–9; ICBS, file 3,795, Godson to ICBS, 17 July 1846; ICBS, file 3,623, Reynolds to ICBS, 1 June 1847.
[44] CC, file 17,789, Rushton to CBC, 22 Jan. 1846.
[45] ICBS, file 3,795, Godson to ICBS, 15 Sept. 1846.

rejoice in observing that some who are not in communion with the Established Church have yet, under the influence of true Christian feeling, come forward to assist their efforts.'[46] In Saddleworth, where the financial pressures were increased by the failure of the metropolitan bodies to provide any grants for new churches, the absence of a multiplicity of local subscribers proved no obstacle because of the generosity of the individual promoters of the projects. In the case of Christ Church, Friezland, the Whitehead brothers, local woollen manufacturers, gave sites for the church, school, and parsonage, contributed the entire sum required to construct the three buildings and to enlarge the church in 1860, established a repair fund, and provided two-thirds of the endowment of the living at a total cost of approximately £16,000. In the case of Denshaw, the generosity of the Gartside family, who built both church and parsonage as well as providing part of the endowment, though less lavish, was still substantial; the parsonage alone cost £1,000 in 1864.[47]

For the less well-supported or more expensive Oldham churches a final resort lay in appeals for assistance from outside the town altogether, and the lists record subscriptions from a total of 134 individuals. Some had local connections, like Miss Currer of Yorkshire, who gave a total of £70 in donations to five of the new churches—she was the chief landowner in Glodwick.[48] Others had ecclesiastical connections, like the Earl of Wilton who was the patron of Prestwich and the most generous of the external subscribers, making three donations of £50 to different local churches. Most of these subscribers, however, had no links with the locality, and like Lord Ashley, who gave £2 to Holy Trinity, Coldhurst, subscribed as part of their general support for charity. These donations were usually quite small, between £1 and £5, but in aggregate they could be quite significant since they tended to be concentrated on a few local churches whose incumbents were particularly active in soliciting contributions. St James's, East Crompton, for example, received the donations of 84 of the 134 external subscribers making a total of £523 11s.—over 16 per cent of its eventual cost. The largest beneficiary, however, was Christ Church, Glodwick, which received among its five external subscriptions a gift of £750 from a 'friend of the Bishop of Chester', making its aggregate £811 1s.—more than 32 per cent of the total cost. Despite the energy expended in prospective fund-raising, only one of the new churches

---

[46] RVR 52, p. 21.

[47] RVR 60, p. 24; Inscription on Whitehead Monument in Christ Church, Friezland; CC, file 26,611, Minute, 28 Jan. 1864.

[48] RVR 52, pp. 143–6, Lowe to Rushton, 17 Feb. 1844.

was able to open free from debt. Sometimes the deficit could be quite small; the accounts of Holy Trinity, Coldhurst, for example, declared a shortfall of only £53, though even this was serious enough considering the poverty of the district. Elsewhere, at East Crompton, Werneth, and Leesfield, the deficit was around £1,000, and, while some help was made available from outside the area (St Thomas's, Leesfield, for example, received a donation of £245 from the Chester Diocesan Fund in 1852), most of the shortfall had to be met from local resources. The collections made at opening services with sermons by famous preachers were vital and, in some cases, their success, together with the continuing generosity of existing subscribers, allowed for a speedy liquidation of the debt. Elsewhere the problem remained a drag on the resources of the parish for years: the debt on Holy Trinity, Waterhead—some £425 on its opening in 1847—still stood at £280 over three years later with little hope of improvement. In 1852 £189 was still owing, although a small school had been built in the meantime, and the whole debt was eventually cleared only through the generosity of Thomas Brideoak, a local coal merchant.[49]

The augmentation of accommodation during the 1840s and 1850s may have been the crowning achievement of the 'reformed' Establishment, but to many of the local clergy it must have seemed a crown of thorns. The problems they faced were enormous: not only did they have to deal with importunate contractors, reluctant subscribers, and recalcitrant bureaucrats; there were also incompetent architects. Some failed because they lacked familiarity with local conditions, but hiring a local man was no guarantee of an adequate design.[50] Shortly after St Thomas's, Friarmere, had been 'improved' by the construction of a new roof and heating system in 1855, a frustrated group of local subscribers was moved to complain that the sexton had to

conduct those parties to *dry seats* whose own pews had the misfortune to be *inundated with water falling from the roof* . . . that the *principal vocalist* . . . has been obliged to make use of her umbrella to protect her from the wet . . . that the *organist* has been compelled to use a *similar protection* for himself and books during his performance! that the whole choir have been driven from their seats by the same cause! and that the head of the *Revd Incumbent* himself has not escaped the 'pelting of the pitiless storm' during his services in the pulpit. . . . Moreover, [they ventured] we trust we may be made acquainted with the name of the '*eminent*

---

[49] RVR 52, pp. 74, 123; RVR 2, pp. 112–13, 137; RVR 53, pp. 141–2; Holy Trinity, Waterhead, MS History, ch. 3; Deem, *St Thomas' Church*, 8.
[50] Ibid. 7–8.

architect' who devised the plan for *warming the inside of a church by placing the pipes of the heating apparatus on the outside of the church wall.*[51]

The additional burden of attempting to finance a church building on top of the usual duties of a densely populated industrial district imposed a prodigious workload on some of the clergy. Reynolds at Waterhead estimated that he had written 7,000 letters to people throughout the country soliciting contributions, many of which were followed up with 'personal calls to press home the appeal'. Added to the workload was the psychological strain of coping with debt and the vagaries of the economy, when a slump might bring subscriptions to a halt, or a boom send the prices of building materials soaring beyond the estimates on which the original applications were based.[52] Most local Churchmen seem to have seen them as essential, but vital time and energy was diverted to the construction of church buildings which might have been better spent in building congregations. Certainly some incumbents felt the tension, and Reynolds must have spoken for many when he told the Commissioners during a particularly frustrating piece of negotiation, 'when I entered the ministry I thought I had nothing to do but to be building the spiritual edifice, but I find now that the contemplation of bricks and mortar form no inconsiderable portion of my lucubrations'.[53]

The Clergymen

In the provision of an adequate number of resident parish clergy, the high standards of the 'unreformed' Establishment seem to have been maintained by its successor. Tables 3.2 and 3.3 show a steady increase in the numbers of clergymen serving in the locality, and in most districts an improvement in the ratio of ministers to their parishioners. The non-resident in 1841 was J. T. Kirkbank of Royton. In 1845 it was F. Gardner of St Thomas's, Friarmere, absent on grounds of ill health, in which category he was joined in the 1855 column by Thomas Lowe of St Mary's, Oldham. All three maintained resident curates, and, in the case of St Mary's, a second, assistant curate as well; so none of the parishes seems to have suffered significantly, and some may have benefited from

[51] RVR 62, p. 81, Circular, 14 May 1855.

[52] Holy Trinity, Waterhead, MS History, ch. 3; RVR 56, p. 125, Littler to Chester Diocesan Church Building Society, 1852.

[53] CC, file 17,254, Reynolds to Commissioners, 19 Feb. 1846. For an extensive discussion of the problems and dangers of over-extension in church-building for both Anglicans and nonconformists, see R. Gill, *The Myth of the Empty Church* (1993).

TABLE 3.2. *Clergy in Oldham and Saddleworth, 1841–65*

	1841	1845	1855	1865
Total number of churches	14	22	23	24
Resident incumbent	13	21	22	24
Non-resident incumbent	1	1	2	—
One additional curate	2	5	5	6
Two additional curates	—	1	1	3
Total number of clergy	16	29	31	36

Sources: *Clergy List* (1841), (1845), (1855); Crockford, *Clerical Directory* (1865); CPAS, *Annual Reports* (1841–65); *Oldham Almanack* (1856–65).

TABLE 3.3. *Numbers of people per clergyman in Oldham and Saddleworth, by district, 1841–1865*

District	Population per clergyman			
	1841	1845	1855	1865
Oldham above town	10,304	5,475	5,300	6,372
Oldham below town	7,329	2,711	4,786	5,531
Chadderton	2,607	1,708	2,700	2,014
Royton	7,186	3,835	4,450	9,670
Crompton	6,729	2,193	2,213	2,370
Middleton	8,078	4,315	2,387	2,527
Saddleworth	4,207	3,450	3,636	2,740

Sources: As for Table 1.1 and 3.2.

the introduction of a young and vigorous pastor. W. Dawson, Kirkbank's substitute at St Paul's, Royton, for example, was described as 'greatly liked . . . a very kindly disposed man and a good preacher'.[54] The numbers of assistant curates gradually increased over the period, mainly concentrated in the larger parishes and supported by the Evangelical Church Pastoral Aid Society (CPAS) or its High Church equivalent, the Additional Curates' Society.[55] This helped to keep the numbers of clergymen relative to the

[54] T. Seville, 'Historical Note', in *Official Handbook to the Grand Bazaar* (Oldham, 1896).
[55] In 1845 the CPAS supported five and the ACS possibly one: *Clergy List* (1845); CPAS, *Annual Report*, x (1845).

size of the local population reasonably steady in most districts after 1845. Although worse than the national figure, which hovered at just less than one clergyman for every 1,000 people throughout the period, the Oldham and Saddleworth districts showed a clerical presence roughly equivalent to the average for the Manchester diocese, which stood at one minister for every 4,000 people in 1861.[56] Thus, while Lowe's dream of a parish church for every 4,000 people had never been realized, his plans came much closer to fruition in terms of the ratio of clergy to the general population. The 'reformed' Establishment could not match the achievement of the eighteenth-century Church, which, even in 1790, provided at least one clergyman for every 2,500 people in Oldham and one for every 2,000 in Saddleworth, but clerical numbers stood up much better to the rising tide of population in the 1850s and 1860s than did the density of seating, and of the two the provision of a resident pastorate in reasonable strength was probably of greater importance.

The clergy of the 'reformed' Establishment were rather better housed than had been their predecessors and by 1865 five of the six incumbents in Saddleworth and eleven of the eighteen in Oldham had been provided with parsonages. However, there was certainly no rush to build prestigious parsonages ahead of churches analogous to that found by Obelkevich in South Lindsey, and, if there was any pressure for larger and more imposing parsonages, it came not from the clergy themselves, but from the Ecclesiastical Commissioners. At St Mary's, Oldham, for example, the Commissioners turned down Lowe's request to build a small house 'sufficient for the residence of the Incumbent'. They required that a larger design be attempted far beyond the available resources, and then put up a series of obstacles that prevented a parsonage being built until 1865, twenty-one years after Lowe had first canvassed the scheme.[57] The familiar story of small grants, crippling conditions, and bureaucratic insensitivity was repeated in the attempt to build parsonages, and the problems faced by many local ministers were summed up in a letter by Littler of East Crompton:

the board can scarcely form an idea of the difficulties a clergyman has to contend with in localities like these . . . It took me two years to get up my church and five or six more to clear it of debt, during which time I wrote with my own hand from one to two thousand letters soliciting contributions in all parts of the country . . .

[56] Chadwick, *Victorian Church*, ii. 245.
[57] *Crockford* (1865); *Oldham Almanack* (1865); Obelkevich, *Religion and Rural Society*, 114–16, CC, file 5,023, Parsonage Correspondence.

Since then I have been raising funds to erect schools and am now on the point of building. They will cost upwards of £1,000. My local resources are consequently dried up besides which I cannot use the same means to raise funds for a parsonage as for a church or schools. Such a course by lowering the clerical character, would tend to impede one's usefulness, to say nothing of personal feeling.

Faced with this sort of choice all the local clergy seem to have preferred pastoral effectiveness to personal comfort.[58]

The cash value of local livings remained more or less constant throughout the 1830s, and the most important advance came with the decision taken by the Ecclesiastical Commissioners in 1841 to augment to the value of £150 poor livings with a resident clergyman, a church, and a population of 2,000 or more. It is a measure of the poverty of local cures that all but three were so augmented. The two largest Oldham parishes were augmented again in 1863 to a value of £300. However, there were many calls on a clergyman's income, and some were clearly feeling the pinch in the 1850s. Littler supported his claim for a grant towards a parsonage with the plea that

the income is insufficient to afford anything like a rent where there is no private means, which I am sorry to say is the case in this instance. My gross income from every source, whether official or private, scarcely exceeds £160 p.a. on which, moreover, there is a continual drain to keep up the services of the church and meet the other wants of a poor and populous parish.[59]

It has been suggested that these low incomes, together with the lack of resident middle-class support, meant that industrial parishes 'attracted few really capable clergymen', but it is difficult to discern such a pattern among the local clergy. They certainly seem to have participated in a general increase during the early nineteenth century in the proportion of Chester clergymen who had received a university education. University graduates predominated among the local clergy and by 1846, of a total of twenty-two active ministers, seventeen were university- and five were theological-college educated.[60]

The churchmanship of these men is, to some extent, indicated by the various religious societies they chose to support. The correlation is by no means straightforward, however, as some organizations, most notably the

---

[58] CC, file 1,886, Littler to EC, 12 June 1856; Deem, *St Thomas' Church*, 9; RVR 56, p. 75.

[59] Best, *Temporal Pillars*, 353; CC, file 1,886, Littler to EC, 12 June 1856.

[60] See Appendix 2; Meacham, 'Church in the Victorian City', 368; Haig, *Victorian Clergy*, 31–3.

Society for the Propagation of the Gospel (SPG), may have been supported in the older churches simply by established local tradition, and
therefore did not indicate any preference on the part of the minister. In
other cases, ministers whose churchmanship can be well established from
a range of sources can be found supporting the 'wrong' society. Richard
Durnford, the High Church Rector of Middleton, for example, was the
chairman of his local auxiliary of the mainly Evangelical Church Missionary
Society (CMS) in 1844.[61] There are, nevertheless, fairly strong indications
of the churchmanship of nineteen of the local clergy in 1846: two of
these may be classified as moderate High Churchmen, and no fewer
than seventeen as Evangelicals, with Evangelicals staffing every church in
Oldham itself and the three nearest out-townships. The balance gradually
changed as time passed; at St Peter's, Oldham, for example, the enthusiastic
Evangelical William Lees was replaced in 1861 by Edward Owen, a High
Churchman, and at St John's, Chadderton, Arthur Keene, an Evangelical
friend of Hugh Stowell, was replaced in 1864 by James Gornall, a Ritualist.
Nevertheless, Oldham's Anglican clergy remained throughout the period
under investigation predominantly Evangelical and, in the crucial formative
years of the mid-1840s, almost exclusively so.[62]

In 1853 Conybeare estimated that there were approximately 6,500
'Low Church' clergymen in the Church of England, or just over two-
fifths of the total number. Professor Chadwick has argued that the true
figure was nearer 3,000, or approximately one-sixth of the total, while
more recent estimates have put the proportion at up to one quarter in
1830 and perhaps one half in 1850.[63] On any of these views, there was, in
Oldham and Saddleworth, a clear imbalance in favour of Evangelicalism
which requires some explanation. In large part, this imbalance can be
attributed to the influence of the bishops of Chester and, after 1848, of
Manchester. The most enthusiastically Evangelical of the Chester bishops
was J. B. Sumner, whose episcopate ran from 1828 until his elevation to
Canterbury twenty years later. He therefore presided over a period which

---

[61] *Manchester Guardian*, 6 Jan. 1844.

[62] See Appendix 2; *Crockford* (1865); E. Owen, *Jottings on the Rubrics for Morning and Evening Prayer* (Manchester, 1874); H. Stowell and A. Keene, *Two Sermons Preached in St John's Chadderton by A. Keene Together with a Biographical Sketch of the Author* (Oldham, 1863); W. A. Westley, *A Brief History of St John's Chadderton* (Oldham, 1945), 16–17.

[63] W. J. Conybeare, 'Church Parties', *Edinburgh Review*, 98 (1853), 338; Chadwick, *Victorian Church*, i. 446; K. Hylson Smith, *Evangelicals in the Church of England 1734–1984* (Edinburgh, 1989), 68; Hilton, *Atonement*, 26. Hilton's estimate rests on a very broad definition of Evangelicalism which is rendered somewhat doubtful by some of his individual identifications.

saw the creation of a good deal of new patronage in Peel parishes. Most of the patronage was officially out of Sumner's control, appointments being placed in the hands of the Crown and the bishop alternately, with the Crown having the right of first appointment. However, this stipulation did not prevent a bishop as determined as Sumner from exercising considerable influence over the choice of clergy. Thus, in 1844, he wrote to inform the secretary of the Ecclesiastical Commission that, 'Under an impression that it will not be possible for the crown, in whom the first nomination to endowed districts is vested, to find a sufficient number of qualified clergy to appoint, I am making it my business to seek out such, that there may be no unnecessary delay in carrying into execution a work of very urgent importance.'[64] This helpful attitude on the part of the diocesan goes some way towards explaining why all eight of the Crown's first appointments in Oldham seem to have been Evangelicals, and at St Thomas's, Werneth, for example, it was remembered that their Crown-appointed first minister 'came on the Bishop's recommendation'.[65] Even mild encouragement from its bishop would have made the Chester diocese a particularly attractive prospect to young Evangelical clergymen, given the hostility they might encounter in other parts of the country like Exeter under Phillpotts, Peterborough under Marsh, or Durham under the successors of Shute Barrington.[66]

Important though it was, episcopal patronage was not the only influence at work. There also seems to have been a strong local demand for an Evangelical ministry, and for Evangelical preaching in particular, and this popular support sometimes found an echo in the attitudes of local patrons. Richard Whitehead, the Evangelical millowning patron of Christ Church, Friezland, was quite certain about the sort of clergyman he wanted for his church: 'He ought not to be too young but should have his character formed and be also free from these new fangled notions, this puseyism which puts forms and ceremonies in lieu of our Saviour. He should be an evangelical, painstaking Parish priest who will take his Bible and preach his Gospel from it.'[67]

A third explanation for the strength of local Evangelicalism is that it may have reflected a more general trend within the Church. The son and biographer of G. D. Grundy, of St John's, Hey, noted that his father was

[64] JRL, Rushton MSS ii, 161, Sumner to EC, 13 Jan. 1844.

[65] Deem, *St Thomas' Church*, 6.

[66] Virgin, *Age of Negligence*, 138; W. B. Maynard, 'The Ecclesiastical Administration of the Archdeaconry of Durham, 1774–1856', Ph.D. thesis (Durham, 1973).

[67] CC, file 45,026, R. R. Whitehead to F. F. Whitehead, 12 Nov. 1844.

attracted towards Evangelicalism as an undergraduate because it was at the time the 'forward party in the church', adding, 'Calvinism was the earnest form of religious life in my Father's undergraduate days, just as Puseyism afterwards was in mine.' If this was the case more generally, then Evangelicals would have been particularly prominent among the most dedicated young clergymen—those most willing to take on the rigours of a new industrial parish.[68]

Although the character of Anglicanism in Oldham and Saddleworth was overwhelmingly Evangelical, it was not without variety, since the local exponents of Evangelicalism were far from uniform in its practical expression. Thomas Lowe, for example, the vicar of Oldham, was quite stiffly Establishmentarian in his attitudes, while his colleague, W. F. Walker at St James's, was a vigorous exponent of pan-evangelical co-operation. Some Evangelicals developed a greater emphasis on sacramentalism towards the end of the period and began cautiously to experiment with richer ceremonial. Thus, Grundy of Hey and Whittaker of Leesfield both adopted the surplice while preaching in the 1860s. Others maintained a more old-fashioned Evangelical approach: Broadbent of Waterhead regarded any robes other than the Geneva Gown as 'the rags of popery', and Thomas Ireland defied his bishop rather than adopt the surplice when required to do so.[69] Nevertheless, whatever their differences on various matters of form, the Evangelicals were united by a common theology, in which moderate Calvinism seems to have been the dominant influence.[70] Local High Churchmanship also appears to have been influenced by the general Evangelical tenor of Anglicanism in Oldham and Saddleworth. The High Churchman Richard Whitelock apparently made no changes when, following the Evangelical F. R. Raines, he became incumbent of St Chad's. Similarly, Cowell at Lydgate may have been a High Churchman of a fairly advanced kind, but was nevertheless sufficiently influenced by the Evangelical tenor of his parish to employ a CPAS curate to run a mission station. Before 1864 local reactions to Tractarianism, at least after

---

[68] Grundy, 'G. D. Grundy', 74. Both Bebbington and Haig record a growth in Evangelical ordinations during the 1830s and 1840s, which Haig ascribes partly to the influence of a number of key Evangelicals at Oxford and Cambridge and which he associates with a new activism among the clergy as a whole: D. Bebbington, *Evangelicalism in Modern Britain* (1989), 78, 105; Haig, *Victorian Clergy*, 13, 47, 356.

[69] Ibid. 91; NS file, Oldham Mumps, Lowe to NS, 21 Dec. 1843; Holy Trinity, Waterhead, MS History, ch. 3; Deem. *St Thomas' Church*, 13. For High Church developments within Evangelicalism, see Bebbington, *Evangelicalism*, 147.

[70] Grundy, 'G. D. Grundy', 87; cf. J. D. Walsh, 'The Anglican Evangelicals in the Eighteenth Century', in M. Simon (ed.), *Aspects de l'Anglicanisme* (Paris, 1974), 92–4.

the first few tracts, appear to have been uniformly hostile even among High Churchmen. Durnford, the High Church supporter of the CMS, was particularly concerned about Tractarian extremism, and Joseph Evans, the moderate High Church incumbent of St Anne's, Lydgate, declared that his intention had been 'to vote against Mr Williams in the recent (1842) contest for the Chair of Poetry at Oxford, had a Poll been insisted on by Dr Pusey and Mr Newman'.[71] There is no evidence of any party strife between High and Low Church groups in the town and none of any problems when High Churchmen and Evangelicals succeeded each other in local cures. This suggests that their styles were more compatible than those which emerged after 1865, when the succession of Tractarians to local Evangelical parishes provoked several secessions from the Establishment.[72]

Church Services

All the local clergy, whatever their churchmanship, were conscientious in liturgical provision and by 1845, apparently in direct response to the growing pressure on Church room, the number of services held in local churches had increased so that it exceeded even the high level revealed by the visitation of 1825. An additional service at St Mary's, Oldham, for example, began in 1840 after seventy-one of the seatholders had petitioned the bishop to 'open Oldham Church for a third service on Sunday

TABLE 3.4. *Sunday services in Anglican churches, 1845–1865*

Number of services	1845	1851	1865
Two services	12	17	12
Three services	6	2	1
No information	4	4	11
TOTAL	22	23	24

Sources: RVR 1–62; PRO HO 129 475, 496; *Oldham Almanack* (1865).

[71] W. R. W. Stephens, *A Memoir of Richard Durnford D. D.* (1899), 83; Raines MSS xv. 58; P. B. Nockles, 'Continuity and Change in Anglican High Churchmanship in Britain 1792–1850', D.Phil. thesis (Oxford, 1982), ch. 7; Hilton, *Atonement*, 27–30.

[72] Westley, *St John's*, 17; Deem, *St Thomas' Church*, 13; anon., *St Margaret's*, 3; Airne, *Lydgate*, 36–8.

evenings with a view to providing further church accommodation'.[73] The apparent fall-off in the number of services thereafter is difficult to interpret. The 1851 figures may indicate an abandonment of the experiment with three services a Sunday, but it is more likely that they merely reflect the timing of the census in March, third services being more frequent during the summer months, especially outside the town centre. By 1865, however, the move back to two services a Sunday as standard practice may have become more pronounced; the intervening period had seen a great increase in the use of mission rooms and these were probably regarded as a more efficient way of increasing accommodation than the provision of a third service.

The characteristic emphases within local services on word and music and opposed to sacrament and liturgy seem to have continued uninterrupted. All the local Sunday services in 1845 were accompanied by a sermon, except the third service at St Mary's, which featured evening prayer followed by a lecture,[74] and the Chester bishops continued their attempts to foster popular preaching of a high quality. In his charge of 1844 Sumner appealed for 'warm and living' preaching in the Evangelical style, which, he argued, would also improve the quality of sacramental worship: 'Preach therefore the cross of Christ, as the only and sufficient satisfaction for sin: and they who are drawn to the cross will not fail to value the ordinance which represents it.' This emphasis was maintained by Sumner's Mancunian successor, Prince Lee, and the Evangelical style retained its popularity throughout the period.[75] None of the local ministers of whose sermons evidence survives seems to have read from a pre-prepared text. Most probably preached from notes, like Whittaker of Leesfield, though some preached extempore or relied on their memory. According to his biography, G. D. Grundy 'had a faculty of keeping several discourses at once arranged in order, each on its own shelf of his memory. He would say "When I went up the pulpit stairs, I had not decided which of three sermons to preach." '[76] Sermons were lengthy, as the popular appetite appears to have dictated, but few can have surpassed the regular exertions of the incumbent of Waterhead: ' "Mr Reynolds did not believe in 15 minute sermons. He was like a steam engine when started, and did not stop till he was run down. Sometimes we had to

[73] MPL M39/23, Manchester Diocesan MSS.   [74] RVR 1–62.
[75] J. B. Sumner, *A Charge Delivered to the Clergy of the Diocese of Chester at the Triennial visitation* (1844), 48, 65; J. P. Lee, *A Charge Delivered at his Second Visitation in December 1855 to the Clergy of the Diocese of Manchester* (1856).
[76] R. Whittaker, *Collected Sermons* (Oldham, 1868); Grundy, 'G. D. Grundy', 84.

hurry home to get back in time for the afternoon service"—on these occasions Reynolds appears to have spoken for about an hour and a half."[77]

Although the sermon remained at the centre of Anglican worship, the sacrament of communion does seem to have been celebrated more frequently then was generally the case before 1830. The rather scattered available evidence indicates that monthly celebrations had become the norm by the middle of the century, perhaps reflecting both the rise of the chapels of ease and new churches to full parochial status and the impact of Evangelical enthusiasm. Popular participation, however, seems in general to have remained at a low level: St Matthew's, Chadderton, which even in the poor conditions of 31 March 1851 recorded an afternoon congregation of 161, averaged only twenty-four communicants at its monthly celebrations between 1857 and 1860. Similarly, St Mary's, Oldham, which recorded a congregation of 970 in March 1851, had only fifty-two communicants at its communion service earlier that month, only eighty-three at Easter, and averaged only sixty-one over the year as a whole.[78] Whether these figures represent a large body of communicants taking the sacrament at different times or a small body communicating regularly is unclear, and it seems likely that a combination of the two—a small body of 'regulars' together with a larger group of occasional communicants—may have been the most common experience.

The low level of communicant figures did not stem from any lack of clerical encouragement. Some made a considerable effort to establish more regular practice; Henry Bunn, for example, the curate of St Paul's, Royton, published a pamphlet in which he sought to reassure those who felt themselves unworthy to receive the sacrament. There were cases where such energetic clerical advocacy had its effect. At Hey, for example, where G. D. Grundy gave catechetical lectures attended by '200 or 250 persons of all ages' on Sunday evenings after church, the number of communicants varied between 250 and 360 during the years 1861–5, with an attendance of 454 communicants at one service during the cotton famine. Grundy was an enthusiastic catechizer of the children in local schools and published his own catechism in serial parts. He also exercised close pastoral supervision over his communicants and both these factors may have helped him break down barriers and achieve a communicant

---

[77] e.g. *Oldham Advertiser*, 28 Aug. 1852, 30 July 1853; Holy Trinity, Waterhead, MS History, ch. 2.

[78] Grundy, 'G. D. Grundy'; SMO, Preachers' Book; St Matthew's, Chadderton, Preachers' Book; PRO HO 129, 475, 2, 31; Rycroft, 'Craven', 287, 313.

roll of over 30 per cent of his congregation compared to the figures of less than 10 per cent achieved elsewhere.[79] Local confirmations followed a national trend in becoming more frequent after the middle of the century. They were also decentralized, the large-scale confirmations at the parish church being replaced by smaller ones in the districts. These were to some extent effective in encouraging greater popular participation in communion: after the first confirmation at St Matthew's, Chadderton, for example, the average number of communicants rose from twenty-four to forty in the following twelve months. Female candidates exceeded males at confirmations, sometimes by as many as three to two, and, if the figures for St John's, Hey are typical, then the female preponderance in terms of regular participation was even more pronounced—often approaching three to one. Perhaps women participated as the representatives of their families, but, whatever the reason for the relative absence of adult men, it is clear that communicants remained an élite group within the congregation, and in 1861 the vicar of Christ Church, Friezland, tried to capitalize on this by establishing quarterly communicant meetings analogous to those held for nonconformist 'members'.[80]

Popular attitudes to the liturgical element of Anglican services seem to have changed little over the period, and, as already noted, Bumstead, the curate of Christ Church, Glodwick, was drawing attention to the problem of inaccessible liturgy as late as the 1850s. Some ministers did make strenuous attempts to make their services attractive, and these were not without effect. According to his biographer, when Grundy prayed, 'In the Divine Service, the "Man-in-the-street" often felt as Archbishop Harcourt felt when His Grace exclaimed at Harewood, "I have never heard the Prayers of the Church so beautifully read."' At Waterhead in the late 1840s members of the congregation responded to the difficulties caused by illiteracy by learning much of the service off by heart. Whether the experience of Grundy and Reynolds, or that of Bumstead, was the more typical, it is impossible to judge, but it was universally acknowledged that a problem existed with the liturgy. Littler at East Crompton felt obliged to commence his ministry by appealing to his congregation 'to join in heartily with the parts of the service to be said together' and

---

[79] H. Bunn, *An Address to Communicants at the Lord's Table* (Kidderminster, 1848); Grundy, 'G. D. Grundy', 86; MPL, Preachers' Book, St John's, Hey; Andrew, *Hey*, 84.

[80] *Oldham Standard*, 2 June, 20 Oct. 1860, 16 Feb. 1861; Chadwick, *Victorian Church*, i. 514–15; St Matthew's, Chadderton, Preachers' Book; *Oldham Chronicle*, 13 July 1861; MPL, Preachers' Book, St John's, Hey; H. M. McLeod, *Class and Religion in the Late Victorian City* (1974), 30–1.

assuring them that 'although to many . . . the house of God appears dull and its services, "a weariness"; his own people find in those services, a rich feast for their souls'.[81] In contrast, the level of popular participation in the musical parts of the service seems to have increased as Anglican practice moved closer to that of the nonconformists. Unlike the small parishes of South Lindsey, none of the new churches in Oldham or Saddleworth experienced any difficulty in raising a choir, and local congregational hymn-singing also seems to have been particularly enthusiastic. There is some evidence that the new prominence of congregational singing, encouraged by the activities of Sunday schools and the popular 'Tonic sol fa' singing societies, may have put a strain on the relationship between the congregation at large and the highly skilled singers and musicians who had previously dominated the musical life of the churches.[82] Nevertheless, relationships in general seem to have been good. Bands of musicians continued to provide the accompaniment for singing in most of the new churches until funds were available for the purchase of an organ. Although organs or harmoniums had become ubiquitous by 1855, the transition, as in the older churches, was managed smoothly and without conflict. The older bands were not entirely displaced, and string and wind instruments were still in occasional use alongside the organ at Holy Trinity, Shaw, in the 1860s.[83] They also frequently appeared at the great popular choral events which still punctuated the musical life of the churches, and the *Oldham Chronicle* reported in 1858 that

the good old custom of having what used to be called 'a great sing' was revived at Saddleworth Church . . . Selections of sacred music were performed by a full choir accompanied by the organ and an effective array of instruments. The church was crowded on both occasions, every aisle and nook being made available and in the afternoon about 1,000 persons went away unable to obtain admission.[84]

Most churches seem to have found a viable musical *via media*, and by the 1860s some Evangelical incumbents were experimenting successfully with occasional full choral services.[85] Thus local Church music continued to

[81] Bumstead, *Church Matters*; Grundy, 'G. D. Grundy', 84; Holy Trinity, Waterhead, MS History, ch. 3; J. Littler, *A Sermon Preached at the Opening of St James East Crompton* (Oldham, 1847).

[82] Obelkevich, *Religion and Rural Society*, 149–50; RVR 1–62; Beswick, *Village School Royton*, 77–83; *Oldham Standard*, 17 Nov. 1860; Elbourne, *Music and Tradition*, 37; Obelkevich, 'Music and Religion', 554–7.

[83] RVR 1–62; Obelkevich, *Religion and Rural Society*, 146–51; Allen, *Shaw Church*, 20.

[84] *Oldham Chronicle*, 26 June 1858.

[85] Grundy, 'G. D. Grundy', 91; Bebbington, *Evangelicalism*, 147.

combine a high level of technical proficiency with great popular appeal and much popular participation.

Educators of the Poor

The local clergy took very seriously their pastoral role as educators of the poor, but the plans for a network of 'National' day and infant schools never came as close to fruition as those for the parochial system which they were intended to supplement. By 1851, when, for Lowe's grand design to have been operative, the Church of England should have been running at least forty schools of both types in Oldham, and eight in Saddleworth, it was actually supporting only thirteen and four respectively.[86] The problem—as ever—was not inertia, but limited resources and the pace of population growth. The burden was a particularly heavy one for the new parishes, whose resources were often heavily committed to the erection and maintenance of church buildings. Long delays were common. None of the new parishes seems to have been able to build schools until the late 1850s, and most not until the late 1860s. Some local school-building projects foundered, or almost did so, on the rocks of bureaucratic obstruction or economic fluctuation.[87] Nevertheless at the census of 1851 the Anglicans returned 2,107 pupils in Oldham, not including those at the Grammar and Blue Coat schools over which the Church exercised considerable influence—far more than the 382 pupils returned by all the other religious denominations put together. In Saddleworth the Anglican monopoly was even more complete, accounting for all 492 pupils who attended schools directly supported by religious bodies. However, although the Church of England had easily outstripped its religious rivals in the provision of daily education, the large number of small private schools in the area meant that only 29.7 per cent of the total day-school population in Oldham and 26.9 per cent in Saddleworth attended Anglican schools. Even after the Factory Act of 1844, the cost for working-class families of sending their children to school remained high; nevertheless, the proportion of the population aged between 5 and 14 attending day school in 1851 was not insignificant, especially among boys. Approximately 44.2 per cent of boys and 27.3 per cent of girls in Oldham, together with 53.4 per cent of boys and 37.9 per

---

[86] PP 1852–3, xc [1692], Census of Great Britain 1851, Education, England and Wales.
[87] NS file, St Mary's Oldham, Lowe to NS, 16 Dec. 1843, Clegg to NS, 26 Jan. 1844; NS file, St John's, Chadderton, Keene to NS, 12 Feb. 1862; NS file, St Margaret's, Hollinwood, Bishop of Chester to NS, 24 Mar. 1846, Bleasdale to NS, 31 Mar. 1846.

cent of girls in Saddleworth, attended day school, the disparity between the sexes being as much the result of daughters being required to look after younger children as of any local doubts about the value of women's education.[88] Moreover, since many children were sent to school intermittently because of fluctuations in their parents' finances, a considerably greater proportion of the local youth would have benefited from at least some day-school education than is suggested by the 1851 census (though the interruptions would have diminished its value), and the influence of the Church would have been correspondingly greater.[89]

Although Lowe's scheme for a complete network of day schools was frustrated by a shortage of resources, his plan for the development of Sunday schooling, which was relatively free from economic disadvantages, was amply fulfilled. The universal adoption in Oldham and Saddleworth of the system of 'gratuitous instruction' meant that collections at special services and occasional congregational subscriptions were sufficient to support even quite large schools, like those attached to St Peter's, which boasted 2,000 pupils in 1834. Consequently, an Anglican Sunday school was formed in all eight of the new districts created in the 1840s, often located in a small cottage or rented room before the construction of the church building. In 1847 a comprehensive survey of Sunday schools in the borough of Oldham (and therefore excluding the parishes of Hey, Leesfield, Tonge, Birch, and Middleton) counted thirteen schools in connection with the Church of England.[90]

This represented a considerable recovery after a major disruption in local Sunday schooling in the mid-1830s, occasioned by the removal of writing from the curriculum. Writing had been taught in most local Sunday schools from their inception in the eighteenth century, and, although from an early date some questions were raised about the propriety of giving a secular education on the sabbath, writing seems to have remained on the curriculum in most schools into the 1830s.[91] Then a succession of new incumbents like Lees of St Peter's and Grundy of Hey challenged the practice. Their reasons are not always clear, though in Grundy's case the motivation seems to have been a combination of sabbatarian sentiment and a fear that the popular Sunday morning writing lessons were proving a drain on the congregation at his morning service. There does seem to have been a resurgence of sabbatarian feeling

[88] PP 1852–3, xc [1692]; NS file, Holy Trinity, Shaw, Brammall to NS, 5 Feb. 1845.
[89] NS file, St Margaret's, Hollinwood, Bleasdale to NS, 31 Mar. 1846.
[90] NS file, St Peter's, Oldham, Winter to NS, 14 Apr. 1834; O'Neil, *Sunday Schools*.
[91] Ibid. 15, 29–30.

in the country as a whole during the 1830s, and this may account for much of the opposition to writing in Oldham. The opposition certainly did not stem from any desire to limit educational opportunities. Grundy offered weekday evening schools in compensation for the withdrawal of Sunday writing and both Grundy and Lees were enthusiastic supporters of day-school education. Like many other contemporary churchmen, 'their scruples forbade teaching writing on the sabbath, not teaching the poor to write'.[92] However, the 'reformers' found it far from easy to secure the desired changes. At Hey the Sunday-school managers made an appeal for public support, pointing out that many scholars 'came from considerable distances, and that it would be extremely difficult, if not impossible, for children to attend on week nights to write, after being at work twelve hours in a mill', and making out a case based on their own theological understanding of sabbath propriety and the sanction of local tradition. This appeal attracted considerable support from the local community. The minister and congregation of the nearby Greenacres Independent chapel allowed a collection to be made in support of the rebels, and in the end only one of the three schools connected with St John's, Hey, bowed to their new vicar's dictum.[93] The Hey schools were following an example set by five of the six schools in connection with St Peter's, Oldham, and the village Sunday school at Royton, which had severed the formal links with their mother churches in 1836—though the children continued to be brought to divine worship at their respective chapels. The rift continued for a considerable period, but most of the rebels were gradually reabsorbed during the 1850s as the growth in day- and evening-schooling began to obviate the need for Sunday writing and the ill feeling engendered by the controversy began to recede.[94]

Even if the seceded schools are excluded from the total, the 1847 survey records a fairly impressive Anglican achievement. The thirteen Anglican schools together mustered 1,827 male and 2,380 female children, representing 17.7 per cent of the whole population aged between 5 and 19 in the relevant districts in 1851 and some 26.5 per cent of the total Sunday-school population. For Saddleworth the best available figures come from the 1851 Education Census, which recorded eight schools

---

[92] Andrew, *Hey*, 39–42, Grundy, 'G. D. Grundy', 84–5; J. Wrigley, *The Rise and Fall of the Victorian Sunday* (Manchester, 1980), ch. 2; Laqueur, *Religion and Respectability*, ch. 5; NS file, St Peter's, Oldham, Lees to NS, 25 Feb. 1843, 29 June 1843.

[93] Circular Letter 1839, quoted in Andrew, *Hey*, 85; Grundy, 'G. D. Grundy', 85.

[94] C. E. Ward, 'Education as Social Control: Sunday Schools in Oldham 1780–1850', MA thesis (Lancaster, 1975), ch. 3; PP 1842, xvii [382], 858; Beswick, *Village School Royton*, 30–1; *Oldham Standard*, 17 June 1865.

with 621 male and 674 female pupils, representing 21.9 per cent of the population aged between 5 and 19 as a whole and 37.5 per cent of all Sunday scholars. The numbers of both schools and scholars under the Establishment continued to increase, and Dunne of St Matthew's, Chadderton, reporting to the CPAS in 1862, noted that 'within two years there have been added to our church here 900 Sunday scholars'.[95] Anglican Sunday scholars may therefore have made up an even greater proportion of the 5–19 age group in 1865 than they did in 1851. Sunday schooling had clearly managed to retain the mass allegiance of the working classes, and W. F. Walker noted in 1842 a 'partiality for Sunday schools which prevails throughout the district'. However, because many of the teachers had only received a Sunday-school education themselves, he felt that 'As a means of religious instruction . . . schools, composed as these are, must be imperfect in the extreme.' Other ministers were much more optimistic about the beneficial effects of Sunday schooling: Dunne of St Matthew's reported a confirmation class of 100 in connection with his Sunday school, while the curate of St Peter's told the CPAS in 1844 that he had great hopes of the 'rising generation' and that 'Many of the children, in whose minds the seeds of Gospel truth have been planted by the Sunday school, are manifesting the soundness of religious principle by the soundness of their lives and their zeal in the service of the Lord Jesus Christ.'[96]

Towards the middle of the century the Anglican Sunday schools began gradually to develop into more complex institutions. At least one printed manual was distributed locally for the benefit of aspiring teachers, encouraging them to develop their own piety and learning, and instructing them in how to inculcate the same qualities in their charges. A Church Sunday-school teachers' association was founded for much the same purpose in the early 1850s, and a host of ancillary institutions grew up which expanded the work of outreach in the community. The teacher was encouraged to visit his or her scholars in their own homes, giving 'an opportunity of introducing religious subjects to the parents and relations of the scholar'.[97] The schools also became centres of tract distribution, and the tract distributors of St Peter's Sunday school recorded in 1860 that they had thirty-seven agents distributing 1,000 tracts per week in St Peter's district, together with another twenty-two assisting in St Thomas's

[95] O'Neil, *Sunday Schools*; PP 1852–3, xc [1692]; CPAS, *Annual Report*, xxvii (1862), 9.

[96] Ibid.; CPAS, *Occasional Paper*, xiv (1844), 3; PP 1842, xvii [382], 858.

[97] J. J. Wray, *The Sabbath School Teacher: What he has to do and how to do it* (Oldham, 1857); *Oldham Chronicle*, 9 Aug. 1856; St Paul's, Royton, Sunday School Minute-Book 1856–60.

and St Mary's districts delivering a further 566 tracts per week. This gave the school a total of '59 distributors calling at 1,584 homes per week and not only leaving about 82,368 tracts per year, but frequently speaking a word of warning or encouragement when an opportunity occurred'.[98] The churches also aimed to draw in adults to the ever popular Sunday-school anniversary services, with their specially commissioned hymns and visiting preachers, followed by anniversary teas and recitations, which annually reaffirmed the position of the schools in local communities. Occasional evening services in schoolrooms could also be a popular success, and Dunne reported that 600 adults regularly attended his services in the Stockbrook branch school—a number probably exceeding his regular congregation at St Matthew's.[99] The schools developed a range of social services including sick and burial clubs and friendly societies, which both proved of benefit to the current generation of scholars and teachers and also allowed the schools to maintain links with former members. The St Peter's Sunday-school friendly society, for example, had 388 subscribers in 1842, comprising 298 current and 90 former members of the school. The recreational activities provided by the schools also multiplied during the 1840s; concerts and tea parties proliferated, creating, especially for the teachers, what amounted to an entire social world. With the arrival of the railway in 1842, the annual treat grew from a parade around the district during the Whitsun weekend followed by a feast for the scholars into a full-scale trip to the seaside constituting, in terms of aggregate popular participation, the biggest regular social event in the town after the annual wakes.[100]

Towards mid-century Churchmen became increasingly concerned about the problem of transition between involvement in the Sunday school and adult membership of the church. This period, therefore, saw the creation of a number of organizations aimed at retaining the constituency created by the popularity of Sunday schooling. Some capitalized on the widespread demand for the means of self-education, like the 'Sunday school and Congregational Lending Library' opened at Holy Trinity, Waterhead,

---

[98] *Oldham Standard*, 10 Nov. 1860.

[99] Beswick, *Village School Royton*, 76–83; St James's, Oldham, Sunday School Anniversary Circular 1838; St Michael's, Tonge, Sunday School Resolution Book 1837–52; St Paul's, Royton, Sunday School Accounts and Reports 1841–60 and Minute-Book 1856–60; CPAS, *Annual Report*, xxvii (1862), 9; PRO HO 129 475, 31.

[100] L. W. M. Hirst, *St Paul's Church Scouthead* (Oldham, 1967); St Paul's, Royton, Sunday School Accounts, Reports 1841–60 and Minute-Book 1856–60; St Michael's, Tonge, Sunday School Resolution Book 1837–52; Laqueur, *Religion and Respectability*, 175–9; *Oldham Standard*, 2, 9 June 1859, 10, 17 June 1865.

in 1849. Others focused more directly on the spiritual interests of their members, like the young men's week evening Bible class, which operated in connection with St Mary's Sunday school, and a third group, like the Shaw church institute, inaugurated in 1861, offered a comprehensive range of activities. Perhaps the most significant institution in this latter group was the interdenominational Young Men's Christian Association (YMCA), which operated as an agency for both education and evangelism and had been established in Oldham because of 'the difficulty of retaining young men when they arrive at certain ages in the classes of the Sunday schools whether as learners or teachers'.[101] This supplementary educational effort also included public lectures conducted by both Anglican clergy and laymen, free evening schools, mechanics institutes, and mutual improvement societies, including the most prestigious local society of all: the Oldham Lyceum, founded in 1837. A different problem, that of reaching children from families that were so poor as to be excluded even from the popular Sunday-school movement, was tackled towards the end of the period by the opening of parish ragged schools.[102]

The dominance of moderate Calvinism, with its emphasis on fallen man's natural resistance to the Gospel, may have helped the local Evangelical clergy to formulate a more realistic assessment of the problems facing their church than that held by many contemporary High Churchmen. For the latter, the simple expansion of church room and the parochial system was often seen as the most appropriate answer to the problem of indifference, an approach exemplified by Blomfield's experiment in Bethnal Green.[103] For a moderate Calvinist, with a stress on resistance to the Gospel stemming from 'Total Depravity', or even for the evangelical Arminian with his emphasis on the need to evoke a personal response to the grace of God, mere expansion of church room was far from sufficient. In order to build up the Church, it was necessary to take the Gospel out into the world. The great nineteenth-century theorist of this approach, at least from the Calvinist point of view, was the Scots Presbyterian Thomas Chalmers. In the second of his three *Lectures on*

[101] Holy Trinity, Waterhead, MS History, ch. 3; *Oldham Standard*, 29 Sept. 1860, 2, 23 Mar., 21 Sept. 1861.

[102] PP 1842, xvii [382], 834; *Oldham Chronicle*, 8 Oct. 1857, 15 Sept. 1860; Holy Trinity, Waterhead, MS History, ch. 3, anon., *Ninth Annual Report of Oldham Lycaeum* (Oldham, 1849); G. D. Grundy, *Episcopacy and the Three-fold Order of the Christian Ministry Proved to be Both Apostolic and Primitive: A Lecture Given in St John's Schoolroom Hey* (Oldham, 1862).

[103] D. M. Lewis, 'The Evangelical Mission to the British Working Class', D.Phil. thesis (Oxford, 1981), ch. 7.

Religious Establishments of 1838 Chalmers stressed that the depravity of man's 'animal self' meant that there was no natural demand for Christianity:

There is no natural hungering or thirstening after righteousness, and before man will seek that the want should be supplied, the appetite must first be created. The less a man has, whether of religion or righteousness, the less does he care for them, and the less will he seek them. It is thus that nature does not go forth in quest of Christianity, but Christianity must go forth in quest of nature.[104]

Chalmers went on to advocate what became known as the 'aggressive approach' as the only effective mode of operation in the new urban environment, and his theological analysis does seem to have been remarkably congruent with the problems facing the churches in the developing working-class communities of Oldham and Saddleworth. His view was shared by Sumner, who quoted Chalmers in his 1832 visitation charge and himself became an advocate of the 'aggressive approach'. Thus, in 1835, he urged that the unchurched must not 'be abandoned':

We do not find them among the Lord's family; they do not come within our care, in our capacity of STEWARDS of God's word. But we have another office, as MESSENGERS . . . we are required to announce to them the riches of divine mercy, and to 'beseech them in Christ's stead to be reconciled unto God' . . . Not waiting till they seek that, which nature, left to itself will never seek whilst it is attainable, and which every year of delay has set at a greater distance from them: but embracing every practicable scheme by which they may be made sensible of their grievous need, and of our readiness and anxiety to supply it, as the accredited guardians of their souls.[105]

Sumner's exhortations met with a ready response in Oldham and Saddeworth. As Whittaker of Leesfield reported, 'The clergy quietly discussed that question some time ago, and considered that if the people did not come to church, the church must be taken into the midst of the people.'[106]

---

[104] T. Chalmers, 'Vindication of a Religious National Establishment, in Opposition to the Reasonings and Opinions of the Economists', in *Lectures on the Establishment and Extension of National Churches* (Glasgow, 1838), 21; S. J. Brown, *Thomas Chalmers and the Godly Commonwealth in Scotland* (Oxford, 1982), chs. 3 and 7; Bebbington, *Evangelicalism*, 118.

[105] J. B. Sumner, *A Charge Delivered to the Clergy of the Diocese of Chester at the Triennial Visitation* (1832), xii. 16–26; *A Charge Delivered to the Clergy of the Diocese of Chester at the Triennial Visitation* (1835), 22–5, 44–50; *A Charge Delivered to the Clergy of the Diocese of Chester at the Triennial Visitation* (1838), 18–20, 58–61; *Charge* (1844), 68–9; on the important role played by Sumner, see Walker, 'Religious Changes', 89; Dell, 'Victorian Archbishop'.

[106] *Oldham Standard*, 6 July 1861.

The theological stress on the godly elect which tended to give a congregational bias to the ministry of some Calvinists was counterbalanced in the minds of local Anglicans by an emphasis on the parish conceived primarily as a focus for evangelism. Thus George Venables, the incumbent of Friezland, commented:

It is much easier work and smoother work to look after the congregation than the parish; but he who does so seems to me to neglect those who most need his visitations and his colloquial preaching. The monastic, or collegiate, or congregational systems cannot penetrate and fail entirely of the force of the command 'Preach the Gospel to every creature'. This is important, and should warn the Church in England now to fully carry out the parochial system.[107]

The 'parochial system' in the hands of the local Evangelicals comprised many features common to all parishes where the clergy conscientiously performed their duty, including the assiduous visitation of the sick and bereaved, itself an extensive task in a densely populated urban parish. This form of ministry seems generally to have been well received, and, when Thomas Lowe left the curacy of St Peter's in 1840,

a purse containing £50. 12. 6., subscribed in a few hours by all classes of his hearers, and particularly by the operative portion, was presented to him . . . as a slight testimonial of respect and approbation of his kind attentions to the sufferings of the sick and distressed, and his assiduity and zeal in administering to the religious comfort of the humble.[108]

However, in most local parishes, visiting was not limited to pastoring the sick and distressed. It was organized, systematic, and evangelistic in intention. Nor was it limited to the clergyman, but involved a mobilization of the laity, which was essential if the Church was to be 'taken out to the people' in industrial communities. Tracts and Bibles were distributed by the thousand through the agency of the two societies set up for that purpose, and hot on the heels of the Bible or tract distributor or the Sunday-school teacher followed the district visitor, lay reader, or assistant curate and the local incumbent himself. Some incumbents presided over what virtually amounted to team ministries, like that run by Lowe from St Mary's with two assistant curates, a lay reader, and a team of district visitors. Others carried out detailed house-to-house surveys in

---

[107] G. Venables, *St Patrick and the Church of Ireland: A Sermon Preached in Christ Church Friezland* (1866).
[108] *Oldham Standard*, 8 Oct. 1859, 2 Dec. 1865; *Manchester Guardian*, 4 July 1840.

order to determine the religious views of their parishioners as a foundation for further action.[109]

Evangelical pragmatism in the employment of laymen as paid scripture
readers or as voluntary workers restored to the Church a measure of the
flexibility it had lost with the withdrawal of the Methodists. Women
often seem to have been regarded as particularly suited to the bringing of
the Gospel into the domestic world of the poor. The period saw a considerable expansion of their influence in this crucial area of the church's
ministry, and figures like Martha Schofield, who, not content with a
vigorous ministry as a Sunday-school teacher and visitor at Waterhead,
started a women's week evening meeting at which she provided biblical
instruction and general advice, must have played a key role in many local
parishes.[110] Local Churchmen certainly seem to have concurred with the
view of the CPAS that 'little good can be effected without constant
domiciliary visitation',[111] and their reports to the society form a representative part of the vast corpus of material attesting to its achievements.
The following excerpt from the journal of a 'lay-Agent' employed in
Waterhead is typical:

This night I met with a case of great indifference and hardness of heart. Before
I entered the house I heard a great noise, loud talking, etc. When I entered I
found six men playing at cards . . . I entreated them to lay their cards aside, and
listen to the Word of God, which I would read. In a short time two of the six
ceased playing . . . I sat down at the same table where the cards were, and determined to read the word of God, confident that I was in the path of duty. I read
for some time, and eventually the cards were laid aside, and the men ceased
playing. I then called their attention to the state in which they were, and assured
them that they were not prepared to die. One of the men said, 'I shall get through
as well as others; and if I go where others go I shall be satisfied.' I told them about
Dives and Lazarus. The substance of this remarkable parable arrested their attention; they listened attentively. I then read the tract, 'The Sunday Idler'. To
this they paid great attention. I then knelt down and prayed with them, gave each
of them a tract, and desired them to come to church.[112]

---

[109] OLIC, Oldham British and Foreign Bible Society (BFBS) Auxiliary Minutes, 1813–
53; MPL L93/2, Box 9, Minutes of the Delph Branch Bible Association 1848–53; *Oldham
Advertiser*, 15 Dec. 1855; CPAS, *Annual Report*, x (1845), 3–5; CC, file 1,443, Lowe to EC,
8 June 1844, Lowe, Application; CPAS, *Quarterly Paper*, lxviii (1866), 8; Haig, *Victorian
Clergy*, 234.

[110] MPL, Delph Branch Bible Association Minutes; F. K. Prochaska, *Women and Philanthropy in Nineteenth Century England* (Oxford, 1980); Shaw, *Local Notes*, 220–1;
Bebbington, *Evangelicalism*, 65–6.

[111] CPAS, *Annual Report*, xx (1855), 34.   [112] Ibid. xxx (1865), 18.

This sort of intrusion into the scarce leisure time and privacy of the working population may not always have been welcome, though the ladies of the Delph Bible Association reported towards the end of a 'general visitation' that 'so far, they had been kindly received'.[113] However, it is certainly a fair reflection of the determination and perseverance with which the Church faced up to the challenge of the new working-class communities. Such visits were intended to lay the basis for further activities. F. B. Broadbent of Waterhead, who employed two lay readers supported by the CPAS, reported in 1864 that 'The lay agents have had many interesting conversations with the families on whom they have called during the year. I directed them during the winter to hold short cottage lectures in some of the poorest districts, and I am happy to say these gatherings promise to be very successful; there is quite a readiness to hear the Word of God read and expounded.'[114]

The introduction of such lectures was strongly supported by Sumner. His 1835 *Charge* effectively suspended (in the Chester diocese) the 71st Canon against preaching in private houses, since a strict interpretation would 'render our establishment unsuitable to the present condition of the country', and, if 'literally acted on, would seriously injure the usefulness of the Church everywhere. In some districts it would utterly subvert it, and could only end in her destruction.'[115] Sumner regarded informal cottage meetings as the best way of evangelizing the naturally resistant poor of the large industrial parishes:

They will not seek the shepherd; they know not why they should. The shepherd must seek them. They will not come for the 'bread of life'; we must take it to them . . . we must carry the Scriptures home, and bring them within their hearing. Excellent results have been found to proceed from a system of this kind: from the simple reading and exposition of Scripture to such a party as can be conveniently assembled in the houses of the poor . . . a lecture of this kind does not presuppose the existence of what it is intended to produce. To attend it, neither requires extraordinary exertion, nor makes an evident manifestation of a change of inveterate habits. This is one of their recommendations. When a spiritual taste is once created, no trouble will be grudged, or self denial spared. But before he submits to either, a man must feel the value of what is to be gained.[116]

This view matched closely the realities of the new parishes of Oldham and Saddleworth, where, moreover, there had been a tradition of such

---

[113] Delph Branch Bible Association Minutes, 25 Apr. 1848.
[114] CPAS, *Quarterly Paper*, lxxii (1864), 3.
[115] Sumner, *Charge* (1835), 44–5.   [116] Sumner, *Charge* (1832), 19, 21.

meetings run by Anglican Evangelicals under Methodist influence. Sumner's urging consequently met with a ready response from the local clergy, and by 1846 the six curates and one lay reader sponsored by the CPAS were alone responsible for eleven cottage lectures in Oldham and one in Saddleworth, including a number located in the large town-centre parishes of St Mary's and St Peter's.[117] The informal nature of cottage meetings seems to have overcome the objections felt by some of the poor towards church attendance and especially their inhibitions about the lack of appropriate clothing. They certainly generated a good response, and the experience of Littler at St James's, East Crompton, was probably typical: 'I have two adult Bible classes of twenty each meet me weekly in a cottage, so willing are these poor people to receive instruction.'[118] The extreme flexibility of the cottage meeting provided an excellent solution to the problems created by the proliferation of communities in Oldham and Saddleworth. In some districts they also provided a valuable link between Sunday school and church attendance and their popularity continued to grow in subsequent decades: in 1871, for example, the incumbent of Waterhead described a packed cottage meeting with a mixed attendance including some he had never seen at church.[119] The development of new pastoral and evangelistic approaches continued apace and by 1859 Anglican laymen could be found preaching to crowds in the open air in Oldham and meeting with a favourable reception. In 1861, at Friezland in Saddleworth, the incumbent established an annual celebration of the anniversary of the church's consecration in an attempt to reinforce the growing identity of his parish, and perhaps in imitation of the very popular nonconformist anniversary services common in the locality. He thus demonstrated the willingness of the local clergy to imitate as well as innovate to advance the interests of the Church.[120]

The more traditional communal role of the Church was fostered by the charitable efforts of the clergy. Local incumbents frequently relieved the poor with gifts of money, in defiance of the ideology of the New Poor Law. The clergy also took a lead in organizing the large-scale relief necessitated by the 'Cotton Famine', and Broadbent of Waterhead noted in 1864 that 'I have given away large and considerable amounts in small sums of money, or in calico, flannel, and linsey, and shoes to my poor people and others. Many of whom would have been compelled, through

---

[117] CPAS, *Annual Report*, xi (1846).   [118] CPAS, *Quarterly Paper*, lxxii (1864), 3.
[119] CPAS, *Occasional Paper*, xiv (1844), 3–4; CPAS, *Quarterly Paper*, xcii (1871), 3.
[120] *Oldham Standard*, 13 Sept. 1859, 1 June 1860.

want of clothing, to stay at home if I had not aided them.'[121] This charitable activity must have contributed to the high degree of popularity enjoyed by many local clergy. Thus, of Lawler, curate of St Michael's, Tonge, who produced bobbins for his silk-weaving parishioners in his spare time, it was noted that 'His ready Irish wit and kindly countenance together with a few bobbins in his pocket for those who were short for their bobbin wheel, always ensured him a hearty welcome.'[122]

There is no evidence of any sustained popular anti-clericalism in Oldham and Saddleworth. Some local clergy did court temporary unpopularity, like G. D. Grundy over the question of Sunday writing, and others, notably Thomas Lowe, became targets for ribald attacks by local ballad singers. As tensions between Church and alehouse developed with the rise of temperance, and clerical professionalism promoted by the Evangelicals became more prominent, it is probable that the old easy relationships of the 'unreformed' period gradually disappeared.[123] However, the same Evangelical attitudes also contributed towards a low level of clerical involvement in the local magistracy, with never more than two of Oldham's incumbents serving on the bench after 1830, and this certainly removed one potential source of unpopularity in a period of considerable turbulence.[124] Some of the clergy were notably concerned to avoid too close an identification with an unpopular political establishment; of G. D. Grundy, his son recalled that 'he seemed morbidly bent on not even seeming to be allied with the employing class'. To this end he inveighed against the truck system and intervened on behalf of the workers in local industrial disputes; a similar ministry was undertaken by Richard Durnford at Middleton.[125] In so far as one can rely on the remarks made at public

---

[121] CC, file 1,886, Littler to Commissioners, 12 June 1856; *Oldham Standard*, 2 Dec. 1865; *Oldham Chronicle*, 16 Aug. 1862; Andrew, *Hey*, 48–51; CPAS, *Annual Report*, xxix (1864), 3.

[122] St Michael's, Tonge, MS History.

[123] Anon., *Parson Lo* (Oldham, n.d.); *Manchester Courier*, 18 Feb. 1832; *Oldham Standard*, 17 Sept. 1859; Bumstead, *Church Matters*, 6; Russell, *Clerical Profession*, ch. 3.

[124] PP 1836, xliii (583), Return of all persons appointed to act as Justices of the Peace in each and every county in England and Wales, 161–262; PP 1840, xli (484), Return of the names, addresses, and residences of Justices of the Peace, Ministers of the Established Church, now in the Commission of the Peace in the several counties in England and Wales, 351–94; PP 1842, xxxiii (524), Return of all persons appointed to act as Justices of the Peace in each and every county in England and Wales since the 21 day of July 1836, 445–70; PP 1863, xlviii (322), A Return of the number of Clergymen placed in the Commission of the Peace in the counties of England and Wales during the last twenty years, 259–79; PP 1873, liv (388), Nominal Return of all the Clerks in Holy Orders in the Commission of the Peace in any county in England or Wales, 33–57; Butterworth, *Oldham*, appendix; Virgin, *Age of Negligence*, 118–25.

[125] Grundy, 'G. D. Grundy', 92; G. B. Grundy, *Fifty-Five Years at Oxford, An Unconventional Autobiography* (1945), 5; Stephens, *Richard Durnford*, 76–7.

meetings and comments in their biographies and obituaries, most of the local clergy, whatever their shade of churchmanship, succeeded in retaining a fair degree of popularity. When Lawler of Tonge died in 1860 an estimated 5,000 attended his funeral, and when Grundy of Hey died in 1901, after sixty-three years' ministry in the area, it was claimed that 50,000 people attended his funeral—mainly mill-hands from Oldham and Saddleworth.[126]

Bearing in mind the challenges it faced, the achievement of the 're-formed' Establishment was impressive. Local Anglicans struggled hard to maintain a reasonable level of church accommodation and a decent number of resident clergy, and, if they lost ground compared to the position achieved by their 'unreformed' predecessors, they were at least still in the race. Full advantage was taken of the additional resources and flexibility introduced by central reforms, but the impetus for change and the dogged determination that saw it through the obstacles were always local. Both clergy and laity pursued a policy of aggressive missionary activity within the parishes with considerable devotion. They also displayed a good deal of initiative in their exploration of new methods of outreach—at times breaking through the traditional Anglican structures that had handicapped their predecessors. Even so, the gathering of a regular congregation could be backbreaking work which was slow to bear fruit, especially when so much time and energy was diverted into the struggle to raise a pile of bricks and mortar. This problem was particularly acute when the local communities were widely dispersed: as Durnford reported in 1837, 'the population though considerable is scattered in little folds of cottages separated by considerable distances, these people have grown up entirely without religious habits and it is very unlikely that at the first, I may say for some years any considerable congregation can be got together. It will require great labour to collect even a few.' Not surprisingly many of Oldham's clergy saw themselves as laying a foundation for the future and placed their hopes for a thorough Christianization of the area in the 'rising generation'—hence their emphasis on education and the concern to strengthen the links between school and Church membership.[127]

Their concentration on the development of a parochial community carried with it the danger of a lapse into parochial attitudes which sometimes manifested itself in a reluctance to support town-wide evangelistic

---

[126] *Oldham Chronicle*, 9 Oct. 1858; *Oldham Standard*, 8 Oct. 1859, 28 Apr. 1860, 2 Dec. 1865; Andrew, *Hey*, 59; Grundy, *Fifty-Five years*, 9.

[127] CC, file 20,833, Durnford to CBC, 3 Apr. 1837; CPAS, *Occasional Paper*, xiv (1844), 3–4.

initiatives. However, the clergy of Oldham and Saddleworth certainly could not be criticized for falling prey to the temptations of a 'life of leisure' in 'the void left by unperformed pastoralia'.[128] No such void existed. They not only ploughed the fields and scattered the good seed on the land, but sought to render the Almighty every assistance at their disposal in feeding and watering the growing crop. It is difficult to see what more could have been asked of them. The men and women of the 'reformed' Establishment were worthy replacements for their 'unreformed' predecessors and that, in Oldham and Saddleworth at least, was a significant achievement.

[128] Obelkevich, *Religion and Rural Society*, 125.

4. Dissent Old and New

The Anglican Church never exercised a monopoly in religious provision for the population of Oldham and Saddleworth. However, the virtual disappearance of residual English Roman Catholicism in the district meant that the Anglican hegemony in the mid-eighteenth century was challenged only by a handful of protestant Dissenters. Dissent had deep roots in Oldham and Saddleworth. The Quakers established a fellowship in Oldham in 1654, and eight years later a body of Presbyterians followed their ejected minister out of the Establishment, and eventually formed their own covenanted church. However, the Quaker community was diminished by a high level of emigration, and by 1725 it had dwindled almost to the point of extinction.[1] The Presbyterians, though more successful, grew only slowly, and their cause at Greenacres was severely weakened by the withdrawal of its Saddleworth members, who built their own chapel at Delph in 1746. Thereafter its problems were exacerbated by theological disputes as two ministers in the 1750s and 1760s attempted to introduce heterodox views on the Trinity. In common with several other Presbyterian congregations in Lancashire, the majority of the Greenacres members resisted this development, and the next minister, William James, swung the church to the opposite extreme, espousing a hyper-Calvinist theology and promoting a drift into Independency. He effected a purge of the few remaining anti-Trinitarians and secured the entrenchment of hyper-Calvinist views which were to keep the church outside the mainstream of the 'evangelical revival' until the 1790s.[2]

---

[1] Lancashire Record Office (LRO), FRM 5, Oldham Preparative Meeting Record of Visiting Friends; J. P. Watkins, 'A Brief History of Greenacres Chapel', in anon., *Greenacres Tercentenary Year Book* (Oldham, 1972), 6; J. Ward, *A Retrospect of the Oldham Meeting of the Society of Friends, its Schools and Kindred Societies* (Oldham, 1911); W. Taylor, *Jubilee Souvenir of the Oldham Friends' First Day School* (Oldham, 1915).

[2] Watkins, 'Greenacres Chapel', 6–8; B. Nightingale, 'Independency a Century Ago', *Oldham Chronicle*, 2, 9 Aug. 1919; R. T. Jones, *Congregationalism in England 1662–1962* (1962), 153–4; G. G. Waddington, *A History of the Independent Church at Greenacres from its First Establishment down to the Present Date* (Manchester, 1854), 60–72; A. Marcroft, *A Historical Account of the Unitarian Chapel Oldham* (Oldham, 1913), 1. For the theological content of hyper-Calvinism, see P. Toon, *The Emergence of hyper-Calvinism in English Nonconformity 1689–1765* (1967).

Hyper-Calvinism enjoyed a brief flowering among local Dissenters in the late eighteenth century, with 'antinomian' pastors occupying the pulpit at Greenacres and a small hyper-Calvinist Baptist cause being established in the Royton out-township. By 1810, however, this tradition had all but disappeared among the Independents, and it was only maintained in Baptist circles possibly by the congregation at Royton and, after 1820, by a small cause in Hollinwood supported by the activity of William Gadsby, the great apostle of early nineteenth-century Baptist hyper-Calvinism.[3] In its manifestation at Greenacres, hyper-Calvinism was clearly a reaction against the threat of Arian heterodoxy, but it may also have been a reaction against the universal 'offers of grace' of the evangelical revival, manifest in the moderate Calvinism of the neighbouring cause at Delph and the increasingly intrusive presence of Methodism and Moravianism in the surrounding communities. It would thus have been an attempt to bar the doors of the sanctuary against a force whose very success in attracting numbers threatened to undermine a hundred years of tradition of the exclusivity of a gathered people—a final fierce affirmation of the peculiarity of 'old Dissent'.[4] This cannot have been the whole story, however, for, ironically, hyper-Calvinism could itself possess considerable mass appeal. Some 'hyper' preachers were, like James at Greenacres, very popular, and Gadsby, the most spectacularly successful of the populist hyper-Calvinists, drew large crowds when he spoke at Hollinwood. It may be significant that hyper-Calvinism in Oldham took root in small villages on the periphery of the central built-up area or in the out-townships—even those without a Dissenting tradition. Here the harsh determinism of a rigid doctrine of election may have held a particular appeal for people in communities experiencing rapid economic and demographic change—not only a source of security in an increasingly uncertain world but, in the old Dissenting political mould, a religious counterpart to the 'radicalism of traditional communities'. At least one minister of the small Baptist church in Royton was deeply involved in Oldham's radical politics.[5]

Nevertheless hyper-Calvinism was the creed of a small minority, even within local nonconformity, and, if it is to be identified in Oldham and

[3] Waddington, *Greenacres*, 60–90; anon., 'Historical Sketch of Bethesda Baptist Chapel Royton', in anon., *Handbook of the Church Bazaar* (Oldham, 1894); J. Gadsby, *A Memoir of the Late Mr William Gadsby Compiled from Authentic Sources* (Manchester, 1844), 83.

[4] See W. R. Ward, 'The Baptists and the Transformation of the Church 1780–1830', *Baptist Quarterly*, NS 25 (1973), 167.

[5] G. G. Waddington, *Historical and Biographical Notices* (Dewsbury, 1886), 283; Gadsby, *Memoir*, 83; Foster, *Class Struggle*, 136; anon., 'Bethesda Baptist Chapel'.

Saddleworth with the last stand of old Dissent, then by 1810 old Dissent was effectively dead. The new evangelicalism was already beginning to permeate local Dissent while the congregation at Greenacres was retreating into its hyper-Calvinist sanctuary in the mid-1780s. Its first prominent locally based Dissenting exponent was Noah Blackburn, who was called to the ministry at Delph in 1787. His pastorate was long and successful and, within four years of his appointment, the congregation at Delph was forced by pressure on its accommodation to build an enlarged chapel. Blackburn was also a prominent figure in the 'Lancashire Itinerant Society' founded in 1801 to promote evangelism in the county, and the decisive moves towards its formation were made in a meeting at Delph in 1796. It was Blackburn's ministry at Delph, rather than that of his contemporary James at Greenacres, which set the tone for the development of nonconformity in the area, and in 1805, with the call of Joseph Galland to the pastorate, Greenacres, the last stronghold of Congregationalist old Dissent, fell to the increasingly confident forces of the revival.[6] Galland, who exercised the first extended evangelical pastorate at Greenacres, found 'the church and congregation . . . in a low and distracted state owing to division and animosity' and responded by tightening church discipline and engaging in a vigorous pastoral ministry. Initially he met with opposition, but under his leadership the church set its face firmly against the tendency to introversion implicit in its previous stance and, together with its sister church at Delph, towards an evangelical theology coupled with an evangelistic ministry.[7]

Although moderate Calvinism was the dominant theological form taken by the evangelical revival in local Dissent, the new evangelicalism did manifest itself in other ways. The Quakers, for example, caught the spirit of revival in the early 1780s, and borrowed Oldham's new Wesleyan Chapel in 1783 to hold an evangelistic meeting—thus reversing the quietist trend which had threatened to confine local Quakerism within the circle of a handful of families.[8] A further element was added to the evangelical mixture in 1772, when itinerant preachers from Dukinfield in Manchester introduced the evangelical Lutheranism of the Moravian

---

[6] Waddington, *Greenacres*, 83–93; W. G. Robinson, *A History of the Lancashire Congregational Union 1806–1956* (Liverpool, 1955), 22–6. On the important role played by itinerant organizations in consolidating evangelicalism within Dissent and in spreading Dissent more widely, see D. W. Lovegrove, *Established Church, Sectarian People: Itinerancy and the Transformation of English Dissent 1780–1830* (Cambridge, 1988), *passim*.

[7] Greenacres Congregational Church (GCC), Church Book, 1806; Watkins, 'Greenacres Chapel', 9.

[8] Ward, *Retrospect*; M. R. Watts, *The Dissenters* (Oxford, 1978), 461–2.

Brethren. For twelve years they preached to a small congregation in Greenacres on the doorstep of the increasingly exclusive old Dissenting cause, before moving to Lees, where they eventually established a permanent presence.[9] Nevertheless beneath this variety of form there subsisted a unity of substance. All the new evangelicals participated in a common vision, a burning commitment to Church expansion, labelled by A. D. Gilbert 'the conversionist priority'.[10] Shamelessly the churches of the revival sought to reach out to society at large in what D. W. Lovegrove has described as 'a promiscuous scouring of the countryside'.[11] A far cry from the peculiarity of the gathered churches of an older nonconformity, this was new Dissent with a vengeance.

The most obvious product of this new commitment to Church growth was the growth of new churches—a process precipitated by the dynamic of the revival and fuelled by twin cycles of fission and fusion operating within existing congregations. A clear example of this process is provided by the origin of the town-centre Baptist church, finally established on Manchester Street in 1816. The church began in 1815 as a secession from St Peter's, where the fusion of Anglican and Methodist enthusiasm had created a congregation whose energy sometimes demanded a greater freedom of expression than could be contained within Anglican structures. Initially the seceders decided to form a Congregational Independent church, and they applied to William Roby, the leading exponent of evangelical Congregationalism in Manchester, for a preacher under the auspices of the Itinerant Society. Roby was, at first, unable to comply with this request, and the majority of the seceders, unwilling to wait, immediately accepted the offer of a preacher from a Baptist church in Rochdale. A few months later a significant portion of the congregation demonstrated the strength of their new-found convictions by trooping down to be immersed, *en masse*, in a local reservoir.[12] Although it began with only a dozen members, the Manchester Street church grew steadily and it became, after 1830, the parent of five other Baptist churches in the locality. Two were produced by divisions in the Manchester Street congregation, the first of which, in 1834, may reflect the influence of Gadsby, since the seceders eventually participated in the formation of the hyper-Calvinist church in Hollinwood.

[9] H. Bintley, *A Brief History of Salem Moravian Church 1824–1974* (Oldham, 1974), 2.

[10] Gilbert, *Religion and Society*, 54; Bebbington makes a similar point in his analysis of evangelical activism and conversionism: *Evangelicalism*, 5–12.

[11] Lovegrove, *Itinerancy*, 150.

[12] King Street Baptist Church (KSBC), Church Register; Manchester Street Baptist Church, Church Register; McOwan MSS; J. Vickers, *A History of Independent Methodism* (Bolton, 1920), 141; Rowbottom Diary, 6 Sept. 1816.

The second secession was the product of a difference of opinion over the propriety of constructing a new and larger church on King Street. When the majority of the congregation moved to their new building in 1863, some twenty members remained behind to form the second Manchester Street church. The other three Baptist churches originated in more peaceful acts of planting by the parent congregation: at Mills Hill in Chadderton in 1845, at Royton in 1861, and at Glodwick in 1864. A further Baptist church, in Middleton, was planted from nearby Rochdale in 1858 with assistance from the Lancashire Baptist Itinerant Society.[13]

Other Dissenting groups were also active in the formation of new causes. By 1801 the Quakers were holding meetings in at least nine different locations in Oldham and Saddleworth, while the Moravians finally established a permanent settlement at Salem near Lees in 1825, and a branch church at Westwood in Chadderton in 1865. Even the local Unitarian congregation might be considered a creature of the revival, since it was a product of the militant proselytizing Unitarianism of the early nineteenth century. The Unitarian missionary Richard Wright visited Oldham in 1812, and succeeded in gathering together a small group of sympathizers who formed a church, which was subsequently supported by the 'Methodist Unitarian' circuit, centred on Rochdale.[14] The most successful of the new Dissenters in Oldham and Saddleworth, however, were the Independents, who, in the early nineteenth century, benefited from a fusion of two separate streams of the revival. In 1806 two local preachers left the Methodist New Connexion in Oldham, having rejected Wesley's position on the doctrine of 'Imputed Righteousness' in favour of one more compatible with moderate Calvinism. In 1807 they founded two congregations, at Uppermill and Springhead, denominated 'Independent Evangelical Methodist Churches'. These churches gradually drifted into association with the Congregationalists, partly because of their need for financial assistance in the late 1820s, and partly from a natural attraction based on the congruence of their doctrine. A similar process of fusion was responsible for the formation in 1815 of Queen Street church in the town centre. This originated in the split from St Peter's, which had

[13] W. T. Whitely, *The Baptists of North West England 1649–1913* (1913), 336–54.

[14] LRO FRM 5, Oldham Preparative Meeting, Record of Visiting Friends; Bintley, *Salem Moravian Church*, 3; I. Packer, *The Moravian Church Westwood 1865–1965* (Royton, 1965), 6–7; anon., *Unitarian Chapel Lord Street Calender*, 1 Nov., 1 Dec. 1896, 1 Sept. 1897; Marcroft, *Historical Account*, ch. 4; H. McLachlan, *The Methodist Unitarian Movement* (Manchester, 1919), 47–8.

produced the Baptist church, being acted on, somewhat belatedly, by William Roby on behalf of the Lancashire Congregational Union. He helped to gather the nucleus of a congregation, found a succession of pastors, and continued to take an interest in the cause into the 1830s. Roby was also instrumental in the formation of a Congregational church in Middleton in 1822, providing similar support, and helping to secure financial assistance.[15]

Two more Congregational churches emerged in the eastern suburbs of Oldham in the 1820s by the more volatile process of fission in existing causes. The first, Hope Chapel, was founded in 1823 largely by the exertions of Samuel Lees, a major employer in the Soho area, who felt that the growing population of his locality merited an Independent church of its own. Lees had been an important supporter of the cause at Queen Street, as were other early members of the new congregation, and their withdrawal inflicted both manpower shortages and financial loss on their rather reluctant mother church. Hope was itself the scene of the second split in 1828, when a 'portion of the congregation', presumably with the support of Samuel Lees, quarrelled with their pastor, Jonathan Fox, who left, accompanied by a number of the members, to form a separate church which eventually established itself on Regent Street in 1829.[16] There was a hiatus in the formation of new Independent churches until 1852, and then a further six were created during the following decade. Five of the new churches were deliberately planted by older causes. Two were the offspring of a single parent church, with the County Union assisting at the birth: Royton, established in 1857 by the minister and members of Queen Street, and Shaw, established by members of the Royton church in 1861.[17] The other three were the product of joint efforts by two or

<hr/>

[15] F. Smith and J. Wilde, *Springhead Congregational Chapel Centennial Souvenir 1807–1907* (Oldham, 1907), 7–10; J. J. Lawton, *Ebenezer Congregational Church Uppermill: Church Memoirs* (Uppermill, 1923), 9–11; Church Book, Uppermill Congregational Church; anon., 'Queen Street Sunday School', in *Queen Street Sunday School Oldham: Handbook of the Grand Bazaar and Fancy Fair* (Oldham, 1879), 32; A. Bridge and G. Lee, *Queen Street Congregational Church Oldham* (Bolton, 1921), 27–35; 'E.', *Historical Account of Providence Chapel* (Middleton, 1871); anon., *History of Providence Congregational Church 1822–1972* (Middleton, 1972), 1.

[16] Ibid. 33; 'Report to the Lancashire Congregational Union' (LCU), 1823, in ibid. 140; J. Jones, *A Century of Hope* (Perth, 1966), 6–9; R. M. Davies, 'History of Congregationalism in Oldham—Incidents in the History of Forty Years' Ministry', *Oldham Express*, 28 July 1883.

[17] Bridge and Lee, *Queen Street*, 6–7; R. B. Maxwell, *A Brief History of the Royton Congregational Church* (Royton, 1961).

more local churches; work began in the village of Hollinwood in the late 1840s sponsored by both the Queen Street and Hope congregations assisted by the Union, and regular worship and preaching commenced in 1852. At the same time, regular preaching began at Dobcross in Saddleworth, and a weekly evening service was introduced in 1861, supported by the Independent churches at Delph and Uppermill. A further cause at Waterhead originated in a cottage meeting and a branch Sunday school established by Galland in 1837. It was, however, abandoned by the Greenacres congregation, probably because of a fear that the resources of the church were insufficient to sustain the work. The school later became dependent on Hope, and was also supported by Queen Street and Springhead. Its first church covenant included former members of all three churches. The emergence of the sixth Independent church, that at Pastures, on the border between Oldham and Saddleworth, was rather less harmonious. It was formed in 1854 from a Sunday school which had previously been supported by the congregation at Springhead, by means of a split which caused a considerable loss of membership at the parent church.[18]

As we have seen, a number of local churches emerged as a product of fission. Some historians have suggested that this process tended to produce checks to Dissenting growth. However, in Oldham this effect seems to have been mitigated by the unifying activities of denominational organizations and the willingness of local congregations to engage in deliberate acts of church-planting.[19] Most of the new foundations were concentrated in the first few decades of the nineteenth century, when the Established Church was relatively inactive in the formation of new congregations, and also in the 1850s and 1860s, after the great Anglican expansion of the 1840s. It would, however, be misleading, even in the 'storm-and-stress' period of early nineteenth-century evangelicalism, to regard these concentrations as sudden responses to new opportunities or to renewed competition. They were rather the maturing fruit of a remarkably sustained evangelistic effort within which virtually the whole corporate life of new Dissent was subsumed.

---

[18] Bridge and Lee, *Queen Street*, 65–9; P. Jones, *The Story of Hollinwood Congregational Church Oldham* (Oldham, 1951), 7–8; LRO CUL 20, 1–3, MS Journal of the Secretary to the Executive Committee of the LCU, i–iii; E. Lewis, 'The Story of Dobcross Congregational Church', *Oldham Chronicle*, Aug. 1970; Uppermill Congregational Church, Waterhead Church Covenent, 1864; H. Bateson, *Providential Lives* (Oldham, 1957), 23.

[19] Koditschek, *Class Formation*, 273; Rycroft, 'Craven', 85–7.

Proclaiming the Gospel

Like Anglican Evangelicals, Dissenters employed a wide variety of evangelistic methods. Some, like the general round of Gospel-preaching, with its offers of grace and calls to conversion, were centred on the church building or the schoolroom, and relied on the willingness of the local population to come in and listen. This preaching was the stock in trade of the revival at most of the local churches. The customary rites of passage, especially baptisms and funerals, often provided opportunities to expose a wider public to Gospel-preaching. For example, the minister of the Moravian church recorded in his diary for 1846 that 'Our sister Newton, having lost an uncle by a fall . . . brought many of her relations and friends to our chapel in the afternoon, that they might hear something that might prove beneficial.'[20] There were also specially arranged evangelistic services like the 'general meetings' held by the local Quakers from the 1770s onwards, and the 'special services' on weeknights organized by the Middleton Congregationalists in the 1860s. In local Baptist and Congregationalist circles, enquirers' meetings were introduced to cater for people attracted by the preaching, and those at Springhead in the 1850s were described as both 'frequent, and numerously attended'.[21]

However, the evangelistic endeavours of the new Dissenters were by no means confined within the walls of their church buildings. Open-air preaching had always been characteristic of the revival, and throughout the period the Dissenters continued to take seriously the divine injunction to 'go out into the highways and byways and compel them to come in'. Among the Congregationalists, the Methodist-influenced church at Springhead pursued this activity with particular enthusiasm, and in the 1830s Mr Morris, the pastor, 'established "preaching stations" at Lees, Waterhead Mill, and Austerlands . . . and on Sunday evenings the believers of Springhead conducted services at these "stations" in fields, barns, and at crossroads'.[22] J. G. Short, the minister of Springhead, in the 1860s held a series of open-air preaching services in the villages surrounding the church, which seem to have excited considerable popular interest, and this approach was pursued by other Independent churches too. The

---

[20] *Oldham Standard*, 13 July 1861; Salem Moravian Church (SMC), Congregational Diary, 17 May 1846.

[21] Taylor, *Friends' First Day School*; Middleton Congregational Church (MCC), Record Book, 3 June 1863; KSBC, Record Book, Nov. 1854; *Congregational Yearbook* (1868), 269.

[22] Bateson, *Providential Lives*, 14.

Oldham Standard reported in 1861 that 'Last Tuesday night from 5[00] to 600 persons, consisting principally of working men and women, assembled in Mill End Square, Shaw, to listen to the Revd Reuben Seddon the Independent minister who held the second of his course of out-door services.'[23] In the 1830s even the local Quakers began to recover the tradition of preaching in the open air, extending an invitation to J. J. Gurney, the prominent Quaker evangelical, who gave evangelistic addresses from a platform on a wagon to large crowds in both Oldham and Middleton.[24]

Open-air meetings were supplemented by evangelistic lectures and preaching in mission rooms, and also by cottage meetings. The Baptists of King Street, for example, established a preaching room in Royton in 1861 and another at Glodwick in 1864, while various Congregationalist churches also hired private rooms, mainly in the out-townships, many of which developed into the new churches of the 1850s and 1860s. In addition, both Unitarians and Congregationalists made considerable use of public assembly rooms, such as the 'People's Hall' in Lees and the 'Temperance Hall' in Middleton, for occasional evangelistic lectures.[25] Cottage meetings, which required even less infrastructure than mission rooms, were probably more widespread. The Queen Street Congregationalists, for example, held cottage meetings in at least five different locations between 1829 and 1832, noting in 1831 that 'the attendance has been gratifying'. The Springhead Congregationalists regularly operated both a mission room and up to seven cottage meetings between 1837 and 1841, with attendance varying between fifteen and eighty at each meeting. The Moravians too organized cottage meetings in the villages and hamlets surrounding their base at Salem, their minister hinting, in 1837, at some of the practical advantages of bringing the Gospel into the homes of his hearers: 'Preached at Waterhead, and at Roundthorn where there was a full house notwithstanding the very forbidding weather and the darkness.'[26]

Although he was a strong supporter of religious establishments, Thomas Chalmers exercised considerable influence among English nonconformists. It is not surprising, therefore, that evangelistic visiting,

[23] *Oldham Standard*, 30 June 1860, 13 June, 13 July 1861.
[24] E. Isichei, *Victorian Quakers* (Oxford, 1970), 3–8; *Manchester Courier*, 4 Aug. 1832; *Manchester Guardian*, 18 Aug. 1832.
[25] KSBC, Record Book, 1 Jan. 1863, 14 July 1864; Lewis, 'Dobcross Congregational Church'; *Oldham Standard*, 25 Feb. 1860, 14 July 1860, 13 Apr. 1861.
[26] Reports to LCU, in Bridge and Lee, *Queen Street*, 142–3, and in Smith and Wilde, *Centennial Souvenir*, 12–13; SMC, Diary, 19 Dec. 1837.

tract and Bible distribution, and the rest of the apparatus of 'aggressive territorial ministry' should have found their place among the activities of new Dissent.[27] It would be wrong to attribute this entirely to the influence of Chalmers—such activity was part of the general methodology of the revival, and many churches were enthusiastically engaged in it almost from their inception. Thus the Queen Street Congregationalists reported in 1822 that 'A Ladies Bible Association, and a Religious Tract Society have been formed, and are now in very active operation . . . These circumstances have excited considerable attention, and it is hoped that they will be the means of bringing many under the sound of the Gospel.'[28] Nevertheless the sources do give a faint impression of a gradual hardening of such activity into a system—a growing professionalism—which may have owed something to the influence of Chalmers. At Salem, for example, the occasional visitation of the surrounding villages to distribute tracts, described in the 1830s as a 'humble attempt to continue our usefulness in the neighbourhood', had given way by 1857 to a fully-fledged tract society distributing 500 tracts a month in an area systematically divided into districts. This certainly represented a move towards Chalmers's territorial approach, and the King Street Baptists adopted a similar system in 1859, while the Greenacres Congregationalists followed suit in the organization of their pastoral visiting in the later 1860s.[29] A similar trend towards professionalization may be detected in the development of salaried full-time ministries, as in the case of the scripture reader employed by the Moravians during the 1850s, and also in the trend towards aiming evangelistic efforts at particular sections of the population. Thus in 1860 J. G. Short argued that the Springhead Congregationalists should exercise a special ministry towards the poor, and in 1861 the 'Dissenting ministers of the town' began a series of lectures in the Ragged school building 'for the benefit of working men'.[30]

It would, however, be misleading to draw a sharp contrast between a charismatic opportunistic Dissenting style in the first half of the period and a more routinized systematic style at its end, or even to present the charismatic and the systematic as mutually exclusive. The germ of a professionalized systematic approach was contained in the organization of

---

[27] LRO CUL 2, 4, LCU Minutes, iv, 8 Dec. 1851; Lancashire and Cheshire Baptist Association (LCBA), *Circular Letter* (1841); Brown, *Thomas Chalmers*, ch. 7.

[28] Report to LCU, in Bridge and Lee, *Queen Street*.

[29] Brown, *Thomas Chalmers*, ch. 7; KSBC, Record Book, 14 Dec. 1859; GCC, *Yearbook* (1869).

[30] SMC, Diary, 22 Aug. 1853; *Oldham Standard*, 24 Sept. 1859, 25 Feb. 1860; *Oldham Chronicle*, 2 Feb. 1861.

the itinerant societies and denominational unions which gave coherence to the revival in its early stages. Conversely, the revivalist fervour which was apparent in the first few decades of the period was reinvoked by the Congregationalists in 1829, and was matched from the later 1860s by a growing interest in, and excitement at, the prospect of a major revival. There is certainly some truth in the suggestion that revival had, partly under American influence, itself acquired a more routinized systematic flavour by the 1850s—what Richard Carwardine has described as 'a more instrumentalist, promotional concept of revival'. However, he also notes that British sympathy for the revival was crucially dependent on an assurance that it was centred on prayer rather than specially devised tactics.[31] Certainly in Oldham the special services and meetings of the late 1850s and early 1860s had been heralded by a wave of prayer meetings. Thus in late 1855 the King Street Baptists noted that 'A special meeting for Prayer has been held for the revival of religion amongst us, we hope accompanied by the blessing of God . . . It was also recommended that two weekly meetings for Prayer and exhortation be established in the out-districts of the town.' Similarly, the pastor of the Middleton Congregationalists recorded in 1857 that 'The subject of revivals is engaging general attention . . . and we are to hold a special prayer meeting next Monday evening. May God grant us a baptism of the Holy Spirit and a powerful revival.'[32] Clearly, the new Dissenters continued to stake their hopes, not merely on the efficiency of their own measures, but on the general grace of God and the special intervention of the Holy Spirit. They thus combined a systematic with an explicitly charismatic approach.

A Gospel Education

The most popular and enduring evangelistic innovation employed by the Dissenters was the Sunday school. Local Dissenters were rather slow to take advantage of this development, and the first school in which they took an interest, that founded jointly by Noah Blackburn of the Delph Congregationalists and John Buckley, the Anglican incumbent of St Thomas's, Friarmere, was not established until the early nineteenth century.[33] However, this initiative was followed by a flood of foundations in

---

[31] LCU Minutes, ii, 9 Apr. 1829; R. Carwardine, *Transatlantic Revivalism: Popular Evangelicalism in Britain and America 1790–1865* (Westport, Conn., 1978), 171; Bebbington, *Evangelicalism*, 116.

[32] KSBC, Record Book, 12 Sept. 1855, 14 July 1864; MCC, Church Book, 2 June 1857.

[33] W. H. Hall, *Delph Independent Sunday School Centennial Souvenir* (Delph, 1918), 3.

TABLE 4.1. *Dissenting Sunday schools, Oldham, 1847:*
Four main denominations

Denomination	Schools	Pupils			Percentage of	
		Male	Female	Total	All Sunday school pupils	All 15–19 year olds in 1851
Baptists	4	503	491	994	6.3	4.2
Congregationalists	6	825	1,154	1,979	12.5	8.3
Moravians	1	56	75	131	0.8	0.6
Unitarians	1	85	64	149	0.9	0.6
TOTAL	12	1,469	1,784	3,253	20.5	13.7

Sources: O'Neil, *Sunday Schools*; PP 1852–3, lxxxvi [1632], 10.

the succeeding decades, so that, as indicated in Table 4.1, all the new
Dissenting churches, with the exception of the Quakers, had by 1847
established at least one Sunday school. Dissenting Sunday schools continued to grow in numbers throughout the 1850s and 1860s. By 1856, for
example, there were, in the borough of Oldham, eleven Independent
Sunday schools. These mustered between them 1,686 male and 1,798
female pupils—an increase of 76 per cent in only nine years which, since
the general population only increased by approximately 28 per cent between 1851 and 1861, must have represented a considerable increase in
the proportion of all 5–19 year olds attending Independent Sunday schools.
The Baptists and Moravians did not increase their number of schools
between the two surveys, but did increase their number of pupils to 1,125
and 165 respectively. Only the Unitarians, who could muster just 52 male
and 3 female pupils in 1856, suffered a decline. The best available data for
Saddleworth come from the 1851 Educational Census, which lists five
Dissenting Sunday schools, all under Independent control, and muster-
ing 471 male and 509 female pupils. This represented 28.3 per cent of the
total Sunday-school population, and 16.6 per cent of all 5–19 year olds in
Saddleworth.[34]

---

[34] Ibid.; PP 1852–3, lxxxvi [1632], Census of Great Britain 1851, Population Tables ii;
PP 1852–3, xc [1692]; PP 1863, liii pt. ii [3221], Population Tables; Butterworth, *Oldham*,
appendix.

Thus the popularity of Sunday schooling among the working classes continued to flourish throughout the period, despite gradual changes in the curriculum. All the early schools seem to have taught writing on Sundays, but attitudes towards such 'secular' education began to diverge in the 1820s—some ten years earlier than the parallel development among the Anglicans. A number of churches remained sympathetic: at Delph in Saddleworth, for example, writing retained its place in the curriculum until 1860, and it was still being taught at Dobcross in 1864. The Oldham Unitarians also seem to have made a point of retaining 'secular instruction'.[35] Other Dissenting churches took a different view, and in the mid-1820s the conductors of the Queen Street Independent Sunday school, 'having regard to the sanctity of the Sabbath, determined contrary to the prevailing custom, to discontinue writing on the Lord's Day', offering instruction three evenings a week in its place. This seems gradually to have become the general pattern in Oldham. The Greenacres school gave up Sunday writing some time around 1850 and its minister, summarizing the situation in 1854, noted 'The necessity for this kind of instruction on the Sabbath, has long since passed away, and as a natural consequence, the system itself has almost ceased in Sabbath Schools of any respectability.'[36] It is difficult to evaluate the suggestion that by the 1850s the need for instruction in writing had disappeared. The provision of daily education had certainly increased significantly, but the Dissenting contribution to this improvement had been small. In 1851 there were only three Dissenting day schools in Oldham, and together their scholars (some 215) numbered less than a tenth of those attending their Anglican counterparts, while in Saddleworth there were no Dissenting day schools at all. Probably more important was the limitation on children's working hours in factories, which increased access to day schooling after 1844 and made attendance at the ubiquitous evening writing classes much more attractive.[37] However, Waddington's contention about a decline in the need for 'Sunday writing' certainly seems to be borne out by the public reaction to its withdrawal. In the early cases major disruptions had ensued. At Queen Street the school, which had previously been in a flourishing condition, 'was almost forsaken'. At Hope, differences over writing disrupted both the school and the church, and its suppression in 1833 provoked 'not only a number of children but many adults to forsake the congregation'. In the

---

[35] Hall, *Delph Independent*, 8–9; Lewis, 'Dobcross Congregational Church'; Marcroft, *Historical Account*, 89.

[36] Anon., 'Queen Street Sunday School', 37; Waddington, *Greenacres*, 15.

[37] PP 1852–3, xc [1692].

1850s, however, there was no such reaction and when the Middleton Congregationalists took over a small Sunday school at Tonge in 1854, suppressing 'secular instruction' as a condition of their support, the numbers in attendance actually increased from 100 to 150, and a year later to 200.[38]

Like their Anglican counterparts, the Dissenting schools benefited from low costs, which enabled them to be supported almost entirely from the proceeds of anniversary collections and occasional money-raising efforts. They also experienced the same gradual process of evolution into more complex institutions. Sunday-school libraries and sick and burial societies had been established in almost all Dissenting schools by 1856. Some schools instituted Juvenile Missionary Societies and many became centres for tract distribution. At Queen Street the 'Tract Distribution Agency' was described as 'one of the most vigorous institutions connected with the Sunday School', and by 1864 it was distributing 38,496 tracts a year. The minute-books of Dissenting Sunday schools reveal a comprehensive social world of tea parties, prayer meetings—especially important as a field of activity for female church members—annual treats, and festivities all of which tended to become more elaborate over the period.[39] Some of these social events themselves seem to have developed an incidental evangelistic function, like the 'open lovefeast' held for Moravian Sunday scholars in 1846, which was 'well attended by strangers', who listened to portions of scripture. However, most of the evangelistic thrust of Sunday schools was carried by regular weekly teaching of the sort described by a Moravian minister reviewing the life of a member of his congregation in 1857: 'One Sabbath afternoon the writer . . . unobserved by Mr Robinson, heard him set forth before his class the great Gospel Truth that Jesus Christ hath brought life and immortality to light through the gospel, and never will he forget the holy animation with which he spoke.'[40] The Dissenters were as sanguine as the Anglicans about the likely effects of such teaching, and the Middleton Congregationalists reported in 1855 that their school at Tonge contained 'about two hundred children and young people and may fairly be expected, with the parent school, largely to augment the congregation, apart from accessions to the world'.[41] As their investment in

---

[38] Davies, 'Congregationalism'; MCC, Record Book, 29 Mar. 1854, 28 Jan. 1855.

[39] SMC, Diary, 18 Mar. 1838, 6 July 1856, 25 Dec. 1857; KSBC, Record Book, 2 Jan. 1865; Bridge and Lee, *Queen Street*, 52; Mills Hill Baptist Church (MHBC), Sunday School Minute-Book, 1854–65; Delph Congregational Church, Sunday School Minute-Book, 1848–60; GCC, Sunday School Minute-Book, 1861–5; *Oldham Standard*, 10 June, 17 Oct. 1865.

[40] SMC, Diary, 25 Dec. 1846, 24 Apr. 1857; Waddington, *Greenacres*, 158–9.

[41] MCC, Church Book, 28 Nov. 1855.

Sunday-school activity increased, so the problem of 'accessions to the world', especially among young men, began increasingly to worry Dissenters. Like the Anglicans they adopted a wide range of measures to deal with it. Libraries, night classes, lectures, and debating societies all proliferated, and mutual-improvement classes also became popular. The class at Springhead, for example, taught writing, grammar, geography, algebra, geometry, and book-keeping to a clientele mainly composed of cotton operatives. These educational pursuits were supplemented by a range of social activities like the 'Springhead fife and drum band' founded in 1860 and by organizations that tried to integrate young adults into specifically religious activity like the Bible and tract Societies and the interdenominational Young Men's Christian Association, with its twin aims of evangelism and reducing 'leakage'.[42]

Some schools do seem to have been quite successful as recruiting agencies. Thus the Moravian minister recorded in 1850 that 'Betty Halkyard, Sarah Hilton and Ann Wrigley called after the class this evening to express their anxiety to give themselves publicly to our saviour, they seemed deeply affected while I endeavoured to shew them the necessity of the new birth.' Certainly by the 1870s the Queen Street Sunday school was able to record considerable success and in 1879 it reported that during the last nine years 'ninety-two of those connected with the School have professed their attachment to the Saviour, and have been received to the fellowship of the church'.[43] Some of these recruits would have been the children of adults already attending the churches, but, given the large number of children passing through the schools, others would almost certainly have been the offspring of people not otherwise connected. This tendency was magnified by the special position of the Sunday schools as bridges between the nonconformist communities of the new Dissenting chapels and the rapidly proliferating residential communities of the new industrial society. Branch schools, often with associated preaching services, allowed the Dissenters to penetrate communities beyond the immediate locality of the chapel, establishing the sort of proximity also facilitated by mission rooms and cottage meetings. Their combination of relative informality with an educative role widely perceived to be beneficial helped to break down many social barriers to involvement in organized religion.

---

[42] LRO FRM 5, Oldham Preparative Meeting Minutes, 26 Feb. 1865; Jones, *Hollinwood Congregational Church*, 13; MHBC, Minute-Book, 29 July 1853; Bateson, *Providential Lives*, 21–5; *Oldham Standard*, 2 Mar. 1861; *Oldham Chronicle*, 2 Mar. 1861, 29 Mar. 1862.

[43] SMC, Diary, 28 July 1850; anon., 'Queen Street Sunday School', 47.

Thus in August 1864 the Moravians started a branch school at Side of Moor and were able to report that about forty children were present on the first Sunday, who were 'exceedingly wild, ignorant, dirty and ragged'. Ten weeks later the school had already begun to make headway in the community and to break down barriers. The minister reported that he had introduced an afternoon preaching service, and explained that 'The necessity for this step was shewn by the desire of some of the mothers to partake of religious instruction. We were prompted to undertake it also by a desire to encourage the older boys and girls, many of whom were very ill clad, to attend the Sunday school. They objected to being taken to Salem chapel on account of their clothes'.[44]

Anniversary services and associated entertainments were important social occasions for local communities, and 1,000 people were present at the evening service of the Springhead Sunday-school anniversary in 1860. According to its historian, the Delph school was often too small to accommodate 'the large number of people who came from the surrounding districts, and who, had they missed the "Christmas Tea Party and Piece-saying at Th'owd Delph" would have felt that nature had cheated them out of one year of their life'.[45] The same communal solidarity is indicated by a general willingness to contribute to the financial support of the schools, even through periods of economic hardship, and by the view, often expressed when districts were canvassed by churches who wished to estimate the likely demand, that each community should have its own school—if only for ease of travel. At least one school, that at Dobcross, sprang from the spontaneous action of 'a group of eight or ten working class men' conscious of the need for a school in their own locality.[46] Clearly, such schools added greatly to the attractive power of the new Dissent. Through them the churches were brought into direct contact with popular culture and enabled to participate in shaping the new identities gradually forming in the emerging communities of Oldham and Saddleworth. The historian of Springhead Sunday school may not be guilty of much exaggeration when he claims that: 'In the middle of last century Springhead Sunday School was the centre of communal life . . . the one unifying influence in a loosely co-ordinated community.'[47]

[44] SMC, Diary, 14 Aug., 30 Oct. 1864.

[45] Bateson, *Providential Lives*, 26; Hall, *Delph Independent*, 10–11.

[46] SMC, Diary, 8 June 1862; MCC, Church Book, Mar. 1854; Lewis, 'Dobcross Congregational Church'.

[47] H. Bateson, *Early Days of Springhead Sunday School* (Oldham, 1930), 6.

Dissenters in the Community

Some impression of the extent to which the new Dissenters had succeeded in penetrating local residential communities can be gauged from
Table 4.2, which has been derived from a survey of the baptism registers
of three Congregationalist churches in Saddleworth during the 1830s,
together with the register of the Delph Independent Sunday school,
plotted against the 1848 Ordnance Survey map of Saddleworth.[48] It is clear
that, although the three chapels each drew heavily from one particular
sizeable community (Delph and Uppermill from the villages where they
were located, and Springhead from the nearby settlement of Lees, over
the border in Oldham), their congregations were not limited to the inhabitants of just one village. The Springhead chapel attracted parents from
a total of thirty-one named settlements, Uppermill from thirty-eight, and
Delph from fifty-eight. If those settlements which sent children to the
Sunday school though not to the font at Delph are included, its total rises
to seventy-three. Naturally these figures can only underestimate the extent
of the penetration achieved by the churches, since there may have been
settlements containing adherents who sent no children to be baptized
during the period. The registers clearly indicate that the bulk of the three
independent congregations came from scattered communities located
between one half and two miles from their respective chapels. The Delph
Sunday scholars, however, display a distribution much more concentrated in the locality of their school. Over 74 per cent resided within half
a mile of the school, perhaps reflecting its central communal role, as well
as a choice determined by convenience. The congregation at Springhead
displays a more concentrated distribution than those of the other churches,
but this reflects the more densely packed settlement pattern of the Oldham–
Saddleworth borderland in its vicinity, rather than any special characteristic
of the church itself. Unfortunately, it is not possible to establish how
far the dispersed spatial distribution of their congregations was a consequence of the aggressive territorial evangelism undertaken by the churches.
There is insufficient information on the location of cottage meetings
during the 1830s to allow a conclusive link to be established between the
presence of such meetings and the clustering of adherents. Nevertheless,
even if no precise causal link can be established between 'aggressive'
evangelistic activity and the spatial distribution of the congregation, the
pattern does at least display the eminent suitability of that approach and

---

[48] OLIC, Microfilm, Non-Parochial Registers, PRO RG 4.3414, 4.2817, and 4.979; Delph
Congregational Church, Sunday School Register, 1849–65.

TABLE 4.2. *Spatial distribution of Saddleworth Congregationalists*

Location of settlements sending children to be baptized	Springhead Congregational			Uppermill Congregational			Delph Congregational			Delph Sunday school		
	Villages	Adherents		Villages	Adherents		Villages	Adherents		Villages	Scholars	
		No.	%		No.	%		No.	%		No.	%
Same as chapel	1	1	1.2	1	12	16.0	1	37	31.4	1	39	31.5
Within												
0.5 mile	7	13	16.0	3	4	5.3	5	11	9.3	9	53	42.7
1.0 mile	16	56	69.1	14	24	32.0	10	17	14.4	7	20	16.2
1.5 miles	5	8	9.9	9	23	30.7	17	24	20.3	7	11	8.9
2.0 miles	2	3	3.7	3	4	5.3	16	18	15.3	1	1	0.8
2.5 miles	0	0	0.0	5	5	6.7	5	7	5.9	0	0	0.0
3.0 miles	0	0	0.0	3	3	4.0	1	1	0.8	0	0	0.0
Over 3.0 miles	0	0	0.0	0	0	0.0	3	4	3.4	0	0	0.0
TOTAL	31	81	100.0	38	75	100.0	58	118	100.0	25	124	100.0

Sources: OLIC, Microfilm, Non-Parochial Registers: Springhead, 1836–7; Delph, 1835–7; Uppermill, 1832–7; Delph Congregational Church, Sunday School register.

one of the reasons why the churches were so orientated towards an evangelistic ministry beyond the settlements in their immediate vicinity. A comparison of the three distributions also reveals that the chapels had each developed a definite sphere of influence in Saddleworth and were not competing with each other in the same communities. Of the total of 274 couples whose residences were traced, only thirty-five resided closer to one of the other chapels than that to which they took their child to be baptized, and then often only marginally. Of the 127 separate settlements to which adherents were traced, only five sent children to be baptized at more than one Congregational chapel, including the large village of Dobcross almost equidistant between Uppermill and Delph. This pattern contrasts sharply with the high degree of overlap between the constituencies of local Congregationalist and Wesleyan chapels described in Chapter 5, and illustrates the gradual development of a denominational consciousness within Congregationalism.

The social composition of nonconformist congregations has commonly been approached through an analysis of the occupational data contained in their baptism registers, and A. D. Gilbert, who used a sample of such registers to make generalizations about the social structure of Dissent on a national scale, concluded that 'no other source permits as clear, comprehensive and quantifiable an answer to questions about the social structure of the movement'. A number of these non-parochial registers have survived for Oldham and Saddleworth, and, in order to facilitate a comparison with a sample of baptisms in the general population drawn from Anglican registers, the occupational evidence they contain has been classified under seven broad categories or groups:

  I industrial employers, landlords, and gentlemen;
  II retailers, master craftsmen, and farmers;
  III professionals and clerical workers;
  IV artisans and craft workers;
  V high status industrial workers;
  VI other industrial workers;
  VII labourers and women with no listed occupation.

The first group comprises those families described as upper class in Foster's analysis, together with a number of the little masters—mainly those operating in the textile trades. Group II comprises the remainder of the little masters, together with the tradesmen and the shopkeepers who made up the bulk of Foster's middle class, while Group III combines the middle-class professionals with a broader band of managers and clerical workers. The remaining groups embrace various sections of the working class and their composition is detailed in Appendix III. The evidence from the registers presents a number of difficulties. Many parents were listed under titles like 'spinner' or 'clothier', which might designate either a workman or an employer, and the same ambiguity extends to craft occupations, with titles like 'tailor', 'plumber', and 'shoemaker' designating anything from an apprentice to a master craftsman employing a number of assistants. A partial solution to this problem can be found by comparing the entries in the baptism registers with those in local trade directories—though this process may fail to identity some smaller employers. Other problems are less susceptible of solution. There were, for example, a range of occupations, mainly in the engineering trades, which can be assigned to either the industrial or the craft category because they were practised in both large engineering firms and small subcontracting workshops. In general, people with these occupations have been assigned to Group IV, comprising artisans and craft-workers. Some groups of industrial workers are also difficult to classify. In cotton-spinning, for example, large variations existed in wages and conditions, and, while a skilled adult spinner in a well-run cotton mill may have been earning over 40 shillings a week in the 1830s and 1840s, his counterpart spinning 'shoddy' in one of Oldham's smaller establishments would have earned only 9–11 shillings a week— less than 'lower status' occupations such as card-room hands in the larger mills. Moreover, there were some occupations whose status changed over the period; handloom weavers, for example, began as skilled artisans, but by the late 1840s were earning less than many labourers.[49] There are also more general problems of interpretation. Occupational status cannot simply be read off from wage rates, nor social status from occupation, nor social and political attitudes from social status. Thus, for example, if Foster's contention about changes in their attitudes were held to be correct, a congregation composed mainly of cotton-spinners would have borne a rather different character in the 'militant' and 'unsegregated' 1830s than in the 'segregated' and 'labour Aristocratic' 1850s and 1860s. Therefore, while the broad categories under which the occupations of local adherents have been classified give a fairly reliable guide to the social constituency of the churches, caution is necessary in assessing the social meaning of the results.

Five registers were analysed, all from Congregational churches, using the occupations of fathers presenting their children for baptism as the

---

[49] Gilbert, *Religion and Society*, 66; Ginswick (ed.), *Labour and the Poor*, appendices 1 and 2.

index of social status (or the occupation of the mother in cases where no father was mentioned in the register). The results, which are displayed in Table 4.3, were compared with a similar analysis of baptism registers for 1838 in eight local Anglican churches, which has been used to represent the social composition of the population as a whole. The various problems of classification mean that Groups I, II, and VI may have been slightly underestimated, and Groups IV and V correspondingly inflated. Nevertheless, some patterns clearly emerge in the composition of Independent congregations during the 1830s. Only some members of Groups I, II, and III belonged to Foster's upper and middle classes; but, even taken together, the three groups still did not compose a high proportion of local congregations—the total varying between 9.3 per cent at Regent Street and 19.3 per cent at Hope. This pattern clearly conflicts with the prevailing impression that nineteenth-century nonconformity was very largely middle class in composition and instead falls much more closely in line with Gilbert's conclusion that the appeal of the new evangelicalism was concentrated largely among the 'lower orders'. However, the local evidence does not support Gilbert's contention that nonconformity in the early Victorian period suffered heavily from the decline of the domestic outworkers who provided a high proportion of its strength.[50] The registers show that many of the churches did recruit reasonably strongly from the 'artisans' of Group IV, but most of these men came from trades like blacksmithing, tailoring, and engineering which did not go into decline in the 1840s. Weavers were quite strongly represented among the 'industrial workers' of Group VI, making up, for example, thirty-seven of the ninety-nine entries in that group for Regent Street; they were, however, heavily outnumbered in Group VI by a combination of factory-based occupations like carding, winding, and reeling. Moreover, it is impossible to ascertain how many of the weavers were domestic out-workers, and how many had already moved within the factory system as power-loom weavers. In fact, in the three churches which recruited most heavily from Oldham the most common single occupation was spinning, although Regent Street and Hope also recruited quite strongly among the skilled engineering

---

[50] Gilbert, *Religion and Society*, 62–7, 146–8. Although a number of local studies have called it into question (see e.g. Rycroft, 'Craven', 203–21, A. M. Urdank, *Religion and Society in a Cotswold Vale: Nailsworth, Gloucestershire 1780–1865* (Los Angeles, 1990), 83), the middle-class image of Dissent remains secure in even the most recent literature: G. Parsons, 'From Dissenters to Free-Churchmen: The Transitions of Victorian Nonconformity', in Parsons (ed.), *Religion in Victorian Britain*, i. 77–8; K. D. Brown, *A Social History of the Nonconformist Ministry in England and Wales 1800–1930* (Oxford, 1988), 2; Koditschek, *Class Formation*, 258.

TABLE 4.3. *Occupational classification: Five Congregationalist chapels*

Occupational group	Springhead		Uppermill		Delph		Regent Street		Hope		Anglican baptisms	
	No.	%	No.	%	No.	%	No.	%	No.	%	No.	%
I	1	1	11	13.3	0	0	4	1.6	5	4.7	41	2.8
II	6	6	3	3.6	13	8.6	15	6.1	11	10.4	137	9.2
III	3	3	1	1.2	2	1.3	4	1.6	5	4.7	19	1.3
IV	9	9	4	4.8	20	13.2	35	14.3	16	15.1	178	11.9
V	29	29	22	26.5	19	12.5	81	32.1	27	25.5	403	27.0
VI	47	47	28	33.7	63	41.4	99	40.4	36	33.9	543	36.5
VII	5	5	14	16.9	35	23.0	7	2.9	6	5.7	168	11.3
TOTAL	100	100.0	83	100.0	152	100.0	245	99.0	106	100.0	1,489	100.0

Sources: OLIC, Microfilm, Non-Parochial Registers: Springhead, 1836–7; Delph, 1835–7; Uppermill, 1832–7; Regent Street, 1830–7; Hope, 1825–37; Parochial Registers: St Mary's, Oldham; St Peter's, Oldham; St Margaret's, Hollinwood; St Paul's, Royton; St John's, Hey; St Chad's, Saddleworth; St Anne's, Lydgate; St Thomas's, Friarmere; Baines, *Directory* (1825); Pigot and Son, *Directory* (1838).

workers of the Soho area. In the late 1830s the churches were thus already doing well among those occupational groups that were to expand in the Victorian period. Moreover, since groups like the spinners and engineers formed a significant proportion of Dissenting congregations during their most militant period in the 1830s, it is difficult to see any increase in church attendance thereafter, in Foster's terms, as part of a process of liberalization. There are some indications of social differentiation between the chapels, with Hope, in Oldham, and Uppermill, in Saddleworth, containing a greater than average proportion of the employers of Group I, while the others, and particularly Springhead and Delph, shared a social constituency more characteristic of the back-street plebeian chapels described by Hugh McLeod.[51] However, the clearest pattern to emerge from Table 4.3 is the close correspondence between the social composition of all five Independent churches and that of the population as a whole, as reflected in the Anglican baptisms. The consequence of this even pattern of recruitment was the numerical dominance of the working classes even in those chapels with a significant middle-class membership.

A shortage of data makes it difficult to estimate the social composition either of the other denominations, or of the Congregationalists after 1840. Statistical evidence is available from only three sources: the baptism register of Waterhead Congregational church from 1856 to 1865, the Middleton Congregational church membership list for 1823–65, which identifies the occupations of church members, and the *First Baptist Church Manchester Street Oldham: List of Members* (1858), which can be linked to the manuscript enumerators' books of the 1861 population census. Together, these sources produced the information displayed in Table 4.4. Only the Waterhead register is directly comparable with the sources used for the 1830s, and, when the position of the village as a centre of craft and metal-working is taken into account, it gives a picture rather similar to that of Hope Chapel. Even allowing for a difference in the basis of calculation, the shift among industrial workers towards the higher status group appears largely to be paralleled by Foster's sample of household heads from the 1861 census. However, the church may have been losing ground among the labourers of an expanding Group VII. The Middleton Congregationalist figures reflect the inner core of the congregation and might be expected to display a constituency weighted towards the first three groups. Although the figure for Group II may be slightly underestimated because of difficulties in cross-referencing the membership list

---

[51] H. McLeod, *Religion and the Working Class in Nineteenth-Century Britain* (1984), 53.

TABLE 4.4. Occupational classification: Three Dissenting chapels in Oldham

| Occupational group | Waterhead Congregationalist | | Middleton Congregationalist | | Oldham Baptist | | | | | |
| | | | | | Household heads | | Others | | Total | |
	No.	%	No.	%	No.	%	No.	%	No.	%
I	0	0	4	1.7	4	12.1	5	9.3	9	10.3
II	7	14	25	10.4	11	33.3	11	20.3	22	25.3
III	0	0	26	10.8	1	3.0	5	9.3	6	6.9
IV	12	24	111	46.0	3	9.1	6	11.1	9	10.3
V	14	28	12	5.0	2	6.1	7	12.9	9	10.3
VI	14	28	46	19.1	8	24.2	14	25.9	22	25.3
VII	3	6	17	7.0	4	12.1	6	11.1	10	11.5
TOTAL	50	100.0	241	100.0	33	99.9	54	99.9	87	99.9

Sources: As described in the foregoing text, together with W. Wheelan and Co., A New Alphabetical and Classified Directory of Manchester and Salford (Manchester, 1852); Foster, Class Struggle, 76, 292; J. O. Foster, 'Capitalism and Class Consciousness in Earlier Nineteenth Century Oldham', Ph.D. thesis (Cambridge, 1967), 303.

with trade directories, and although the list displays an above-average number of Group III mill managers and clerical workers, its main feature, nevertheless, is the high number of workers in Group IV. Most of these (85) were the silk handloom weavers who dominated the local occupational structure, and this, together with a reasonable showing among workers in Group VII, suggests that the Middleton Congregational church may have been recruiting even its membership fairly broadly from among the general population. The Oldham Baptist figures share the same tendency to be weighted towards the first three groups as those from Middleton, a tendency almost certainly accentuated by the process of linking the list to the census. Only eighty-seven, just over a third of the 258 resident members recorded in the list, were successfully traced; thirty-three of these were household heads and they have been classified separately to provide a set of data more comparable with that derived from the baptism registers and with Foster's sample than is the list as a whole. The remaining fifty-four were classified under the occupation of their household head, if one was stated in the census, and otherwise under their own occupation. Considering the nature of the evidence, it is not surprising that Groups I and II feature particularly strongly, especially among household heads, but, since the percentage in those groups is approximately three times the average for the general population, this may represent a genuine bias within the membership. More surprising is the relative weakness among craft and high-status industrial workers, and the strong showing in Group VII, which, although below Foster's average of 19 per cent, is the more remarkable because of the problems of census linkage. Certainly the statistical basis for any change in the composition of Dissenting congregations seems rather narrow, and the figures above, taken in conjunction with those produced by Foster from a survey of marriage certificates between 1846 and 1857, suggest that, although Dissent may have been disproportionately strong among shopkeepers and employers, the nonconformist constituency continued largely to be congruent with the population as a whole.[52] There is no statistical evidence of any great influx of 'Labour Aristocrats' beginning in the late 1840s, and the bulk of most nonconformist congregations continued to be composed of the lower-status industrial workers who dominated the occupational structure of Oldham and Saddleworth.

This conclusion is reinforced by a review of the qualitative evidence for the nature of the Dissenting constituency. Thus Goodier, the Unitarian

---

[52] Foster, *Class Struggle*, 215.

minister, writing in 1816, commented: 'Most of those who join us are poor people, but we have one or two families of property.' According to their pastor, most of the Moravians were mill-hands, and the minister of the Independent Chapel in Middleton reported in 1855 that 'the congregation mainly belongs to the working class'.[53] This recognition may have had a significant effect on the self-image of the denomination in the locality. Thomas Binney and the Congregationalists as a national body may have believed that they had a 'special mission' to the educated middle classes, but the local Independents took a rather broader view. They eschewed any special mission and in 1855 confidently asserted that 'There is no Christian community in the town in so good a position for reaching the outstanding population of all classes as ourselves.'[54]

Although they possessed a well-balanced social composition, most of the local Dissenting chapels had a distinct asymmetry in the gender balance of their membership. Despite some variation from church to church, local Dissent clearly tended to recruit its membership more widely among women than men, and, although in some cases the difference was marginal, the usual situation seems to have been one in which women outnumbered men by at least three to two.[55] This imbalance need not necessarily imply that women were more easily attracted into evangelical churches than men, since adherents, among whom men may have preponderated, could have been just as committed to their chapel, in terms of regular church-going, for example, as the members themselves.[56] It does suggest, however, that women were more prepared to make a formal commitment to church membership—a phenomenon already observed in relation to Anglican communicants. The reasons for this are obscure. It may be that, as tensions increased between the relatively secularized culture of work and beer house and the counter-culture of the chapel, men found it especially difficult to make such a formal commitment, while women, for a much greater proportion of whom life revolved around the home rather than an external workplace, would have been less susceptible

---

[53] Goodier to Anon., 29 Jan. 1816, in Marcroft, *Historical Account*, 33; SMC, Diary, 21 Mar. 1855; MCC, Church Book, 28 Nov. 1855.

[54] C. Binfield, 'Thomas Binney and Congregationalism's Special Mission', *Transactions of the Congregational Historical Society*, 21 (1971), 1–10; MCC, Church Book, 28 Nov. 1855.

[55] SMC, Diary, 25 Dec. 1850; GCC, Minute-Book, 1790; Uppermill Congregational Church, Minute-Book, 1830, 1865; Ward, *Retrospect*, 44–5; MHBC, Minute-Book, 1857. A similar pattern among nonconformists in Craven and Baptists in Nailsworth has been noted by Rycroft, 'Craven', 286, and Urdank, *Nailsworth*, 287.

[56] R. Chadwick, 'Church and People in Bradford and District', D.Phil. thesis (Oxford, 1986), 146.

to negative cultural pressures. This cultural influence may have been reinforced by the positive effect of the traditional domestic focus of much nonconformist piety, which was frequently reasserted during the nineteenth century, and by the opportunities for public activity which churches provided at a time when women were relatively deprived of such opportunities.[57] Finally, it is possible that some women, in the same way as others may have participated in Anglican communion, took on the responsibilities of formal membership not as individuals only, but as the representatives of their families.

Churches and Buildings

The absolute number of Dissenters increased markedly over the period, from a few hundreds at most in the 1780s to several thousands in the mid-nineteenth century, and this necessitated a corresponding multiplication of accommodation. In 1780 Oldham and Saddleworth combined mustered two Independent chapels, which, together with the small Quaker and Baptist meeting houses, probably seated just under 1,000 people. By 1851, as can be seen from Table 4.5, the level of accommodation had increased markedly. Nevertheless, although a considerable effort had been made, the new Dissenters were far from matching the places provided in Anglican churches. In 1851 the total Dissenting provision, some 6,837 seats, could have accommodated only 6.5 per cent of the whole population: 5.8 per cent in Oldham and 10.3 per cent in Saddleworth, compared with 18.9 per cent in the area as a whole for their Anglican colleagues. A building boom in the 1850s and early 1860s went some way towards closing the gap, with a very large absolute increase in the provision of seating which is displayed in Table 4.6. This produced a considerable improvement in the density of Dissenting accommodation, the totals rising to around 9.3 per cent for Oldham, 12 per cent for Saddleworth, and 9.7 per cent for Oldham and Saddleworth combined. However, the uneven geographical distribution of the Dissenting effort makes figures for overall density an unsatisfactory indication of its impact. Taken together, the accommodation provided by the new Dissenters was spread fairly evenly in Oldham, but the spread of accommodation provided by the individual denominations was much less even. Over half of the Baptist seating was located in Oldham below town, where it represented 46.1 per cent of all new Dissenting accommodation; almost half of

---

[57] Chadwick, *Victorian Church*, i. 407; LCBA, *Circular Letter* (1862).

TABLE 4.5. *Accommodation in 'new Dissenting' chapels 1851*

	Oldham				Saddleworth			
	Chapels	Seats		Total	Chapels	Seats		Total
		Free	Rented			Free	Rented	
Quaker[a]	1	—	—	155	—	—	—	—
Moravian	1	400	84	484	—	—	—	—
Unitarian	1	48	140	188	—	—	—	—
Baptist	4	567	603	1,170	1	200	—	200
Independent[b]	8	1,005	2,010	3,015	3	160	1,465	1,625
TOTAL	15	2,020	2,837	5,012	4	360	1,465	1,825

[a] The Quakers did not specify the nature of their seating.

[b] The Independent totals include two 'preaching rooms' with regular Sunday services but underestimate the total accommodation because one of these rooms did not complete the relevant portion of the return.

Source: PRO HO 129 475, 496.

TABLE 4.6. *Accommodation in 'new Dissenting' chapels 1865*

	Oldham		Saddleworth		Total	
	Chapels	Seats	Chapels	Seats	Chapels	Seats
Quaker	2	500	—	—	2	500
Moravian	2	975	—	—	2	975
Unitarian	1	188	—	—	1	188
Baptist	8	3,400	1	200	9	3,600
Independent	11	5,930	4	2,100	15	8,030
TOTAL	24	10,993	5	2,300	29	13,293

Sources: PRO HO 129 475, 496; *Oldham Chronicle*, 4 Aug. 1860, 10 Dec. 1864; *Oldham Standard*, 21 Oct. 1865; anon., *Bethesda Baptist Chapel*; LCU, *Annual Report* (1867); Whiteley, *Baptists*, 133–354; Congregational Union, *Religious Statistics of Eight Towns in South Lancashire* (Oldham, 1880), 6; Bateson, *Providential Lives*, 23.

the Congregationalist seating was located in Oldham above town, where, contributing 80.4 per cent, they dominated new Dissenting provision. However, the Congregationalists' efforts were still outmatched by the Anglicans, who, in the same area, could muster almost twice as many seats.

It is, of course, inappropriate to make a direct comparison between the results of the Anglican and Dissenting building efforts, since their objectives were rather different. The Anglicans, as the logic of their parochial system dictated, built in order to stimulate demand; the nonconformists, on the other hand, generally built in order to supply an existing demand, even if the scale of the building sometimes anticipated future growth. Most Dissenting congregations spent their early days in makeshift accommodation in barns, or upper rooms, moving like hermit crabs into progressively larger homes as they grew. Purpose-built chapels were constructed only when the congregation had grown too large for makeshift premises and large enough to make such a permanent presence viable; insufficient room for the existing congregation seems to have been the invariable reason for extensions to Dissenting chapels or decisions to rebuild on a larger scale.[58] Thus, the Independents at Uppermill had to

[58] e.g. J. D. Mansley, 'Queen Street Church Looks Back 100 Years', *Oldham Chronicle*, 22 Oct. 1955; LRO CUL 20, Journal of the Secretary to the Executive Committee of the LCU, i–iii.

extend their chapel in the 1830s because of the popularity of their minister Reuben Calvert. 'So great was his influence that on account of the large congregations who gathered to hear him every Sunday the church was nicknamed the "Squeezemites", and it became necessary to enlarge the building by two windows.'[59] Some churches went to great lengths to estimate the likely demand for accommodation before they committed themselves to building, and it was only after a canvass of the church, two separate reports of a special committee, and much anxious discussion that the Manchester Street Baptists rejected a planned enlargement of their chapel and resolved to rebuild. The anxiety that lay behind much of this sort of discussion was financial. The costs of constructing a chapel in the eighteenth and early nineteenth centuries may have been relatively low: the Unitarians built Lord Street in 1816 at a cost of only £500, while the Congregationalists built their first chapel on Queen Street in 1824 with 470 seats for £1,200.[60] This represented a considerably more efficient use of funds than in the Anglican St James's, Oldham, which though four times as large was eight times as expensive. Low costs, however, were a function of simplicity of construction and this advantage was gradually sacrificed, especially after mid-century, as more complex and impressive buildings became the fashion. In part, this complexity reflected the new functional diversity of church organization, with a plethora of auxiliary institutions requiring rooms for meetings and social activities, but it was also the product of what Parsons has described as a search for a more characteristically churchly architecture. In the 1850s and 1860s, especially in local Congregational circles, the emphatic functional evangelicalism of the sanctified barns of the revival gradually gave way to the pseudo-Anglican synthetic medievalism of 'Dissenting Gothic'. When Greenacres Chapel was rebuilt on an enlarged scale in 1855, it was reported that 'one grand feature of Gothic architecture has been revived: namely, that five massive arches overarch the nave and transepts, and abutting on the walls of the cross support the roof: these arches by their bold and lofty curves, add considerably to the dignity of the interior effect'. The chapel seated 800 people at a cost of £2,100 and was thus still relatively economical at only £2 12s. per seat. The Gothic of the new Queen Street, with its prominent spire, was particularly admired, though its seats each cost £3 7s. to provide in 1855. However, the most ambitious project in the locality was the rebuilding of Hope Chapel in 1865–6,

[59] Lawton, *Church Memoirs*, 11.
[60] KSBC, Minute-Book, Jan.–June 1859; *Manchester Chronicle*, 8 July 1815; Bridge and Lee, *Queen Street*, 33.

complete with an elaborate tower. It seated 1,100, and cost between £4,500 and £5,000, so that the seats each cost £4 2s. at the lowest estimate. This extravagant use of resources presented a stark contrast with the much less ostentatious 'plain brick' Baptist chapel at Royton which provided 600 seats at a cost of 13s. each in 1865.[61]

Unlike the Anglicans, the new Dissenters had no large central funds on which to call, and they were, therefore, thrown back almost entirely on local resources. Most of the funds for new building were raised from subscriptions among the members and congregation of the chapel concerned, and this placed a heavy burden on the richer members. A few chapels benefited from a handful of rich subscribers. Hope, for example, was attended by both Samuel Lees and James Platt, the great engineering magnates, and Lees provided most of the finance for the first chapel in 1823. Similarly the Moravian chapel at Salem was built largely through the generosity of John Lees of Clarksfield.[62] Not all local congregations could muster such supporters, however, and the first chapels at Springhead and Uppermill, for example, were built from the aggregate of small subscriptions, as was the Lord Street Unitarian chapel. At Uppermill there is also some evidence that the congregation reduced the costs by working on the building themselves.[63] In several cases, appeals for subscriptions were extended beyond the congregation either to the community at large or further afield using a network of contacts provided by the denomination. Thus in 1806 the promoters of Springhead 'canvassed the district collecting money', in 1815 Goodier, the Unitarian minister, undertook a collecting tour throughout north-west England, and, when in 1842 the Salem Moravians decided to buy their chapel from the executors of John Lees, William Okeley, their minister, made an extensive money-raising tour though the Moravian congregations of Yorkshire and south and west England.[64] The new Dissenters used a variety of means to tap the resources of the locality and of visiting friends. The King Street Baptists, for example, resolved in August 1859 'That there be held on 31st inst. a Public Tea Meeting to promote the building of a new chapel', and

[61] Cf. C. Binfield, *So Down to Prayers: Studies in English Nonconformity 1780–1920* (1977), 145–61; *Congregational Yearbook* (1855), 266–7; Bridge and Lee, *Queen Street*, 48; LCU, *Annual Report* (1867), 78–9; Jones, *Hope*, 14; *Oldham Standard*, 21 Oct. 1865; Parsons, 'Dissenters to Free Churchmen', 101.

[62] Jones, *Hope*, 6–12; Bintley, *Salem Moravian Church*, 2–3.

[63] Lawton, *Church Memoirs*, 9–11; Smith and Wilde, *Centennial Souvenir*, 9; Bateson, *Providential Lives*, 7–9; Marcroft, *Historical Account*, 22–6.

[64] Bateson, *Providential Lives*, 7; Goodier to Anon., 4 Sept. 1815, in Marcroft, *Historical Account*, 23–4; SMC, Diary, 1 Sept.–19 Oct. 1842.

a similar event was held in November of that year 'in connection with the recent alterations at the Independent Chapel Hollinwood'. Bazaars were also popular, and the 'Greenacres Independent Bazaar', for example, raised £450 over three days in 1856 in aid of various building projects undertaken by the congregation. The most popular events of all, however, were foundation-stone laying ceremonies and opening services. The former were widely reported in the local press and provided invaluable publicity. The latter, with their attendant collections, were vital; chapels were often crowded, and at Springhead in 1855 £170 was collected at the opening—over 8 per cent of the total cost.[65]

The most significant departure in the financing of chapel-building during the period was the endorsement by the Lancashire Congregational Union, in 1852, of a plan to subsidize the building of fifty new chapels. Subscriptions were canvassed and several local churches benefited from large grants. Springhead, for example, received £700 towards its new chapel in 1855. These funds were boosted in the early 1860s by the campaign to build a series of 'memorial chapels' to mark the bicentenary of the 'great ejection' of 1662, for which approximately £20,000 was raised. Together, these new sources of finance gave the Independents their first equivalent of the large central funds available to support Anglican church-building. At least three Oldham chapels were assisted by this fund, which provided a welcome relief for hard-pressed local congregations.[66] Nevertheless, a general survey of the Dissenting chapel-building effort suggests that the most consistent feature of its financial arrangements was debt. Almost all Dissenting subscriptions fell short of the total required, and the remainder had to be borrowed. Sometimes the money was provided from the internal resources of the congregation, like the £175 borrowed in 1845 by the Queen Street church from its own Sick and Funeral Society in order to meet the shortfall on a new school. However, probably more typical was the resolution of the King Street Baptist church meeting in 1862 that 'The Deacons will borrow at 5 per cent as much as is necessary to pay the unsettled accounts on the new chapel.'[67]

---

[65] KSBC, Minute-Book, 12 Aug. 1859; *Oldham Standard*, 10 Nov. 1860, 2 Nov. 1861; *Oldham Advertiser*, 28 June, 5, 12 July 1856; *Oldham Chronicle*, 22 July 1854, 14 Apr. 1855, 10 Dec. 1864; Smith and Wilde, *Centennial Souvenir*, 16. For similar successful Dissenting appeals for subscriptions from the whole community, see Rycroft, 'Craven', 271.

[66] LRO CUL 2, 4, LCU Minute-Book, 8 Apr. 1852; Smith and Wilde, *Centennial Souvenir*, 16; Robinson, *Lancashire Congregational Union*, 52–3.

[67] Bridge and Lee, *Queen Street*, 42; KSBC, Record Book, 5 May 1862; Rycroft, 'Craven', 273–4.

The possession of a chapel certainly gave a Dissenting congregation a substantial asset—a valuable base for its activities and a symbol of its permanent presence in a locality. Some churches felt that their work was hampered by the lack of a suitable building, and the Greenacres Congregationalists, for example, recorded a marked improvement in church attendance following the opening of their new chapel in 1854.[68] However, just as for the Anglicans, the increasing diversion of resources into chapel-building could also carry with it significant disadvantages. The effort of building, even on a modest scale, could impose serious financial strain on a congregation, and the consequences of failure, for a cause with little or no support from a strong central body, could be devastating. Thus at Queen Street the withdrawal of Samuel Lees left the cause in severe financial trouble; by 1829 the church was insolvent and it had to be rescued by the efforts of William Roby. It was the Unitarian cause at Lord Street, however, that best illustrated the danger of over-extension. Despite the efforts of Goodier to clear the debt, the congregation still owed £60 on its chapel in 1825, and in 1828, with little prospect of being able to pay off this sum, the Unitarians were forced to relinquish occupation of their building, which was rented first to the Roman Catholics and then to the Wesleyan Association. The congregation did not get its chapel back for over ten years, and then only with the support of the Methodist Unitarian Village Missionary Society.[69] Even where the size of a debt did not cause an immediate crisis, it could drag on for years, absorbing the energies of a congregation and hampering its work. The church at Springhead reported in 1845, for example, that their attempts 'more widely to extend the gospel' were being 'crippled by the debt upon their chapel'.[70] The funds established by the Congregationalists to stimulate chapel-building and the enthusiasm of the memorial chapel movement may have been indirectly responsible for some of these problems, since they encouraged churches to attempt projects for which they were ill-equipped. At Hollinwood, 'the people few and poor shrunk from undertaking any works involving pecuniary liabilities they would not be able to meet; but they felt that unless their action was prompt they would lose the receipt of the Bicentenary grant. To the utmost of their power they contributed, and ventured to raise a chapel . . . at a cost of £1,800.' It is perhaps not surprising that, despite generous opening collections and a grant of £500,

---

[68] Waddington, *Biographical Notices*, 332–59.

[69] Mansley, 'Queen Street', 37; Marcroft, *Historical Account*, 52; Lord Street, *Calendar*, Dec. 1897–July 1898.

[70] Report to LCU (1845), in Smith and Wilde, *Centennial Souvenir*, 15.

'the chapel was opened with a crippling debt of some £900, and on and off for the next forty years heavy debts hung over the church'.[71]

The decision to rebuild a chapel could lead to serious divisions within its congregation, and in the case of the Manchester Street Baptist church, despite the immense care taken to consult the congregation, the eventual decision to build a new chapel on King Street provoked a schism. A more general problem, however, was the diversion of attention and resources into chapel-building. Over-investment of resources in their chapels, especially towards the end of the period, probably eroded the flexibility of the churches, cutting down the freedom of movement within the locality that had been such an asset in the eighteenth and early nineteenth centuries.[72] Some local Dissenters were certainly uneasy about this development and among the Congregationalists doubts were expressed about the propriety of the renewed building effort even during the period of greatest enthusiasm in the early 1860s. J. G. Short, for example, declared that 'A century ago, Methodism did what the free churches ought to have done, namely they made the Gospel felt to those around them. But we ought to think less of buildings and organization and more of men.'[73]

Fellowship, Worship, and Identity

The impact of the revival in promoting 'the conversionist priority' has already been noted, but the new evangelicalism also had a more general effect on the theological identity of the churches. Individual issues, especially that of election, continued to be controversial, but the vast majority of the churches interpreted their doctrine in a thoroughgoing evangelical manner. Thus the Greenacres Congregationalist 'Confession of Faith', although it declared that 'God from all eternity did ... freely and unchangably ordain whatsoever comes to pass', noted that this was done, 'so as thereby neither is God the author of sin nor is violence offered to the will of the creatures'.[74] A number of writers have pointed out that a key factor in the growth of new Dissent was its willingness to give the spread of the Gospel priority over the minutiae of doctrinal orthodoxy, and certainly a broad evangelical consensus did emerge in Oldham and

[71] LCU, *Annual Report* (Manchester, 1867); Jones, *Hollinwood Congregational Church*, 12.
[72] KSBC, MS Statement, 1862; G. A. Weston, 'The Baptists of North-West England 1750–1850', Ph.D. thesis (Sheffield, 1969), 442. A similar schism, provoked by a move to relocate a Congregationalist church, is noted in Urdank, *Nailsworth*, 89. For general problems occasioned by the development of large congregations in prestigious chapels, see Lovegrove, *Itinerancy*, 156–9.
[73] *Oldham Standard*, 28 Jan. 1860.
[74] Bateson, *Providential Lives*, 12; GCC, Church Book, 1790–1865.

Saddleworth. Even in churches with a detailed doctrinal basis, an eirenic attitude was often adopted towards individuals who differed from the confession. At Springhead it was decided in 1831 that the pulpit should be available to any who 'hold and preach the doctrine of the fall of man by the sin of our first parents, redemption by the atonement of the Redeemer, and holiness of heart and life'. The chapel would therefore have been open both to evangelical Calvinists and Arminians. The Oldham Quakers, too, were thoroughly permeated by evangelical theology, welcoming a visit from Isaac Crewdson in August 1829, though they do not seem to have provided any recruits for his 'evangelical schism' seven years later.[75]

This catholic enthusiasm permeated local Dissenting attitudes towards participation in communion. Thus, the doctrinal basis of the Hollinwood Congregationalists was qualified by a statement that, 'Although these doctrines and principles are binding on church members, they are not intended to prevent communion at the Lord's Table with other Christians holding such views of divine truth as are consistent with the saving faith of the Gospel.' The Oldham Baptists probably practised 'open communion' from their formation, and this policy seems to have been maintained in local Baptist causes throughout the period, despite the various cross-currents within the denomination. The cause at Mills Hill, for example, shortly after its constitution as a separate church, resolved 'that members of other churches, not Baptist, be allowed to sit down at the Lord's table with us'.[76] For any covenanted community the operation of a policy of 'open communion' represented considerable commitment to evangelical inclusiveness which may have been rare among Independents before the 1830s. The issue was even sharper for the Baptists, since, for them, believer's baptism as a condition for participation in communion was not only a sacramental, but also a confessional issue. To the supporters of 'strict communion', therefore, 'open communion' seemed to threaten the integrity of the whole Baptist denomination. In this context, its smooth run in Oldham and Saddleworth was a considerable tribute to the continuing integrative power of the revival with its unifying emphasis on the

---

[75] Smith and Wilde, *Centennial Souvenir*, 10; Ward, *Retrospect*; Isichei, *Victorian Quakers*, 44–52; O. C. Robison, 'The Particular Baptists in England 1760–1820', D.Phil. thesis (Oxford, 1963), 153; I. Sellers, *Nineteenth Century Nonconformity* (1977), 57; Parsons, 'Dissenters to Free Churchmen', 72; Bebbington, *Evangelicalism*, 17.

[76] Jones, *Hollinwood Congregational Church*, 10; A. H. Stockwell, *The Baptist Churches of Lancashire* (London, 1910); Robison, 'Particular Baptists', 260–73; A. M. P. LeBarbour, 'Victorian Baptists: A Study of Denominational Development', Ph.D. thesis (Maryland, 1977), 82–4; MHBC, Minute-Book, Jan. 1854.

centrality of evangelism—a power made explicit by the Lancashire and Cheshire Baptist Association in 1825, with its declaration that the issue of baptism was much less important than preaching the Gospel.[77]

The inclusive approach seems also to have been extended to the doctrinal conditions for membership of local Dissenting churches. The Baptist church at Mills Hill, for example, in 1856 formally declared its membership open to those who had not undergone believer's baptism. No such declarations have been traced for other churches, but their actions indicate that, in practice, they adopted a similar attitude. Thus, in 1855 the Middleton Congregationalists were prepared to accept the direct transfer of a Methodist member across the Calvinist–Arminian divide, noting at their Church Meeting, 'J. Summersgill was admitted by vote without the formality of a month's probation on the testimony of Mr J. Taylor and Mr W. Holden as to his Christian character as having been in consistent fellowship with the Wesleyans.' The Waterhead Congregationalists adopted the same approach towards a Methodist member from Middleton in 1864, and the Manchester Street Baptists were quite prepared, in 1862, to transfer members to the Independent church at Hollinwood. Clearly the Oldham Baptists were not excessively concerned with their 'Baptistness', and much the same point could be made about the other denominations, although their dilemmas were less sharply posed.[78] In this attitude lies exposed a crucial characteristic of local nonconformity. Its congregations were children of the revival, and their heritage was the inclusive evangelicalism of new Dissent rather than the exclusive peculiarity of the older tradition. These were not so much gathered as gathering churches.

There may have been a gradual relaxation of the conditions for entry into membership of some Dissenting churches, but church discipline in general was maintained at a high level. The nature of their ecclesiastical position gave nonconformists much greater freedom to exercise discipline within their membership than that enjoyed by the Anglicans, who lacked the ultimate sanction of exclusion. Dissenters applied this sanction in response to a wide variety of offences: among the reasons given at Manchester Street Baptist church during the 1820s were neglecting the means of grace, immorality, antinomianism, inconsistency, and Sunday

[77] Jones, *Congregationalism*, 226; Binfield, *Down to Prayers*, 25–6; W. R. Ward, 'The Baptists', 177; LCBA, *Circular Letter* (1825).

[78] MHBC, Minute-Book, Apr. 1856; MCC, Church Book, 4 Oct. 1855; Waterhead Congregational Church, Church Meeting Minutes, 23 June 1864; KSBC, Record Book, 9 July 1862; Binfield, *Down to Prayers*, 25.

trading. A review of Dissenting church minute-books suggests that neglect of attendance at the Sunday services or at communion was the most common reason for exclusion, followed by sexual immorality.[79] However, the minute-books probably give a misleading picture of the implementation of church discipline, since only the most serious cases were recorded and a much more low-key approach must have sufficed for many lesser offences.[80] Even expulsion was not regarded as a permanent condition, and normally its expressed aim was to bring the offender to repentance, after which he could again be 'given the right hand of fellowship'. The minute-books record several such reinstatements, and at Mills Hill Baptist church one member was expelled and reinstated on several occasions during the 1850s.[81] Nevertheless it must have required a considerable commitment to maintain the moral standards and level of regular attendance required of nonconformist members in an environment that was not always conducive to such activity. The culture of much of the working class may have exposed its members to greater temptations, especially to drink and irregular attendance, than that of the more outwardly respectable middle class. There is, however, no evidence of unfair discrimination in the treatment of rich and poor members like that described by MacLaren in Aberdeen, and local churches do seem to have been prepared to discipline and even exclude influential members of their own fellowship.[82] Discipline was not regarded merely as a question of the treatment of individuals, but as crucial to the well-being of the whole body. It was imposed, as the Greenacres Congregationalists noted, 'for purging out that leaven which might infect the whole lump, for vindicating the Honour of Christ and the Holy profession of the Gospel and for preventing the wrath of God which might justly fall upon the church if they should suffer this Covenant . . . to be profaned by notorious and obstinate offenders'.[83] Discipline was thus an important component of the vital fellowship that characterized local Dissenting churches, a sign that, however individualistic the Dissenting ethos might be, it still implied commitment to a community.

The central institution of this community was the church or society

[79] KSBC, Register, Record Book; MHBC, Minute-Book; SMC, Diary; GCC, Minute-Book.

[80] e.g. SMC, Diary, 9 Apr. 1851.

[81] e.g. GCC, Minute-Book, 27 June 1860; Uppermill Congregational Church, Church Book, Feb. 1836; MHBC, Minute-Book, 1853–60.

[82] McLeod, *Religion and the Working Class*, 61; A. A. MacLaren, *Religion and Social Class: The Disruption Years in Aberdeen* (1974), 135–8; KSBC, Record Book, 18 Mar. 1862; SMC, Diary, 4 June 1837.

[83] GCC, Church Book.

meeting, and a survey of the minute-books shows that most local Dissenting churches were holding twelve such meetings a year in the nineteenth century. These monthly meetings continued to provide the main forum in which the business of the fellowship was conducted, and also to supply a focus for the devotional life of church members. However, as the churches began to pursue a greater range of activities, there seems to have been a tendency towards compartmentalization which eroded the central importance of the church meeting. Especially in the larger local churches, much activity was carried out by semi-autonomous societies like the Sunday school, which would submit a detailed report to the whole church at the 'Annual Congregational Meeting' rather than to the membership in the church meeting. Increasingly, much important work was delegated to committees, which, though they might report to the church meeting, were nevertheless clearly cutting across its role in conducting regular church business.[84] How typical this development was, it is difficult to assess, and certainly in the small Baptist church at Mills Hill the church meeting retained a significant business role throughout the period, though even there an active committee conducted much Sunday-school business. Nevertheless, it seems that the church meeting as an institution probably became more heavily dependent on its role as a focus for devotional and social activity. Thus, in 1854, the Greenacres Congregationalists noted 'The church meetings in Jun. 29th, Aug. 3rd and Aug. 31st were conducted simply as the usual week evening services.'[85] Even in its social and devotional roles the church meeting suffered increasing competition from a proliferation of alternative institutions. The tea party became the archetypal social event in the churches and took several different forms. Some were focused on particular groups, like the Sunday school, and some celebrated particular events, like New Year's Day, while others had fundraising functions. Most of the earlier tea parties seem to have been limited, like church meetings, to members only, but from the mid-1850s it became increasingly common to invite the congregation—especially at the annual tea party—to join in the entertainment afterwards if not in the tea itself. The social life of the covenanted community was thus further diluted by the presence of those gathered in by the evangelistic activities of the church. The same pattern was apparent in the development, during the 1850s and 1860s, of a whole range of social activities which extended beyond the membership to the congregation at large, like the

---

[84] J. H. Taylor, 'The Survival of the Church Meeting, 1691–1901', *Transactions of the Congregational Historical Society*, 21 (1971), 31–44; Lord Street, *Calendar*, 1 Jan. 1899; GCC, Church Book, 25 May 1859.

[85] MHBC, Sunday School Teachers' Minute-Book; GCC, Church Book, 31 Aug. 1854.

'maternal meeting' established by the Manchester Street Baptists in 1858, or the cricket club founded by the Springhead Congregationalists in 1868.[86]

The devotional activities of the churches were closely integrated with their social life, and some devotional meetings possessed a specific social function. These included the 'reading meetings' held by the Quakers in the 1860s, and the love-feasts of the Moravians. The latter varied considerably, from relatively solemn devotional occasions, sometimes associated with the celebration of communion or with funerals, to rather lighter occasions like the feasts held for the 'committee, chapel servants, Sunday- and day-school teachers and tract distributers' in 1855.[87] Other devotional activities played a social role incidental to their explicit purpose of building up the spiritual life of the churches. These also proliferated from the late eighteenth century onwards and included Bible classes, lectures, and, among all denominations with the probable exception of the Unitarians, meetings to promote foreign missions. Missionary meetings developed an appeal which stretched beyond the membership to the congregation, and beyond the congregation to the population at large. Thus the Salem Moravians attracted almost 200 people to a missionary love-feast in March 1851, and in 1857 they publicized their annual missionary meeting by delivering 500 handbills around the vicinity of their chapel.[88]

Missionary meetings grew in importance over the period, but the most characteristic evangelical devotional activity, the prayer meeting, was already prominent at the beginning. Even the young Congregational church at Queen Street, for example, had a well-established pattern of meetings in the 1820s. Some meetings were occasional and directed towards some particular purpose, like prayers for a special outpouring of the Holy Spirit, but most local evangelical churches seem to have run regular prayer meetings, often on a weekly basis. The Greenacres Congregationalists had a centrally located Wednesday evening prayer meeting, and the Manchester Street Baptists a well-established Monday evening prayer meeting; the Moravians, on the other hand, preferred a large evening

---

[86] Taylor argues that they effectively replaced church meetings in some places: 'Church Meeting'; KSBC, Minute-Book, 3 Mar., 26 Dec. 1852, 29 June 1863; MCC, Church Book, 31 May 1854, 29 June 1863; MHBC, Minute-Book, 19 Sept. 1853, Aug. 1854; Bateson, *Springhead Sunday School*, 5.

[87] Taylor, *Friends' First Day School*; SMC, Diary, 6 Aug. 1837, 29 Apr. 1838, 14 Jan. 1855.

[88] Ibid. 14 Oct. 1850, 30 Mar. 1851, 29 Nov., 25 Dec. 1857; Taylor, *Friends' First Day School*; Butterworth Diary, 8 Sept. 1830, *Oldham Standard*, 29 Oct. 1859, 2 Nov. 1860, 2 Feb. 1861; LRO FRM 5, Oldham Preparative Meeting Minutes, 29 Sept. 1861.

'meeting for intercession' held quarterly. The routine centrally located prayer meetings were supplemented by a mass of 'district prayer meetings' held in cottages. At Springhead in the 1830s, for example, the evangelistic cottage preaching of the Congregational church was supported by prayer meetings in several parts of the district. Similarly, the Mills Hill Baptists held regular cottage prayer meetings in the outlying hamlets of Jumbo and Summer Hill, and almost the first duty of George Waddington, when he assumed the pastorate of the Greenacres Congregational church in 1850, was to attend a similar meeting at Waterhead.[89] The format varied from simple meetings for intercession to the more elaborate meeting with Bible study, singing, and prayer run by the Moravians. Hymn-singing was probably an integral part of many such meetings and it was certainly well enough established at Manchester Street Baptist prayer meetings for two brothers to be delegated 'to attend to the singing' in 1854.[90] Prayer meetings provided the engine of much evangelical activism and were central to the spirituality of the revival. Their presence in outlying hamlets, and in the cottages of ordinary members, meant that the church as well as the Gospel was being taken out to the people at large.

Most Dissenting church covenants committed the fellowship to the relief of its poor members and this commitment successfully survived the new extroversion of the covenanted community. At Greenacres Congregational church, for example, twelve collections were taken for poor members between February and December 1851. Members and adherents were also protected against some of the most common causes of secondary poverty by sick and funeral societies organized by the churches, and that at Greenacres mustered 525 members in 1868.[91] However, such charitable activity was not limited to the membership or even the congregations of nonconformist churches, and at times of local crisis, most notably during the 'cotton famine' of the early 1860s, churches were central to the organization of general relief. As well as organizing the efforts of their own churches, nonconformist clergymen were also prominent in the co-ordination of national relief schemes, and R. M. Davies of Hope was described as 'either the leader of or very active in Causes which

[89] LCU Report 1828, in Bridge and Lee, *Queen Street*, 141; SMC, Diary, 28 Apr. 1837; KSBC, Minute-Book, 23 Feb. 1853; GCC, *Yearbook* (1869); LCU Report 1838, in Smith and Wilde, *Centennial Souvenir*, 12; MHBC, Minute-Book, July 1854; Waddington, *Greenacres*, 108.

[90] SMC, Diary, 13 Sept. 1846; KSBC, Minute-Book, Dec. 1854.

[91] Weston, 'Baptists', 284; GCC, Church Book, 1851; GCC, *Annual Report* (1868).

raised over £30,000 to help the destitute'.[92] The pastoral activities of the Dissenting churches also included visiting the sick and more general visitation to ensure the spiritual well-being of their members and adherents. Visits could occupy a great deal of time, especially in the larger churches, even when the minister was assisted in the work by a group of elders or deacons. At King Street Baptist church the minister reported, in 1864, that over the last seven years he had personally paid an average of between 1,000 and 1,100 visits per annum, and it is not surprising that some ten months later the church meeting set up a committee of six to assist the pastor and deacons in this work. Pastoral visitation was important because it tied the church together, especially for those members who might feel isolated from the fellowship because, for example, they had fallen sick or had been sent to the workhouse. Moreover, while Dissenting attitudes to visitation never seem to have approached the territorial consciousness of the Anglican parochial system, pastoral visits were sometimes extended to people outside the congregation and occasionally provided the visitor with evangelistic opportunities. Visitation could also bring the pastor much needed encouragement, as the Moravian Minister noted in 1859: 'I have had much pleasure in visiting . . . William Bennett and Joshua Bentley, the latter is a well instructed Christian and amidst the mournful ignorance which prevails, visits to such are like cold waters to a thirsty soul.'[93]

There is insufficient evidence to form an estimate of the social composition of the diaconate and the various church committees, though it is probable that men and women of relatively high social status took a disproportionate share of the positions of influence, if only because of their more extensive self-confidence, education, and leisure time. However, Weston has concluded that among Lancastrian Baptists most lay preachers and deacons were working men and that, although in some wealthy churches the middle class tended to dominate the diaconate, the Sunday schools and evangelistic work of the churches was, particularly during periods of revival, largely free from class bias.[94] The new evangelicalism was therefore responsible for a democratization of church activity. There were so many organizations and meetings that it was impossible to run a new Dissenting church without a massive mobilization of the talents of its ordinary members and adherents, both men and

[92] Ward, *Retrospect*, 123–4; Smith and Wilde, *Centennial Souvenir*, 17; *Oldham Chronicle*, 16 Aug. 1862; Jones, *Hope*, 14.

[93] KSBC, Minute-Book, 19 June 1864, 26 Apr. 1865; SMC, Diary, 30 Oct., 1, 13 Nov. 1837, 13 Apr. 1850.

[94] Weston, 'Baptists', 273–8.

women. The revival also produced a democratization of the spirituality of Dissent. In part this was an accentuation of a pre-existing characteristic. Binfield has pointed to the individualistic nature of much Dissenting spirituality; and personal piety, both felt and acted, was stressed by the evangelicals as the essence of each individual's relationship with her or his redeemer. Thus Noah Blackburn, preaching at Delph in 1807, announced 'I will not my brethren, even suppose that you omit any duty ... but that you are punctual in surrounding the family altar, and in attending to the devotions of the closet, and that on these occasions you read the sacred Scriptures, and pour out your desires to God by prayer and supplications, in the best manner you are able.'[95]

Similarly, the Moravians extolled members who had a lively personal devotional life, and the Lancashire and Cheshire Baptist Association published a *Circular Letter* on 'Family Prayer'.[96] This development was a corollary of theological change, for the rise of evangelical Calvinism and Arminianism meant that neither the spiritual benefits, nor the responsibilities, of an intimate relationship with God could be confined within the narrow circle of a covenanted community. The democratization of spirituality was made concrete, however, in the activity of the revival in the cottages of the poor. It was in cottage meetings, and especially in cottage prayer meetings, that the poor could express their spirituality and develop their gifts—and, according to the Lancashire and Cheshire Baptist Association, such meetings served to 'call into exercise and improve the gifts of the brethren, and are thus very frequently the first introduction to ministerial and pastoral labours and usefulness'.[97] Cottage prayer meetings offered the ordinary convert, within a few hundred yards of his or her own home, the possibility of the sort of fellowship previously enjoyed only by the covenanted elect, and they must have provided vital encouragement, especially for working-class adherents struggling to maintain their faith in an unamenable culture.

The new evangelicalism also had a levelling effect on the regular Sunday worship of the churches, replacing some of its earlier variety with a clear evangelical style. There is little information available about the number of Sunday services in the first half of the period, though it is probable that two services a Sunday, one in the morning and one in the

---

[95] Binfield, *Down to Prayers*, 23; N. Blackburn, *Attachment to the World Lamented and a Throne of Grace Petitioned or the Distressed Saint Seeking Quickening Grace: A Sermon Preached in the Independent Chapel Delph* (Manchester, 1807).

[96] e.g. SMC, Diary, 2 Apr. 1857; LCBA, *Circular Letter* (1862).

[97] LCBA, *Circular Letter* (1831).

afternoon, were the norm. Judging by the 1851 Religious Census, two services remained usual at the end of the period, although the Queen Street Congregationalists and the Moravians were running three, and the Quakers, together with some of the smaller Independent and Baptist churches, only one service a Sunday. There had, however, been a shift in the timing of the services, especially among the Congregationalists, since four of the eight churches which offered a second service in 1851 were holding it in the evening, along with two of the four Baptist churches.[98] Chadwick has suggested that the move to evening services was a direct product of the evangelical revival, replacing an older Dissenting tradition of Sunday evenings spent in 'quiet meditation and prayers in the home'. However, the continuing popularity of afternoon services in country areas, even among churches heavily influenced by the revival, suggests that geographical location and the time of year were probably the vital determining factors.[99]

Communion services were usually held at monthly intervals, or slightly less frequently at branch churches. To share in these services was both the privilege and the responsibility of church members, and despite the 'open communion' policy it remained central to fellowship in the covenant of the church. Attendance was rigorously enforced, and the Baptist church at Mills Hill issued 'communion cards' to all its members in 1854 as a means of regulation. The only discernible change over time was the increasing influence among Baptist and Independent churches of the temperance movement. This produced anxious debate in some fellowships, and in a few places individuals were permitted to take communion without drinking the wine, while in others a second 'unfermented cup' was introduced.[100] Nonconformist communicants remained an élite group within the congregation, and, even with a few 'guests' introduced by open communion, celebrations of the Lord's Supper could still be powerful and unifying devotional exercises. Here, even among the most evangelical of the Dissenters, something of the old power and resilience of the covenanted community could be glimpsed mingling with the warmth of the revival. Some of this was caught by the Moravian minister in 1854: 'In the Holy Communion special nearness of our Lord was granted to not

[98] Lawton, *Church Memoirs*, 10; Marcroft, *Historical Account*, 39; PRO HO 129, 475, 496.
[99] Chadwick, *Victorian Church*, i. 407; e.g. Delph, Springhead, and Uppermill Congregationalist.
[100] MHBC, Minute-Book, 12 Sept. 1853, June 1854; MCC, Church Book, July 1852; KSBC, Minute-Book, 10 Dec. 1863; GCC, *Yearbook* (1869); Bintley, *Salem Moravian Church*, 5; Watts, *Dissenters*, 313; Robison, 'Particular Baptists', 265.

a few. A deep conviction of the necessity of the anointing of the Spirit rested upon all. Oh that it may be fruitful in substantial blessing to this flock and may the desire be awakened for an outpouring of the Holy Spirit on all the agencies in the congregation.'[101] For nonconformist adherents, though they were excluded from participation in communion, the year was punctuated by a series of special services. Some, like missionary and Sunday-school and chapel anniversary services, had, together with watchnights and harvest festivals, entered with the revival. Others, like ordination and recognition services, stood in an older Dissenting tradition, along with those which celebrated the traditional festivals of the Christian year.[102]

With the partial exception of the Moravians, no local nonconformist churches seem to have adopted a liturgy, and most of their services must have comprised the usual nonconformist elements of Bible readings, extemporary prayer, music, and a sermon. Although Dissenters were spared the difficulties of a dubiously intelligible liturgy, the traditional 'long prayer' of the nonconformist service came under criticism in the nineteenth century. Thus C. M. Birrell, the influential evangelical Baptist, argued in 1845 that 'It might also be considered whether, instead of extending any one prayer, there might not be several shorter ones introduced into every service', and this new style probably became the general pattern among Victorian Baptists. This seems to be a clear example of a popular, charismatic, evangelical approach overriding the older tradition, and this sort of ministry in prayer certainly seems to have been appreciated in Oldham.[103] The strong local tradition of popular 'art music' that nurtured Anglican church choirs and musicians also supported their Dissenting counterparts, and even small churches, like those at Springhead and Uppermill, seem to have had little trouble in raising choirs and bands. Some choirs were of very high quality. The historian of Queen Street Congregational church noted that 'In the early and middle parts of the last century, part singing was much cultivated . . . and family parties and choirs often met at each others houses to practice part songs, glees, rounds, etc. These meetings most undoubtedly stimulated a love of music for its own sake.' Consequently the church choir which in the 1850s

---

[101] SMC, Diary, 1 Jan. 1854.

[102] Ibid. 3 Dec. 1855, 4 Oct. 1857; KSBC, Minute-Book, 10 Feb. 1858; GCC, Church Book.

[103] SMC, Diary, 25 Dec. 1857; LCBA, *Circular Letter* (1845); LeBarbour, 'Victorian Baptists', 70–1; D. Thompson (ed.), *Nonconformity in the Nineteenth Century* (1972), 6; Smith and Wilde, *Centennial Souvenir*, 17.

'consisted of eight voices, all excellent readers of music . . . was noted for the beauty of its part singing'.[104] At the beginning of the period most Dissenting choirs were accompanied by instrumental bands. Some were quite varied. At Uppermill, for example, 'music for worship was led by a band of fiddles, flute, bassoon and trumpet', and at Springhead music was provided by a 'pipe and string band'. However, the nineteenth century saw the gradual introduction of organs. This happened remarkably early and smoothly in Oldham and Saddleworth—the Manchester Street Baptists, for example, introducing an organ in 1816 only a few months after the foundation of the church. Both Regent Street Independent and Salem Moravian—churches founded in the 1820s—were using organs in the 1830s, and almost all local Dissenting churches had introduced organs by 1860. This process was completed virtually without opposition, protests being recorded only at the Uppermill Independent church in 1854, where some members 'looked upon such an instrument as a worldly innovation'.[105] In fact, just as in the Anglican churches, the old instrumental bands who elsewhere in the country led the protests were rarely displaced by the introduction of organs in Oldham and Saddleworth. The Delph Independent accounts for 1856 record payments both for the organist's salary and for the repair of the chapel's bass fiddle. The major obstacle to the introduction of organs was not opposition but expense. Cheaper instruments like seraphines and harmoniums were much in evidence, and some churches borrowed or hired their organs. The purchase of an instrument could require a major financial effort: a Bazaar at Springhead Independent in 1866, for example, raised several hundred pounds to wipe off the debt on the chapel organ, and 'organ openings' joined school and chapel openings as major public events from the 1830s onwards.[106]

The popularity of their music helped nonconformists build bridges towards the community at large, as Dissenting choirs and bands took part in oratorios as well as many lesser, public musical occasions. Music also developed a broader base within the churches themselves with the

---

[104] Bateson, *Springhead Sunday School*, 3–5; Lawton, *Church Memoirs*, 13; Bridge and Lee, *Queen Street*, 126–7; *Oldham Standard*, 14 Apr. 1860.

[105] Lawton, *Church Memoirs*, 13–14; Bateson, *Springhead Sunday School*, 3–5; Whiteley, *Baptists*, 350; Bintley, *Salem Moravian Church*, 6; Butterworth Diary, Nov. 1836; LeBarbour, 'Victorian Baptists', 73; Jones, *Congregationalism*, 225; *Oldham Chronicle*, 11 July 1857, 2 Oct. 1858; Bridge and Lee, *Queen Street*, 126–7; Lord Street, *Calendar*, Feb. 1899.

[106] Delph Congregational Church, Trustees' Cash Book, 1856; KSBC, Minute-Book, Jan. 1851; Waddington, *Greenacres*, 115; Bridge and Lee, *Queen Street*, 126–7; MCC, Church Book, 30 June 1852; Lord Street, *Calendar*, Feb. 1899; Bintley, *Salem Moravian Church*, 6; Smith and Wilde, *Centennial Souvenir*, 16; Butterworth Diary, Nov. 1836; *Manchester Guardian*, 26 June 1844.

development of congregational singing. Hymn-singing was probably an important feature of evangelical-influenced new Dissent from the start. Early services at Springhead, for example, always included three hymns. R. T. Jones has argued that 'All the evidence goes to show that right down to the middle of the [nineteenth] century congregational singing was bad', and, hampered as they were by the practice of lining out (reading out the hymns two lines at a time before they were sung by the congregation), hymn-singing may sometimes have been an unsatisfactory musical experience even among northern congregations. Nevertheless the singing was at least enthusiastic. According to R. M. Davies, it was said that 'when they sang at Springhead Chapel they could be heard at Lydgate Chapel', and we should be wary of concluding from its low musical standard that hymn-singing was not acceptable as an act of congregational praise. Standards probably did improve over the period, and the music certainly became more varied, especially in local Baptist churches, where the chanting of psalms was introduced in the 1850s. The improvement in standards must have come, in part, through the influence of the Sunday schools, though, after 1860, just as in the other local churches, the most significant influence was probably the immensely popular 'tonic sol fa' singing system.[107]

Ministerial Labours and Denominational Identities

Lay preaching was common practice among all the local denominations. The Quakers and Baptists had a long tradition of such activity, but it also appeared increasingly among Moravians, Congregationalists, and Unitarians as the only way in which a ministry based on cottage meetings and local preaching rooms could be operated.[108] However, especially in the chapels themselves, most of the weight of the regular preaching ministry must have fallen on the shoulders of the pastor. Like their Anglican counterparts, nonconformist sermons seem to have been fairly lengthy. John Birt, the Baptist minister, usually spoke from brief notes or extempore for about three-quarters of an hour, while Dixon, the Independent

[107] Bateson, *Springhead Sunday School*, 3–5; Jones, *Congregationalism*, 223–4; LeBarbour, 'Victorian Baptists', 69; KSBC, Minute-Book, 5 June 1853; MHBC, Minute-Book, Sept. 1855; GCC, *Annual Report* (1867). On the development of nonconformist singing, see Obelkevich, 'Music and Religion', 553–7.

[108] Ward, *Retrospect*, 82; KSBC, Minute-Book, July 1860; D. W. Lovegrove, 'Particular Baptist Itinerant Preachers during the Late Eighteenth and Early Nineteenth Centuries', *Baptist Quarterly*, 28 (1979), 127–41; SMC, Diary, 25 Dec. 1857; Lawton, *Church Memoirs*, 10; Bridge and Lee, *Queen Street*, 53; Marcroft, *Historical Account*, 33–8; Lovegrove, *Itinerancy*, 27.

minister at Springhead, was remembered for his 'very long' though 'soul-stirring' sermons. Most local preaching, even in the late eighteenth century, was popular in style, having broken away from the older nonconformist tradition to become 'more emotional, existential and gospel centred'. Only one local minister is remembered for having maintained the older style: Joseph Glendenning, who occupied the pulpit of Hope Congregational from 1829. 'He was a man of refined intellect, scholarly and well read; his compositions were chaste and highly rhetorical, but his productions lacked the point and force which would favourably impress those who heard him', and this seems to have helped to provoke a decline in the size of the congregation. On the other hand, Jonathan Fox, the first minister of both Hope and Regent Street Independent churches, was an original preacher who 'embodied his ideas in sentences which were easily comprehended by the comparatively untutored minds that surrounded him'. Richard Jessop, who followed Glendenning at Hope, 'was of a different stamp to his predecessor—a plain preacher, saying strong things in strong language'. Similarly, J. G. Short, the minister at Springhead in the 1860s, was 'a rather emotional preacher who attracted and moved large congregations'. However, popular 'plain preaching' was not always highly charged with emotion, and of Birt, who probably addressed one of the largest regular congregations in the locality, it was noted: 'His manner in the pulpit is anything but animated, seeing that he rarely uses any gestures . . . His language is strong and energetic and his sentences are more distinguished for strength and solidity than for brilliancy or elegance of diction.' This sort of variety at the local level was a function of the talents and capacities of individual ministers and tends to undermine the notion that particular styles were characteristic of each denomination.[109]

Some sermons were directed at specific groups, like the annual sermon to young men preached at Uppermill Independent during the 1850s. However, the main preaching effort was the regular round of two sermons preached in each church every Sunday, a burden only sporadically relieved by visiting preachers, like the escaped negro slave who addressed the Congregational church at Middleton in 1860. For a minister who might have to preach over a hundred sermons a year, it must have been difficult to maintain a uniformly high standard. In 1860 the congregation at Springhead were warned that they should not expect a good sermon every time their minister spoke, and 'if he preached one good sermon in

[109] J. Eavans, *Lancashire Authors and Orators* (Manchester, 1859), 24; Smith and Wilde, *Centennial Souvenir*, 19; Jones, *Congregationalism*, 166–7; Davies, 'Congregationalism'.

a month he would do well'. However, in 1883 R. M. Davies noted that in forty years of ministry he had 'preached in Oldham more than 3,800 times, and never without a prepared sermon', and, according to the historian of his church, Davies's 'sermons were always acceptable to the congregation and more often than not were a matter of great inspiration to those who heard him'. Similarly, one of Dyson's hearers at Uppermill remembered 'few if any preachers of any denomination I should prefer to listen to for seven years sabbath after sabbath'.[110] Much of this preaching was evangelistic. At Greenacres, Thomas Hale's preaching was 'Evangelical in the true sense—Jesus the Christ—from whom all truth radiate and resolve—Sinners faithfully and earnestly invited to him . . . these topics were the staple', while J. G. Short 'was attached to the pure gospel, and preached it with great earnestness and power'.[111] When not directly evangelistic, most sermons seem to have been expository and often systematic. There is no evidence in Oldham and Saddleworth of the general abandonment of doctrinal preaching through the Bible held responsible by Sellers for the importation of theological liberalism into nonconformity. Thus of Birt's preaching it was claimed, 'If there is a truth or a series of truths to be extracted from any passage in the Bible . . . Mr Birt will not remain content till he has brought them fully before your notice.' Similarly, one of Dyson's hearers suggested 'A review of his pulpit labours at Uppermill does not preclude the probability that at the outset of his ministry he laid his plans of intellectual labour, apportioning to the varied sections and departments of Biblical truth their fair and legitimate share of attention.'[112]

Dissenting critics of the revival lamented the disappearance of traditional intellectual standards as the learned ministry was eroded by 'men in a hurry'. However, the evangelical revival seems to have produced an increase in the number of Dissenting academies, especially in the north, and K. D. Brown has demonstrated that both the Baptists and the Congregationalists maintained a reasonably well-educated ministry even in the early nineteenth century.[113] Certainly, all the local ministers on

---

[110] Eavans, *Lancashire Authors*, 23–4; Uppermill Public Library (UPL), Hewkin MSS: 2b, Reminiscences of Revd S. Dyson; *Oldham Standard*, 14 Apr., 27 Oct. 1860; Davies, 'Congregationalism'; Jones, *Hope*, 13; Parsons, 'Dissenters to Free-Churchmen', 77.

[111] Waddington, *Greenacres*, 77–8; *Congregational Yearbook* (1867), 312. Dissenting academies placed a high premium on the development of Evangelistic preaching in the first half of the nineteenth century: Lovegrove, *Itinerancy*, 77.

[112] Sellers, *Nonconformity*, 21–2; Eavans, *Lancashire Authors*, 23; Reminiscences of Revd S. Dyson.

[113] Jones, *Congregationalism*, 163, 236; Brown, *Nonconformist Ministry*, 64.

whom information is available seem to have received at least three years' training at an academy. Most of these men were probably, like Benjamin Longley of Greenacres, respectable scholars, but the area could also boast a few ministers of greater intellectual distinction. John Morris, for example, the minister at Springhead between 1837 and 1842, was 'a man of intellect and scholarship' who eventually became a professor at the Independent College in Brecon.[114] However, the need to provide ministers for the multiplying congregations of the new industrial towns probably did lead to changes in curriculum or standards within the academies. For a man like Richard Williams of Hollinwood, risen to the pastorate from the loom after some years as a Primitive Methodist local preacher and combining his part-time course at 'Lancashire College' with his pastorate at Hollinwood, a classical education can have held few attractions. It certainly seemed of little value to Joseph Galland, who, after his first two years at Rotherham, 'requested permission from Dr Williams to discontinue his attention to classics and devote himself entirely to subjects more immediately connected with the ministry'.[115]

The concerns of a nonconformist pastor extended far beyond his preaching ministry. Thus, when Revd Stokes was appointed as minister of King Street Baptist Church in 1864, he agreed 'That as often as practicable and his health permits he shall . . . preside at our church meetings, lead our prayer meetings, lecture, preach, exhort, visit our sick, and in every other way, seek to promote the increase, the peace and the prosperity of the church.' Such a wide ministry required enormous energy coupled with great personal gifts, and all the most popular local ministers seem to have been notable for one or both of these characteristics. Benjamin Goodier, the Unitarian minister, was a 'hard worker' and had a 'winning and persuasive way'. J. G. Short of Springhead was 'fervent' and 'energetic', and John Smith, the first Moravian minister, was 'energetic and self-sacrificing'.[116] Some ministers achieved considerable success, and, on J. W. Ashworth's first six months among the Manchester Street Baptists, the church reported:

[114] Bridge and Lee, *Queen Street*, 23; *Congregational Yearbook* (1869), 105, 278; Bateson, *Providential Lives*, 13–15.

[115] Jones, *Hollinwood Congregational Church*, 9, 16–17; anon., *History of Failsworth Macedonia* (Oldham, 1925); Waddington, *Greenacres*, 92; Brown, *Nonconformist Ministry*, 57–74.

[116] KSBC, Church Book, 2 Oct. 1864; Marcroft, *Historical Account*, 36; Smith and Wilde, *Centennial Souvenir*, 17; Bintley, *Salem Moravian Church*, 4.

His labours amongst us have been attended with remarkable success, the Gospel as preached by him has been attended in a large degree by the outpouring of the Holy Spirit, so that many whose love had waxed cold have been aroused to a lively sense of their duties and privileges as members of the church of Christ, others who had been excluded many years since after deep repentance have been restored to church fellowship, many others who had been struggling with religious convictions and then hesitating on the threshold of the church have been led to decide for God whilst others who were living without God and without hope in the world have been led to ask what they must do to be saved.[117]

These were certainly impressive results, but the style of leadership exercised among nonconformists could also be an important weakness. Theoretically the burden was shared by the minister, deacons, and other members of the church. Nevertheless, in practice, much of the 'heat of the day' was borne by the minister alone, and, isolated from the fellowship of the church by this leadership role and deprived of much of the institutional support and automatic authority conferred on their Anglican counterparts, some found the burden too much. In a remarkably high number of cases the health of the minister or that of his family broke down. Okeley, the Moravian minister who worked so hard to raise money to buy the chapel, resigned after four years because of illness in his family, and his successor died after only three years' ministry. Similarly, of William Dixon, the Springhead minister, the *Congregational Yearbook* noted: 'His inquirers' meetings were frequent, and numerously attended, and everything was hopeful and full of promise, when, in consequence of heavy pastoral duties and the exertions he put forth to clear off the debt of the chapel, his health broke down and he was laid aside by illness, from the effects of which he never afterwards fully recovered.'[118]

A second consequence of the weight placed on ministers and the uncertainties of their relationship with deacons and members was an increased danger of dissension through misunderstanding, lack of consultation, or the clash of powerful personalities striving for authority. The Oldham Baptist split of 1862, which eventually led to the resignation of Ashworth, exemplified the first two sorts of problem, and the secession from Hope which led to the formation of the Independent church at Regent Street almost certainly exemplified the third. These were not isolated

[117] KSBC, Minute-Book, 10 June 1857.
[118] Bintley, *Salem Moravian Church*, 6; *Congregational Yearbook* (1868), 269. For the strain put on ministers and their families and the consequent high rates of ill health and premature death, see Brown, *Nonconformist Ministry*, 171–85.

examples, however, and in August 1865 George Waddington called a special meeting 'to take into consideration the relation of the pastor to the church and the church to the pastor . . . because of discouragements, annoyances, insults, and injuries, to which I have been subjected for some time past'— a move which ended with his resignation. Sometimes the two sorts of ministerial problems converged, as at Delph in the 1860s, where 'misunderstandings arose between the Trustees and the church in which Mr Shawyer became involved, which continued many months, and seriously affected the health and the spirits of the pastor', leading first to his removal and soon afterwards to his death.[119]

Despite such difficulties, most churches considered the services of a full-time professional minister essential. In 1853 the Mills Hill Baptists, for example, expressed their desire for a regular pastor because 'the desultory kind of preaching, the result of having a different individual to supply the pulpit every week, was found far from profitable'.[120] Most churches were, therefore, willing to make considerable efforts to provide a salary, though the size of stipend varied considerably, in proportion to each congregation's ability to pay. The pastors of large prosperous churches might receive as much or more than their Anglican counterparts: the King Street Baptists resolved in January 1864 that their minister should receive between £140 and £200 per annum, depending on the financial health of the church, and even the medium-sized Congregational church at Springhead could offer J. G. Short £100 a year in 1860. On the other hand, the pastors of small churches could be much worse off. Mills Hill could offer only £60 per annum in 1854, and the Unitarians offered the same sum to C. W. Robberds, their minister, in 1853. Both of these ministers would have been earning less than some skilled workers, and much less than any of the middle-class members of their own churches. The direct relationship between ministers' salaries and their churches' ability to pay meant that a successful ministry often brought direct financial rewards. Thus Robberds' annual salary was 'soon increased to £80', and by 1858 Knightly at Mills Hill was being paid £100 a year. However, salaries could also decrease in times of hardship. In 1840 the Moravian minister was paid only £14 and Knightly's stipend fell to just over £80 in 1859.[121]

[119] GCC, Church Book, 13 Aug.–7 Sept. 1865; *Congregational Yearbook* (1869), 278; Brown, *Nonconformist Ministry*, 161–2.

[120] MHBC, Minute-Book, 29 Aug. 1853.

[121] KSBC, Minute-Book, 1 Jan. 1864; Bateson, *Providential Lives*, 24; MHBC, Minute-Book, April 1854, Accounts, 1859–60; Lord Street, *Calendar*, Feb. 1899; Bintley, *Salem Moravian Church*, 6.

The general running costs of Dissenting churches seem to have remained extremely low, and the minister's stipend formed a great proportion of their annual expenses. At Mills Hill the minister's salary made up £100 out of total running costs of just over £164 in 1858, and at Delph Independent in 1865 the pastor's salary made up £86 4s. 3d. from a total expenditure of £116 16s. 2d.[122] Most of this money came from pew rents, and a high proportion of nonconformist seating was therefore appropriated: 66.7 per cent of seats in Congregationalist chapels in Oldham and 51.5 per cent of seats in Baptist chapels were subject to a rent in 1851, though there was considerable variation in individual cases. At the small Congregationalist church in Hollinwood, for example, all 130 seats were free, while the Unitarians had the highest proportion of appropriated sittings of any denomination in the town—some 74.5 per cent of their seats being subject to a rent. Rents were generally higher than in Anglican churches, though they were still kept within the range of most local families. Among the Mills Hill Baptists, rents were set at 1s. a quarter in 1849; at the Middleton Congregational chapel rents were set in 1860 at between 1s. and 4s. depending on the position of the seat, and the same sort of differential payments were also in operation at Hope.[123] Historians have tended to concentrate on the propensity of differential pew rents to reinforce social differentiation within the chapels, while ignoring its corollary that the richer attenders were effectively being persuaded to subsidize the sittings of the poor. Certainly rents do not seem to have provided a major obstacle to popular participation in the Dissenting congregations of Oldham and Saddleworth. However, from the mid-1850s local Baptists and Congregationalists began to substitute weekly offerings and envelope schemes, either for rents or for incidental collections. Thus, the Middleton Independents resolved to adopt weekly payments for pews in 1864, 'for the convenience of the congregation and especially for that of the great majority who can more easily pay small sums often than larger sums less frequently'. Similar schemes were adopted at Queen Street in 1861 and among the Baptists at Manchester Street in 1855 and Mills Hill in 1857. Elsewhere churches retained the standard combination of rents with quarterly or half-yearly collections and occasional special subscriptions towards particular projects.[124]

[122] MHBC, Accounts, 1859; Delph Congregational Church, Trustees' Cash Book.
[123] PRO HO 129 475 MHBC MS History; MCC, Church Book, 25 June 1860; Jones, *Hope*, 14.
[124] MCC, Church Book, 29 June 1858, 27 June 1864; Bridge and Lee, *Queen Street*, 51; KSBC, Minute-Book, 2 Oct. 1855, 2 Jan. 1858; MHBC, Minute-Book, 18 Jan. 1857; SMC, Diary, 29 Jan. 1850, 4 Oct. 1857, 31 Oct 1860; Marcroft, *Historical Account*, 89.

Most churches probably derived an income from the occasional letting of their chapel or schools for public meetings or daily education, and a few possessed additional property. The Moravians, for example, owned a house, the rent from which helped to pay the minister's salary.[125] However, the only other regular income available to most churches took the form of donations from wealthy members. Some donations were quite large, like those of the three members who paid most of the incidental expenses of the Second Manchester Street Baptist church in 1865. Others took the form of smaller amounts given on a regular basis, like the regular subscription of 30s. a year received by the Congregationalists at Dobcross. Some churches became extremely dependent on such income,[126] and this dependence may have given a disproportionate level of influence to wealthy members. It seems likely, for example, that the ascendancy of evangelicalism among the Oldham Friends was partly due to the influence of the evangelical Emmott family, the major financial backers of local Quakerism, and J. T. Cheetham seems to have used his large financial contribution to the Mills Hill Baptists in 1857 to secure a position of authority within the church. In 1822 the Lancashire and Cheshire Baptist Association was concerned enough about the disturbing effect of such men to warn its members that

there may probably be some few among you whose rank in life . . . whose pecuniary assistance or whose religious views, as standing connected with a love of power, and a disposition to interfere with your rights, may prove a great snare to you; and by their influence over you in a great variety of ways, of which you may not be fully aware, so entangle and corrupt you, as to reduce you to a most deplorable state of spiritual desolation.

This advice seems to have been taken to heart in Oldham, and Cheetham's influence in local Baptist circles was not sufficient to secure his immunity from church censure in 1862.[127]

The shortage of local resources led Dissenting churches to turn to their denominational associations for support, and almost all the new nonconformist foundations of the nineteenth century felt the need to make such appeals during the early part of their history. In 1839 only aid from the

---

[125] Ibid. 88; MHBC, Minute-Book, Feb. 1857; SMC, Diary, 23 Jan. 1850.

[126] Glodwick Baptist Church, Second Manchester Street Baptist Church Treasurer's Accounts; Lewis, 'Dobcross Congregational Church'; SMC, Diary, Nov. 1842.

[127] MHBC, Minute-Book, Sept. 1857; LCBA, *Circular Letter* (1822); Weston, 'Baptists', 267; KSBC, Record Book, 18 Mar. 1862; anon., 'Queen Street Sunday School', 35–7. Similar problems were noticed by Koditschek, *Class Formation*, 271, and Rycroft, 'Craven', 324.

'Provincial Helpers' Conference' allowed the Moravians to retain a resident minister, and the Mills Hill Baptists had to ask their county association for financial assistance in 1856. However, ironically, the best organized
and most interventionist of the denominational associations was that of
the Independents. The Lancashire Congregational Union played a significant role in the establishment of Independent churches in Oldham, and
many received large grants over a considerable period. The Middleton
Congregationalists received over £516 in grants between 1822 and 1844
and the church at Queen Street £560 between 1818 and 1834.[128] Associational support was another product of the revival, born out of the
activity of men like Roby and their desire to plant churches where local
resources, at least initially, were inadequate for their support. All the
churches, therefore, began to move towards a denominational structure,
which, whatever formal disclaimers might be made, tended to blunt the
independence of local churches. Causes supported by the Congregational
Union, for example, had to submit to a regular inspection and, in some
cases, to criticism of their activities. Moreover, the grant was sometimes
made only on conditions, and Middleton was offered £50 in 1831 only
when they had a minister 'who shall make Middleton the centre of an
active itinerancy'.[129]

This erosion of the autonomy of the local cause represented a considerable breach with tradition for the Baptists and Independents, and
Oldham and Saddleworth seem to display to an exaggerated extent the
submerging of the old Dissenting ethos under the flood of new converts
with no tradition. The leading churches were creatures of the revival and
in several cases, while they were evangelical by conviction, they were
Baptist or Congregationalist almost by accident. Binfield has argued for a
continuity with the older ethos, maintained by unbroken Dissenting family traditions and transmitted to the new converts swept in by the revival:
'The evangelical outpouring had profound implications for churchmanship
and attitude, but however massive, it was still an infusion of individuals
caught up in families; of common experience understood even where
not shared.'[130] However, in Oldham and in Saddleworth, where whole

---

[128] Bintley, *Salem Moravian Church*, 6; MHBC, Minute-Book, Jan. 1856; LCU Minutes,
23 Sept. 1806, 25 Oct. 1815, 11 Apr. 1822; LRO CUL 5, 1, LCU Visitation Committee
Minutes 1844–5.
[129] Robinson, *Lancashire Congregational Union*, 31–47; Journal of the Secretary to the
Executive Committee of the LCU; LCU Annual Meeting Minutes, 7 Apr. 1831; Lovegrove,
Itinerancy, passim.
[130] Binfield, *Down to Prayers*, 3–29; C. Binfield, 'The Place of Family in a Felt Religion',
Journal of the United Reformed Church Historical Society, 2 (1978), 4.

congregations were new branches grafted into the vine, the common experience was simply evangelical, and at most nonconformist, rather than Dissenting. That a resurgence of denominational consciousness did replace the undenominational evangelical Christianity of the heyday of the revival has become a commonplace of nonconformist historiography, and this process was certainly visible in Oldham and Saddleworth. The denominational missionary societies and county associations played a crucial role by creating a bond between churches with rather disparate origins. They also provided a larger stage for the activity of ministers who, like R. M. Davies, became leading lights in their denomination at a county level, and a common focus of allegiance through their annual meetings and circular letters. By the second half of the nineteenth century, some local churches had even begun to accumulate their own Dissenting family tradition, and events like the 1662 bicentenary, intended as a positive celebration of Dissenting tradition, allowed academy-trained ministers to act as bearers of this tradition to their own congregations.[131] Thus, while there was a resurgence of denominationalism in the nineteenth century, denominational identities were very much a new creation in the local churches. They overlay, and in some cases—judging by policies on communion and membership—overlay rather thinly, a basic set of inclusive evangelical commitments.

Beyond the Mainstream

Beyond the mainstream of new Dissent lay two small groups nourished by the popular millenarian tradition of the north. The Swedenborgians arrived in the first decade of the nineteenth century, and by 1832 had gained sufficient strength to enable them to embark on the construction of a small 'temple' in the Middleton out-township. There, perhaps reinforcing the perennial appeal of millenarian enthusiasm with a combination of political radicalism and folkloristic visionary spirituality, they made limited progress among the weavers in the local silk industry. Rather like its sister church in Failsworth, the Middleton Swedenborgian congregation was so dominated by silk-weavers that, uniquely among the churches of Oldham and Saddleworth, it came close to becoming a religious expression of a single occupational group, and, though its growth remained strictly limited, the church survived to make a small but

---

[131] Robinson, *Lancashire Congregational Union*, 56; Jones, *Hope*, 11; J. H. Taylor, 'The Bicentenary of 1662', *Transactions of the Congregational Historical Society*, 19 (1960), 18–25; *Oldham Standard*, 7 Jan. 1860, 2 Feb. 1861; *Oldham Chronicle*, 29 Mar. 1862.

distinctive contribution to local nonconformity throughout the period.[132] The impact of Mormonism, though it rested on similar millenarian foundations, was rather more widespread. Although Mormon missionaries failed to maintain a foothold in the central township of Oldham itself, they had by 1860, nineteen years after their arrival, established five small preaching rooms in the out-townships, together with at least one Sunday school. This development provoked a strong reaction from the mainstream churches, including the staging, by the local Primitive Methodists, of an anti-Mormon camp meeting in 1858. Nevertheless, like the Swedenborgians, after an initial period of success, the Mormons failed to recruit strongly in the locality, and the influence of their church, weakened as it was by periodic waves of emigration to America, remained strictly limited.[133] With the exception of a few unsectarian Sunday schools with occasional preaching services (two each in Oldham and Saddleworth according to the religious census), the only other non-Methodist alternative to the Established Church was Roman Catholicism.

Roman Catholicism was, to all intents and purposes, itself a new form of Dissent in Oldham and Saddleworth after 1800. Native recusancy had all but disappeared during the eighteenth century, and when local incumbents first noticed a significant Catholic presence in their parishes, in 1825, it was attributed almost entirely to Irish immigration. Thus, the incumbent of St Mary's reported 'The Roman Catholics consist chiefly of Irish labourers, they are not numerous, some suppose about a hundred', and the incumbent of St Peter's remarked that the number of Catholics was not known, 'because all are strangers from Ireland'.[134] This limited constituency tied the Catholics closely to the development of the Irish community, which was itself numerically insignificant, at least before the 1850s. At first, the size of the local Catholic population did not merit a mission of its own, although occasional masses were said in a room above the Harp and Shamrock public house. Then, in 1829, the priest in charge of the Ashton mission negotiated a five-year lease on the recently constructed Unitarian chapel and established an independent mission in Oldham. The average regular attendance remained small—around forty —and, after the lease ran out in 1835, the congregation returned to its

---

[132] *Manchester Courier*, 30 June 1832; LRO MJ1 81.3582, Wood Street Baptism Register; W. R. Ward, 'Swedenborgianism: Heresy, Schism or Religious Protest', *Studies in Church History*, 9 (1972), 303–9; P. Lineham, 'Restoring Man's Creative Power: The Theosophy of the Bible Christians of Salford', *Studies in Church History*, 19 (1982), 207–23; J. F. C. Harrison, *The Second Coming: Popular Millenarianism 1780–1850* (1979), 69–74.

[133] *Oldham Almanack* (1860); *Oldham Chronicle*, 8 Aug. 1857, 30 Oct. 1858; Butterworth Diary, Mar.–July 1841; Harrison, *Second Coming*, 188–9.

[134] CVR 1825, 368, 369.

upper room and the resident priest was withdrawn. However, the mission's baptism register suggests a rising Catholic population in the later 1830s, and a letter to the *Orthodox Journal* in 1838 claimed that the congregation amounted to upwards of 1,000 and consisted of poor Irish.[135] This increase encouraged the building of a Catholic chapel in Oldham, which was eventually opened in March 1839 with 450 free and forty appropriated seats. The rapid growth of the Irish population in the 1850s provoked further expansion. The church was enlarged in 1855 and a chapel of ease to seat 350 was established in 1858. In 1851 the work spread to Saddleworth, and a garret with sittings for eighty was taken to cater for a Catholic population estimated at 300 strong. In 1864 Middleton, too, was made into a separate parish, with a 'mass centre' being established in a house.[136]

The proportion of the Irish population attending the Catholic chapels on a weekly basis is difficult to estimate. In Oldham it may have been quite low, and the incumbent of St Peter's reported in 1844 that

In some instances I have found the people totally ignorant of the first principles of the religion which they profess to believe. I have also found some superstitious to a deplorable degree; and in my conversations with such persons, I have traced much of it to the Irish Romanists who have settled amongst them, and who like themselves go nowhere on the Sunday, and, in some cases, have ceased to call themselves Romanists.[137]

In 1851 the Roman Catholic priest reported an average regular mass attendance of 400—around 13 per cent of Foster's estimate for the total Irish population. In Saddleworth, on the other hand, 50 per cent attendance had been achieved after only a month's work among a much smaller, and therefore more easily supervised, Catholic population. However, as Connolly has pointed out, it is dangerous to judge the impact of Catholicism by conformity to a tridentine discipline essentially foreign to the popular religion of the Irish peasantry, and a more occasional attendance may have been characteristic of a much larger proportion of the community.[138]

The essential Irishness of the Catholic community had a number of important consequences. It meant that the social composition of Catholic

[135] T. Curley, *The Catholic History of Oldham* (Market Weighton, 1911), 22–40; LRO QDV 9, MS Return of the Total Number of Places of Worship not of the Church of England, 1829; LRO RCO 1, 1, St Mary's Roman Catholic Baptism Register, 1829–52.

[136] *Manchester Guardian*, 9 Mar. 1839; PRO HO 129, 475, 16; 496, 12; *Oldham Advertiser*, 23 June 1855; *Oldham Chronicle*, 16 Oct. 1858; anon., *Our Lady of Mount Carmel and Saint Patrick: Oldham Centenary Souvenir* (Farnworth, 1958); anon., *St Peter's, Middleton, Centenary Souvenir* (Ashton-under-Lyne, 1967).

[137] CPAS, *Occasional Paper*, xiv (1844), 3.

[138] PRO HO 129, 475, 16; 496, 12; Foster, *Class Struggle*, 244; G. Connolly, 'Irish and Catholic: Myth or Reality?', in R. Swift and S. Gilley (eds.), *The Irish in the Victorian City*

congregations was much less balanced than that of other local churches, and, judging by Foster's survey of Catholic marriages, the congregation was massively skewed towards the labourers of occupational Group VII, who made up 63 per cent of Catholic, but only 8 per cent of all marriages. Though its Irishness provided the Catholic church with a ready-made urban working-class base, it also limited opportunities for proselytization among the general population, and it left the church open to hostility produced by communal tensions, which in 1861 erupted in a serious riot and damage to the two Catholic chapels in Oldham.[139] When these differences are allowed for, local Roman Catholicism displayed many of the same characteristics as other Dissenting churches. There was a Sunday school in connection with the mission from 1831 at the latest, and by 1865 it mustered 230 boys, 440 girls, and 24 teachers. It therefore required some mobilization of the laity in active church work. A day school was opened in 1840, and in 1858–9 a large purpose-built school to hold 850 scholars was constructed at a cost of over £400, while a second school was begun in temporary premises in Lees in 1863. These educational efforts were supplemented in 1854 by the foundation of a branch of the 'Catholic Young Men's Society', which seems to have operated in much the same way as analogous Anglican and Dissenting societies.[140] For the congregation there were lectures and social events, like the 'Grand Catholic Tea Party' which attracted an attendance of 700–800 in February 1861, and the chapel was also central to a good deal of charitable activity, especially during the cotton famine.[141] The church was very active in evangelism and, according to its historian, 'In the September of 1862 a very successful mission was given at St Mary's by the Redemptorist Fathers, every inch of space in the church being occupied each night by devout congregations.'[142] In Sunday services, although the traditional Catholic emphasis

---

(1985), 225–54; G. Parsons, 'Victorian Roman Catholicism: Emancipation, Expansion and Achievement', in Parsons (ed.), *Religion in Victorian Britain*, i (Manchester, 1988), 146–83.

[139] J. O. Foster, 'Capitalism and Class Consciousness in Earlier Nineteenth Century Oldham', Ph.D. thesis (Cambridge, 1967), 282; *Oldham Chronicle*, 8 June 1861; E. Norman, *The English Catholic Church in the Nineteenth Century* (Oxford, 1984), 283–5; Parsons, 'Victorian Roman Catholicism', 163–4.

[140] Butterworth Diary, 10 July 1831; *Oldham Standard*, 10 June 1865; Curley, *Catholic History*, 46–52; *Oldham Chronicle*, 10 Apr. 1858, 10 Jan. 1863.

[141] *Oldham Standard*, 24 Mar. 1860, 16 Feb. 1861; Curley, *Catholic History*, 65–6.

[142] Ibid. 68. The Passionists also visited Oldham in 1859: ibid. 54. On the role of the new orders in promoting protestant-style catholic revivalism and the central role assumed by missions in Roman Catholic parochial life, see Norman, *English Catholic Church*, 223–4; Parsons, 'Victorian Roman Catholicism', 153, 172; Parsons, 'Emotion and Piety: Revivalism and Ritualism in Victorian Christianity', in *Religion in Victorian Britain*, i (Manchester, 1988), 223–5.

on the sacraments remained strong, the popular appeal of the sermon was not neglected, and music also played a major part in worship, with the choir being accompanied at first by a seraphine and then by an organ together with an instrumental band.[143]

The Roman Catholics also shared many of the problems of the other churches. There was the same diversion of energy away from the urgent task of preventing 'leakage' into expensive building projects. The absence of rich attendants placed the Catholics in a poor financial position—a problem which persisted to the end of the period. Although one wealthy family was able to subscribe 500 guineas, the rest of the £6,000 involved in building the new school and the chapel of ease in the late 1850s was only raised with 'much labour and anxiety'. A few subscriptions towards the school were received from local protestants, including £10 from James Platt, and the congregation made considerable exertions—resolving each to give a day's wages in the first two months of fund-raising. However, much of the burden fell on the priest, and, 'Desirous of leaving no stone unturned, Fr. Conway travelled far and wide throughout the country seeking the help of the faithful.'[144] There was no parallel in Oldham and Saddleworth to the struggles for leadership between priest and laity characteristic of those parts of Lancashire where residual English Roman Catholicism remained strong. This accentuated the tendency towards solo leadership implicit in contemporary concepts of priesthood, and brought with it all the associated problems of such a leadership style. At least one priest gave up his post in Oldham partly because of the strains induced by his exposed position.[145]

All in all the Dissenting achievement in Oldham and Saddleworth was considerable. A few churches like the Unitarians and the Mormons failed to make any significant headway. Others, like the Swedenborgians and more especially the Roman Catholics, were handicapped by the distinctive nature of their doctrinal position and limited by their particular appeal to a single occupational or ethnic group. However, most of the churches, imbibing the spirit of the revival, broke out of the constraints of traditional structures and achieved spectacular growth. They adopted a flexible approach to evangelism and church-planting which allowed

---

[143] Butterworth Diary, 27 June 1830; Curley, *Catholic History*, 36; *Manchester Chronicle*, 3 Aug. 1833.

[144] Inglis, *Churches and the Working Classes*, 122–30; Curley, *Catholic History*, 36, 52; J. Conway to the editor, *Oldham Standard*, 8 Aug. 1861; *Oldham Chronicle*, 11 July 1857, 10 Apr. 1858.

[145] Connolly, 'Irish and Catholic', 237–40; J. Conway to *Oldham Standard*, 8 Aug. 1861; Parsons, 'Victorian Roman Catholicism', 153.

them to penetrate many of the proliferating communities of Oldham and Saddleworth and, in defiance of traditional historiographical stereotypes, to develop a broad appeal to all social classes. In the course of this achievement, however, there was a change in the character of Dissent. The rise of evangelical Calvinism submerged many traditional theological distinctives and facilitated the relaxation of conditions for membership. A common evangelical culture nurtured in Sunday schools, tea parties, and prayer meetings linked all the churches, and the rise of county unions, while they provided new access to denominational traditions, tended to blunt the autonomy of local churches. From a position of relative insignificance, the new Dissenters grew until they represented a genuine alternative to the Anglican Establishment. In the process, however, the Dissenters also grew in many respects to resemble that Establishment.

5. *Wesleyan Theme and Methodist Variations*

The Methodists were the 'first born' of the revival and, more completely than any other group in Oldham and Saddleworth, they embodied the full force of the conversionist priority. In the eighteenth and nineteenth centuries the Methodist churches combined revivalist zeal with the most streamlined and effective machinery for penetrating communities with the Gospel that any church could bring to bear on the locality. Nevertheless, while they represented the pragmatic, evangelistic genius of the revival at its most inspired, the Methodists also displayed its inherent tendency to fission at its most extreme.

Many Methodisms

The first Methodist preachers penetrated the area in the mid-1750s, when classes were founded in Chadderton and Middleton. In 1763 a Wesleyan preacher reached the central township, but his reception was so outrageously hostile that further attempts to mission the town were suspended until the early 1770s, when a second wave of preachers succeeded in establishing a society which was sheltered by its close relationship with the Evangelical incumbents of St Peter's chapel of ease. Once established, the Wesleyans began rapidly to expand their mission: in 1778 the incumbent of Shaw reported that a few of his congregation were 'methodistically inclined'; Saddleworth was penetrated a year later; and in 1787 the establishment of a society in Royton completed the roll call of Oldham's out-townships.[1] Oldham was made the head of a circuit in 1791, which claimed 950 members six years later, and, despite disruptions in the 1790s, the membership total climbed to 1,100 by 1806. The Wesleyans not only grew more rapidly than any other nonconformist denomination in Oldham and Saddleworth, they also achieved a more extensive geographical spread. In 1826, despite considerable losses consequent on disruption, war, and

[1] MARC, McOwan MSS; *Methodist Magazine*, 39 (1816), 9; CVR 1778, Holy Trinity, Shaw; *WMM* 76 (1853), 785.

economic depression, the Oldham circuit mustered 900 members in four-teen societies with a total of twenty-four preaching places on its plan. A separate Saddleworth circuit was created in 1828, and in 1865 the two circuits combined mustered 1,516 members, although the number of regular preaching places had fallen to twenty.[2] The development of Methodism was not solely a question of the progress of Wesleyanism, and the years between 1796 and 1851 saw the appearance of at least a dozen non-Wesleyan groups in Oldham and Saddleworth, producing a Method-ist mosaic as varied as that of the rest of the churches put together. A few of these groups developed independently of the Wesleyans in Oldham and Saddleworth, being planted more or less peacefully by their parent bodies, using pioneering missionary techniques virtually identical to those employed earlier by the old connexion. Most of the new Methodist groups, however, sprang from divisions in existing Methodist societies. This process, described in detail below, reveals not only the general suscept-ibility of Methodism to secession, which connexional structures helped to promote on a national scale, but also the crucial role of local factors in determining the specific character of division in individual circuits.

Ties between Anglicans and Wesleyans were very close in Oldham, and this made the issue of holding services in Church hours and the administration of communion in Methodist chapels especially divisive. In 1794 the Conference gave permission for the Sacrament to be adminis-tered in the chapels at Delph and Middleton, and this development may have contributed to a small secession in the same year. However, when, following the adoption of the 'Plan of Pacification' in 1795, both com-munion services and meetings in Church hours were extended to the chapel in Oldham, a vocal 'church party' grew up in the society. Although they began by combining attendance at Wesleyan meetings and Church, most of the members of this group gradually drifted into secession between 1796 and 1798 and, joining the earlier seceders, 'attached themselves to St Peter's Chapel'.[3] 'Church Methodism' has received less attention than the contemporaneous Methodist New Connexion split, and the majority of its chroniclers, their eyes firmly fixed on a prominent Church Methodist

---

[2] *Wesleyan Methodist Conference Minutes (WMCM)* (1797), (1806), (1826); anon., *Oldham Wesleyan Methodist Circuit Plan* (Ashton-under-Lyne, 1825); MARC, Wesleyan Manchester District Meeting Minutes (WDM), 20–2 May 1828; anon., *Oldham Wesleyan Methodist Circuit Plan* (Oldham, 1865); anon., *Saddleworth Wesleyan Methodist Circuit Plan* (Uppermill, 1864).

[3] *WMCM* (1794); McOwan MSS. An excellent account of the various Methodist divi-sions can be found in D. Hempton, *Methodism and Politics in British Society 1750–1850* (1984).

dispute at the 'old room' chapel in Bristol, have regarded it as a rather conservative force. Commitment to the exclusive right of episcopally ordained ministers to administer communion has thus been represented as the prerogative of rich trustees or conservative 'High Church Preachers' and as incompatible with popular expansion.[4] However, negative reactions to the introduction of the Sacrament could also stem from a popular desire to retain the old informality of Methodism as a religious society and to prevent the clericalization of the Wesleyan ministry. In Ireland, the Primitive Wesleyan Methodists (a new connexion formed after a Sacramentarian split in the early nineteenth century) were a notably expansionist body whose rapid growth was marked by 'remarkable outpourings of the divine spirit'. In Oldham, too, where the Establishment could be both Evangelical and popular, adhesion to the Church could be construed as a radical reaction to the elevation of the Wesleyan itinerancy. John Walsh has pointed out that Wesley's autocracy tended to check the pretensions of his travelling preachers,[5] and it is not inconceivable that, after his death, some members regarded the Church as a substitute. The reservation of presidency at the Eucharist to Anglican clergymen certainly diminished the growing distinction between professional Itinerants and local preachers, and would have imposed a significant check on the incipient development of the Wesleyan doctrine of the 'pastoral office' which enshrined this distinction. The Church Methodist secession in Oldham was clearly popular in character. The seceders pursued their Methodist activities with considerable enthusiasm in St Peter's, where 'they introduced Class and Band meetings, prayer meetings also and were useful in a considerable degree in promoting the work of God'. In the early nineteenth century they successfully fostered 'a revival in this congregation similar to those that frequently take place in Methodist societies', and the subsequent career of many of the group as proletarian Independent Methodists with no paid Itinerancy is highly suggestive about the attitudes behind the original division. Equally suggestive was its effect on the local impact of the Kilhamite Methodist New Connexion schism of 1797–8. Several of the outlying societies were badly damaged by the split. Middleton, for example, suffered a net loss of thirty-eight members between 1797 and 1798, and the Chadderton society 'was rent in the time of Kilham'.[6] In

---

[4] Ibid. 59–67; W. R. Ward, *Religion and Society in England 1790–1850* (1972), 27–34.

[5] J. D. Walsh, 'Methodism at the End of the Eighteenth Century', in R. E. Davies and E. G. Rupp (eds.), *A History of the Methodist Church in Great Britain*, i (1965), 283; A. Stewart and G. Revington, *Memoir of the Life and Labours of the Revd Adam Averell* (1849), 355–66, 372 ff.

[6] McOwan MSS.

Oldham, however, the agitation was pre-empted by the Church Methodist secession; no Kilhamite society was established in the town until 1800 and even then it could muster only seven members. At Middleton, where the schism divided several classes into two, the Kilhamites survived into the early nineteenth century, but in 1805 they got into serious financial difficulties in trying to buy an old Wesleyan chapel. In 1808 the *New Connexion Magazine* reported the successful opening of a chapel in Middleton, but the financial strain may have been too great, the cause dwindled, and by 1826 at the latest it was extinct.[7]

In Oldham, though the New Connexion got off to a later start, its efforts were rather more enduring. It gained further recruits by a series of minor secessions from the Wesleyans during the first decade of the nineteenth century, especially in 1804 when Daniel Lees, one of the richest supporters of the Old Connexion, joined their society and the membership rose to about eighty. Lees financed the erection of the first chapel in 1805, but shortly afterwards rejoined the Wesleyans — perhaps finding the calls on his support too great. The society dwindled to a membership of only fourteen, and lost two of its most energetic local preachers to the 'Independent Evangelical Methodists'. They struggled on for several years in hired rooms and the membership sunk at one point to nine, but, freed of financial problems, the cause began to grow. A further small secession from both the Wesleyans and the Primitives in 1827 and the return of some members from the Independent Evangelical Methodists allowed a second society to be established at Lees, and lifted the cause in Oldham. More reinforcements came from the Wesleyan disruptions of the 1830s and chapels or preaching rooms were established in Lees, Oldham, and at Delph in Saddleworth. Membership in Oldham doubled between 1834 and 1837, when a circuit was created, based on Mossley, whose five societies included those at Oldham, Lees, and Delph.[8] The early 1840s were troubled and the new circuit suffered a severe check from the Barkerite secession. Between 1840 and 1843 the membership fell from 751 to 185 with the cause in Oldham being particularly badly affected, but thereafter the circuit experienced steady growth. At the end of 1856, though the Delph society numbered only nine, Oldham mustered 162

---

[7] MPL L92, Union Street, Methodist New Connexion Church, MS History (USMH). Oldham was a blackspot in an area of great MNC strength: Ward, *Religion and Society*, 37; McOwan MSS; Popilius, *A Statement of Facts Relative to the Purchase of the Methodist Chapel at Middleton from the Old Connexion* (Manchester, 1806); *Methodist New Connexion Magazine* (*MNM*), 11 (1808), 45.

[8] USMH, MARC, J. McOwan to J. Everett, 12 Feb. 1827; W. Walker, *Builders of Zion* (1914), 30–46; *MNM* 40 (1837), 42; 42 (1839), 6.

and Lees 230 members, while in 1858 further reinforcements arrived from a local secession in the Wesleyan Association. A spate of chapel building and alteration filled the 1850s and 1860s, and a new cause at Werneth was established in 1862. In 1863 Oldham was made the head of a circuit, and the *Oldham Almanack* of 1865 recorded five places in which the New Connexion held regular Sunday preaching, to which must be added at least one place in Saddleworth.[9]

The next Methodist group to establish themselves in Oldham were the Independent Methodists, who emerged in 1805, an expression of what David Hempton has described as an indigenous tradition of revivalistic Methodists in Lancashire. The local Church Methodists, having fostered a revival at St Peter's, discovered that their close relationship with the Church denied them legal protection for lay preaching. This occasioned a dispute between the advocates of lay preaching and the advocates of Church discipline, and the former party moved out to set up their own separate congregation in a hired room. In June 1806 they were visited by Lorenzo Dow, and his itinerancy brought contacts with similar revivalist groups which gradually coalesced into a loose federation and followed Oldham's lead in adopting the title 'Independent Methodist'.[10] Thereafter the Independent Methodists grew steadily. A chapel was opened on George Street, and a circuit plan for 1832 recorded nine regular Sunday preaching places in Oldham and its out-townships. The Independent Methodists betrayed their popular revivalist and radical Church Methodist origins by employing no paid Itinerants, and their 'cheap gospel' approach seems to have been successful as their denomination grew in both numbers and geographical spread. In 1835 a new society was established at Smith Street in Greenacres; in 1840 the George Street society could claim 175 members in nine classes meeting around the central township, and by 1842 a presence had also been established in Saddleworth. In 1854 the Independent Methodists suffered their only serious secession—occasioned by a dispute over the issue of 'total abstinence'. The hard-line Teetotallers moved out of George Street, formed their own church, and in 1855 built a school and preaching room on King Street. However, the new church was able to remain part of the Independent Methodist

[9] *Methodist New Connexion Conference Minutes* (*MNCM*) (1840–3); *MNM* 47 (1844), 37; USMH; MPL L92, Union Street; Methodist New Connexion Leaders' Meeting Minutes (USLMM), 26 Jan.–1 Mar. 1858; *Oldham Almanack* (1865), 47.

[10] McOwan MSS; anon., *Independent Methodism*, 1–2; L. Dow, *History of Cosmopolite: or, The Writings of Revd Lorenzo Dow: Containing his Experience and Travels in Europe and America* (Cincinatti, 1849), 272; A. Mountfield, *A Short History of Independent Methodism* (Wigan, 1905), 1–26; Hempton, *Methodism and Politics*, 94–6.

Connexion, revealing the resilience of its loose federal approach, and King Street was one of five regular Independent Methodist Sunday preaching places in Oldham recorded in the *Almanack* of 1865.[11]

The local Calvinistic Methodists of the Countess of Huntingdon's Connexion also originated in a secession from the Established Church. They began as a small religious society comprising a few members of the congregation of St Leonard's, Middleton, who, 'desirous of engaging more actively in religion, agreed to meet in each other's houses on the evening of the Sabbath, for the purpose of singing and praying and of reading the Holy Scriptures or a Sermon'. In 1808 a small revival increased their numbers and they established regular Monday evening meetings in Middleton Grammar School by permission of the curate. These meetings were extremely popular, entirely composed of 'people of the labouring classes', and attendance sometimes exceeded the congregation at the parish church. However, during the political agitation of 1816 some members were implicated in radical activity and the society was denied the use of the school room. The members of this 'Church Meeting Company' then began a classic drift from Anglican religious society to nonconformist church, renting a small chapel and inviting preaching from a 'Countess of Huntingdon's minister'. In 1824 they built St Stephen's Chapel, and began to employ a full-time minister. Thereafter the cause prospered, apart from a secession in 1854 which badly damaged the Sunday school, but the denomination remained localized in Middleton.[12]

The first Primitive Methodist preachers arrived in Oldham in 1820 shortly after the formal opening of their mission to Manchester, and their aggressive evangelistic style achieved rapid success. Before the end of the year a class had been formed, and in 1821 John Verity preached to thousands in the open air, and the membership of the Oldham society increased to 160. In 1822 their first camp meeting attracted a crowd estimated at 14,200 and the town was made the head of a circuit which, with the exception of Middleton, took in the whole of both the Oldham and Saddleworth Poor Law Unions.[13] By 1835 the Primitive Methodists

[11] Mountfield, Short History, 96; anon., *Independent Methodism*, 2–12; Vickers, *Independent Methodism*, 224; Independent Methodist Church, George Street (IMGS), Account Book; *Oldham Almanack* (1865).

[12] Anon., *History of St Stephen's Church, Middleton 1803–1938* (Middleton, 1938), 2–8; *Manchester Guardian*, 14 Aug. 1824.

[13] J. S. Werner, *The Primitive Methodist Connexion* (Madison, Wis., 1984), 132; W. E. Farndale, *The Story of Primitive Methodism in Lees* (Oldham, 1911), 6–7; H. B. Kendall, *The Origin and History of the Primitive Methodist Church*, ii (1906), 41–3; anon., *Primitive Methodist Manchester Circuit Plan* (Bemersley, 1827).

in Oldham and Saddleworth could boast 644 members in twenty-four societies and outlying classes—only 144 fewer than the Wesleyans, a difference probably attributable to the larger area covered by the Wesleyan circuits. This represented a considerable achievement after less than fourteen years' work, and the Primitives probably remained the largest Methodist group in Oldham and its out-townships until the 1860s. One significant factor in this advance was the relative freedom of the local Primitives from disruption. There was an abortive attempt to take a chapel over to the Wesleyan Methodist Association in 1836 and, more seriously, the defection of almost an entire society at Royton in 1842. However, the Primitives never suffered a check as severe as that which the Wesleyans were to experience between 1833 and 1836, and in 1862 they felt strong enough to divide the circuit into two parts, which in 1863 mustered 500 and 640 members respectively.[14]

In July 1830 the Wesleyan Protestant Methodists (the denomination that emerged from the Leeds organ dispute) established a preaching room in Oldham, but thereafter disappear from the record, and may have merged with the Wesleyan secession of 1834–6.[15] This schism was the joint product of local tensions that surfaced in the secession of the Stephensites in 1834 and national tensions that produced the Wesleyan Methodist Association in 1835–6. It ended in a merger of the two seceding bodies and a severe disruption of the Oldham circuit. The occasion for the first of these divisions was the suspension by the Wesleyan Conference in 1834 of J. R. Stephens, the popular minister of the Ashton-under-Lyne circuit. In May 1834 annoyance at this suspension provoked many Oldham members to threaten to withhold their financial contributions, and later in the month 140 members requested a circuit meeting to consider the question. An impromptu meeting was convened in the Independent Methodist Chapel on George Street which condemned the actions of the Conference, but at the next circuit leaders' meeting Mr Wolsey, the Itinerant minister, against the wish of the majority of the leaders and amidst cries of 'Popery! Popery!', expelled two local preachers, William Knott and George Jacques, on a charge of 'having promoted a meeting contrary to the established rules of Methodism'. This produced an escalation from widespread protest into outright secession, with eight

---

[14] MARC, C. Hallam, MS Circuit Book, 1834–5; *WMCM* (1835–65); MPL, Oldham Wesleyan Methodist Circuit Steward's Accounts (WMCSA), 1835–57; *Primitive Methodist Conference Minutes* (PMCM) (1835–65); MPL L26/3, Primitive Methodist Quarter Day Board Minutes (PMQ), 5 Sept. 1836, 27 June 1842; *Oldham Almanack* (1865), 47.

[15] Butterworth Diary, 14–27 July 1830; Ward, *Religion and Society*, 144–6.

leaders and local preachers resigning on the spot, soon followed by a large number of members. Now that the expulsions were of well-known local figures, greater interest was stirred, and a much more numerously attended protest meeting declared Wolsey's action to be 'unscriptural' and resolved to stop financial contributions to the circuit. For the next few months the expelled preachers fought a guerrilla campaign against the circuit authorities — preaching by request in outlying chapels and Sunday schools. Finally, they hired a preaching room in Oldham, formed a committee to reform the Wesleyans, and advised seceders to form their own church or to join another body according to local circumstances.[16]

In 1834 the membership of the Oldham circuit fell from 836 to 641, a net loss of 195, and at the end of the year the troubled Wesleyan societies were swept by a fresh wave of agitation deriving from a row over the creation of a new Wesleyan theological institution, and the suspension of Dr Warren, a prominent figure in the Manchester District. The proceedings against Warren were heralded by the Stephensites as another example of Wesleyan popery, and they reported at the beginning of February 1835 that 'Mr Wolsey's flock are many of them very uneasy under the conference yoke and if they had a leader or two, there would be a rebellion'. Warren found considerable sympathy in his home district, and he received a warm welcome when he came to Oldham in February to address a joint meeting of 'Warrenite' and 'Stephensite' seceders.[17] In terms of numbers the Warrenite secession was rather less significant than that of the previous year, with the circuit sustaining a net loss of ninety-one members. However, it seems to have spread the agitation to parts of the circuit that had previously escaped. At Cowhill in Chadderton, for example, a small society which had been established in 1828 was more or less wiped out. The Saddleworth circuit weathered the Stephensite division without any major problems and even recorded a net gain of fifteen members during 1834. However, in 1835, under the additional stimulus of the Warrenite agitation, problems began to emerge, culminating in the expulsion of a local preacher and a net loss of thirty-eight—some 16 per cent of the total membership.[18]

[16] WDM 28 Apr. 1834; Ward, *Religion and Society*, 156–9; *Manchester Courier*, 7–24 May 1834; *Manchester Guardian*, 24, 31 May, 27 Sept. 1834; Butterworth Diary, June–Aug. 1834; *Manchester Chronicle*, 21 June, 20 Sept. 1834.

[17] *WMCM* (1834–5); D. A. Gowland, *Methodist Secessions: The Origins of Free Methodism in Three Lancashire Towns* (Manchester, 1979), 42–66, 162–70; *Manchester Chronicle*, 7 Feb. 1835; Butterworth Diary, Jan.–Feb. 1835.

[18] *WMCM* (1834–6); J. Fletcher, *Cowhill School 1849–1949* (Manchester, 1949), 7; MPL L93/1, Saddleworth Wesleyan Methodist Local Preacher's Minutes, 2 Jan.–23 Sept. 1835.

Although the secessions of the early 1830s were occasioned by ministerial suspensions, and exacerbated by the expulsion of their supporters, the causes ran much deeper. The virtual disappearance of the Oldham circuit records makes it difficult to identify the detail of the argument, but clearly there was considerable resentment about the changing relationship between ministers and people. Such resentment had deep roots in the Oldham circuit—it had surfaced in the Church Methodist split and probably fed periodic secessions to the New Connexion. Thus the circuit minister had noted in 1815 that 'The worst of it is, some of our leading people have got a notion into their heads that a Quarter Day is a kind of House of Parliament which has a right to legislate for and rule the circuit, and some of the preachers I fear have too much countenanced the idea.' This notion was alive and well in the 1830s, with the Stephensites recommending that supply should be withheld until the 'people' had brought forward their resolutions on Quarter Days. There was also resentment of high-handedness in the administration of discipline and of the growing expense and pretensions of the Wesleyan ministry. The separated Stephensites declared that 'We are as happy, as useful and far more independent than we were before: and the money we were compelled to pay before to men who lorded it over us, will soon build our chapels and schools and when we have got fitted with these, we can please ourselves in the choice of our preacher, if we choose to have one.'[19]

It also seems probable that beneath the irritation with the weight and expense of the Wesleyan superstructure lay growing doubts about its pastoral effectiveness. Oldham was a large circuit and the 1826 circuit plan shows a clear tendency for the Itinerants to concentrate on the main chapels and largest societies. Among the seventeen smallest or more remote places in the six months between September 1825 and January 1826, William Knott, one of the future dissident local preachers, was planned for eight sermons—as many as all three Itinerant ministers put together. Both the Oldham Itinerants were newly stationed in 1833, and had little opportunity to build up local contacts in a circuit which, in the twelve months before the storm struck, had just suffered its first serious net loss for ten years. The resentment engendered by the expulsion of two well-known local preachers against the express wish of the leaders' meeting and at the hands of two unknown Itinerants of doubtful competence in an already agitated circuit may easily be imagined. Particularly

[19] MARC, W. France to T. Jackson, 24 Oct. 1815; *Manchester Chronicle*, 7 Feb. 1835; Gowland, *Methodist Secessions*, 42–66; Ward, *Religion and Society*, 159–76; R. Currie, *Methodism Divided* (1968), 46–8.

revealing are the membership figures, which had been carefully entered in the Account Book each quarter since the middle of 1811. At the end of 1832 there were thirteen societies in the Oldham circuit, plus a 'school class': two large societies with membership of over 100, four medium-sized societies, and seven small societies. The figures come to a halt in mid-1833, and when they resume in June 1836 the difference is startling. The two largest societies recorded a net gain of two members and the long-established medium-sized society at Shaw had lost only two members. However, the membership of the medium-sized societies at Failsworth and Heyside fell from 65 to 39 and 66 to 28 respectively, while the medium-sized society at Lees, all seven small societies, and the school class—which combined had mustered 207 members in December 1832—had ceased to exist altogether. It was almost always the outlying societies that invited the dissident preachers to speak, and Wesleyan recovery in these areas was long delayed. Clearly the agitation of 1830s was not so much an expression of 'radical Oldham' as a 'revolt of the provinces'.[20]

The subsequent fortunes of the seceders are a little unclear: some probably drifted back to the Wesleyans, and others joined the Methodist New Connexion. However, the main body of Stephensites and Warrenites coalesced in 1835, and established their base in the former Unitarian chapel. A Stephensite circuit plan of 1835 recorded a total of eight places with regular Sunday preaching and a further three with weeknight services. In 1841 they leased a former Primitive Methodist chapel on Grosvenor Street, which remained their headquarters in the town until the construction of a new chapel on King Street in 1861. Oldham was granted circuit independence in 1847, and thereafter a fairly stable membership of between 75 and 108 was maintained until the early 1860s, when a period of rapid growth began. By 1865 there was considerable ground for optimism with a membership of 165, twenty-four more on trial, and three regular Sunday preaching places recorded in the *Oldham Almanack*.[21]

The next two Methodist groups to appear on the scene in Oldham were planted in a peaceful manner by missionary activity rather than by secession in existing circuits. However, neither succeeded in establishing

---

[20] Anon., *Oldham Wesleyan Methodist Circuit Plan* (1825); *WMCM* (1823–34); MARC, T. Dunn to J. Bunting, 29 July 1836; Gowland, *Methodist Secessions*, 73.

[21] Ibid. 57–8; Butterworth Diary, Jan.–Feb., July–Aug. 1835, Dec. 1840–March 1841; Marcroft, *Historical Account*, 62–78; anon., *Oldham Lord Street Circuit Preachers' Plan* (Oldham, 1835); *Wesleyan Methodist Association Magazine* (*WAM*) 4 (1841), 487–8; *Oldham Standard*, 20 July 1861; Gowland, *Methodist Secessions*, 77; *Wesleyan Methodist Association Conference Minutes* (*WACM*) (1838–56); *United Methodist Free Church Conference Minutes* (*UMFCCM*) (1857–66); *Oldham Almanack* (1865), 47.

a permanent presence in the area. The first of these groups, a sect calling itself the 'Bible Christians', appeared in 1837 and seems to have been a revivalist Methodist group rather than an offshoot of the heterodox Salford Bible Christians. However, after just over a year's work, they gave up the attempt to maintain an independent existence and applied to join the Primitive Methodists. Similarly shortlived were the 'Welsh Methodists' who hired the Oldham theatre as a place of worship in January 1840. The local Welsh Methodist constituency must have been extremely limited, and, though a permanent preaching room was opened early in 1841, they drop out of the record thereafter.[22] At the same date, Oldham found itself close to the centre of a convulsion in the New Connexion. Joseph Barker was a popular minister in the Mossley circuit and his expulsion, in 1841, produced an effect on the New Connexion societies of the north similar to that of the expulsion of Stephens among the Wesleyans. The Mossley circuit, where Barker had many friends, was particularly badly hit, and between the conferences of 1840 and 1843 numbers fell from 749 to 185 —a net loss of 75 per cent. Both Oldham and Lees were affected, and in 1842, according to one report, the Union Street 'Chapel estate was a complete wreck through the great disturber and agitator of our connexion . . . Through his schism we were mowed down from 210 members to about 30 or 40 with a debt of about £1,200 or £1,400.'[23] The Union Street society had suffered a secession by between 81 and 86 per cent of its membership —higher than average even for the badly damaged Mossley circuit. The seceders only just failed to take legal possession of the chapel, and by early 1842 feeling was running so high that a brawl erupted in the chapel yard. Lees was rather less badly affected; it could still muster sixty members at the end of 1843 and by 1844 had recovered to ninety-two members compared to fifty-nine at Union Street. W. R. Ward has suggested that Barker's complaints were similar to those of the Wesleyan radicals, with a special stress on the gap between poor members and the rich lay aristocrats of the New Connexion. At Lees, there was certainly an emphasis on cheap gospelism among the seceders, for whom Barker's exclusion was the occasion for the expression of pre-existing tensions:

a nucleus was already being formed in the cottage meeting, and in the development of a feeling . . . that ministerial power at the conference was becoming too strong for the lay element . . . They also saw that the poor people absented themselves from the house of God because of the expenses being increased. Our elders

[22] PMQ 4 June 1838; Butterworth Diary, May–June 1837, Nov. 1839–Jan. 1840, Dec. 1840–Mar. 1841.
[23] *MNCM* (1840–3); *MNM* 60 (1857), 157–8.

were thus influenced by a desire to open a place where people could hear the word of God preached at a very limited cost.[24]

In the Oldham circuit, the Barkerite schism was not a ministerial revolt against the authority of the trustees, but a lay revolt formed in the cottage meeting and led by local preachers and class leaders against the authority of the Itinerant minister. Moreover, though the seceders failed to seize control of the chapel, the Connexion was so doubtful of the loyalty of the Oldham trustees that they were removed and a new set inserted, 'to secure the premises to the connexion and prevent further unpleasantness'. Some Barkerites may eventually have returned to Union Street, which by the end of 1846 was claiming a membership of ninety-two. Others may have joined other Methodist groups, or drifted away altogether, but in 1841 the main body established the 'Christian Brethren' church at Lees on 'strictly free church principles'. There were no pew rents or paid ministers, and leadership was democratically controlled by the church meeting. Although the church was at first part of a Barkerite circuit, its polity was virtually identical to that of the Independent Methodists, with whom it gradually moved into association.[25]

The Wesleyan Reform secession of the early 1850s established the last Methodist body to appear in Oldham. Nationally, the Reform split was the most damaging schism in Methodist history. It raised many of the same issues as the earlier divisions and Oldham was close to the storm centre of the agitation. However, the Oldham circuit was not badly affected: between the conferences of 1849 and 1851 the circuit membership fell from 770 to 725, a secession by less than 6 per cent of the membership (considerably less than the national average), and by 1854 the membership had reached 774—a rapid recovery. The Reform agitation may partly have been pre-empted by the earlier divisions and by losses sustained during the economic depression of 1842. It also seems likely that the Oldham ministers adopted a conciliatory approach aiming to reduce tensions in the circuit, and the resolutions concerning the crisis in the Stewards' Account Book end, not with a list of expulsions, but with a call to prayer for unity.[26] The influence of the Reform division on the Saddleworth circuit, however, was more serious because the national problems converged with local ones. The circuit had already been disturbed in

[24] USMH; Butterworth Diary, Dec. 1841; Ward, *Religion and Society*, 274; anon., *Historical Account of the Christian Brethren Chapel, Lees* (Lees, 1891), 8.

[25] Ward, *Religion and Society*, 274–5; anon., *Christian Brethren*, 7–9; USMH.

[26] Currie, *Methodism Divided*, 71–80; Chadwick, *Victorian Church*, i. 380–5; *WMCM* (1841–54); WMCSA, June 1851; Gowland, *Methodist Secessions*, 62.

1845, when the Uppermill Sunday school invited a Warrenite to preach its anniversary sermon and the Itinerant minister, in intervening to prevent this, provoked 'a rupture in his congregation'. In 1847 the District authorities provoked further unhappiness when they attempted to interfere with the Delph Sunday-school trust and in 1850 the situation was further complicated when John Avison, a wealthy member of the Uppermill society, offered to provide a permanent residence for the circuit minister if he would move from his rented lodgings in Delph and come to live in Uppermill. This prospective move caused considerable resentment at Delph and a secession ensued. In the middle of 1850 the Saddleworth circuit had mustered 194 members, and by mid-1851 the total had fallen to 117—a net loss equivalent to 40 per cent of the membership. At first sight this might appear a simple consequence of the Reform division, but when the figures are examined in more detail the influence of local factors comes into sharper focus. In 1850 there were three societies in the Saddleworth circuit: Uppermill with 52, Greenfield with 73, and Delph with 66 members, plus a society class at Cherry Clough near Delph with 3 members. In mid-1851 the 117 members were distributed as follows: Uppermill 54, Greenfield 58, and Delph 5, the class at Cherry Clough having been absorbed into the Delph total. Clearly, the 'Reform secession' in Saddleworth had much to do with local resentments. In the mid-1830s the Oldham societies had revolted partly because they were outlying places; in 1851 Delph revolted against the prospect of becoming an outlying place, and the Wesleyan society did not recover its 1850 membership level for another thirteen years.[27]

The complex structure of local Methodism not only vindicates Alun Howkins's observation that 'there were many Methodisms in many places and times', but also demonstrates that there could also be many methodisms in one place and at one time. The Methodist experience, even within the same denomination, might be widely different depending on whether one attended a large chapel-based society frequented by the Itinerant minister or an outlying Sunday-school preaching room dependent on local preachers. Moreover, the example of Methodism in Oldham and Saddleworth illustrates the danger of generalizing about the meaning of secession. Connexional structures may have had the effect of spreading disputes throughout the societies on a national scale, but local factors could completely overshadow the infuence of more general ones. It is difficult, for

[27] Ward, *Religion and Society*, 271; MPL L93/1, Saddleworth Circuit Schedule Book; WDM 19–21 May 1847, 14–17 May 1850; E. Hudson, 'History of Delph Methodism 1770–1850', serialized in *Oldham Chronicle*, Feb. 1902, 18;

example, to classify the dispute at Delph in 1850–1 simply as part of the 'Reform' agitation with which it coincided. Nevertheless, though the character of individual divisions might be obstinately local, the Methodism of Oldham and Saddleworth did share with Methodism at large the fact of secession: the tendency, as John Kent has pointed out, for almost any stimulus to produce a sharply divided response.[28] The case of local Methodism illustrates a number of sources of tension which, in the first half of the nineteenth century, were common to Methodism as a whole. In particular, there was the problem of the large circuit, like Oldham with its multitude of outlying societies, in which the fabric of the Wesleyan pastoral structure was stretched too thin to resist the strains imposed by the Wesleyan constitution. A second problem derived from a shift in the relationship between the Itinerant minister and the people. Here the tension was not just between two rival views of Methodism: an official view stressing the importance of an independent, clerical, pastoral superintendence, and a popular view stressing the importance of a cheap gospel and presenting an idealized picture of primitive Wesleyanism as 'a band of brothers'. It was also a tension between different forms of Methodist experience. Despite Currie's suggestion that 'The chapel is the central fact of Methodism', for many early nineteenth-century Wesleyans the most important institutions were the society and the class, and the most important officials were the leader and the local preacher. Both were valid expressions of the Wesleyan tradition: William Knott, the Oldham radical, was as much a Methodist as Jabez Bunting, the Oldham Itinerant. It is one of the more remarkable features of E. P. Thompson's portrait of Methodism that, while he concedes that 'there was a sense in which working people could make it their own' and readily admits that 'what the orthodox Methodist minister intended is one thing; what actually happened in many communities may be another', he does not recognize Wesleyan radicalism as a valid expression of Methodism. For Thompson, the 'orthodox Methodist' was a conservative Buntingite; in the late eighteenth century, Wesleyanism's 'democratic tendencies' were 'alien', and largely 'drained' by the Kilhamite secession. There would certainly have been little conflict had Thompson's official Methodism in 'new-brick Brunswick and Hanover chapels' not existed. There would have been little conflict either, but for the Wesleyan radicalism perenially developed

[28] J. D. Walsh, 'Methodism and the Common People', report by R. Colls in R. Samuel (ed.), *People's History and Socialist Theory* (1981), 354–62; J. Kent, 'The Wesleyan Methodists to 1849', in R. E. Davies, A. R. George, and E. G. Rupp (eds.), *A History of the Methodist Church in Great Britain*, ii (1978), 223.

in Sunday schools, in cottage meetings, and in some chapels too, where a Wesleyanism of the poor received as vital expression as that of the Conference. Had Conference not guaranteed the inner cohesion of Wesleyanism, it might have fallen apart, with the weaker circuits going to the wall. Had the societies not continued to nurture the lay energies that came into conflict with the Conference, its finest evangelistic cutting-edge would have been lost. The combination was essential to Wesleyan growth; secession was the corollary of success.[29]

Evangelism and Revivalism

Although the missionary activity of the other churches was impressive, for sheer intensity of commitment to aggressive evangelism none matched the Methodists. Most of their activities had some evangelistic implication, and the most characteristically Methodist of these was open-air preaching. In 1827, for example, the Independent Methodists preached in the open air at Lees 'to a goodly company', their missioner reporting that 'the people seemed to feed on the word and thanked me for the sermon'. Similarly, the New Connexionists began a series of special services in Oldham market place in 1852, and in 1856 arranged for open-air preaching in the town square with the aim of drawing a crowd to a subsequent evangelistic sermon in the chapel. The most enthusiastic open-air preachers of all, however, were the Primitive Methodists. In 1835 they began regular preaching in the market place assisted by a 'praying company', and in 1840 the Oldham leaders planned 'open-air missioning' throughout the circuit once a fortnight.[30] The Primitives also pioneered that most spectacular form of open-air religious activity, the camp meeting. Such meetings exercised an extraordinary drawing-power, and some approached the scale of popular festivals embracing whole communities. The first local camp meeting, in 1822, featured 'two preaching stands, five praying companies', and drew an estimated attendance of 14,000. They remained popular throughout the period and Butterworth recorded a series of large camp meetings between 1829 and 1841, with an attendance varying from 'very numerous' to 'an immense multitude'.[31] As time passed

[29] Ward, *Religion and Society*, 100–4, 240; Currie, *Methodism Divided*, 44–6; Kent, 'Wesleyan Methodists', 255; Thompson, *The Making*, 47–50, 386–7, 415–7.

[30] *Independent Methodist Magazine* (*IMM*), Jan. 1827, July 1827; USLMM 27 July 1852, 5 July 1856; PMQ 9 Mar. 1835, 20 Sept. 1840.

[31] Werner, *Primitive Methodist Connexion*, 45–6, 147–8; Kendall, *Primitive Methodist Church*, ii. 41; Butterworth Diary, 19 July 1829, 30 May 1830, 26 May 1833, July–Sept. 1835.

the focus shifted from large central meetings to a series of smaller events staged on a regular basis in various parts of the locality usually during the summer. The attendance at these local events could be quite small and the *Oldham Standard* reported only 200–300 at a meeting in Hollinwood during August 1863.[32] Nevertheless the Primitives retained the ability to draw large crowds and in 1856, for example, the press reported

3[00]–400 Oldham members assembled at Boardman Street Chapel at 8.30 and were joined by those from the country. After a short service held in the chapel, they perambulated the principal streets in real Primitive Methodist style. The congregation on the edge was unusually large, especially in the afternoon when competent persons estimated the assembly to number at least 15,000. The preaching was plain, pointed and practical, and well adapted to so diversified a company. In the evening a special service was held in the chapel, and was largely attended. A considerable accession was made to the church at night, and it is hoped much spiritual good was done during the day.[33]

The Primitive Methodists were soaked in the spirit of revivalism, and in 1839 the Oldham Primitives introduced a new revivalist technique to their connexion—a systematic series of 'protracted meetings'. These long meetings of preaching and prayer were held in seven or eight places in the circuit, each preceded by a day of prayer, and seem to have produced a considerable effect. At Lees, for example, after the society had engaged in a 'powerful prayer meeting', 'poor sinners flocked to the chapel like doves to the windows', and twelve converts were recorded. After a similar series of meetings at Delph, the society's membership increased from fourteen to forty-nine, and so much interest had been created that the chapel was packed and people could not get in. At the end of the programme, they reported that 'The whole place is moved; the chapels which were but poorly attended are now reported to be quite full', and that numbers in attendance had increased from 548 to 687.[34] Given this sort of tradition, it is not surprising that the wave of revivalist excitement that swept 'new Dissent' in the later 1850s was anticipated among the Primitives by more than a decade. In 1842 they noted, 'Every leader is requested . . . to give it out in his class that every member is requested to pray mightily for a revival, and never rest till we have one.' In 1845–7 a 'revival meeting' was planned at every place in the circuit, and at Middleton they were

---

[32] PMQ 16 June 1856; *Oldham Standard*, 22 Aug. 1863.

[33] *Oldham Advertiser*, 17 May 1856.

[34] *Primitive Methodist Magazine* (*PMM*) 21 (1840), 250–2, 297–9; the Oldham meetings thus anticipated the meetings held by Caughey in Liverpool; Carwardine, *Transatlantic Revivalism*, 111.

supported by large prayer meetings and 'missionary processions'. The same pattern was repeated in the 1850s, and the Primitives were also in the forefront of the revivalist excitement of the early 1860s. At Lees in November 1861 a series of missionary and revival services attracted an average attendance of 200 each night for a week, and in 1863 every place in the newly formed second circuit had at least one week's protracted meetings. By 1865 the Primitives were also supporting the activities of a professional female revivalist, Mrs Tolson. A considerable revival ensued at Lees, the membership of the society was doubled, and in Oldham as a whole the membership increased from 700 in 1859 to 1,157 in 1864—a net gain of 457 or over 65 per cent in five years.[35]

Although the Primitives were the most consciously revivalist Methodist group in the town, the other denominations did not lag far behind. After 1822 the organization of camp meetings, for example, became a standard practice not only among the Primitives, but also among all the younger Methodist groups. In 1827 the Oldham Independent Methodists reported that 'holding camp meetings, and preaching in the open air have been the happy means of convincing many who declare they are now the adopted children of God', and such meetings were a regular feature of Independent Methodist activity in the 1840s and 1850s. In 1855 the Wesleyan Associationists described a camp meeting preceded by early morning prayer, singing, open-air preaching in the market place, and a procession. At the camp ground, there was a sermon for the young and several other addresses, all of which met with a favourable reception: 'The people paid strict attention to the Word of God—the power of the most high came down, the Divine Glory rested upon us, and there was a shout of a King in the camp.' The first local New Connexion camp meeting, in August 1838, was a joint effort with the Primitives and 'a large number of members of other Dissenting societies who are favourable to their opinions'. Thereafter, camp meetings became a regular part of the New Connexion programme.[36] The younger Methodist denominations were also close behind the Primitives in their pursuit of revival. There were prayers for revival in the Association circuit in 1849, which registered 'a general expectation . . . that the Lord is about to pour out his Holy Spirit',

---

[35] MPL L26/3/1, Oldham Primitive Methodist Circuit Committee Minutes, 2 Dec. 1842; *PMM* 28 (1847), 241; MPL L22, Box 1, Irk Street Primitive Methodist Chapel Middleton, Leaders' Meeting Minutes, 28 July 1845; PMQ 2 Sept. 1850, 15 Sept. 1856; *Oldham Standard*, 16 Nov. 1861; A. Auty, *Annie, Being a Faithful Account of the Life, Experience and Labours of Annie Auty, the Yorkshire and Lancashire Revivalist*, 4th edn. (1888), 95–9; Farndale, *Primitive Methodism*, 14; *PMCM* (1859–64).

[36] *IMM* (1827); IMGS, Accounts, 1845, 1850, 1856; *WAM* 18 (1855), 456; Butterworth Diary, July–Aug. 1838.

and in 1855 the Associationists reported that a series of revival meetings had regenerated the circuit. There was a revival at the Independent Methodist church on Smith Street in 1853, and in 1855 the whole circuit was praying for a revival and employing a special evangelist to promote it. The New Connexion churches were also engaged in this sort of activity more or less continuously from 1854. In the 1860s a fresh impetus was imparted by the general revivalist excitement, and the meetings were supported by a massive effort in prayer, typified by the resolution of the leaders of the Werneth cause 'that we hold a week of prayers for the outpouring of God's spirit upon the church and the salvation of souls'.[37]

It is often suggested that the Wesleyan leadership's suspicion of its uncontrolled aspects led to a falling off of revivalism in the old connexion, with some notable exceptions like the circuits of West Cornwall.[38] The local Wesleyans, however, were far from squeamish about open-air preaching. In 1832, despite the unrest caused by the agitation for parliamentary reform, the Saddleworth Wesleyans nominated five places to hold field preachings; in 1847 the Oldham Wesleyans re-established their cause at Cowhill by a programme of open-air preaching in the village; and in the early 1850s they began preaching from a wagon like those used at camp meetings.[39] Clearly, whatever the reasons for the success of Primitive Methodism in the area, it was not the consequence of any major slackening of the Wesleyan commitment to the streets and fields. The local Wesleyans had experienced revivals in the 1780s and 1790s, and, in Saddleworth at least, the new measure revivalism of the mid-nineteenth century received an enthusiastic reception. The Primitive Methodist protracted meetings introduced in 1839 were immediately copied by the local Wesleyans, and both Oldham and Saddleworth circuits were also heavily involved in the revivalist activity of the 1860s.[40]

Although revivalism was an important feature of local Methodism, its

---

[37] *WAM* 12 (1849), 552; 18 (1855), 101; Independent Methodist Church, Smith Street (IMSS), MS History; *Independent Methodist Conference Minutes* (*IMCM*) (1855); Vickers, *Independent Methodism*, 293–4; USLMM 1 Aug. 1854–7 Sept. 1858; MPL L93, Werneth Methodist New Connexion Leaders' Meeting Minutes (WLMM) 18 Nov. 1862.

[38] Carwardine, *Transatlantic Revivalism*, 107; Werner, *Primitive Methodist Connexion*, 33, D. H. Luker, 'Revivalism in Theory and Practice: The Case of Cornish Methodism', *Journal of Ecclesiastical History*, 37 (1986), 601–19.

[39] Saddleworth Wesleyan Methodist Local Preacher's Minutes, 2 Apr. 1832; Fletcher, *Cowhill School*, 7; N., 'A Century of Methodism at Hollins', serialized in *Oldham Chronicle*, 8–21 May 1937.

[40] *Arminian Magazine*, 9 (1786), 664–5, anon., 'Methodism in Oldham', in *Christian Journal*, 22 Apr. 1885; McOwan MSS; *Primitive Methodist Magazine* (*PMM*) 21 (1840), 297–9; J. J. Norcross, *Brunswick Wesleyan Chapel* (Oldham, 1912), 10–11; *WMM* 86 (1863), 945; 87 (1864), 467; 88 (1865), 84. On the continuing importance of Wesleyan revivalism in Cheshire, see Walker, 'Religious Changes', 91.

success rested on the relentless commitment to evangelism that informed all Methodist activity. Thus the Primitives, reporting over 100 conversions at a series of protracted meetings in 1847, noted: 'The means employed to produce these pleasing results have been faith in God, fervent prayer, pointed addresses, singing in the streets, ministerial family visitation, special attention to Sunday scholars and the force of powerful union among the brethren.'[41] The sort of systematic visiting, preaching, and mobilization of the laity to take the Gospel into the homes of the poor that constituted the 'aggressive approach' was commonplace among the Methodists. In 1828, for example, the Saddleworth Wesleyans listed five places where village preachings were held, and in 1830 two classes of 'exhorters' were planned to attend the 'smaller places'. Similarly, in the twenty-seven months between March 1832 and June 1834 the Primitives held such preachings in no fewer than thirty-four places in Oldham and Saddleworth. The Methodists also participated enthusiastically in Bible and tract distribution, supporting the Oldham auxiliary of the BFBS and forming their own societies to supplement its work. By the 1850s all the main denominations were running tract societies, and in 1865 even the small Barkerite cause at Lees was regularly distributing tracts round the village. These organizations were quite effective, and, according to its historian, through the agency of the New Connexion Bible society at Lees, 'there was not a house from Hartshead Pike to Bardsley, from Althill to Glodwick without a Bible'.[42] By the early 1850s Bible and tract societies had begun to develop a more sophisticated organization, parallel to that appearing among their Dissenting counterparts. In 1851, for example, the 'Saddleworth Wesleyan Tract Society', which had been in existence since 1834, was reorganized on a new basis. The villages were to be divided into 'convenient districts of from 15–40 houses each', distributors were to visit regularly, every week, and, 'affectionately endeavour to check immorality, lead all in their districts to Christ, sympathise with the distressed and to increase attendance on public worship and at the Sabbath school'.[43]

These organizations mobilized a large proportion of the Methodist laity in active evangelism, and in 1865 the Oldham Wesleyans reported

[41] *PMM* 28 (1847), 241.

[42] Saddleworth Wesleyan Methodist Local Preacher's Minutes, 6 Oct. 1828, 29 Mar. 1830; PMQ 12 Mar. 1832–9 June 1834; Oldham BFBS Minutes; *IMCM* (1850); MPL L22, Box 1, Irk Street Primitive Methodist Leaders' Meeting Minutes, 23 Oct. 1859; USLMM, 23 Jan. 1855; *Oldham' Chronicle*, 29 July 1865; 96; Walker, *Zion*, 63.

[43] MPL L93/1, Box 5, Saddleworth Wesleyan Methodist Tract Society minutes, 12 Dec. 1851.

that a recently formed tract society 'is worked vigorously and prayerfully by our young people, and will prove a great blessing to the population'.[44] In 1849 the Wesleyans also began to employ a professional 'home missionary' in Oldham who eventually operated from a specially designated 'mission chapel'. In the early 1860s a similar missionary was employed to help establish the New Connexion cause at Werneth,[45] and in 1865 the Wesleyans reported, 'The home missionary on this circuit has been highly successful during the year. The minister and those who have co-operated with him have displayed much zeal and efficiency in domiciliary visitation in holding cottage and other services and in the distribution of religious tracts and these labours have been crowned with God's prospering blessing.'[46]

All the Methodist groups operated cottage meetings as an instrument of evangelism, and some of them very extensively. In Saddleworth, where the relatively dispersed settlement pattern made them a virtual necessity for any extensive penetration, the Wesleyans by 1822 were running seventeen regular cottage meetings, with five bands going out fortnightly to conduct them. Similarly, in the 1830s the Independent Methodists were holding such meetings in at least seven different locations around Oldham. The evangelistic activity of the 1860s also made great use of cottage meetings. Thus, among the Oldham New Connexionists, 'a number of leaders and pious young men formed themselves into companies for the purpose of holding cottage prayer meetings'; at Copster Hill, where two members offered the use of their houses, 'the numbers attending weekly increased, until it was with difficulty that even standing room could be obtained. Several, principally householders, were converted to God.' A society was formed and within a year a membership of thirty, a congregation of 200, and a Sunday school of 109 were meeting regularly in a school room.[47] The Wesleyans demonstrated similar vigour, and in 1864 reported that

The Journal of the Revd Henderson . . . narrates several instances of conversion to God, resulting from visitation and the influence of numerous cottage services . . . Some of the prayer meetings have been seasons of great power, many present being deeply convinced of sin; and on some occasions 9 or 10 have

[44] *WMM* 88 (1865), 468; Bebbington, *Evangelicalism*, 10.
[45] USLMM 25 Mar. 1862, 24 Jan. 1864.   [46] WDM 15–19 May 1865.
[47] PMQ 3 Sept. 1838, 15 Sept. 1862; IMSS, MS History; Walker, *Zion*, 64–7; WLMM 10 Nov. 1863; J. Marrat, *A Centenary Memorial or Brief Record of the Origins and Progress of the Wesleyan Sunday Schools in Oldham and the Neighbourhood* (Oldham, 1885), 26–7; Hudson, 'Delph Methodism', 16; IMGS, MS History; *MNM* 68 (1865), 183–4.

professed to find peace with God through faith in Christ . . . More than 50 cottage services have been held during the quarter, in which the Missionary minister has been assisted by 16 earnest and faithful friends. The meetings have been well attended and are sometimes crowded.[48]

The emphasis on cottage meetings, which seems to have developed furthest among the Methodists, provided an extremely flexible evangelistic tool. When any member's home, or even the house of a sympathizer, might become the nucleus of a new cause, the penetration of rapidly proliferating communities was made much easier than for churches more sharply focused on chapels or preaching rooms. The evasion of immediate expenditure on material infrastructure meant that many more places could be missioned at the same time and more readily abandoned, if no response was forthcoming. The informal atmosphere created in cottage meetings also lowered barriers to attendance and made it easier for Methodism to become a religion of the people.[49]

The preparation for much Methodist evangelism was made in Sunday school. The Wesleyans were heavily involved in the first schools in Oldham in the 1780s, and, having eliminated the main financial constraints on their development by the adoption of 'gratuitous instruction', the Wesleyan schools grew rapidly. Between 1785 and 1828 there were at least seven new foundations, and in 1831 a total of 1,998 scholars and teachers took part in Jubilee celebrations. The younger Methodist groups were equally enthusiastic about Sunday schooling. The Independent Methodists, for example, established a school as soon as they separated from the Church in 1805. Similarly, the Countess of Huntingdon's cause at Middleton was claiming 600 pupils by 1824. Secession groups also tended to recruit heavily among Sunday schools, which were often centres of resistance to the imposition of minsterial authority. The Oldham Barkerites, for example, caused a considerable secession from the New Connexion school linked with Union Street. Sunday schooling was therefore an important feature of all branches of local Methodism, and there was certainly none of the slowness to invest time and energy in Sunday schools during the first half of the nineteenth century found by Obelkevich in South Lindsey.[50] The

---

[48] *WMM* 87 (1864), 467.

[49] Bamford, *Early Days*, 125–31; D. M. Valenze, *Prophetic Sons and Daughters* (Princeton, NJ, 1985), *passim*.

[50] O'Neil, *Sunday Schools*, 10–13; Marrat, *Centenary Memorial*, 9; S. Whitehead, 'The Rise and Progress of Methodism in Glodwick', in *Handbook of the Grand Bazaar in the Town Hall Oldham* (Oldham, 1884), 55; IMGS, MS History; anon., *St Stephen's*, 4; Ward, *Religion and Society*, 135–44, 158–9; USMH; Obelkevich, *Religion and Rural Society*, 193.

extent of the Methodist achievement in Oldham was revealed by the O'Neil survey of 1847, displayed in Table 5.1.

Clearly, although the survey omitted areas of considerable Methodist strength, the overall Methodist contribution to Sunday schooling in Oldham was very impressive. Only the combined Anglican schools could boast more pupils than the Wesleyans, and the combined Methodist total was greater than that of the Established Church, or that of all the other nonconformist churches combined. The early adoption of Sunday schooling certainly makes Obelkevich's suggestion that Sunday schools emerged 'as the outward evangelistic impulse weakened and was turned inward' inapplicable to Oldham. Sunday schools were never aimed solely at the children of existing members and in practice their appeal was so widespread that it is better to see them as part of an integrated system of evangelism aimed at the population as a whole.[51] In Saddleworth, where the first Wesleyan Sunday school was founded in the mid-1780s, growth was rather slow and the result less impressive: the Independents and the Anglicans could each muster more scholars than all the Methodists put together. However, 1851 was a bad year for Wesleyanism and this, taken together with a Sunday-school defection at Uppermill in 1845, may account for the relatively poor performance of Methodist schools in the census survey presented in Table 5.2. The survey may also have missed a small Primitive Methodist school established at Delph in 1837.[52]

The Methodist schools seem to have undergone the same sort of institutional development as those of the Anglicans and new Dissenters. By 1856 most schools boasted libraries and 'sick-clubs', some of which clearly provided a continuing link with former members. There was the same growth of tract distribution agencies, emphasis on the pastoral responsibility of teachers, and support for the Sunday-school union, the same social world of tea parties, and the same pattern of Christmas parties, recitations, and Sunday-school outings.[53] Methodist schools were very cheap to run, and in 1858 the Oldham Wesleyan circuit was supporting

[51] Ibid. 193, 228.

[52] Hudson, 'Delph Methodism', 18–19; PMQ 4 Dec. 1837.

[53] Butterworth, *Oldham*, appendix; USMH; MPL L26, Add'n 6, Primitive Methodist Irk Street Sunday School Minutes, 2 Sept. 1849; *IMCM* (1863); MPL L26/18, Higginshaw, United Methodist Free Church, Sunday School Minute-Book, 15 Apr. 1863; *Oldham Standard*, 11 Feb. 1860, 17 July 1865; *Oldham Chronicle*, 1 Feb. 1862; IMGS, Sunday School Accounts, 1823; MPL L92, Werneth Methodist New Connexion, Sunday School log book, 2 Jan. 1859; anon., 'St John's Methodist Church Hollins', published in *Oldham Chronicle*, 27 May–2 June 1939; MPL L26, Add'n 5, Cowhill Wesleyan Methodist Sunday School Superintendent's Minute-Book, 19 July 1863.

TABLE 5.1. *Methodist Sunday Schools in Oldham 1847*

| Denomination | Schools | Teachers | Scholars | | | % of all Methodist scholars | % of all Sunday scholars | % of all 5–19 year olds in 1851 |
			Male	Female	Total			
Wesleyan Methodist	9	303	1,145	1,443	2,588	38.1	16.3	10.9
Primitive Methodist	6	170	682	793	1,475	21.7	9.3	6.2
New Connexion	2	56	225	239	464	6.8	2.9	2.0
Independent Methodist	4	147	611	830	1,441	21.2	9.1	6.1
Wesleyan Association	4	122	376	451	827	12.2	5.2	3.5
TOTAL	25	798	3,039	3,756	6,795	100.0	42.8	28.6

Source: O'Neil, *Sunday Schools.*

TABLE 5.2. *Sunday Schools in Saddleworth 1851*

Denomination	Schools	Scholars				% of all Methodist scholars	% of all Sunday scholars	% of all 15–19 year olds
		Male	Female		Total			
Wesleyan Methodist	4	308	382		690	95.2	20.0	11.7
New Connexion	1	14	21		35	4.8	1.0	0.6
TOTAL	5	322	403		725	100.0	21.0	12.3

Source: PP 1852–3, xc [1692], Census of Great Britain 1851; Education.

twelve schools with 3,280 scholars at a total annual cost of only £215. These costs were easily met from a combination of public subscriptions and collections at special anniversary services which, along with Methodist Sunday-school openings, developed into vastly popular public occasions. In 1847, for example, the Middleton Primitive Methodists printed 1,000 double hymn sheets and 200 single ones for their anniversary services and in 1855 the Wesleyan Association Chapel was completely filled for the Sunday-school anniversary.[54] As was the case with the other denominations, the Methodist schools also experienced changes in their curriculum, with lectures and singing classes, for example, becoming especially popular. Inevitably, the most controversial of these developments was the suppression of the teaching of writing. 'Secular instruction' came under increasing pressure within the Wesleyan connexion during the first decades of the nineteenth century as part of a general sabbatarian reaction.[55] Nevertheless, in Oldham opposition to the teaching of writing was relatively slow to gather force, and in February 1831 the Independent Methodists hosted a meeting to debate the issue at which the Baptist minister put the sabbatarian case, and the two Wesleyan Itinerants opposed him, declaring that the teaching 'was extremely just and good'. Sunday writing remained a regular feature of most Methodist schools in Oldham for at least a decade after its abandonment in the generality of Anglican and Dissenting schools. Not until 1841, when a meeting of teachers in the circuit voted 'by an overwhelming majority' to end the practice and arranged to open on two nights each week in compensation, was there any significant move towards the elimination of 'secular instruction' on the sabbath. There were exceptions. The Middleton Wesleyans, for example, got out of step in 1839 by banning writing, and they paid a heavy price in the form of a considerably reduced anniversary collection. Rather more common, however, were those Wesleyan schools that continued to teach writing into the second half of the century despite the decisions taken at circuit level. Writing formed a central part of the curriculum of the Wesleyan School at Hey Top, for example, at its foundation in 1845, and in the Wesleyan school at Lane End writing was taught until

[54] WDM 18–22 May 1858; Fletcher, *Cowhill School*, 9–13; MPL L92, Union Street, Methodist New Connexion Trust Treasurer's Accounts, 1838; anon., *Christian Brethren*, 11; Primitive Methodist Irk Street Sunday School Minutes, 25 June 1848, 11 July 1848; *WAM* 18 (1855), 504.

[55] USMH; *IMCM* (1850); Marrat, *Centenary Memorial*, 10; anon., *St Paul's Methodist Church, Shaw* (Shaw, 1961), 10; Ward, *Religion and Society*, 137–40; Hempton, *Methodism and Politics*, 91.

1860.[56] The younger Methodist bodies probably retained Sunday writing even longer than the Wesleyans; it certainly formed part of the curriculum of the Primitive Methodist school at Bardsley in 1850 and the Independent Methodists of King Street were teaching writing until well after 1850. There is no evidence that schools that abandoned writing after 1850 suffered any great unpopularity and the Wesleyan school at Cowhill was able to raise £350 for a new building in 1855, by public subscription.[57] The resources mobilized by connexional structures gave the Wesleyans a considerable advantage over the Dissenters in the redirection of their long-standing commitment to Sunday education into the compensatory provision of day schools. In 1851 the Oldham Wesleyan circuit, gradually recovering from the economic difficulties of the 1840s and the impact of the Reform secession, had only one day school with 166 male and eleven female pupils. Thereafter, the mid-century Wesleyan educational initiative took off. By 1858 the Wesleyans were supporting nine schools with 1,592 scholars. In 1844 the Lees New Connexionists also established a school supported by the British and Foreign School Society and the Primitive Methodists of Hollinwood followed suit in the mid-1860s.[58]

There must have been a considerable difference in the experience of scholars attending the largest Sunday schools—like the Wesleyan one at St Domingo Street which mustered 630 pupils in 1847—and the smallest—like the Primitive Methodist school at Knott Lanes, where a committee of colliers attempted to convey the rudiments of literacy and the Gospel to 150 children from the local mines. Nevertheless, despite a developing concern at the end of the period about 'leakage' which issued in the growth of Bible classes, Young Men's Associations, and Mutual Improvement Societies,[59] all the schools seem to have been reasonably successful as evangelistic agencies. There were, for example, no fewer than twenty-five conversions at the Wesleyan School in Middleton in one

[56] Butterworth Diary, 13 Feb. 1831; *Manchester Guardian*, 26 Feb. 1831, 25 May 1839, 21 Jan. 1841; anon., *The Chapel in the Valley: The Centenary Handbook of Greenfield Methodist Church* (Uppermill, 1945), 14; R. O. Ball, *One More Light: A History of Middleton Junction Methodist Church* (Wigan, 1951), 7; Laqueur, *Religion and Respectability*, 142.

[57] MPL L26, Add'n 5, Lane End Sunday School Minutes, 1850; anon., *A Centenary History of King Street Independent Methodist Church Oldham* (n.p., 1954), 7; Fletcher, *Cowhill School*, 8–10.

[58] *Manchester Guardian*, 14 Oct. 1843; Hudson, 'Delph Methodism', 27; PP 1852–3, xc [1692]; Hempton, *Methodism and Politics*, 171–3; WDM 18–22 May 1858; Walker, *Zion*, 75–87; PMQ 30 Mar. 1866.

[59] USLMM 24 Nov. 1863; MPL L26/3/3, Oldham Primitive Methodist Leaders' Meeting Minutes, 17 Nov. 1865; WDM 18–22 May 1851; *Oldham Standard*, 7 Apr. 1860, 24 July 1861; *Oldham Chronicle*, 8 May 1858, 2 Mar. 1861.

year during the 1790s, and in 1858 the Wesleyan schools in Oldham reported 294 of their pupils as society members and a further 135 in select classes, comprising 17.7 per cent of the Wesleyan Sunday-school population. Similarly, in the 1840s the Associationists reported: 'Our hopes of success largely rest on our Sunday schools . . . Many scholars are savingly converted . . . and their consistent conduct manifests the fruits of Genuine Christianity. Others of the scholars, are the subjects of serious impressions and will we trust, ere long become decided for Christ.'[60] Converted scholars could act as a channel of the Gospel to the adults in their families. Not only did they invite their parents to special services, they might also make an effective witness in their own homes. Thus in 1850 an Independent Methodist teacher reported, 'young babes in Christ, having been taught by the pious Sabbath school teacher and feeling themselves freed from sin, in their turn become the instructors of their parents; and, by the mild endearing and anxious words they address unto them, they succeed in turning them to Christ'.[61]

There is some evidence of a change in the style of Methodist evangelism and revivalism towards the middle of the nineteenth century. Like the new Dissenters they displayed an increasing tendency towards the adoption of a more systematic approach and to the appointment of professionals. Revivals were often planned with considerable care and occasionally with an ulterior motive. The programme of protracted meetings initiated by the Primitive Methodists in 1839, for example, began as a means of rescuing their flagging society at Delph.[62] However, like the new Dissenters, the Methodists also retained an explicitly charismatic approach to revival. As the New Connexionists put it in 1853:

if we do not unite our hearts and voices in prayer for the outpouring of the Holy Spirit, we shall labour in vain. It is neither plainness nor splendour in our places of worship, neither poverty nor riches in our congregations, neither commonplace language nor thrilling eloquence in our pulpits, that will turn sinners from darkness to light, and from the power of Satan unto God. When men are convinced of sin and righteousness, and judgement, it is by the Holy Spirit; when men are born again, they are born of the Spirit; and when men are seen walking in newness of life they walk in the Spirit.[63]

[60] PP 1842, xvii [382], 854; R. Jones, *A Short History of the Wesleyan Methodist Sunday-School Middleton* (Middleton, 1886), 3; WDM 18–22 May 1858; *WAM* 10 (1847), 134–5.

[61] MPL L26, Add'n 5, WM Sunday School Cowhill, Minutes, 5 June 1864; *The Free Gospel Advocate*, Sept. 1850.

[62] *PMM* 21 (1840), 297–9.   [63] *MNCM* (1853), 59–60.

The Methodists may have been confident that their prayers would be answered, but it was a confidence produced less by a 'routinized' approach to revivalism, than by a charismatic triumphalism.

The Methodist Constituency

An impression of the spatial distribution of the two main Wesleyan congregations in Saddleworth can be derived from a comparison of their baptism registers with the 1848 Ordnance Survey Map. As was the case with the Congregationalists, the Methodists not only drew heavily on the villages in which their chapels were situated, but also on a scatter of surrounding settlements, mostly spread between one-half and two-and-a-half miles from the chapels. The pattern of spatial distribution also reflected clear spheres of infuence established by the two chapels. Of the 140 adherents plotted, only five resided closer to another Wesleyan chapel than to the one they attended, an even tighter division of space than among the Congregationalists. When Congregationalist and Wesleyan distributions are compared, however, a considerable overlap becomes apparent. At least twenty Congregational adherents, or 7.3 per cent of the total, lived closer to a Wesleyan chapel than to the Congregational chapel they attended. At least twenty-five Wesleyan adherents or 17.9 per cent of the total lived closer to a Congregational chapel than to the Wesleyan chapel they attended. It is possible that this differential reflects the greater efficiency of the decentralized Wesleyan evangelistic and pastoral system, but it is clear that the inhabitants of Saddleworth certainly did not simply attend their nearest nonconformist chapel. There was a strong element of competition between the different denominational representatives of the evangelical revival, and, of the fifty-six Saddleworth settlements that sent more than one adherent anywhere, twenty-four sent them to both Wesleyan and Congregationalist chapels.[64]

Something of the extent to which the Methodists succeeded in penetrating local communities may also be gauged from the opposition they provoked. In Oldham, early Wesleyan preachers were commonly subjected to violence at the hands of both the mob and the constables. This opposition often simply reflected the activities of local hooligans, but it may also sometimes have indicated a degree of communal attachment to the parish church. Other attacks represented an urgent response to the

---

[64] Ordnance Survey Map (1848); OLIC, Microfilm, Delph and Uppermill Wesleyan Methodist Baptism Registers.

removal of people from traditional familial and communal relationships into the sectarian Methodist community of faith. In 1775, for example, it was reported of one George Scholes that incensed by 'the union of his son Samuel to the Methodists he has used the poker in a very free manner to clear the house of his son Samuel, of the persons attending a prayer meeting there'. Similarly, at Royton, 'for two or three years the mob continued to persecute [the Methodists] in going to their little class meeting, and occasionally they would surround the house with strange noises during that time'.[65] Such opposition was not limited to the early Wesleyans. Violence was a common response to Primitive Methodist attempts to penetrate new communities in the 1820s and 1830s. Their preachers met heavy opposition when they preached in the village of Luzley Brook because their behaviour 'seemed strange', and, significantly, this opposition 'increased mightily' when they succeeded in forming a class. As late as 1850 the Independent Methodists, trying to establish themselves in the small settlement at Fir Lane near Royton, could report that 'Persecution has raged violently.' Perhaps more surprisingly, when the Wesleyans attempted to re-establish their cause at Cowhill by open-air preaching, 'For several months [they] were roughly handled by the villagers, who threw sods and mud at them.' The new society was particularly vulnerable to communal hostility because it was based in the village school, the 'antagonism of the villagers grew worse, and eventually, at a crowded meeting, they decided that these troublesome Wesleyans should be denied the use of the school'. When the Methodists barricaded themselves in to hold a service, the villagers came to enforce this decision with the traditional sanction of rough music. It was not until 1855, when their Sunday school received generous local subscriptions, that the Wesleyans could feel assured of communal acceptance.[66] Clearly, the Methodists possessed a genius for getting under the skin of local communities—in both senses of the phrase.

Information on the occupational structure of the Methodist congregations was derived from their baptism registers using the methods described in Chapter 4, and the results are displayed in Table 5.3. Bearing in mind the distortions consequent on the sources and system of classification, it appears that the Oldham Wesleyans, like the Congregationalists,

---

[65] J. D. Walsh, 'Methodism and the Mob in the Eighteenth Century', *Studies in Church History*, 8 (1972), 213–27; McOwan MSS; *Arminian Magazine*, 16 (1793), 283.

[66] Werner, *Primitive Methodist Connexion*, 98–9; *PMM* 15 (1834), 215–18; *IMCM* (1850); Fletcher, *Cowhill School*, 6–10. On the polarizing effects of Methodism in some communities, see Rule, *Labouring Classes*, 164.

TABLE 5.3. *Occupational classification of seven Methodist chapels*

Occupational group	Chapel															
	Delph Wesleyan		Uppermill Wesleyan		Shaw Wesleyan		Manchester Street Wesleyan		George Street Independent Methodist		Zion Methodist New Connexion		Henshaw Street Primitive Methodist		Anglican Baptisms	
	No.	%	No.	%	No.	%	No.	%	No.	%	No.	%	No.	%	No.	%
I	3	3.1	4	6.8	4	3.7	0	0.0	1	1.0	5	7.1	0	0.0	41	2.8
II	11	11.3	10	16.9	7	6.5	12	15.6	5	4.8	4	5.7	5	4.5	137	9.2
III	3	3.1	0	0.0	0	0.0	4	5.2	0	0.0	1	1.5	2	1.8	19	1.3
IV	15	15.5	4	6.8	14	13.0	8	10.4	17	16.3	5	7.1	20	18.0	178	11.9
V	12	12.4	4	6.8	28	25.9	21	27.3	24	23.1	26	37.1	22	19.8	403	27.0
VI	45	46.4	35	59.3	49	45.4	30	38.9	49	47.1	23	32.9	51	46.0	543	36.5
VII	8	8.2	2	3.4	6	5.5	2	2.6	8	7.7	6	8.6	11	9.9	168	11.3
TOTAL	97	100.0	59	100.0	108	100.0	77	100.0	104	100.0	70	100.0	111	100.0	1,489	100.0

Sources: OLIC, Microfilm, No-Parochial Registers: Delph Wesleyan Methodist Chapel, 1825–37; Uppermill Wesleyan Methodist Chapel, 1825–36; Manchester Street Wesleyan Methodist Chapel, 1829–37; Zion Methodist New Connexion Chapel, 1829–37; George Street Independent Methodist Chapel, 1835–7; LRO, Microfilm, 1/90, Shaw Wesleyan Methodist Chapel, 1826–37; MPL L26 12/3/1, Henshaw Street Primitive Methodist Chapel, 1836–8.

recruited fairly evenly from the population at large. Although the sample of baptisms did not pick up its employer clientele, the town-centre Manchester Street cause did predictably recruit a greater than average proportion of shopkeepers and professionals. However, its occupational structure was hardly dominated by these groups, and at Shaw both were under-represented. Even if all the members of Groups I–III are regarded as upper and middle class, both the Manchester Street and Shaw churches would have been numerically dominated by working-class adherents. Neither was it the case that the majority of working-class Methodists came from declining artisan trades. Many of the Group VI workers were weavers, some of whom may still have been domestic workers, but they were outnumbered by a range of factory-based occupations among the industrial workers, and even the 'Artisans' of Group IV were almost all from developing trades like shoemaking, or craft work in engineering. Thus, while the Oldham Wesleyans fell roughly in line with Gilbert's national sample, they were, like the new Dissenters, already doing well among those occupational groups that were to expand in the Victorian period.[67]

In Saddleworth, the Wesleyan chapels seem to have outperformed their Congregationalist rivals among the tradesmen and master craftsmen of Group II, although, when Groups I and III are taken into account, there is perhaps a hint of social differentiation, with the Wesleyans having the slightly more fashionable chapel in Delph and the Congregationalists the more fashionable chapel in Uppermill. However, these small differences should not obscure the fact that the adherents of both Wesleyan churches were overwhelmingly working class in character—82.5 per cent of the congregation at Delph and 76.3 per cent at Uppermill falling in Groups IV–VII. Group VI was very large at both churches because it included a large number of men describing themselves as clothiers, many of whom would have been working in factories by the 1830s. The case of Oldham and Saddleworth clearly casts doubt on the consensus about the social structure of Wesleyanism described by David Hempton: 'All are agreed . . . that Wesleyanism made little impact on the unskilled masses.' If the 'unskilled' are limited to the labourers of Group VII, then, at 11 per cent of household heads, they could hardly be labelled 'the masses'. If 'the masses' are to be taken to include the lower-status workers of

[67] Gilbert, *Religion and Society*, 66, 146–8. The same pattern of even recruitment across the population at large has been traced by Rycroft in the Methodist churches of Craven: 'Craven', 221.

Group VI, then the Wesleyans were making a major and in some places more than proportionate impact.[68]

The occupational structure of the three non-Wesleyan chapels tends to reinforce existing stereotypes. The New Connexionists, for example, in keeping with their reputation for attracting rich laymen, had a higher proportion of adherents in Group I than any other Methodist church. Similarly, the Independent and Primitive Methodists maintain their proletarian reputation with a high proportion of workers in Group VI. Perhaps rather surprising, however, is the significant under-recruitment, even among the New Connexionists, of the shopkeepers and master-craftsmen of Group II. All three chapels were numerically dominated by adherents in the clearly working-class Groups IV–VII: 85.7 per cent for the New Connexionists, 93.7 per cent for the Primitives, and 94.2 per cent for the Independent Methodists. The Primitive and Independent Methodists both did well among weavers—a sector of textile manufac-turing that was to contract in the area, and the Independent Methodists additionally recruited strongly among operative hatters, who were badly affected by the slump of the 1840s. Nevertheless, these chapels were also doing well among factory-based occupations, especially among cotton-spinners, and both recruited strongly among the local coal-mining popu-lation. Just as in Dissenting chapels, this pattern tells against Foster's assumption that increased church-going among 'Labour Aristocrats' was a component of the decline of local radicalism.[69] If radical groups like weavers, spinners, and hatters were all well represented in the churches during the radical 1830s, any increase in church-going could more plau-sibly be interpreted as a radicalizing force!

Statistical evidence concerning the occupational make-up of Methodist Congregations after the 1830s is scarce, and the available information, relating to the Henshaw Street Primitive Methodist church and the New Connexion Methodist Sunday school at Union Street, is presented in Table 5.4. There is some evidence of 'social lift' among the Primitive Methodists, with increases in the proportion of adherents in Groups I–III and Group V. In part this was due to a decline in the number of weavers who were replaced as the largest occupational category at Henshaw Street by colliers. There was also an increase in various high-status factory occupational groups like the 'mechanics' in engineering. Equally striking is the increase in the labourers of Group VII, who by the mid-1850s had

---

[68] Hempton, *Methodism and Politics*, 14. See also Bebbington, *Evangelicalism*, 25; Koditschek, *Class Formation*, 258.

[69] Foster, *Class Struggle*, 214–16.

TABLE 5.4. *Occupational classification of Primitive and New Connexion Methodists 1854–65*

Occupational group	Henshaw Street Primitive Methodist		Union Street New Connexion Methodist Sunday School	
	No.	%	No.	%
I	2	1.5	1	1.1
II	7	5.1	9	10.2
III	4	2.9	5	5.7
IV	24	17.5	24	27.3
V	30	21.9	17	19.3
VI	48	35.0	18	20.5
VII	22	16.1	14	15.9
TOTAL	137	100.0	88	100.0

Sources: MPL, Henshaw Street Primitive Methodist, Baptism Register, 1854–6; L92, Union Street Methodist New Connexion, Sunday School Register, 1864–5.

become the third largest occupational group in the church. To a certain extent this development reflected changes in the general occupational structure of the town. Nevertheless, the Primitive Methodists were clearly maintaining their appeal among these lowest status workers into the mid-1850s. The figures for Union Street New Connexionists are not directly comparable with the New Connexionist figures from Table 5.3 because, deriving from parent's occupations listed in a Sunday-school register, they probably represent people more loosely connected with the church than those taken from the baptism register. However, the constituency of the Sunday school at least was clearly proletarian in character, with only 17 per cent of parents coming from groups that might not be regarded as working class. The only significant deviation from the occupational distribution of the general population was over-recruitment among Group IV: mainly craft-workers in engineering, one of Oldham's most rapidly expanding industries. The serious effects of economic depression on Methodist societies are indicative of the marginal economic position occupied by many of their members, and the continuing strength of the Methodist appeal to the working classes is also confirmed by anecdotal evidence. In 1849, for example, the Lees Primitives reported, 'our society is small, composed chiefly of poor operatives, who can with difficulty maintain themselves and their families by hard labour'. The Greenfield Wesleyans in the 1840s were 'poor and humble folk', and in the 1860s the 'Free Methodists' of Oldham had 'not a rich man among them, [being] all poor, hard working, industrious people'.[70]

A shortage of membership lists for local congregations makes information on their gender balance rather sparse. However, the intimate spirituality of Methodist bands and classes and the domestic focus of much Methodist devotional activity may have proved particularly attractive to women—producing an asymmetry even greater than that found among the Dissenters. Certainly, the available evidence from Independent Methodist and New Connexion churches suggests that a situation in which females in membership outnumbered males by two to one was not uncommon.[71] Some information about the age and circumstances of Methodist conversions can be gleaned from an analysis of some 133 obituaries of local Methodists in denominational magazines between 1780 and 1890. Most conversions took place between the ages of 16 and 25, although the New Connexion and Primitive Methodists also recruited fairly strongly among 26–35-year-olds, and there is no evidence of a drift towards a younger age of conversion analagous to that detected by Obelkevich in South Lindsey.[72] Table 5.5 displays information about the circumstances of these conversions. It is not clear how far the seventy-two obituaries which contained conversion narratives constitute a representative sample. Obituaries tend to over-represent members prominent in the life of the churches and may therefore have over-represented those converted early, through the influence of their parents or Sunday schools, and who therefore had longer to become established. Nevertheless, the strongest impression conveyed by the survey is the sheer variety of circumstances under which local Methodists 'found liberty'. Relatively few conversions occurred in the heightened atmosphere of revivals, band meetings, and love feasts. Most occurred in the context of the regular Methodist means of grace, in the family, and—the most numerous category of all—while spending time alone in prayer. The obituaries also indicate the cumulative effect of a whole range of Methodist activities. One Wesleyan, for example, after being 'convicted' by a sermon in the chapel, went first

---

[70] *PMM* 7 (1826), 47; 30 (1849), 439; anon., *Chapel in the Valley*, 5; *UMFCCM* 4 (1861), 58. *IMCM* (1863); anon., *Christian Brethren*, 12.

[71] IMSS, Register; MPL L92, Union Street, Methodist New Connexion, Membership List, 1869; G. Malmgren, 'Domestic Discords: Women and the Family in East Cheshire Methodism, 1750–1830', in Obelkevich, Roper, and Samuel, *Disciplines of Faith*, 55–70.

[72] Obelkevich, *Religion and Rural Society*, 241–2.

TABLE 5.5. *Circumstances of conversion of Methodist members*

Means	Wesleyan Methodist	Primitive Methodist	New Connexion Methodist	Other Methodist	Total
Revival or camp meeting	1	1	3	1	6
Sunday school	2	2	—	1	5
Prayer meeting	2	2	2	2	8
Regular preaching services	1	6	2	—	9
Cottage meeting	1	1	—	—	2
Class meeting	—	4	1	2	7
Band meeting	—	2	1	—	3
Love-feast	—	1	1	1	3
Open-air preaching	—	1	—	—	1
Funeral sermon	—	1	1	—	2
Charity sermon	—	1	—	—	1
Watchnight Service	—	1	—	—	1
Own illness or death of relative	—	2	3	—	5
Parental influence on children	5	1	—	1	7
Children's influence on parents	—	2	—	—	2
Praying or reading alone	2	7	3	1	13

Sources: IMM (1825–65); *PMM* (1820–90); *MNM* (1800–90); *WAM* (1838–57); *UMFCCM* (1858–90); *AM*, 1780–97; *MM*, 1798–21; *WMM* (1828–90).

to a class, then the following week to a band meeting, and finally 'gained liberty' in a prayer meeting after the band. Similarly, a Primitive Methodist who was 'convicted of sin' at a chapel opening in 1827 'a day or two afterwards . . . found peace with God in her own home'. It is easy to forget that even those swept over the threshold of commitment during the course of a revival had a personal history, and one Associationist was converted, aged 61, at a revival meeting after several years' attendance on the means of grace.[73]

[73] *WMM* 70 (1847), 108; *PMM* 32 (1851), 186; *WAM* 19 (1856), 518–19.

Some future members made their first acquaintance with Methodism through their neighbours or workmates, but the process that led towards conversion usually gained its initial impetus from Methodist preaching, Sunday schooling, or parental influence.[74] Another important influence was provided by events which emphasized the insecurity of temporal existence—often personal illness or the illness or death of a relative. James Rhodes of Lydgate, for example, began to attend a New Connexion chapel after the death of his son, and was converted during a morning service while the preacher was giving out a hymn. Some of these events were rather more colourful. Sarah Ashworth of Hollinwood, for example, had joined the Primitives from Sunday school, but had fallen away during a period of doubt; she recovered her faith during a violent thunderstorm and thereafter remained a regular attender on her class. Even more spectacularly, Mark Neild of Oldham was convicted of sin in a minor earthquake that set his house shaking, and thereafter joined an Independent Methodist class of which he subsequently became a prominent member.[75] Clearly, the Methodists of Oldham and Saddleworth could rely on a large variety of means in the mobilization of their wide-ranging constituency.

Chapels and Societies

In 1780 the Methodists of the Oldham circuit owned only two chapels, with seating for at most 1,000 people.[76] By 1851, as indicated in Table 5.6, there had been a massive expansion. Wesleyan accommodation alone had increased to at least thirteen chapels and preaching rooms, with seating for 5,790. The Primitive Methodists could claim at least ten chapels and rooms with over 2,700 seats, and the other Methodist groups combined could muster some fourteen chapels and rooms with 4,178 seats at the lowest estimate. Altogether this represented a greater than twelve-fold increase—approximately twice that achieved by the combined forces of new Dissent over the same period. Methodist chapels contained the usual mixture of free and rented seating. However, the total of appropriated seats significantly exceeded the total of free seats only among the Wesleyans and the Countess of Huntingdon's Connexion. In the New Connexionist chapels the balance was fairly even, the Associationists and

---

[74] *PMM* 15 (1834), 215–18; 36 (1855), 268; *WMM* 70 (1847), 206, 831; 78 (1855), 763–4.

[75] *MNM* 45 (1842), 510–12; *PMM* 22 (1841), 102–4; *IMM* (1847), Memoir; Malmgren, 'Domestic Discords', 62.

[76] McOwan MSS.

TABLE 5.6. *Seating in Methodist chapels 1851*

Denomination	Saddleworth	Oldham above town	Oldham below town	Royton	Crompton	Middleton	Chadderton	Total
Wesleyan chapels	4	2	1	1	1	3	1	13
Free seats	620	170	300	357	284	438	200	2,369
Appropriated seats	1,102	150	1,070	156	202	741	—	3,421
Total seats	1,722	320	1,370	513	486	1,179	200	5,790
% density of seats	9.6	1.2	4.8	6.0	7.6	13.0	2.0	5.4
New Connexion chapels	1	3	1					5
Free seats	140	450	84					674
Appropriated seats	70	260	358					688
Total seats	210	710	442					1,362
% density of seats	1.2	2.6	1.5					1.3
Primitive chapels		3	1		1	2	3	10
Free seats		520	158		250	350	640	1,918
Appropriated seats		203	361			201	28	793
Total seats		723	519		250	551	668	2,711
% density of seats		2.7	1.8		3.9	6.1	6.7	2.5

Independent Methodist chapels								
		2	1					3
Free seats		640	550					1,190
Appropriated seats								
Total seats		640	550					1,190
% density of seats		2.4	1.9					1.1
Associationist chapels								
			2		2	1		5
Free seats			200		387	350		937
Appropriated seats			188		63			251
Total seats			388		450	350		1,188
% density of seats			1.4		7.1	3.9		1.1
Calvinistic Methodist chapels								
						1		1
Free seats						120		120
Appropriated seats						318		318
Total seats						438		438
% density of seats						4.8		0.4
Total Methodist chapels								
	5	10	6	1	4	7	4	37
Free seats	760	1,780	1,292	357	921	1,561	840	7,511
Appropriated seats	1,172	613	1,977	156	265	957	28	5,168
Total seats	1,932	2,393	3,269	513	1,186	2,518	868	12,679
% density of seats	10.7	8.9	11.4	6.0	18.6	27.7	8.7	11.8

Source: PRO HO 129 475, 496.

Primitives were heavily weighted towards free seats, and the Independent Methodists prided themselves on avoiding seat rents altogether. In fact, the most significant difference lay not between, but within, the Methodist denominations. Among the Wesleyans, for example, most of the appropriated seats were concentrated in the older chapels or in prestigious ones with central locations. Elsewhere, the balance was rather more even, and no fewer than five Wesleyan chapels and preaching rooms contained no appropriated seats at all—again reflecting the different character of prestigious and less prestigious societies. Among the Primitives, appropriated outnumbered free seats only in the centrally located Boardman Street building; a similar pattern could also be discerned in New Connexion and Associationist chapels. Table 5.6 certainly underestimates the level of Methodist accommodation. The 1851 census failed to pick up an Independent Methodist room at Greenacres with at least 300 seats, and many more of the small chapels, preaching rooms, and cottages favoured by the Methodists may also have slipped through the census net. Some indication of the scale of this problem is conveyed by the Primitive Methodist preaching plan for 1852. This recorded fourteen places with regular Sunday preaching and another with regular weeknight preaching of which only eight were included in the census and only one had been established since census Sunday 1851. The missing six included a chapel at Waterhead that had been in Primitive Methodist hands since 1847 and was planned for two services every Sunday in 1852.[77] The absence of mid-century plans for the other denominations makes it difficult to estimate the level of omission more widely. However, when at least one in four Independent Methodist and three in seven Primitive Methodist preaching places remained undetected, the 1851 census must be regarded as a very defective instrument for assessing Methodist accommodation in Oldham.

After 1851 there was an expansion of Methodist accommodation at least comparable to that engineered by the new Dissenters. The Independent Methodists opened a new chapel on King Street in 1855. In 1852 the 'Free Methodists' built a chapel for 500 in Middleton, and in 1861 they opened a new town-centre chapel in place of Grosvenor Street, with 560 additional seats. The New Connexionists rebuilt Zion Chapel in 1852–3 with 340 additional seats, enlarged Union Street in 1854, and built a new chapel at Werneth in 1861 to seat at least 650. Similarly, between 1859 and 1865, despite the economic difficulties produced by the cotton famine, the Primitives undertook at least seven major chapel-building or

[77] IMSS MS History; anon., *Primitive Methodist Itinerant and Local Preachers' Plan for the Oldham Circuit* (Oldham, 1852); PRO HO 129 475, 496; PMQ 24 Mar. 1851.

enlargement projects. These included a chapel at Fir Lane in 1865, and the rebuilding of Lees Road chapel in 1863 with about 737 extra seats. The Wesleyans were also heavily engaged in building during this period. In 1855, for example, a school/chapel was built at Hollins and the Wesleyan presence in the district of Oldham above town was greatly strengthened by the construction of a chapel on Greenacres Road with seating for around 1,000. When all the new projects are added in, the Methodist total must have approached at least 20,000 in 1865—a figure not far short of the Anglican total at the same date.[78]

The scale of Methodist church-building projects may, like those of the Dissenters, sometimes have reflected anticipated growth. However, the trigger for new building was almost always increasing pressure on existing accommodation. A meeting of the Oldham Wesleyans in 1862, for example, decided that a new chapel was required because, even with extra services in their schools, the existing accommodation could no longer satisfy the demand for church room.[79] The average cost of such a project in the period 1780–1865 seems to have been approximately £750–£1,000. In the later 1850s and the 1860s there was a trend towards more expensive buildings with the new Primitive Methodist chapel on Lees Road opening in 1865 at a cost of £2,000. Some chapel designs may have become more complex in order to accommodate a wider range of activities, but few Methodist buildings followed the mid-nineteenth-century Dissenting trend towards the adoption of a more elaborate architectural style. In general, the local Methodists remained faithful to the functional approach that had characterized their earliest efforts to construct preaching houses, and even at Lees Road the seats cost only £2 each to provide — a most efficient use of resources when compared to the Congregationalists.[80]

In a few cases, Methodist chapels were financed by a single wealthy subscriber. Thus Daniel Lees of Bankside paid for the first Methodist New Connexion chapel in Oldham, and the Wesleyan chapel opened at Rhodes in 1833 was financed by John Burton, a local millowner.[81] More

[78] Anon., *Independenet Methodism*, 11–12; *WAM* 15 (1852), 245; *UMFCCM* 3 (1860), 258–9; *MNM* 56 (1853), 229–31; 60 (1857), 157–8; 62 (1861), 307–10; S. Richardson, *On Zion's Hill* (Rochdale, 1965), 16–17; *PMM* 44 (1863), 750; WDM 15–18 May 1854, 5–18 May 1855; *Oldham Chronicle*, 24 Apr. 1858.

[79] Ibid. 2 Feb. 1861.

[80] Hudson, 'Delph Methodism', 15; *WAM* 15 (1852), 245; *PMM* 43 (1861), 335–6; 46 (1865), 371–2; 50 (1869), 620–1; anon., 'Wesley Chapel and Schools Greenacres Road Oldham Jubilee History', in *Souvenir of the Grand Springtime Bazaar* (Oldham, 1926), 9; WDM 13–17 May 1861, 2–16 May 1862; *MNM* 64 (1861), 307–10; *Oldham Chronicle*, 20 July 1861.

[81] USMH; *Manchester Chronicle*, 12 Oct. 1833.

usually, however, the whole of the congregation was asked to contribute. At Middleton in 1834, for example, the Primitive Methodists adapted the local working-class institution of wakes savings clubs as a means of raising cash for a new chapel. Some congregations also contributed their own labour, and as late as 1865 the Primitive Methodists of Bowlee dug the foundations and assisted in the construction of their own chapel. The Methodists employed all the usual methods of drawing support from the surrounding neighbourhoods, with canvasses, tea meetings, lectures, recitals, and bazaars. They also matched the new Dissenters in the development of opening services as large-scale public fund-raising events. The Primitive Methodists printed 1,500 hymn papers for one set of opening services in 1860, and the New Connexionists at Zion Chapel garnered over £350 in collections at a series of services that stretched between 20 and 27 February 1853. In the nineteenth century the Methodists seem often to have attracted a good deal of support from the population at large. Canvassers were frequently well received, and the New Connexionists in Werneth noted in 1861 that 'We confidently reckon on the sympathy and support of the surrounding inhabitants, by whom the need of religious ordinances is felt as strongly as is our desire to supply it.'[82]

Although they relied heavily on local subscriptions, the Methodists' success in chapel-building was also underpinned by the provision of additional resources through their Connexional structures. This gave the Methodists a clear advantage over their Dissenting rivals. In 1799 thirteen local Wesleyans toured societies in Yorkshire, Lancashire, and Lincolnshire, collecting for their second chapel, and they succeeded in raising more than £290—almost one-third of the total cost. This sort of support was common and could also be supplemented by more direct donations from Connexional funds like the 'liberal grant' made by the Countess of Huntingdon's Trustees towards the construction of St Stephen's Chapel.[83] Connexional support inevitably entailed a restriction in the freedom of local societies. However, even among the Wesleyans, Connexional control was restricted to authorizing the initiation of new projects and the enforcement of conference rulings about the proportion of the total cost that must be raised before building could begin. Moreover, the Manchester Wesleyan District Meeting minutes are a testament to the ease with

[82] Ibid. 4 Oct. 1834; Walker, *Zion*, 46; J. Verity, *Primitive Methodist Chapel Bowlee Jubilee Souvenir and Historical Sketch* (Middleton, 1914), 11; Butterworth Diary, Jan.–Feb. 1835; *Oldham Standard*, 3 Dec. 1859, 16 Feb., 6 Apr. 1861; PMQ 25 Jan. 1861; *MNM* 56 (1853), 223–31; 64 (1861), 307–10; 67 (1864), 193.

[83] Hudson, 'Delph Methodism', 12; *UMFCCM* 4 (1861), 57–8; anon., *St Stephen's*, 5.

which societies could evade Connexional control. They regularly disregarded the maximum permitted cost and the approved level of debt. Sometimes they simply went ahead with building projects without bothering to consult the authorities at all. In most cases, the District Meeting responded to such open flouting of its authority with a rather ineffectual protest, and ultimately always seems to have provided the necessary support. The contrast with Anglican bureaucratic inflexibility and the precipitate action induced by the more sporadic efforts of Dissent is striking.[84]

Nevertheless, debt remained a ubiquitous feature of Methodist chapel-building. Sometimes the debt formed a high proportion of the total cost, and the Mount Pleasant Wesleyans actually borrowed the entire £800–900 expended on their chapel in 1832. More usually, the debt was around a third of the total—like the £300 borrowed by the promoters of the Delph Wesleyan chapel in 1799 against an expenditure of just over £980. Sometimes the money was borrowed from wealthy members or from well-disposed neighbours, like the interest-free loan of £160 made in 1841 to the Primitive Methodists at Rhodes by a local manufacturer.[85] More usually, however, mortgages were raised on the open market. Debts could hang on for years; the struggling Primitive Methodist Society at Knott Lanes, for example, still owed £130 out of £250 expended on its chapel nine years after its completion and had little hope of future reduction. Debts became the focus of considerable activity as means were sought to reduce and eventually to liquidate them—usually adopting the same methods as were employed to build the chapels in the first place. The Connexions played an important role in supporting 'distressed chapels' from central funds; Royton, for example, received at least four grants from Wesleyan funds between 1825 and 1829. Other grants were made to prime the pump of local efforts, like the £300 offered to Oldham in 1850 by the New Connexion if the society could raise £150 to meet it.[86] Although there is one example of a society over-reaching itself, the position even of the smaller Methodist churches seems to have been rather more secure than that of the new Dissenters. The effort of building, and of reducing debt, did absorb considerable energies, and for the Hollins

[84] WDM 19–23 May 1846, 18–22 May 1851, 20–1 Sept. 1854, 17–20 May 1859, 14–18 May 1860, 12–16 May 1862, 9–13 May 1864.

[85] Anon., 'Wesley Chapel', 9; Hudson, 'Delph Methodism', 13; *WMM* 76 (1853), 79; M. Wrigglesworth (ed.), *There is Holy Ground: A History of Methodism in Middleton 1760–1850* (n. p., 1950), 19.

[86] PP 1842, xvii [382], 854; PMQ 9 Dec. 1833, WLMM 10 Nov. 1863; WDM 21 Sept. 1825, 26–8 May 1829; *MNM* 53 (1850), 89.

Wesleyans the debt was a source of so much anxiety that only when it was cleared could they really settle down to 'spiritual enterprises'.[87] Nevertheless, the greater use of cheap preaching rooms, the relative inexpensiveness of their buildings, and the ease and efficiency with which they disposed central funds all made the Methodists less vulnerable to this problem than either Anglicans or Dissenters.

Chapel Services

The holding of three services each Sunday had already become the norm in the main Wesleyan chapels by 1778–9, with one or two services being held at the smaller places. The Oldham circuit plan for 1825–6 demonstrates that this pattern was maintained into the first half of the nineteenth century. In contrast to the practice of the other denominations, morning services seem to have been the least, and evening services the most common among the Methodists—a pattern which probably reflected the influence on the Methodist devotional tradition of their early practice of refusing to hold services in Church hours. A similar pattern is also discernible in the 1832 Independent Methodist, and the 1835 Associationist plans.[88] However, as direct links with Anglicanism weakened, there was clearly a trend towards the provision either of three services on a Sunday or two services morning and evening, and by the mid-1860s only among the Primitive Methodists did Sunday worship remain overwhelmingly a feature of the second half of the day.[89] The Methodists made much more use of week evening services than any other religious group. The two surviving eighteenth-century Wesleyan plans recorded appointments for their respective travelling preachers on almost every evening of some weeks, and the later plans indicate that in the mid-1860s almost every Methodist preaching place had at least one week evening service. This level of activity required a good deal of commitment from Methodist congregations, and, as a greater proportion of the population became subject to factory discipline in the 1830s, services had to be carefully timed to facilitate attendance. When Hugh Bourne visited the Primitive

---

[87] Hudson, 'Delph Methodism', 15; N., 'Methodism at Hollins'; Brown, *Nonconformist Ministry*, 142.

[88] MARC MS Circuit Plans of J. Farrar and J. Bunting; anon., *Oldham Wesleyan Methodist Circuit Plan* (1825); 'Oldham Independent Methodist Cricuit Plan' (1832), in Mountfield, *Short History*, 95; *The Preachers' Plan Lord St. Oldham* (1835).

[89] PRO HO 129 475, 496; anon., *Oldham Wesleyan Methodist Circuit Plan* (1865); anon., *Saddleworth Mesleyan Methodist Circuit Plan* (1864); *Oldham Almanack* (1865); Obelkevich, *Religion and Rural Society*, 225.

Methodists at Cowlishaw in 1833 he noted: 'The preaching this evening did not begin till after 8 o'clock; the people work so late in the factories.'[90]

The regular round of Sunday and weeknight worship was supplemented by a series of special services. Some, like the chapel anniversary services, could become important communal occasions: the first anniversary sermons of the Werneth New Connexion chapel had to be preached in the open air because the building could not contain the congregation.[91] Other special services were innovative products of the revival, especially watchnights—particularly popular among the Primitives—and missionary meetings. Most local Methodist groups formed missionary auxiliaries from the early nineteenth century onwards, and the ubiquity of such organizations, even among the aggressively evangelistic Primitive Methodists, tells against the suggestion that they served as a diversion from the potentially revolutionary mission to evangelize the nation. However, they were certainly popular, and the annual missionary sermons frequently attracted considerable support from the community at large.[92] A third class of special services was specifically limited to the congregation or the membership. This included the annual covenant service—probably the nearest point of contact between Methodism and the gathered tradition of old Dissent—and also the celebration of occasional fast days. When to all these meetings are added the annual renewal of tickets and various special sermons and collections, a distinctively Methodist or at least evangelical calendar of 'sacred time' emerges. Nevertheless, Obelkevich's judgement, that the 'calendar was in some respects more Methodist than Christian',[93] seems rather extreme, and the new Methodist occasions were counterbalanced by the increase in the regular performance of Holy Communion, encouraged by the evangelical revival.

In the early nineteenth century Wesleyan members, like those of Anglican and Dissenting churches, were in theory encouraged to take communion on a monthly basis, but the Wesleyan plans of the 1820s record sacrament services in the main chapels only every two months on average. The smaller chapels had only quarterly celebrations, and they were absent altogether from the smallest chapels and rooms—probably because

[90] *PMM* 14 (1833), 146.

[91] G. H. Christie, 'Werneth Church Oldham', *The Methodist Evangelist*, 1 Jan. 1898. The adoption of Methodist anniversaries as communal festivals was paralleled in the industrial villages of Craven: Rycroft, 'Craven', 269–70.

[92] *Manchester Mercury*, 13 June 1815; USMH; B. Semmel, *The Methodist Revolution* (1974), 146–69; Butterworth Diary, 25 Apr. 1831, Apr.–June 1832; USLMM, 11 Mar. 1856.

[93] Obelkevich, *Religion and Rural Society*, 230.

celebration was the preserve of the Itinerant preachers. The plans of the mid-1860s reflect an unchanged picture, with the exception of the introduction of monthly celebrations in the main chapels in Oldham. Celebration once every two months was still common among the Wesleyan Associationists and the Independent Methodists in the 1860s. The Primitives, on the other hand, had already moved to monthly celebrations in their main chapel by 1838.[94] The democratization of spirituality produced by the revival penetrated among the Methodists even to the level of sacramental practice. Although the administration of communion was limited to travelling preachers and participation to members, the large-scale revival of the primitive Christian agape provided a more open sacramental alternative. The love-feast, describe by John Walsh as 'a domesticated, democratized folk-Eucharist', was very popular among the Methodists, and before the middle of the century was celebrated in more places than communion—probably a consequence of the freedom extended to local preachers to preside at love-feasts.[95] By minimizing the dangerous mystery of the Eucharist (emphasizing instead the experience of corporate celebration) and by presenting something new to which no traditional cautions attached, the Methodists side-stepped many popular reservations about participation. Love-feasts could be enormously powerful occasions, witnessing to the communal dimension of evangelical spirituality and manifesting the spirit of revival. Sometimes love-feasts were opened to the general public as the sequel to camp meetings. There are several reports of chapels being 'crowded to excess' for these events, which could be powerfully charged, as the Associationists reported in 1854:

In the evening we held a general love feast. The time was taken up, by mutual and sound Christian experience . . . and the unction of the Holy Ghost richly descended upon the people, 'our upper room' . . . was filled from end to end . . . the people . . . sung in the spirit and prayed in the exercise of mighty faith; and verily God, even our own God, was in the midst of us. Poor trembling sinners were

[94] N. P. Goldhawk, 'The Methodist People in the Early Victorian Age: Spirituality and Worship', in Davies, George, and Rupp (eds.) *Methodist Church*, ii. 134–8; anon., *Oldham Wesleyan Methodist Circuit Plan* (Lees, 1819), (1825), (1865); anon., *Saddleworth Wesleyan Methodist Circuit Plan* (1864); anon., *Oldham United Methodist Free Church Circuit Plan* (Oldham, 1868); anon., *George Street Independent Methodist Circuit Plan* (Oldham, 1861); PMQ 5 Mar., 3 Dec. 1838. This represents a much more frequent pattern of administration than in South Lindsey: Obelkevich, *South Lindsey*, 228.

[95] J. D. Walsh, 'Religious Societies: Methodist and Evangelical 1738–1800', *Studies in Church History*, 23 (1986), 288; anon., *Oldham Wesleyan Methodist Circuit Plan* (1825); anon., *Oldham Wesleyan Methodist Association Circuit Plan* (Oldham, 1835); anon., *Oldham IM Circuit Plan* (1832); anon., *Oldham Primitive Methodist Circuit Plan* (1852).

converted, backsliders were restored, and the saints of the Most High shouted aloud for joy.[96]

There is little evidence concerning liturgical practice, but most local Methodists probably used abridgements of the Anglican liturgy and extempore prayer in addition to the usual elements of music and preaching. It appears that, as was the case with their sacramental practice, the generality of Methodist services was characterized by an unusually high level of popular participation.[97] Enthusiastic congregational singing was one of the keynotes of Methodism, and, though its general musical quality may not have been very high, the singing was certainly popular. Thus, at the small Wesleyan cause at Glodwick in the 1860s, 'The singing . . . was with the spirit, but not always with the understanding, and, though not art music, it was, with many the music of the heart.' The prevalence of barely literate congregations prolonged the use of 'lining out', which was still in regular use among the Wesleyans at Hollins in the 1850s. One might expect this practice to have faded out gradually, under the influence of musical training and the development of literacy in the Sunday schools. However, among the Primitive Methodists, at least, it long persisted. At Boardman Street Chapel in 1863, for example, it was ruled that all hymns were to be given out two lines at a time except for the second hymn, which might be sung right through. The antiphonal effect produced by lining out must have played an important part in drawing attention away from the music and towards the words of Methodist hymns. The famous 'sung creeds of Methodism' were at the same time spoken catechisms, if not liturgies.[98]

Local Methodists, however, were not without provision for 'art music', and none of the local churches seems to have had any difficulty in raising a good choir. By the mid-nineteenth century, a little later than their Anglican and Dissenting counterparts, Methodist choirs had introduced anthems and psalm-chanting, and were performing oratorios and holding special musical services. Some of these were a great draw and, even in the case of the small Wesleyan cause at Bowlee, 'crowds from great distances

[96] *Oldham Chronicle*, 12 June 1858; *Oldham Standard*, 20 July 1861; *WAM* (1854), 456; D. Hempton, 'Methodism in Irish Society 1770–1830', *Transactions of the Royal Historical Society*, 5th ser. 36 (1986), 121.

[97] Goldhawk, 'Spirituality and Worship', 123–34.

[98] Whitehead, 'Methodism in Glodwick', 37; anon., *Centenary History of Smith Street Sunday School* (Oldham, 1937), 9; N., 'Methodism at Hollins'; PMQ 14 Sept. 1863; Walsh, 'Religious Societies', 289.

flocked' to hear the annual 'sing'.[99] As choirs became more prominent, the potential for conflict between the singers and other participants in the services increased. At the Wesleyan chapel in Rhodes, 'The choir was the most important feature of the church life in the years 1850–54. Trouble started when on one occasion "an elegant programme was cut" by the minister and the choir walked out in protest.' In response to these tensions some societies introduced specially appointed committees to supervise the singing in their chapels, like the one established at the New Connexional chapel in Union Street after a virtual mutiny among the choir.[100] Although singing was unaccompanied in the small Wesleyan chapel at Uppermill as late as 1864, most chapels provided musical accompaniment in the form of instrumental bands. Some bands were very small. At Hollins Wesleyan in the 1840s music was provided by two violins, reinforced, for anniversary services, by a large bass fiddle brought specially from Middleton. Others amounted to small orchestras, with as many as eleven violins accompanying singing for the New Connexionist meeting in Alt School in the 1830s, while for anniversaries in the 1840s the Greenfield Wesleyans mustered a band of bass fiddle, cello, violin, fiddle, flute, and accordion.[101] An organ was introduced into the Countess of Huntingdon's chapel in 1824, and in 1837 a 'small organ' was introduced by a local Wesleyan Society without requesting the permission of the District meeting according to conference rule. In the 1840s organs or harmoniums became much more widespread in chapels of most Methodist denominations. The Zion New Connexionists acquired an organ in 1844, followed by their sister church on Union Street in 1847. In the same year an organ was opened in the Grosvenor Street Primitive Methodist chapel and the George Street Independent Methodists acquired a harmonium around 1850. In the 1850s and 1860s organs and harmoniums became standard equipment even in small Methodist chapels and, as in Anglican and Dissenting churches, the innovation appears to have been well received. The Union Street New Connexionists, for example, believed their organ would prove 'a useful auxiliary to congregational singing', and even the

[99] Verity, *Bowlee Souvenir*, 12; *UMFCCM* i (1858), 618; anon., *Primitive Methodist Sunday School Anniversary Service Sheet* (29 Sept. 1844); USLMM 17 Sept. 1861; IMGS, MS History; Wrigglesworth (ed.), *Holy Ground*, 22–3.

[100] Ibid. 19; USLMM, 19 Sept. 1865.

[101] anon., *Wrigley Mill Wesleyan Chapel and Sunday School History and Jubilee Souvenir* (Uppermill, 1914), 7; IMGS, Account Book, 1827–60; anon., 'St John's'; N., 'Methodism at Hollins'; Walker, *Zion*, 64; anon., *Chapel in the Valley*, 15.

poorer members subscribed towards its introduction.[102] In Methodist churches as elsewhere organs did not entirely displace the old instrumental bands. The New Connexionist meetings in Alt School were accompanied by both harmonium and strings—the same combination persisted among the George Street Independent Methodists at least until 1860, and was still being employed by the Cowhill Wesleyans in 1868.[103]

It was in the other major feature of chapel services—the sermon—that Methodist practice most differed from that in other local churches. Just as in Anglican and Dissenting churches, some sermons were adapted to particular audiences, like the special quarterly sermon to the young established by the Primitive Methodists in 1841, and the Methodists also invited a similar range of special preachers.[104] Nevertheless, the regular round of Methodist preaching was distinctive in that most of it was undertaken by laymen. An average Sunday in 1825, for example, saw eight sermons in four places by the three Oldham Wesleyan Itinerant ministers and twenty-two sermons in seventeen places by seventeen of the thirty local preachers in the circuit. With the exception of the Countess of Huntingdon's Society, which operated like a Dissenting cause with a resident pastor, and the Independent and early Association Methodists, who employed no Itinerants, this pattern was repeated in all the Methodist denominations.[105] The majority of local preachers, like their congregations, probably came from working-class occupational groups, but clear occupational data are available on only four nineteenth-century local preachers—two weavers, a miner, and a plasterer's labourer—and it would be unwise to draw firm conclusions from such inadequate data.[106] In most Methodist denominations men monopolized the preaching ministry, but among the Primitives a small group of female preachers persisted throughout the period, some of whom were very well received by their hearers.[107]

[102] Anon., *St Stephen's*, 5; WDM 22–4 May 1837, 18–22 May 1858, 14–18 May 1860, 12–16 May 1862; Walker, *Zion*, 75; *MNM* 1 (1847), 236; *Manchester Guardian*, 5 May 1847; IMGS, MS History; Irk Street Leaders' Meeting Minutes, 21 Mar. 1865; *IMCM* (1862).

[103] Walker, *Zion*, 64; IMGS, Account Book, 1827–60; Fletcher, *Cowhill School*, 13.

[104] PMQ 27 Sept. 1841; *Primitive Methodist Magazine* (*PMM*), 14 (1833), 146; Butterworth Diary, May–June 1842.

[105] Anon., *Oldham Wesleyan Methodist Circuit Plan* (1825–6); anon., *St Stephen's*, 4; anon., *Oldham Wesleyan Methodist Association Circuit Plan* (1835); anon., *Oldham Independent Methodist Circuit Plan* (1832); anon., *Ashton Methodist New Connexion Circuit Plan* (Ashton-under-Lyne, 1832).

[106] *Oldham Standard*, 27 Oct. 1860; anon., *Christian Brethren*, 8–15; Walker, *Zion*, 129; PMQ 2 Jan. 1847.

[107] PMQ 12 Mar. 1832, 22 Sept. 1845, 22 June 1857.

Whether preached by 'professional' or 'amateur' ministers, Methodist sermons were probably shorter on average than others in the locality. This was especially the case among the Primitives, who limited their local preachers to a maximum of half an hour.[108] The theology of Methodist sermons also differed from that of most of those preached by Anglicans and Dissenters because of their espousal of Evangelical Arminianism and the characteristic Methodist optimism about the possibility of achieving, by the grace of God, the charisma of 'entire sanctification'. The approved Methodist sermon was simple, enthusiastic, anecdotal, and expressed in plain language. Thus the biographer of Philip Garratt, the Wesleyan minister in 1811 and 1812, claimed that 'His style was easy, natural and impressive; remarkable for freshness, raciness and originality. His sermons were expository and practical; rich in evangelical truth, and replete with faithful and sometime pungent application. He spoke from the heart to the heart.' Similarly, Wright Burton, the Barkerite Independent Methodist, preached sermons notable for 'sterling honesty and genuine simplicity'.[109] Ostentatious displays of learning, like those which characterized some of the earlier Dissenting sermons, were discouraged by the Methodists, and their ministers were probably less scholarly than their university- or academy-trained rivals. The 'men in a hurry' of the revival were more likely to be Methodists than Dissenters. However, learning was not despised, especially when it was clearly linked to effective ministry, and the theological studies of some preachers did stretch beyond standard works of Methodist divinity, like Wesley's notes and sermons. Extensive reading was not the preserve of the paid ministry, and of one local preacher, William Drummond, it was reported that, 'altho' a working man, with a large family dependent on him', he spent £16 on Adam Clarke's commentary on the Bible. His sermons nevertheless seem to have been in traditional Methodist, existentialist style: 'As a preacher he was what is called a "weeping prophet", tender, winning and successful. He scarcely ever preached without shedding tears; and frequently the congregations were similarly affected'—a style and reaction common even among Wesleyans, at least until the middle of the nineteenth century.[110]

The Methodist structure of ministry introduced several problems into

[108] PMQ 11 Mar. 1833.

[109] MARC PLP 43.32.5, Obituary of Philip Garratt; WDM 18–22 May 1858; anon., *Christian Brethren*, 12.

[110] PMQ 10 Mar. 1834; *MNCM* (1845),. 39; *PMCM* (1855), 33; MARC PLP 42.24.7, W. France to Thomas Jackson, 17 Nov. 1816; *WAM* 16 (1853), 485–7; Obelkevich, *Religion and Rural Society*, 187–92.

local societies. The relatively short period of time for which ministers were stationed in Oldham and Saddleworth limited their knowledge of, and sensitivity to, local conditions—a particular problem in a large circuit, with many scattered societies. It was compounded, especially among the Wesleyans, by the development of the doctrine of the pastoral office, which created a widening gap between the supervisory functions the ministers were required to perform, and the knowledge and the quality of relationships required to perform them effectively.[111] This gap probably made a significant contribution to the various divisions among the Wesleyans, and the Primitive Methodist ruling in 1832, 'that the term Mr be used at Oldham and not Reverend', seems calculated to minimize this problem in their denomination. However, difficulties with ministers were not limited to the Wesleyans, and the Primitives twice, in 1855 and 1865, successfully petitioned against the stationing of ministers they found unacceptable.[112] A number of Itinerants complained about various strains imposed by their job on their health and their family relationships. The Wesleyan William France felt both that his circuit was too large and that he was bearing an unacceptable burden because his colleague was not pulling his weight, and one Associationist minister resigned in 1854, because of his wife's ill-health. There were also problems with lay preaching —sermons were not always of the highest quality, appointments were not always kept, and the strong local loyalties it generated increased the fissile quality of Wesleyanism. However, the Connexional structure had its compensations: periodic restationing, while it certainly disrupted ministerial family life, must have helped to relieve accumulated tension, and the important role played by local preachers and class leaders also spread the ministerial load over many more shoulders. Many local preachers worked extremely hard, and one Oldham Wesleyan, for example, walked 6,500 miles and gave at least 1,600 sermons in a twenty-four-year preaching career, in addition to pursuing his occupation as a coal-miner.[113]

The historiographical concentration on conflicts within Methodism makes it easy to exaggerate the unpopularity of the professional ministry. As Philip Rycroft has pointed out, most Methodists met their ministers as preachers rather than as disciplinarians, and the first Wesleyan minister

---

[111] Ward, *Religion and Society*, 103–4, 142–65; Brown, *Nonconformist Ministry*, 143–5.
[112] PMQ 12 Mar. 1832; MARC, Primitive Methodist MS Conference Journals (1855), 256 (1865), 274.
[113] MARC, W. France to T. Jackson, 24 June 1815, 17 Nov. 1816; *WACM* (1854), 9; PMQ 10 Sept. 1832, 9 Apr. 1834; USLMM 6 Dec. 1859; *Oldham Standard*, 27 Oct. 1860. See also Brown, *Nonconformist Ministry*, 138–85.

in the Saddleworth circuit, for example, was extremely well received. Mr Wolfenden, the Associationist minister, was presented with a gold watch chain in 1857 in appreciation of his three-year ministry, and so popular was William Antliff, perhaps the most successful of all the local Primitive Methodist ministers, that he was pressed in 1861 to stay an extra year, thus extending his term of service to five years.[114] Nevertheless, Methodist Itinerants were on average the worst-paid professional ministers in the locality. In the 1820s the Countess of Huntingdon's minister in Middleton received a stipend of £60 per annum, a sum comparable to the ministers of smaller Dissenting churches. Single Primitive Methodist preachers, on the other hand, received only £16 a year. Wesleyan ministers were the best paid among the Methodists, and the Saddleworth circuit minister received a stipened of £120 in the mid-1860s, while his Primitive Methodist colleague in Oldham received less than £60. However, not even the Wesleyan ministers could boast a stipend comparable to the earnings of their middle-class members, and the Primitives would have earned rather less than the skilled factory workers in their congregations. Certainly it would have been difficult for most Methodists to feel alienated by the economic preferment of their ministers, even if their financial demands did increase during the period.[115]

Although average chapel running costs were similar to those of other nonconformists, most Methodist churches bore greater financial burdens because they supported elaborate circuit and connexional structures. The regular source of circuit income was the weekly contribution of its members meeting in class. It was thus extremely vulnerable to the effects of economic depression, and 'circuit debts' soon developed when trade stagnated.[116] The main source of chapel income was the renting of its pews. Methodist rents tended to be slightly lower than those in Dissenting chapels, and in 1834, for example, the Primitives set the rent for the seats in their main chapel in Oldham at $7\frac{1}{2}d.$ per quarter, while in the Wesleyan chapel at Uppermill rents varied between 10*d.* and 1*s.* 3*d.* a quarter in 1841. Rents at this level are unlikely to have deterred the skilled workers, or even the generality of Methodist attendants, from taking a seat in a

---

[114] Hudson, 'Delph Methodism', 17; *WAM* 20 (1857), 494; PMQ 29 Mar. 1861; *PMCM* (1857–61); Rycroft, 'Craven', 254.

[115] Anon., *St Stephen's*, 4; *PMCM* (1822), 10; MPL L93/1, Box 1, Saddleworth Wesleyan Methodist Quarterly Meeting Minutes, 26 Dec. 1865; MPL L26, Add'n 5, Box 1, Oldham Primitive Methodist Second Circuit, Quarterly Meeting Minutes, 13 Sept. 1862; Rycroft, 'Craven', 245.

[116] MPL L26, Add'n 15, Union Street, Methodist New Connexion Trust Treasurer's Accounts, 1840–52; IMGS, Accounts, 1825–65; PMQ 12 Sept. 1834.

chapel. Both chapel trust and circuit incomes were augmented by a variety of special collections, levies, donations, and sales. However, the most important additional support came from connexional funds. The Delph Wesleyan circuit, for example, received grants from the district, varying between £20 and £40 almost every year between 1828 and 1865. Few circuits received support on so regular a basis, but the knowledge that local societies did not stand alone must have done much to reduce anxiety.[117]

The Life of the Society

The Methodists betrayed their origins as religious societies in the emphasis they placed on devotional meetings. The lively communal atmosphere of the band meeting was an important feature of early nineteenth-century Wesleyanism, and it persisted, at least in the society at Cowhill, until after the middle of the century. A band meeting was among the first institutions to be established by the New Connexion society at Werneth in 1862. However, it was the Primitive Methodists who seem to have made the most use of bands. Their meetings varied in size, from the small ones held in private houses around the chapel at Mount Pleasant in the 1840s, to the much larger ones that almost filled the chapel in Oldham during the 1830s.[118] The most basic meetings for Methodist members, however, were those held weekly in class for mutual support, the sharing of experience, and spiritual direction. The long-term decline in the vitality of the class meeting remarked on by Methodist historians was not evident in Oldham and Saddleworth before 1865. Obituaries suggest that participants found them a valuable and in some cases a formative experience. There is no evidence that, even among the Wesleyans, classes had become 'boring and unhelpful', and some class leaders, like the 'Free Methodist' William Holt, who made great use of his 'good knowledge of Scripture and sacred song' and 'quaint and witty sayings', became particularly popular.[119] However, after 1810, larger meetings for the whole society gained in favour, especially among the non-Wesleyan denominations.

---

[117] MPL L26, Box 1, Irk Street, Middleton, Primitive Methodist Finance Committee Minutes, 1 Dec. 1865; MPL L93/3/1–5, Uppermill, Wesleyan Methodist Seat Rent Books, 1841–7; anon., *Oldham Wesleyan Methodist Circuit Plan* (1865); PMQ 4 Dec. 1837; anon., 'Wesley Chapel'; *MNM* 67 (1864), 193; WDM 1828–65.

[118] Fletcher, *Cowhill School*, 9; WLMM 4 Feb. 1862; PMQ 28 Jan. 1848; *PMM* 11 (1830), 189–90.

[119] Goldhawk, 'Spirituality and Worship', 141; *WMM* 70 (1847), 108, 743–4; 89 (1866), 192; *WAM* 10 (1847), 558–9; 13 (1850), 550–1; Obelkevich, *South Lindsey*, 192; *UMFCCM* 21 (1878); *PMM* 18 (1837), 372–3.

Initially they followed the Wesleyan pattern of quarterly or monthly meetings limited to members, but by the 1850s some churches had established
meetings on a weekly basis, competing with the class as the major devotional
focus of the society. By the mid-1860s the Primitives were even inviting
adherents to join with members at some meetings—a development parallel
to the dilution of church meetings among the Dissenters during the same
period.[120]

The Methodists were also enthusiastic exponents of prayer meetings.
Like the Dissenters, most Methodist churches ran a centrally located
prayer meeting based in the chapel or preaching room, sometimes on a
Sunday but more frequently on weeknights. Many more were held in the
cottages of members and sympathizers scattered in residential communities all over the area, and often supported by specially mobilized praying
companies or prayer leaders. The pastoral and devotional enthusiasms
of the revival thus broke out of the chapels and also burst the bonds of
Methodist societal discipline in what was probably the most determined
attempt to sacralize the locations of everyday life that the area had ever
seen. Sometimes these meetings penetrated or even took over traditional
local gatherings for social intercourse. Giles Bradbury, for example, a
New Connexionist Prayer Leader in Uppermill during the 1820s, persuaded a neighbour, whose house was a regular meeting place for the
local youth, to allow him to hold a prayer meeting, and the house soon
became the regular location of a crowded weekly meeting. These meetings provided the context for the development of ministries as powerful
on a small scale as those of the most popular preachers. Thus, of James
Wild, a Primitive Methodist, it was recalled that 'His tact in conducting
a prayer meeting, and his fervour and power in prayer were extraordinary. "He was decidedly", says one of our travelling preachers . . . "the
most powerful man in prayer that I ever knew except Father Clowes"
. . . [he was] changed from Glory into Glory in prayer.'[121]

The Methodists developed much the same range of social events as the
other local churches. There were the same annual tea parties and recitals,
like the 500–strong Christmas tea party at Union Street New Connexion
chapel in 1863, open free to the poorer members. There was also the

---

[120] PMQ 7 June 1835; Goldhawk, 'Spirituality and Worship', 141; anon., 'St John's';
USLMM 2 Mar. 1852; MPL L26, Add'n 5, Box 1, Oldham Primitive Methodist Second
Circuit, Quarterly Meeting Minutes, 4 Sept. 1863.

[121] PMQ 9 Sept. 1833; WLMM 7 July 1863; G. E. Butterworth, *Greenfield Methodist
Church Jubilee Souvenir* (Manchester, 1932), 4; PMQ 19 Mar. 1849; *IMM* (1826), Memoir;
USLMM 18 Mar. 1856; *PMM* 17 (1836), 349–50; 26 (1845), 515–18; *MNM* 63 (1860),
515–18.

usual range of lectures and debates on diverse subjects, which attracted audiences both from within the churches and from the population at large. The Wesleyan schoolrooms on St Domingo Street in Oldham and at Delph in Saddleworth also seem to have been the most popular venues for public gatherings in their respective areas—both being let for a vast range of functions.[122] The Methodists were particularly enthusiastic about 'temperance'. Its advocates had a stronghold in the Saddleworth Wesleyan circuit from 1834 onwards, and both the Associationists and New Connexionists supported various temperance functions in the 1840s. However, temperance was both most prominent and most controversial among the Primitive and Independent Methodists. The first significant temperance meeting in the area was held in the Independent Methodist chapel on George Street in 1833; in 1835 a very large meeting was held in the Primitive Methodist chapel on Boardman Street, and thereafter the involvement of the two denominations remained both heavy and prominent. Perhaps the more overwhelmingly proletarian their constituency, the more the Methodists felt the need to distance themselves from the alternative proletarian culture based on the beerhouse and the hush shop. This stance produced serious tensions within churches, and in 1849 the Primitives, worried about a potential loss of balance, ruled 'That our preachers preach the Gospel and not Total Abstinence'. Its disruptive power within Independent Methodism was even greater, leading to the division of 1854.[123]

The visitation of the sick, and the general charitable work carried out by members of Methodist societies, had a significant impact on the surrounding communities. One Wesleyan, Ben Brierley of Shaw, for example, 'spent much time in visiting the sick, not only those of his own church, but others. By the residents in that district he was looked upon as a saintly character, and his prayers were often sought for the afflicted.'[124] Support for more public charity was expressed in two ways: the preaching of charity sermons in aid of public causes and, in co-operation with

---

[122] *Manchester Guardian*, 13 Apr. 1844; IMSS, Elders' Committee Minute Book, 27 Feb. 1864; *WAM* 79 (1856), 198; USLMM 6 Oct. 1857, 1, 21 Dec. 1863; Butterworth Diary, 13 July 1829, Feb.–Mar. 1839; *Manchester Courier*, 8 Aug. 1829–27 Mar. 1837; MPL L93/2, Box 10, Delph Wesleyan Methodist Sunday School Accounts, 1860–3.

[123] Saddleworth Wesleyan Methodist Quarterly Meeting Minutes, 26 Mar. 1834; *Manchester Guardian*, 7 Mar. 1835, 15 Oct. 1845; Butterworth Diary, 6 Feb. 1833, May–July 1841; *Oldham Standard*, 17 Sept. 1859; PMQ 19 Mar. 1849, 19 Sept. 1853, 15 Sept. 1862; Koditschek, *Class Formation*, 301–7.

[124] U. Sellers, *A Short History of the Wesleyan Sunday School, Shaw* (Shaw, 1911), 13; *PMM* 43 (1862), 592.

Anglicans and Dissenters, the direct organization of large-scale relief, especially during the cotton famine of the early 1860s.[125] Most of the churches' charitable resources, however, went towards trying to relieve the poverty of their own congregations, which, in normal times, meant the donation of sacrament, or love-feast collections to poor members, augmented by occasional gifts in money or in kind. Methodist churches also developed institutions to provide against the main causes of secondary poverty—sickness and death—and in 1837 the Primitive Methodists even provided work cleaning the chapel for members who were unemployed.[126] The cotton famine highlighted the phenomenon of mutual support within the societies, and the Wesleyans of the Manchester District felt that the relief effort had promoted 'a deep sympathy between all classes, and especially between the richer and poorer members of Christ's flock'. Similarly, according to the historian of the Primitive Methodists at Waterhead, such was the degree of mutual aid in the society that it 'even approached that earlier day when "they had all things in common". The church funds did not suffer, in some departments they actually increased.' John Wesley would, no doubt, have been delighted.[127]

Methodist societies and congregations, like those of the Dissenters, were tied together by regular pastoral visitation. However, the Methodists seem to have been more successful than other churches in mobilizing the membership of their societies to assist their preachers in this vital task. In 1843 the Wesleyan Association conference stressed that visiting should be undertaken by both preachers and members, and the New Connexion followed suit in 1844. Among Independent and Wesleyan Methodists, too, large numbers of members were active in this work, but it was probably among the Primitive Methodists, with their stress on 'conversation ministry', that it was given most emphasis. In 1847 the Oldham circuit ruled that their preachers should visit non-society members most frequently, thus placing the emphasis in pastoral oversight on those outside the mutual supervision of the class. Two years later they adopted the 'class visiting system'. This involved nominating two or three members of each class to follow up absentees and perhaps to support the

---

[125] *Manchester Mercury*, 27 Mar, 24 Apr. 1792; *Oldham Chronicle*, 16 Aug. 1862; *UMFCCM* (1862), 71–2.

[126] PMQ 10 Dec. 1832, 5 June 1837; USLMM 17 Nov. 1857, 28 Feb. 1860; Hudson, 'Delph Methodism', 13; IMGS, Sick Club Accounts, 1825–47; Union Street, Methodist New Connexion Trust Treasurer's Accounts, 1847; Fletcher, *Cowhill School*, 9.

[127] WDM 11–15 May 1863; W. Upright, *The Story of Primitive Methodism in Washbrook* (Oldham, 1916), 2; Walsh, 'Methodism and the Common People', 358.

preachers in visiting more widely.[128] Some pastoral visiting was directly associated with the exercise of church discipline. Local Methodist churches imposed sanctions against a wide variety of misbehaviour and though, among the Primitive Methodists, whose discipline records are the most complete, the most usual misdemeanours were linked to alcohol or sexual relationships, members could also be disciplined for disturbing the fellow-ship by 'lying and backbiting' and commercial sharp practice like selling short-weight. The sanctions employed also varied, from arbitration between aggrieved parties to official admonishment or reprimand from the circuit authorities and, in the most serious cases, the ultimate sanction of expulsion —it was presumably this that lay behind the otherwise rather extreme verdict of the Irk Street leaders in 1847, that four persons were 'to be dismembered'![129] Pastoral discipline was seen as vital to the good health of the societies. Methodism had never been dominated by an obsession with numerical growth, but had sought to strike a balance between an emphasis on the universal availability of salvation and the need to produce Christian perfection. Methodism sought not simply the greatest number of adherents, but the greatest holiness of the greatest number. As John Walsh has put it, 'If the societies recruited they also expelled . . . Wesley's societies were not intended as modern free-expression psychotherapy groups but as disciplined pilgrim companies pressing along a strenuous path to perfection.'[130]

There may have been a tendency for local Methodist decision-making bodies to be dominated by middle-class members, or at least those from the upper reaches of the working class, with more education and greater leisure time. However, the whole Methodist system would have ground to a halt without the mobilization of the time and talents of a great swathe of the membership. There was simply too much to do, too many posi-tions of activity and responsibility to fill, to permit any other course. This mobilization of the laity was a corollary of Methodist spirituality, and in particular of the Arminian stress on man's responsibility to co-operate with divine grace. The Methodist was on a spiritual pilgrimage with clearly defined landmarks from conviction of sin to conversion, and, through growth in grace, to 'entire sanctification' or at least a holy or

---

[128] *WACM* (1843), 187; *MNCM* (1844), 71; *IMM* (1847), Memoir; anon., *Wrigley Mill*, 6; MPL L26/3/3/1, Oldham Primitive Methodist Circuit Committee Minutes, 18 June 1847; PMQ 19 Mar., 31 Aug., 1849.

[129] PMQ 10 June 1833, 22 June 1846; MPL L26/3/3/1, Oldham Primitive Methodist Leaders' Meeting Minutes, 30 Sept. 1842, 6 Jan. 1843; USLMM 11 Feb. 1862; Irk St Leaders' Meeting Minutes, 23 June 1850.

[130] Walsh, 'Religious Societies', 290.

'triumphant' death.[131] This upward movement depended not only on regular attendance on the public 'means of grace' but also on a lively personal devotional life. Such devotions were frequently noticed in obituaries. The *Wesleyan Methodist Magazine* noted that Ellen Burton 'delighted in private prayer', and of William Whitehead that 'in the secret exercises of devotion he especially delighted'. This devotion was fed by the Bible and the Methodist hymn book. Thus, James Firth of Shaw was notable for 'love for his Bible': he had learnt much of it by heart and this 'enriched his prayers and addresses'. Hannah Brooks, a New Connexionist servant girl, learnt to read so that she could study the Bible, and Edward Mills, a Primitive Methodist nightwatchman, died quietly while reading his Bible at work.[132] Hannah Dyson of the Wesleyan Association knew many of the Wesleyan hymns by heart, and the strength gained from private worship was a resource available to Methodists even when they could no longer enjoy communal worship in the chapel. According to the obituary of Anne Nutter, for example, 'When from feebleness of age she was prevented from attending the public means of grace, the Bible (especially the psalms) and the Wesleyan hymn-book were her constant companions.' This sort of private devotion made the Methodist pilgrimage literally a daily walk with God and its individual focus was balanced by its extension into family worship.[133]

If much Methodist spirituality was expressed quietly in private, much was also expressed in public and sometimes with considerable exuberance. At a New Connexion love-feast in the early 1820s, 'partaking much of the spirit of primitive Christianity, the worshippers assembled together in one room with one accord, expressed their overflowing joy by stamping with their feet etc.', and were subsequently expelled by the owners of their room on the ground that they made too much noise. It was perhaps among the Primitive Methodists, however, that Methodist worship appeared at its most exuberant. For example, rhythmic jumping during worship as an expression of religious excitement was a feature of Primitive Methodist worship at least during the Connexion's first twenty years in Oldham. One eyewitness to a love-feast in December 1829 reported: 'We had not long been in the chapel when the jumping began. It soon

---

[131] Walsh, 'Methodism in the Later Eighteenth Century', 312–14; *WMM* 64 (1841), 236; 66 (1843), 418; *MNM* 49 (1846), 516; 72 (1869), 629–30; *WAM* 10 (1847), 558–9; *PMM* 26 (1845), 360; 36 (1855), 268; Bebbington, *Evangelicalism*, 74.

[132] *WMM* 63 (1840), 52; 78 (1855), 763–4; 83 (1860), 92; *MNM* 55 (1852), 442–6; *PMM* 51 (1870), 689.

[133] *WMM* 66 (1843), 245; 89 (1866), 192; *WAM* 17 (1854), 493–4; Obelkevich, *Religion and Rural Society*, 232–6; *MNM* 27 (1824), 253–5.

spread and became general all over the chapel'; nor was this activity the prerogative of recent converts or adherents, but was 'confined to the best and most devoted members of the society'. A similarly powerful display was witnessed at the renewal of tickets in the following year: 'Some were seeking entire sanctification, others enjoyed it; the power of God was amongst us; some fell to the ground, others were praising God.'[134] Primitive Methodism at least was not ashamed of its role as a religion of the poor, catering to the popular temperament. However, the revivalism of the 1850s and 1860s and the popular services and love-feasts held in places like Cowhill,[135] demonstrate that even at the end of the period Methodism as a whole, including the old connexion, had retained its position as an organization within which it was still possible that 'the mournful broken hearts rejoice, the humble poor believe'.

Taken together, the Methodists were perhaps the most successful of all the churches in Oldham and Saddleworth. Starting from a base even lower than that enjoyed by the Dissenters, the Methodists had, by 1865, achieved a massive expansion of their accommodation so that it rivalled even that of the Establishment. However, it is not in terms of seats in chapels that Methodist success should be judged. The true strength of Methodism lay in the immense flexibility of its pastoral and evangelistic structures, its zest for innovation, and the highly participative nature of its corporate devotional practice. All of these features could be found to some extent in other local churches, but nowhere else could they be found in the extreme form that characterized the Methodists. There was also another side to the coin of Methodist success, for nowhere outside the Establishment could be found such an extensive underpinning to the local missionary enterprize as that provided by the Connexion. Methodist denominational structures compared favourably with those of the Anglicans and Dissenters. The relatively decentralized nature of its decision-making structure made the Connexion particularly responsive to local circumstances, and, though connexionalism helped to import national tensions into the circuits of Oldham and Saddleworth, even in the sphere of conflict, local factors usually determined the outcome. The various branches of Methodism—not least the Wesleyans—developed a broad appeal to all sections of the community. Some of the more prestigious

---

[134] *MNM* 55 (1852), 201–2; PMQ May 1835; Kendall, *Primitive Methodist Church*, ii. 44; Obelkevich, *Religion and Rural Society*, 233–4; *PMM* 11 (1830), 189–200; C. B. Turner, 'Revivalism and Welsh Society in the Nineteenth Century', in Obelkevich, Roper, and Samuel (eds.), *Disciplines of Faith*, 311–23.

[135] Fletcher, *Cowhill School*, 7–12.

chapels offered a relatively restrained form of worship, while elsewhere, in smaller chapels, preaching rooms, and cottage meetings, the Methodists developed a vibrant popular spirituality—sometimes raucously expressed. This diversity of experience—more apparent within than between the Methodist denominations—matched closely the realities of a society in which a variety of subcultures were beginning to emerge, and it both reflected and refuelled the dynamic of Methodist success.

6. *An Evangelical Consensus*

Undenominational Enthusiasms

The churches of Oldham and Saddleworth have in the preceding chapters been considered more or less in isolation from each other. However, none of the denominations operated in a vacuum, and the process of interrelation both played a prominent part in their activities and reveals much about their character. The prevailing view of interdenominational relationships during this period is one of enthusiastic co-operation at the beginning, especially among Dissenters, followed first by a descent into gradually intensifying conflict in the early nineteenth century, and then by a cautious re-emergence of co-operative activity in the later 1850s. The first wave of co-operation is supposed to have been the product of the undenominational enthusiastic idealism of the evangelical revival—'there was general euphoria at the end of bigotry and the triumph of Catholic Christianity'.[1] At a national level, this atmosphere stimulated the creation or rejuvenation of a number of undenominational societies for home or foreign missions. In the localities it produced auxiliaries to the national societies and also numerous forms of direct co-operation, including pulpit exchanges and joint Sunday schools.[2]

This sort of undenominational activity was certainly characteristic of Oldham and Saddleworth between 1760 and 1830. In Saddleworth it emerged clearly in 1792, when Anglican and Dissenting ministers joined in promoting a petition against the slave trade. In Oldham its most prominent institutional expression was an auxiliary to the BFBS, established in 1813, with support from a mixture of Anglicans and nonconformists.[3] There was even some all-party support for specifically denominational projects like Anglican church-building, and in 1821 the *Manchester Mercury* reported that many Dissenters in Oldham had contributed liberally towards Anglican church extension. The most

---

[1] D. M. Lewis, *Lighten their Darkness: The Evangelical Mission to Working-Class London 1828–1860* (Westport, Conn., 1986), chs. 1–2; Ward, *Religion and Society, passim.*

[2] Ibid. 44–51; R. H. Martin, *Evangelicals United; Ecumenical Stirrings in Pre-Victorian Britain 1795–1830* (Metuchen, NJ, 1983), 14–33; Laqueur, *Religion and Respectability*, 21–42.

[3] *Manchester Chronicle*, 3 Mar. 1792; OLIC, Oldham BFBS Minutes, 1813–30.

conspicuous field of co-operation, however, was Sunday schooling. The early schools were almost all co-operative efforts—often between Methodists and the Anglicans (from whom they were not yet formally separated), sometimes between Anglicans and the emergent forces of new Dissent. By the early nineteenth century even schools clearly under the patronage of a single denomination were commonly integrated into undenominational Sunday-school unions. The Saddleworth Sunday School Union, for example, was founded in 1810 by the joint efforts of Noah Blackburn of Delph Independent and 'his close friend, the Reverend John Buckley of Heights'—the neighbouring Anglican minister.[4]

It is generally argued that undenominational activity came under increasing strain at the end of the century as tensions mounted between the Established Church and Dissent. Throughout the country, Anglicans and Methodists began to drift apart in the 1790s, while greater concern for church order gradually weakened undenominationalism among Anglican Evangelicals. At the same time, Lord Sidmouth's attempts to introduce legislative controls on itinerancy seemed to herald a general Tory High Church reaction. On most views the old undenominationalism was in ruins by 1830, while the churches headed for at least two decades of 'the warfare of denomination and party'.[5] Both Oldham and Saddleworth displayed signs of interdenominational strain. The local Methodists followed the national trend towards institutional disengagement from the Establishment in the 1790s, and the Moravians, who had also operated in close co-operation with local Anglicans, followed suit some thirty years later. Undenominational Sunday-school activity also came under pressure. The new foundations of the 1820s seem to have been strictly denominational in nature, and they increasingly became integrated into the life of their parent churches rather than operating as separate co-operative agencies. In 1817 the undenominational Sunday-school union in Saddleworth broke up—a victim of an imbalance in its membership, which comprised one Independent and four Anglican schools. This gave the latter a preponderance of votes on the management committee which was used to introduce the Church catechism, provoking, after much heart-searching, the withdrawal of the Independents.[6] There was thus little to suggest that interdenominational relations in Oldham and Saddleworth

---

[4] *Manchester Mercury*, 25 Sept. 1821; Hall, *Delph Independent*, 1.

[5] Lewis, *Lighten their Darkness*, ch. 1, p. 265; Ward, *Religion and Society*, 54–62, 177; Machin, *Politics and the Churches*, 15–16; Gilbert, *Religion and Society*, 168–71; Lovegrove, *Itinerancy*, 132–7.

[6] Bintley, *Salem Moravian Church*, 2–5; Hall, *Delph Independent*, 2–3.

would not follow the pattern for the rest of south-east Lancashire, described by W. R. Ward as 'notorious not merely for the politics of class confict, but for conflict within and between denominations'.[7] However, in the event, church activity in Oldham and Saddleworth during the four decades after 1825 was characterized much less by conflict than by enthusiastic interdenominational co-operation.

Consensus and Co-operation

Alan Gilbert has argued that in the early industrial period nonconformists developed an 'evangelical consensus' based on a common theology and on a common set of evangelical values—the 'conversionist priority' and the importance of 'a religion of the heart'.[8] This would certainly appear to be a fair characterization of the new Dissenters and Methodists in Oldham and Saddleworth. However, the strong, and increasingly preponderant presence of Evangelicals within the Church of England in the locality also made possible the development of a wider consensus into which both nonconformists and Anglicans were increasingly integrated. This consensus crystallized gradually from five major components: a common theology combined with common origins, a common culture with common preoccupations, and, perhaps most importantly, a common approach to those preoccupations.

The local Methodists, Moravians, and Quakers did not share the moderate Calvinism espoused by the Evangelical Anglicans, Baptists, and Independents, but their differences in theological approach had little effect on their practice, and all these groups clearly displayed those characteristics identified by Bebbington as central to evangelical belief.[9] Individual denominational emphases did persist, but they gradually assumed less prominence than the core doctrines which were held in common, and the willingness of Dissenters to welcome Methodists unconditionally into the membership of their churches demonstrated the openness that flowed from growing mutual theological confidence. The consensus in theology was reinforced by the common origins of the major congregations in Oldham and Saddleworth. As we have seen, there were by 1830 four main nonconformist congregations in Oldham town centre: the Manchester

---

[7] Ward, *Religion and Society*, 49. [8] Gilbert, *Religion and Society*, 51–3.
[9] Bebbington, *Evangelicalism*, 2–17. On the components of evangelical consensus, see also G. Parsons, 'Liberation and Church Defence: Victorian Church and Victorian Chapel', in Parsons (ed.), *Religion in Victorian Britain*, ii. 161.

Street Wesleyans and Baptists, the Queen Street Congregationalists, and the George Street Independent Methodists. All of these churches were the product first of a fusion of Methodist enthusiasm with the Anglican Evangelicalism of St Peter's, and then of fission as the Anglican structures and the law both proved too inflexible to contain the energy thereby created. A similar process can be traced in the origins of the local Moravian congregations, the Methodist churches in Saddleworth, and the Calvinistic Methodists in Middleton. These common origins laid the foundation for common sympathy and activity. Although some secessions and splits did engender considerable bitterness, this was far from being the universal rule, and secession, by relieving tension within churches, could often facilitate better relations between separated groups in the longer term. Thus, the Independent Methodists of King Street remained in close contact with the other Independent Methodists after their split over temperance, and the Barkerites of Lees rapidly established good relations with the local New Connexionists after their secession in 1842. Moreover, the extent to which the splits represented a complete divorce can be exaggerated. In 1814–15, for example, George Cussons was elected Chapel Warden by the seatholders of St Peter's and also served as steward for the Oldham Wesleyan circuit—some twenty years after the two institutions had officially drifted apart.[10]

Perhaps more important, however, was the effect of common origins on local nonconformist tradition. In Oldham and Saddleworth, the vast majority of nonconformist causes were precipitated by the revival. Dissenting tradition was a relatively late accretion formed only gradually during the nineteenth century and there was, in consequence, rather less at stake in the defence of traditional denominational positions. For causes like Manchester Street Baptist, which had Anglican–Methodist origins and was Baptist almost by accident, it must have been difficult to feel any great sense of continuity with seventeenth-century Baptists when the heritage of inclusive evangelicalism in its recent past overshadowed the more distant influence of denominational tradition. This heritage shaped a common evangelical culture with common preoccupations. In part, this was a matter of a pervasive evangelical spirituality which coloured all the forms in which it was practised. In some cases as time passed even the forms were intermingled, with organs, choirs, and eventually anthems and psalm-chanting becoming widespread among the local churches. By the late 1840s the most popular hymn at Holy Trinity, Waterhead, was Charles Wesley's 'Lo He Comes with Clouds Descending', and all the

[10] McOwan MSS; Walker, *Zion*, 73; Owen, *St Peter's*, 20.

bitterness of the 'Calvinistic controversy' could not obscure the evangelical appeal of Toplady's 'Rock of Ages Cleft for Me' for the local Wesleyans. Moreover, at the centre of almost every evangelical service stood the sermon, and, with so much attention focused there, the characteristic features of different forms of worship must often have assumed relative insignificance. This common culture was also incarnated in a variety of social activities. As we have already seen, almost all the local churches ran the same range of tea parties, lectures, Sunday-school trips, societies, and prayer meetings. These in combination amounted to a virtually comprehensive social world which, given the composition of local congregations, may sometimes have transcended social barriers especially between different sections of the working class. This common social world was reflected in a high degree of intermarriage between members of different denominations. Foster found a striking example of this phenomenon in his study of tradesmen's marriages, but interdenominational marriage was visible at all levels of the social structure.[11] Individual families could frequently contain members of more than one evangelical denomination. J. R. Dunne, for example, reporting to the CPAS in 1866, recorded considerable traffic between the churches caused by short-distance migration, some people 'having been brought up to attend the Church, when in their native parish, have removed to another, and for the sake of convenience have attended some Dissenting Chapel. Then again, there are others who were formerly Dissenters, but on removing into another parish have attended the Church.' This state of affairs, compounded by the influence of Sunday schools, meant that 'frequently there will be as many as two or three sects in one family'.[12] In such cases, even family prayers must have been major pan-evangelical exercises.

The common preoccupations of this evangelical culture were both social and religious. Churchmen and nonconformists faced the same problem of church debt, and adopted the same means to relieve it. They shared the problems of recruiting from Sunday schools and established the same sorts of institutions in an attempt to deal with them. All evangelical groups confronted the issue of drink, and the need to encourage proper observance of the Sabbath. They also fostered an interest in charity and in foreign missions. However, their most constant preoccupation was with the fate of their unconverted neighbours. As one lay pamphleteer, addressing all the Christians in Oldham, put it in 1852, 'We have around

---

[11] Holy Trinity, Waterhead, MS History; *WMM* 89 (1866), 192; Obelkevich, 'Music and Religion', 554; Foster, *Class Struggle*, 168–9; Jeremy, *Dictionary of Business Biography*, iv. 725–8; SMC, Diary, 5 Dec. 1854.

[12] CPAS, *Quarterly Paper*, 78 (1866), 67.

us thousands to whom the Gospel requires to be carried with nearly the same degree of urgency as to many of the heathen abroad.'[13] In response to this preoccupation, there emerged the most important feature of the evangelical consensus—its common methodology. At the level of denominational structures, this can be seen in the gradual *de facto* abandonment of Independency by the Congregationalists and Baptists as, in the cause of more effective church-planting, the operations of their county associations blurred the practical differences between the various ecclesiological systems within which local evangelicals operated. The methodological consensus became even stronger at the level of local pastoral and evangelistic practice. Partly as a consequence of the influence of Thomas Chalmers, and partly in pragmatic response to the problems with which they were confronted, all the evangelical churches adopted a very similar range of pastoral and evangelistic techniques. Wherever one looks in the records of local churches, there emerges the same pattern of cottage meetings and prayer meetings, tract and Bible distribution, evangelistic visiting, and lay preaching. Open-air preaching, lectures, revival meetings, and special evangelistic services were almost universal practice, and, by the 1840s at the latest, it seems clear that all the churches were doing all the same things all the time. Already in 1835 the Anglican 'aggressive approach' was so similar to that of the nonconformists that Sumner had to answer the charge that he was advocating the methods of Dissent: 'It has been urged, I know, in regard to the domestic mode of teaching or lecturing, that it . . . approximates us to the habits of Dissenters. If this be so, it only proves that they have been quicker than ourselves to discover what is needed by the wants of the people, and what is suited to their habits.'[14] Judging by the attitudes of their 'customers', evangelical Sunday schools too were regarded as little different from one another, and Thomas Lowe reported in 1843, on the basis of a thorough visitation of his locality, that even committed members of local churches would send their children to Sunday schools run by other denominations.[15]

The breadth of the evangelical consensus in Oldham and Saddleworth made possible a good deal of practical co-operation as a new eirenic pan-evangelicalism arose from the ashes of the old undenominational enterprise. In face of the sharpening denominational identities of the period, its exponents sought not so much to ignore the differences between denominations as to co-operate with those from whom they avowedly differed, on the basis of those things about which they did agree, spurred

[13] Oliver, *Appeal*, 1.   [14] Sumner, *Charge* (1835), 25.
[15] CC, file 1,443, Lowe, Application.

on by the enormous needs of their locality. For the Anglicans, the tone was set in the 1840s by their diocesan: 'I have considered it as no part of my business to inveigh against Dissent, in a diocese where the Establishment was avowably inadequate to supply the spiritual food which the mass of the people needed.'[16] Despite tensions in the early 1840s, the Methodists remained generally sympathetic to the Establishment, and other nonconformist groups also adopted an eirenic approach to their Anglican Evangelical colleagues. In 1825 the LCBA noted, 'we rejoice to find that in the National Establishment are many who faithfully and successfully preach the Gospel of Christ', and in 1851 the LCU condemned 'work in a sectarian spirit, as if the evangelization of the people were to be effected by ourselves alone'.[17]

Pan-evangelical co-operation embraced most aspects of the social and religious life of the town. Evangelical interest in the abolition of slavery remained strong and produced a remarkable joint effort in the general election of 1832, when a coalition of local evangelicals promoted George Stephen, one of the most radical of the young anti-slavers, as a candidate for one of the seats in the newly enfranchised borough. His candidature, explained his sponsors W. F. Walker (Anglican) and T. F. Jordan (Baptist), was not in opposition to the Radicals, Fielden and Cobbett, but aimed to prevent a pro-slaver taking the seat. Stephen's campaign was directed mainly against William Burge, the Tory candidate, who had slaving interests, and, judging by that gentleman's protestations, it did him considerable damage. The evangelicals succeeded in making slavery a central issue in the campaign, and the return of Fielden and Cobbett represented a victory for the evangelical anti-slavery lobby, which continued to keep up pressure for abolition by holding meetings and organizing petitions well into the following year.[18] Pan-evangelical political action was not restricted to the slavery issue, and in 1843, for example, an anti-Corn Law festival in Oldham was addressed by Anglican, Baptist, and Congregationalist ministers, who declared the tax on food to be unscriptural. Again, in 1855 a petition urging Parliament to legislate for the closure of all public houses on the sabbath was signed by ministers of all the main denominations in the town.[19]

[16] Sumner, *Charge* (1844), 25.

[17] LRO CUL/2/1/4, LCU Annual Meeting Minutes, 8 Dec. 1851; LCBA, *Circular Letter* (1825).

[18] *Manchester Guardian*, 15 Dec. 1832; *Manchester Courier*, 8, 22 Dec. 1832, 16 Feb. 1833; Butterworth Diary, 11 Feb.–12 Apr. 1833; Weaver, *John Fielden*, 62–3; E. M. Howse, *Saints in Politics* (1953), 19, 126, 163.

[19] *Manchester Guardian*, 28 Jan. 1843; *Oldham Advertiser*, 2 June 1855.

Pan-evangelical co-operation was also a feature of many local educational and cultural institutions. The 'National School' at Cowhill, for example, included both Anglicans and Wesleyans among its trustees, and by the 1850s a secondary school, Primrose Mount Academy, was being supported by Anglicans, Wesleyans, and Independents, all of whom had a right of inspection.[20] The rise of denominational Sunday-schooling had produced several separate Sunday-school unions in the locality. However, here, too, interdenominational co-operation emerged as the unions combined for joint marches at Whitsuntide followed by treats or outings. Sometimes such ventures reflected the common feeling of a residential community. In 1864, for example, the Primitive, New Connexion, and Independent Methodists of Lees, together with the Anglicans and Congregationalists, joined in arranging a Whitsuntide trip for local scholars. More widespread co-operation could be mobilized for special events, as in 1853, when a series of lectures delivered by various ministers of the town, both Dissenting and Anglican, to the teachers and senior scholars of all the Sunday schools generated considerable interest.[21]

The provision of charity especially in periods of economic crisis also produced bursts of activity that transcended denominational boundaries. A meeting to raise 'Indian Relief', for example, attracted support from Anglicans and Congregationalists in Saddleworth in 1857. More local distress, during the winter of 1857–8, produced a similar response from the clergy of Oldham, and during the cotton famine of the early 1860s all the local churches participated in the co-ordination of relief on a town-wide basis.[22] Support for foreign missions had been fundamental to the earlier, undenominational phase of co-operation, and it remained one of the spheres of activity in which local evangelicals found it easiest to co-operate. The Baptist Missionary Society meeting in 1854, for example, was supported by both Baptists and Independents, and in Oldham the usually exclusively Anglican CMS frequently welcomed the assistance of the Moravians at its annual meetings. However, it was in binding together the various strands of Methodism that support for foreign missions had its most prominent integrative effect. The Primitive Methodists were particularly catholic, sending their ministers to support the Methodist New Connexion missionary meeting from as early as 1838—a gesture which

---

[20] Ward, *Religion and Society*, 14–5; Fletcher, *Cowhill School*, 6–7; *Oldham Advertiser*, 27 May 1852; *Oldham Chronicle*, 21 June 1856.

[21] Ibid. 9 Aug. 1856, 6 Feb. 1858, 1 Feb. 1862, 18 June 1864; *Oldham Standard*, 2 June 1859; *Oldham Advertiser*, 3 Dec. 1853.

[22] *Oldham Chronicle*, 24 Oct., 26 Dec. 1857, 2 Jan. 1858, 16 Aug. 1862.

the New Connexionists soon began to reciprocate on a regular basis. There were similar exchanges with the Wesleyans and various Dissenting groups in the 1840s, and by 1850 the Primitive Methodist annual missionary meeting had become a neutral ground on which Dissenters, New Connexionists, Free Methodists, and Wesleyans could all gather.[23] Evangelical co-operation was also visible in regular pulpit exchanges among nonconformists at revival meetings and in interdenominational support for church-building activities. Thus in 1860, when the Quaker Thomas Emmott laid the foundation stone of the Primitive Methodist School at Lower-moor, he was moved to remark that 'the Catholicity of the spirit which had animated all [its supporters], both Churchmen and Dissenters, was to him very encouraging'.[24]

Evangelical solidarity was often manifested in good relations between local clergymen. The young Wesleyan Itinerant, Jabez Bunting, had in 1799–1801, along with his superintendent minister, arranged a series of dinner parties in which he 'enjoyed religious fellowship and theological conversation with the Congregational and Baptist ministers of the neighbourhood'. Similarly, a flourishing friendship between the Congregationalist Noah Blackburn of Delph and the Anglican John Buckley of Heights had been productive of a good deal of practical co-operation during the period of undenominational enthusiasm. This tradition was maintained during the pan-evangelical period by good relations between F. B. Broadbent, the Anglican minister of Waterhead, and successive ministers of the Salem Moravian church.[25] The most influential of these friendships, however, was that between W. F. Walker, the incumbent of St James's, Oldham, and R. M. Davies, the Independent minister of Hope. Walker was the moving spirit behind much pan-evangelical co-operation and Davies recalled:

His appointment was an epoch in the history . . . of the town . . . In politics he was liberal; in theology a Calvinist, holding views strictly in accordance with the doctrinal articles in his church, and was prompt in vindicating the principle of an establishment whenever required to do so while he wished that establishment to be so broad as to comprehend all those that faithfully preached the Gospel. He cordially co-operated with his nonconformist brethren, and was foremost in all

---

[23] Ibid. 21 Oct. 1854, 14 Apr., 2 June 1860; SMC, Diary, 14 Mar. 1837; PMQ 6 Apr. 1838; Oldham Primitive Methodists' Circuit Committee Minutes, 2 Apr., 18 Sept. 1847, 25 Jan. 1850.

[24] *Oldham Chronicle*, 4 Aug., 20 Oct. 1860, 12 Jan., 19 Oct. 1861.

[25] SMC, Diary, 24 Apr. 1857; W. R. Ward (ed.), *The Early Correspondence of Jabez Bunting 1820–1829* (1972), 11.

movements for the mental and moral improvement of the people . . . When he died I lost a priceless friend.[26]

When Walker fell seriously ill in 1847, his congregation paid a spontaneous visit to their friends at Hope and held a joint prayer meeting to request that he might be granted an additional ten years of life. His death in 1857 was 'improved' by Davies on the text 'He being dead yet speaketh'—appropriately enough, because his name was invoked for years after, in support of numerous local pan-evangelical projects.[27]

Together with Birt the Baptist minister, and Antliff the Primitive Methodist, Davies and Walker were the leading lights in most of the pan-evangelical organizations whose operations provided the bedrock of practical co-operation in the locality. The longest-established was the Oldham auxiliary to the BFBS, whose minutes, together with those of the Saddleworth auxiliary, are a testimony to a sustained if unspectacular exercise in pan-evangelical co-operation. The local annual meetings of the society and those of its sister organization, the Religious Tract Society, resounded with statements of evangelical unity. In 1856, for example, the BFBS chairman celebrated the fact that, 'while differing in religious opinions', local evangelicals 'were ready to meet and help each other to promote the common interest of all'.[28] Early in the 1830s Walker helped to establish a regular fortnightly 'prayer meeting for the ministers of all denominations'. This met in rotation at St James's Vicarage and the homes of local Baptist, Independent, and Moravian ministers right through the troubled 1830s and 1840s. In 1832 Walker was 'unanimously elected' chairman of a temperance society which persisted, with pan-evangelical support, throughout the period, and in 1856 Davies led a local pan-evangelical initiative to promote Sabbath observance. On a grander scale, Birt and Walker were founder members of the Evangelical Alliance (EA) in 1847, and in the following year they were joined by Davies and several other Independent ministers and subsequently by representatives of various Methodist groups.[29] Although Walker, Birt, Davies, and Antliff took a leading role, they were by no means the only enthusiastic pan-evangelicals in the locality, as the annual meetings of the various organizations demonstrated. Interdenominational co-operation was clearly alive and well in

---

[26] Davies 'Congregationalism', 4.   [27] *Oldham Standard*, 23 Mar. 1861.
[28] Oldham BFBS Minutes; Delph Branch Bible Association Minutes, 1848–53; *Oldham Chronicle*, 26 Apr. 1856, 28 Aug. 1858.
[29] *Manchester Courier*, 18 Feb. 1832; *Oldham Standard*, 17 Sept. 1859; *Oldham Chronicle*, 17 May 1846; SMC, Diary, 27 Mar. 1837, 17 May 1846; EA, *Conference Reports* (1847–61).

Oldham throughout the 1830s and 1840s.[30] It reached a climax during the 1850s with the establishment of the local YMCA and the foundation of the Oldham Ragged School and Town Mission. The YMCA attracted very broad support and was certainly ecumenical in spirit, as the Anglican F. B. Broadbent explained at its annual meeting in 1861: 'It signified not to him, to what denomination a man belonged; he was certain of one thing, so far as they could be in this world, that they belonged to Christ, and that the Spirit of God . . . had breathed into them the breath of life.'[31] The Ragged School, established in 1859, was aimed at those children, an estimated 1,000–2,000, who did not attend Sunday school. It, too, was thoroughly interdenominational in ethos, as one of the committee explained: 'They wished to throw it open to all who would come forward to give a helping hand, as they felt that . . . they could shirk the minor differences of sect and meet on the broad basis of their love for Christ.' Within a year the school had developed into a fully fledged town mission, employing lay missionaries and eventually a team of 'Bible women'. In 1863 the staff made 4,484 sick and 18,618 evangelistic visits, distributed 25,356 tracts, and held 524 cottage meetings with an aggregate attendance of 19,328 and an average attendance of 37, as well as making 415 visits to the workhouse. There was considerable resistance among some Anglican clergy to involvement in the school and mission. Their reluctance was based, however, not on any doubts about the propriety of co-operation with Dissenters but on the town-wide scope of the mission, which, they feared, might undermine the new parochial structure they had established with so much effort. However, by 1863 these concerns had faded and the mission was being supported by several Anglican ministers and leading laymen. All the main evangelical denominations were represented by vice-presidents on the mission's executive committee, and the eirenic spirit successfully survived the initial controversy.[32]

Interdenominational co-operation occasionally extended beyond the orthodox evangelical community. The Middleton Swedenborgians, for example, participated in general Dissenting political agitation in 1843, and in 1855 the Roman Catholics were involved in the petitioning for closure of public houses on the sabbath. Temperance had a particularly broad appeal, and in 1844 there was a meeting in the Independent Methodist chapel to raise money for Father Matthew—the Catholic temperance

[30] Butterworth Diary, 11 Oct. 1831.   [31] *Oldham Standard*, 2 Mar. 1861.

[32] Ibid. 24 Sept. 1859, 24 Nov. 1860, 7–28 Dec. 1861, 4 Jan. 1862, 4 Apr., 28 Nov. 1863; *Oldham Chronicle*, 15 Sept., 1 Dec. 1860, 19 Jan., 23 Mar. 1861, 4 Apr., 1 Nov. 1863; anon., *These Fifty Years 1859–1909* (Oldham, 1909), *passim.*

campaigner. The cause of Bible distribution could also command unusually wide support. In 1860 a prominent evangelical layman, assisted by a number of other subscribers, made a gift of fifty Douai Bibles to the local Catholic priest for the benefit of his congregation.[33] However, relationships between the evangelical and non-evangelical churches were rarely cordial, and relations with the Roman Catholics, complicated by inter-ethnic strife, were often tense. St Peter's, which stood in a district with an unusually large Irish population, became a stronghold of the Orange order in the early nineteenth century, and popular anti-Catholicism grew in step with Irish immigration in the 1850s. It was not until the early 1860s, however, that the uneasy relationship between Catholics and evangelicals degenerated into open conflict. Then Oldham experienced its own miniature 'Papal Aggression', as a newly arrived priest, Father Conway, opened the propaganda battle with a series of lectures, arguing that salvation was only possible within the Roman Catholic church and that there was 'no Christianity without the Pope'. In some places Dissenting suspicions about the influence of Tractarianism within the Established Church made calls to the defence of a common protestantism rather divisive. In Oldham they were entirely cohesive. A sharp response followed, led by local Anglicans and Congregationalists, who organized counter-lectures, bombarded the press with correspondence, and finally revived an 'Oldham Evangelical Protestant Association' to co-ordinate their activities, which commanded wide support among Churchmen, Methodists, and Dissenters. Anti-Catholicism also retained a popular and potentially uncontrollable aspect, and, in the tense atmosphere of 1861, a clash between Roman Catholic and Protestant Sunday-school processions produced a serious riot during which major damage was done to the Catholic chapel.[34]

Consensus, Competition, and Conflict

Even among the evangelicals, not everything went smoothly after 1830. There remained frictions between denominations, and these sparked small 'crises' in 1833–4, 1843, and 1861–2. In 1833–4 the issue was Church rate, complicated by alleged mismanagement of the huge sums raised to

[33] *Manchester Guardian*, 14 May 1843, 20 Nov. 1844; *Oldham Advertiser*, 2 June 1855; *Oldham Chronicle*, 1 Sept. 1860.

[34] *Oldham Standard*, 24 Mar., 21 Apr., 5, 12 May 1860, 16 Feb. 1861; J. Wolffe, 'Protestant Societies and Anti-Catholic Agitation in Great Britain 1829–1860', D.Phil. thesis (Oxford, 1984), 259; *Oldham Chronicle*, 12 Mar. 1859, 24 Mar. 1860; Foster, *Class Struggle*, 219–20, 243–6.

rebuild St Mary's, Oldham. In 1843 the educational clauses of Graham's Factory Bill provoked a national storm, and in 1861–2 the bicentenary of the 'great ejection' focused local attention on the issue of establishment, while the activities of rival societies raised the temperature of debate.[35] However, what is most striking about all three of these 'crises' is the low level of conflict that actually ensued, and the absence of straightforward confrontation between Anglicans and nonconformists. In 1833–4 most of the opposition to the Church rate was the product not of sectarian disputes but of rivalries between local communities as the out-townships proved unwilling to support church-building in the central township. There were also genuine problems with the stewardship of the Trustees, about which Anglicans themselves were still complaining as late as 1846.[36] Moreover, any hope of a united nonconformist front was dashed by the decision of the Wesleyans to line up behind the Establishment in favour of the general principle of Church rate. Although almost all the local nonconformists backed the opposition to the 1843 Factory Education Bill, this apparent unanimity masked wide differences about the issues at stake. At the first public meeting against the Bill in April 1843, a coalition of Dissenters opposed the projected legislation because it contravened the voluntary principle. The Wesleyans and New Connexionists, on the other hand, merely objected to the extension of clerical control. By 1861–2 the Methodists had reverted to their previous stance of support for the Establishment, and public confrontations were restricted to the Anglicans and Congregationalists.[37]

In sharp contrast to the great co-operative effort, the conflicts of 1834 and 1843 produced little in the way of permanent organization. An Anti-State Church association was established in 1834, but it was not very active, and, far from being an anti-Anglican body, it expected to recruit members from among sympathetic Churchmen. Its successor, the Liberation Society, made little impact on the locality until 1860, when it launched a literature distribution campaign. The society also arranged lectures against Establishment in 1861–2 and it was holding public meetings as late as December 1863, although the interest and attendance were small.[38] The rival Anglican Church Defence Association (CDA) originated

[35] Butterworth Diary, 27 Feb.–31 Mar. 1834; Machin, *Politics and the Churches*, 151–9; *Oldham Chronicle*, 16, 23 Mar. 1861.

[36] *Manchester Chronicle*, 7 Sept. 1833; *Manchester Guardian*, 31 Sept. 1833; CCs, file 5,203, Lowe to EC, 3 Sept. 1846.

[37] *Manchester Guardian*, 15 Apr. 1843; *Oldham Chronicle*, 2 Feb., 16 Mar. 1861.

[38] Butterworth Diary, Mar.–Apr. 1834; *Oldham Chronicle*, 15 Dec. 1860, 23, 30 Mar. 1861; *Oldham Standard*, 19 Dec. 1863.

in popular resentment against the activities of the Liberation Society, and quickly gained the support of an impressive array of Evangelical clergymen. However, after organizing lectures in support of Establishment, the CDA soon changed its focus and as early as July 1861, had become preoccupied with questions of Church reform rather than the ambitions of political Dissent.[39] Conflict and co-operation clearly tended to operate at different levels: conflict at the level of what the churches were talking about, co-operation at the level of what the churches were doing.

The rhetoric of conflict is also illuminating. Abusive language seems generally to have been avoided, and very critical speeches against the Established Church were generally made only by a few radical politicians, visiting speakers, and, in 1834, Methodist seceders, whose virulence was perhaps generated largely by the experience of conflict within their own denomination.[40] Local Anglicans, too, adopted moderate positions and were equally careful in their use of language. They were also capable of conciliatory gestures, and in the 1830s, for example, the rector of Middleton himself took the initiative in abolishing the Church rate in his parish and substituting a voluntary levy, to the delight of the local Dissenters.[41] Dissenters were careful to insist that they were opposed to church establishments in principle rather than to the Established Church as they encountered it in the locality. Thus Allanson, the Baptist minister, explained to a public meeting in 1834 that 'he had not the least animosity against the members of that church he was only against its principle', while Glendenning, the Independent minister, explained, 'the Dissenters cherished no hostility to Churchmen, but they deprecated their errors. Their quarrel was with the system, not with the men.' During the more widespread agitation of 1843 the nonconformists were careful to restrict their attacks to Graham's proposed legislation rather than the Anglican church in general, and the same distinction between opposition to the principle of Establishment and hostility to its local exponents was constantly reiterated during the confrontations of 1861–2.[42] In this respect the evangelical consensus cut across the agenda of mainstream popular radicalism and it is not surprising that one frustrated local radical was moved to accuse the Dissenters of Oldham of 'apathy in the cause of civic and religious liberty'. That this charitable practice of condemning the 'sin' of Establishment while continuing to love the Anglican 'sinner' was

[39] Ibid. 2 Mar., 13 Apr., 4 May, 6 July 1861; *Oldham Chronicle*, 16 Mar. 1861.
[40] Butterworth Diary, 22 Mar. 1834.
[41] *Manchester Guardian*, 15 Apr. 1846; Raines MSS xl. 251.
[42] Butterworth Diary, 22 Mar. 1834, 12 Apr. 1843; *Oldham Standard*, 2, 9 Mar. 1861.

not mere rhetoric is indicated not merely by continuing efforts at co-operation, but also by the fact that, when in 1845 a voluntary levy was substituted for the Oldham Church rate, many local Dissenters made substantial contributions.[43]

This moderation stemmed from a growing confidence that ultimately all local evangelicals were proclaiming the same Gospel—that they were in competition rather than in conflict. J. G. Short, one of the sharpest Dissenting controversialists, summed this up when, in 1861, addressing a meeting in Lees, he declared:

Go to Springhead Chapel and what did they hear preached—'Believe in the Lord Jesus Christ and thou shalt be saved—one God, one Christ and one way to heaven.' Go to Zion Chapel, they heard the same, go to Leesfield Church, they heard the same. Go to Hey Chapel, they heard the same. Go to the Christian Brethren's place and they heard the same; and the same at the Primitive Methodist Chapel. They were not different religions but different forms of church government.[44]

Even local disputes were carried out within a framework of evangelical consensus. There was a certain geniality and much mutual respect, even when controversy was at its height. R. M. Davies caught this mood while delivering a voluntaryist lecture in 1861:

He regretted the necessity of such a controversy . . . A little acrimony would no doubt arise out of it, and he regretted it, which would last until a common danger to their Protestantism arose, and then they would be again as in former times, addressed as 'their dear Dissenting brethren'. When that time came, he would not respect Churchmen less for having defended their principles, and he trusted they would not respect Dissenters less for having done the same.[45]

David Bebbington has noted that during the 1830s interdenominational co-operation in evangelism was 'fraught with bickering'. In evangelical Oldham, however, the problem for potential sectarian warriors was that the bickering was fraught with co-operation. What is most striking when the record is examined closely is the frequency with which opponents might be found, in the middle of some agitation or controversy, sitting round a table to co-ordinate Bible distribution or sharing a platform to promote some other pan-evangelical cause. The periodic 'crises' were

---

[43] *Manchester Guardian*, 20 May 1843, 18 Jan. 1845. For similar attitudes to Church rate among Dissenters in Croydon, see J. Morris, *Religion and Urban Change: Croydon 1840–1914* (Woodbridge, 1992), 86–7.

[44] *Oldham Standard*, 13 July 1861.   [45] Ibid. 13 Apr. 1861.

only waves on the surface. The great mass of water underneath remained in a state of calm.[46]

How far Oldham might be said to reflect the situation in the rest of England is open to question. Clearly, other towns did experience sectarian strife. However, conflict by its very nature tends to be more prominent than co-operation—it has always been more newsworthy. If the work of bodies like the BFBS was studied more closely, it might well reveal a surprising amount of practical co-operation in the parishes. Moreover, the application of the stereotype of conflict has tended to obscure the fact that there were many possible positions short of co-operation with the Establishment that did not imply animosity to the Anglican Church as such. Even in the neighbouring parish of Rochdale, notorious for interdenominational conflict, the local nonconformists contributed liberally to the Church rate once it had become voluntary.[47] The activities of 'political Dissent' have, in the past, been given great prominence, but the views of the average Dissenter may be better reflected in the position taken by the LCBA in 1840:

Whether our efforts be strenuous or weak, they are our own, and are necessarily characterized by our particular views; as are the efforts of all religious communities by theirs, and we think rightly so. That against which we would guard brethren, is unlovely conduct towards those from whom we differ, a spirit of unholy and envious rivalry, which would alike indispose us to love them and to rejoice in their success . . . We must perceive that we can render no more essential service to the universal church, than by a diligent and consistent cultivation of the field which we call our own. And we can by no means more effectually call forth the hallowed sympathies and affections of our hearts toward our brethren, than by entering with them into the most energetic conflict with the powers of darkness.[48]

This commitment to the development of unity in diversity certainly produced fruit in Oldham and Saddleworth, and the categories of co-operation and competition suggested by the experience of their churches may take us much further in understanding interdenominational relations in England as a whole than has the stereotype of conflict.

---

[46] Oldham BFBS Minutes, Oct. 1833, July 1834; *Manchester Guardian*, 29 Mar. 1834; *Oldham Standard*, 13 Mar., 13 Apr. 1861.

[47] Ward, *Religion and Society*, 183–9; *Manchester Guardian*, 2 Sept. 1843.

[48] LCBA, *Circular Letter* (1840), 7.

7. 'And Was Jerusalem Builded Here'?

The leading characteristic of the churches in Oldham and Saddleworth between 1740 and 1865 was their commitment to growth. They built and prayed for growth, and they mobilized an increasing proportion of their membership within a wide variety of social milieux to go out into the urban mission field and work for growth. Some of their commitment derived from denominational competitiveness, and some from a concern about the moral health and general stability of the new industrial society. Its compulsive force, however, derived mainly from the evangelical concern of many individuals and church fellowships to share with their neighbours the felt benefits, both moral and spiritual, of a personal relationship with God, and thus to secure their eternal destiny. In the course of their mission these evangelical activists developed and exploited a variety of points of contact with the population at large which were at the same time the means and the measure of their success.

Churches and Church-goers

The most direct and most important of these points of contact were the church buildings, mission rooms, and converted cottages which provided accommodation for worship on Sundays and a variety of other activities during the rest of the week. By the end of the period virtually every community in Oldham and Saddleworth had been provided with some form of religious accommodation by one or other of the evangelical churches, and sizeable communities usually boasted a number of places of worship. In Oldham, the churches and mission rooms of the main denominations contained well in excess of 50,000 seats in 1865, allowing at least 50 per cent of the adult population to be seated at any one time. In Saddleworth the scale of provision was even more generous, with seating being provided for at least 60 per cent of the adult population. The majority of this seating was available either free of charge or at a very low rent, and it was supplemented by a mass of informal cottage meetings and occasional schoolroom services. If the population of Oldham and Saddleworth stayed away from the activities of organized religion, it was not because the churches had failed to accommodate them.

It is difficult to be certain about the number of people who joined the churches and attended their services. Nevertheless it is clear that the vast majority of local churches were in a flourishing condition throughout the period. Only the Unitarians, and a few small sectarian groups, ever came close to extinction, and most congregations increased in absolute size. Unfortunately, good series of membership statistics are available only for the Baptists and some of the Methodist groups. John Foster attempted to use communicant figures recorded in visitation returns to construct an Anglican series between 1778 and 1825 roughly equivalent to nonconformist membership and concluded that Anglican influence declined over the period. A. D. Gilbert used a similar technique for parishes in Oxfordshire producing similar results, and, more recently, I. R. Christie has used Foster's evidence to argue for a very low level of Anglican influence in 1789.[1] However, the tenuous nature of the link between figures for communicants and numbers in attendance at Anglican churches makes it extremely difficult to draw any reliable inferences from this data. Moreover, when the additional complications produced by the gradual withdrawal of the Wesleyans from communion with the Church are taken into account, the figures for Oldham and Saddleworth may indicate a slight increase rather than a decline in Anglican strength.

The available nonconformist data for Oldham are displayed in Fig. 7.1. The Baptists, apart from minor fluctuations associated with the formation of new churches, experienced fairly steady growth in membership throughout the period. The trace for the Free Methodists, on the other hand, confirms their failure to capitalize on the 'Wesleyan Reform' agitation of 1851, and indicates that they continued to experience considerable difficulty in recruiting members until the early 1860s. Both the Methodist New Connexion and Wesleyan Methodist traces demonstrate the checks to growth produced by schism. The disastrous effect of the Barkerite secession is spectacularly displayed by the New Connexionist trace, as is the permanent damage done to the New Connexion's challenge for the numerical leadership of local Methodism. Periodic losses in Wesleyan membership left the total for the old connexion oscillating around a mean of 889 for the fifty-six years between 1796 and 1851, and constantly stalled any take-off beyond 1,150. Some of the troughs were associated with secessions, especially the splits of the later 1790s, the Stephensite and Associationist schisms of the mid-1830s, and the Reform agitation of

[1] Foster, *Class Struggle*, 29; Gilbert, *Religion and Society*, 27–9; I. R. Christie, *Stress and Stability in Late Eighteenth-Century Britain* (1984), 197.

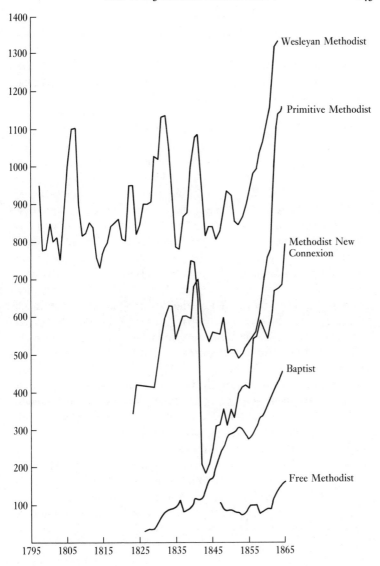

the early 1850s. Other low points seem to represent the effects of economic depression, especially in the period 1801–13. Local wages fell again in 1825, and there were steep falls from the late 1820s to the later 1830s, and again in the 1840s, which also seem to have coincided with checks to Primitive Methodist recruitment.[2] However, this correlation is weakened by evidence of economic crises which did not significantly check recruitment—most notably the cotton famine of the 1860s. Given the complicated pattern of economic fluctuation and internal Methodist dynamics, it is difficult to establish any correlation between recruitment to Methodist societies and radical political activity in the tradition either of Eric Hobsbawm or of E. P. Thompson. There is no evidence of any consistent decline of interest in Methodism during periods of high radical activity or of what Thompson termed the 'chiliasm of despair'. Local Methodism recruited strongly throughout the radical 1790s, and it also did well from 1814 to 1819, when, according to Foster, Oldham was in a state of popular ferment. The 'failure' of these activities was not followed by any surge in recruitment and neither was the collapse of the great strike of 1842. However, only tentative support can be given to Hobsbawm's suggestion that peaks of radical and Methodist strength tended to coincide, because some peaks of radical activity, especially in the 1830s, were coincident with periods of Methodist decline.[3]

The one characteristic undoubtedly shared by the traces for all five denominations in Fig. 7.1 is a trend, during the later 1850s, towards a more sustained pattern of growth. In part this may have been a consequence of new stability—both in the local economy and in Methodist politics—which removed the brakes of depression and schism from the continuous evangelical drive towards recruitment. This acceleration in growth produced a recovery in the density of Methodist membership within the population at large. Membership of the three main Methodist groups expressed as a proportion of the whole population stood at 2.8 per cent in 1841; it declined to only 1.6 per cent in 1851, but had recovered to 2.1 per cent ten years later. When these figures are modified in order to express Methodist membership as a proportion of the population aged 10 and over and multiplied (following the usual convention) by a factor of between three and five to allow for the large number of adherents, we might speculate that in 1841 between 12 and 20 per cent of the adult population had come within the ambit of the three main Methodist groups.

[2] Foster, *Class Struggle*, 36–46, 80–4.
[3] Ibid. 107–16, 142–6, 205–9; Hempton, *Methodism and Politics*, 74–5.

The recovery of the 1850s was more than proportionate to population growth, and density also probably continued to increase after 1861—the very next year was one of revival and record growth.

The only large-scale survey of church attendance carried out during the period under consideration was the religious census of 1851. However, the evidence produced by the census, and still available in the manuscript returns collected by the enumerators, is extremely difficult to interpret. The census recorded the total attendance of adults and Sunday scholars at each service in participating churches on 30 March 1851. It is, therefore, impossible to be certain about how many individuals went to church on that Sunday, because some people attended more than once, and would consequently have been counted twice or even three times. It is possible, however, to establish the range within which the figure for individual attenders would have fallen. The lower end of the range is given by calculating the numbers of adults and of Sunday scholars present at the best-attended service on census Sunday 1851—usually the morning service—and ignoring attendances at other times to avoid the possibility of multiple counting. The upper end of the range is given by aggregating the attendances at all the services and treating each attendance as though it represented a single individual. These statistics have been calculated for the two divisions of Oldham's central township, each of the four out-townships, and for Saddleworth; they have then been expressed as a proportion of the population eligible to attend. The eligible population is assumed to have been equivalent to that part of the population aged between 5 and 19 for Sunday scholars and that part aged 20 and over for adults. In each case the total has been reduced by 5 per cent to allow for people prevented from attending church by illness or unavoidable responsibilities at work or at home.[4] The results of this analysis are presented in Table 7.1. The two districts of the central township display similar characteristics, with total attendance varying between 20 per cent at the lower and 48 per cent at the upper end of the range. The out-townships, on the other hand, vary markedly, with Chadderton and Royton displaying a much lower level of attendance than Crompton and Middleton. To some extent the figures may reflect a genuine difference in the impact

---

[4] This calculation gives a higher figure for the eligible population than the method employed by Horace Mann, the original interpreter of the census data, who estimated that only 58% of the population was free to attend any single church service and only 70% was free to attend at any time on census Sunday. The method used here should be regarded as a relatively conservative one for the purpose of assessing the general influence of the churches, especially with respect to the calculation of the lower end of the range.

TABLE 7.1. *Minimum and maximum attendance at church in Oldham and Saddleworth 30 March 1851*

District		Minimum attendance			Maximum attendance		
		Sunday scholars	Adults	Total	Sunday scholars	Adults	Total
Oldham below town	No.	2,220	3,607	5,827	3,476	7,283	10,759
	% density	24.6	24.6	24.6	38.6	49.8	45.5
Oldham above town	No.	2,226	2,220	4,446	4,480	6,312	10,792
	% density	25.7	16.1	20.0	51.7	46.5	48.5
Total central townships	No.	4,446	5,827	10,273	7,956	13,595	21,551
	% density	25.2	20.7	22.4	45.0	48.2	47.0
Middleton	No.	1,144	1,710	2,854	2,170	3,660	5,830
	% density	43.5	42.4	42.8	82.6	90.7	87.5
Chadderton	No.	760	389	1,149	1,237	721	1,958
	% density	24.0	7.7	14.0	39.1	14.3	23.9
Royton	No.	414	590	1,004	785	1,331	2,116
	% density	15.2	14.0	14.5	28.9	31.5	30.5
Crompton	No.	963	683	1,646	1,703	1,286	2,989
	% density	47.0	21.0	31.0	83.2	39.5	56.3
Total out-township	No.	3,281	3,372	6,653	5,895	6,998	12,893
	% density	31.1	20.4	24.6	55.8	42.3	47.6
Total Oldham Poor Law Union	No.	7,727	9,199	16,926	13,851	20,593	34,444
	% density	27.4	20.1	23.2	49.1	46.0	47.2
Saddleworth	No.	896	2,450	3,346	1,694	4,247	5,941
	% density	15.5	26.0	22.0	29.3	45.0	39.0

of the churches. Chadderton's population had grown much more rapidly than that of the other out-townships in the ten years since 1841, and in 1851 it possessed much the largest and most dispersed of any of the out-township populations. This rapid population growth created difficulties for the churches, many of which were relatively recent foundations and had been given little opportunity to gather impetus. Royton, which also had a large population, had something of a reputation for irreligion and was long considered a particularly difficult mission field, especially by the Methodists. However, the figures for Royton and Chadderton also reflect the influence of statistical anomalies. The Independent Methodist church at Fir Lane in Crompton recruited heavily from Royton, thus boosting the attendance figures in the former and reducing those in the latter township.[5] Similarly, a significant number of Chadderton church-goers would have attended places of worship like St John's, Chadderton, St Thomas's, Werneth, and St Margaret's, Hollinwood, in Oldham below town, while others would have attended church in the Middleton township. Middleton congregations would also have been boosted by attendants from parts of the parish located outside the Oldham Poor Law Union—thus accounting, in part, for its unusually high attendance figures. A more reliable estimate for church attendance in the out-townships is probably provided by averaging the figures for all four. This produces a set of attendance statistics similar to those for the central township and for Saddleworth—suggesting that the churches were, in general, equally effective in ministering to the densely packed communities of Oldham and to the more dispersed populations of Saddleworth and the out-townships.

Any attempt to estimate the precise number of individual attenders on census Sunday 1851 can be no more than an educated guess. Some writers have simply estimated the number of attenders at two-thirds of the total attendance.[6] However, this method of analysis would be inappropriate for a study using the manuscript returns for individual churches—it would, for example, certainly underestimate the number of attenders at churches holding only one service on the Sunday. The approach adopted here has been to use a modified version of the formula employed by the original interpreters of the census data. This counts the whole attendance at the best-attended service in each church, half that at the next best, and a third at the next, if any, treating adults and Sunday scholars separately. The results, disaggregated by denomination and by

[5] Foster, *Class Struggle*, 138; MARC MAM PLP 36.31.1, T. Dunn to J. Bunting, 29 July 1836; Richardson, *On Zion's Hill*.

[6] Joyce, *Work*, 244; Perkin, *English Society*, 201.

district, are reproduced in Table 7.2. There is, unfortunately, little evidence which would allow the reliability of this formula to be confirmed. It is clear that a proportion of the church-going population did attend more than once on a Sunday (a practice especially prevalent among the more enthusiastic Methodist churches), but there is also evidence that Sunday scholars, in particular, attended only once on the Sunday. In some churches boys' classes were taken to the morning service and girls' classes to a service in the afternoon, while, in others, Sunday-school classes were taken to different services according to the age of the participants.[7] It appears likely, therefore, that any overestimate among the adult attenders would have been more than counterbalanced by an underestimate among Sunday scholars, and it would not be unreasonable to conclude that 37 per cent of the population of Oldham and 31 per cent of the population of Saddleworth aged 5 and over were both able and willing to attend church on census Sunday.

Many contemporary observers were depressed by the census results. Some historians, pointing to the large numbers who did not attend church, have seen the census as proof of failure. This tendency has been accentuated in the case of Oldham because, in reliance on a defective printed return for the borough, it has been calculated that the town had the second lowest church attendance in urban Lancashire.[8] However, only in the context of the ultimate ambition of the churches to draw in all of the people could the census be construed as revealing failure. On any other view, the attendance figures clearly indicate extraordinary success. It is, to paraphrase Jeffrey Cox, difficult to imagine any other institution, except perhaps the public house, that could have mobilized 37 per cent of the eligible population to attend an ordinary weekly meeting. Moreover, the figures derived from the census certainly underestimate the church-going population of Oldham and Saddleworth because of the incompleteness of the survey. Three of the nineteen Anglican churches made no attendance return, indicating an underestimate of around 10 per cent in the Anglican total. More serious were the wholesale discrepancies in the Primitive Methodist returns, which, even allowing for the fact that it was mainly the smaller places that were missed, suggest an underestimate of around a third. The strength of other denominations with many attendants in small meetings may also have been seriously underestimated.[9]

---

[7] PRO HO 129 475, 1, 14,

[8] Joyce, *Work*, 244; K. S. Inglis, 'Patterns of Religious Worship in 1851', *Journal of Ecclesiastical History*, 11 (1960), 74–86.

[9] Cox, *English Churches*, 5; see above, p. 206.

TABLE 7.2. *Estimated church attendance and percentage density among the eligible population in Oldham and Saddleworth March 1851*

Denomination	Oldham central township		Middleton		Chadderton		Royton		Crompton		Total		% of all attendances	Saddleworth	
	No.	%	No.	%	No.	%	No.	%	No.	%	No.	%		No.	%
Anglican	5,872	12.8	1,279	19.2	515	6.3	844	12.2	889	16.8	9,399	12.9	34.3	1,357	8.9
Independent	3,145	6.9	487	7.3			128	1.8			3,760	5.2	13.7	1,408	9.3
Baptist	898	2.0			473	5.8	40	0.6			1,411	1.9	5.2	30	0.2
Unitarian	162	0.3									162	0.2	0.6		
Moravian	456	1.0									456	0.6	1.7		
Quaker							28	0.4			28	0.0	0.1		
Wesleyan	1,555	3.4	1,204	18.1	130	1.6	611	8.8	520	9.8	4,020	5.5	14.7	961	6.3
Methodist New Connexion	1,179	2.6									1,179	1.6	4.3	70	0.5
Primitive Methodist	1,051	2.3	543	8.1	510	6.2			253	4.8	2,357	3.2	8.6		
Wesleyan Association	510	1.1	158	2.4					371	7.0	1,039	1.4	3.8		
Independent Methodist	677	1.5							294	5.5	971	1.3	3.5		
Calvinistic Methodist			562	8.4							562	0.8	2.1		
Roman Catholic	675	1.5									675	0.9	2.5	120	0.8
Swedenborgian			359	5.4							359	0.5	1.3		
Mormon			90	1.4			50	0.7			140	0.2	0.5		
Other	862	1.9									862	1.2	3.1	852	5.6
TOTAL	17,042	37.2	4,682	70.3	1,628	19.9	1,701	24.5	2,227	42.0	27,380	37.5	100.0	4,798	31.5

Source: As Table 7.1.

It is clear that attendances on census Sunday were unlikely to have been particularly representative of attendances during the rest of the year. In one or two local churches the timing of anniversary services meant above average congregations on 30 March, but in most of the churches attendances were lower than usual. The reasons for this are well documented, and included an influenza epidemic and the timing of the census in March, when the shorter days would have produced a lower attendance than in the summer. These problems were compounded by the appalling weather conditions on the day, with driving rain which, in the case of one local church, flooded its only access road, significantly reducing the size of its congregation. These difficulties probably had a particularly severe effect on Saddleworth and the out-townships, but a further factor affected the whole area—the coincidence of the census with mid-Lent Sunday. This was a traditional day for family reunions throughout northern England and would consequently have produced perhaps the *lowest* church attendance of the year.[10] To a certain extent the influence of these factors can be assessed by basing calculations on figures returned by the churches for 'Average attendance'. This was usually considerably higher than attendance on census Sunday, and one Oldham congregation reported that it had been underestimated by 260 per cent. Unfortunately, just over half of the churches failed to return an average total. In some cases this was probably because there was little difference between the average attendance and that on census Sunday and in others because the difference was impossible to calculate with sufficient accuracy. In addition a number of returns for average attendance have been lost. When the surviving average returns are totalled and substituted for the census Sunday figures for the same churches, the density of attendances among the eligible population increases to 40 per cent in Oldham and 37 per cent in Saddleworth. However, the average figures cannot solve the problems created by incomplete returns and missing churches, and the averages may themselves be too low. In Saddleworth the figures for average attendance were based on congregations over the previous year, but in Oldham many were calculated on a three- or six-month basis—thus providing figures for winter congregations which would probably have been lower, especially in the out-townships, than summer ones.[11] Taking into account all the foregoing considerations, we might conservatively suggest that an average

[10] PRO HO 129 475, 11, 13, 23, 38, 50; W. S. F. Pickering, 'The 1851 Religious Census—A Useless Experiment?', *British Journal of Sociology*, 18 (1967), 382–407; D. M. Thompson, 'The Religious Census, Problems and Possibilities', *Victorian Studies*, xi (1967), 87–97.

[11] PRO HO 129 475, 23, 50.

of around 45 per cent of the eligible population of both Oldham and Saddleworth were able and willing regularly to attend church during 1851.

The absence of other comparable surveys makes it difficult to be certain about the extent to which church attendance in 1851 was typical of the period as a whole. There is little worthwhile statistical information from the early nineteenth century,[12] but it is probable that attendance in the 1830s and early 1840s was lower than in 1851. During these decades the gap between Anglican provision and the size of the local population was at its greatest, and several Methodist groups were suffering from the effects of schism. Nevertheless, 1851 was far from being an auspicious year in which to assess the strength of the churches. It marked a low point for the Wesleyans, and also seems to have been a bad year for other Methodist groups. Moreover, many of the new Anglican churches were still struggling to establish themselves, and a census taken in the mid-1850s, which would have given them greater time to gather substantial congregations, would probably have produced a stronger showing. Most of the local churches shared in the steady growth and enthusiasm of the early 1860s, and regular church attendance in Oldham and Saddleworth may have exceeded 50 per cent of the eligible population during much of the second half of the nineteenth century. Something of the effects of this Church growth can be glimpsed from a survey of the parish of Waterhead undertaken in 1859 by an Anglican churchwarden and a local surgeon. Of 753 resident families, 285 attended no place of worship and 292 attended the Anglican church. There were also 133 Independent, 29 Wesleyan, and 8 Roman Catholic families, together with 6 others—mainly Moravians. Thus 62 per cent of families in the parish were regularly in attendance in the local churches—though how this figure would have converted into individual attendances, comparable with the figures for 1851, is unclear.[13]

Regrettably, the census provides little information about the identity of the people who attended church. The evidence from baptism registers and membership lists indicates that the churches recruited fairly evenly from all social classes, though the middle classes may have been slightly over-represented in some denominations. Both Anglican communicant rolls and nonconformist membership lists suggest that the churches may

---

[12] Foster used estimates of attendance drawn from the 1821 visitation returns and a survey of non-Anglican places of worship carried out in 1829 to compile a set of figures for the earlier nineteenth century. However, neither of these surveys is sufficiently complete or exhaustive to warrant direct comparison with the census: Foster, *Class Struggle*, 214, 313.

[13] Holy Trinity, Waterhead, MS History.

have recruited particularly strongly among women, and the figures for Sunday scholars attending church on census Sunday indicate, at least in Oldham, a slight over-recruitment among 5–19 year olds. The traditional concentration of historiographical interest on the culture and politics of the adult male working class has led to a relative lack of interest in churches perceived as institutions primarily concerned with the middle classes, and with working-class women and children. It is important to note, therefore, that adult working-class men in 1851 formed at most only 25 per cent of the population aged 5 and over. This included both the unskilled workers who are traditionally assumed to have had little contact with the churches, and the skilled workers for whom the churches are often regarded as having had considerable appeal. If the churches were over-represented among the middle classes, and working-class women and children, then they were appealing particularly strongly to those groups which at any one time comprised the vast majority of the population.

The 1851 census does provide a basis for some reasonably firm conclusions about the relative strength of the various churches in the locality. The Anglican church, although it had lost its near monopolistic position, was still by far the largest church in Oldham, recording well over twice as many attendance as its nearest rival—the Wesleyans. Attendance in the town could be divided into three roughly equal parts—one-third Anglican, one-third Methodist, and one-third comprising other Dissenting denominations, mainly Independents and Baptists. The Unitarians and other heterodox religious groups were numerically insignificant. Only the Anglicans and Wesleyans were represented in all districts of Oldham; other groups, especially the Independent and New Connexion Methodists, were quite restricted in their geographical spread. Perhaps the most significant variation in strength, however, was to be found among the Congregationalists, who concentrated almost two-thirds of their attendances in Oldham above town, where they closely challenged the Anglicans as the major ecclesiastical presence. In Saddleworth the Anglicans were in a weaker position than in Oldham, and recorded fewer attendances than the Independents. However, while the latter were boosted by the presence of the mainly Lees-based congregation of Springhead, the former were depleted by attendances at churches beyond the Saddleworth border, and were particularly badly affected by the special circumstances of census Sunday.[14] Even so, the ecclesiastical balance was much more even in Saddleworth than in Oldham, with the Anglicans, Wesleyans, and

[14] PRO HO 129 496, 14.

Congregationalists each accounting for roughly a quarter of the attendances, the remainder being made up by a number of smaller churches and undenominational preaching rooms. The evangelical revival in nonconformity had decisively shifted the ecclesiastical balance in Oldham and Saddleworth. The Anglican church, though both active and powerful, was no longer a preponderant—much less a monopolistic—presence on the ecclesiastical scene. Denominational pluralism and thus religious voluntaryism had become the most prominent feature of the local ecclesiastical ecology.

Churches and Communities

Church membership and attendance were, for the adult population of Oldham and Saddleworth, their most significant points of contact with organized religion. They were not, however, their only points of contact, for the churches exercised an influence on the public life of local communities, the extent of which is difficult to overestimate. Not only did the churches continue to preside over private rites of passage, maintaining an easy superiority of appeal over the secular alternatives; they also authenticated public rituals for a broad range of local organizations, from friendly societies and Orange lodges to the Oldham regiment of volunteers, and the town council of the newly incorporated borough.[15] The churches also played a particularly important role in local politics. Religious issues— like disputes over Church rate and religious establishments—and moral crusades—like those against slavery and drink—remained high on the political agenda throughout the period. Religion may have been a particularly potent influence on the politics of the upper ranks of the town's bourgeoisie, providing a focus of loyalty which sometimes reinforced and sometimes cut across alternative sources of allegiance based on other social and political formations. However, churches and church-goers also played a crucial role in the politics, both radical and conservative, of the emergent middle and working classes. In the eighteenth century, popular conservatism was most often expressed as acquiescence in the existing social and political order, punctuated by an occasional riot as 'Church feeling' overflowed in the violence of a Church and King mob. Mob activity was generally low key, and directed on an occasional basis against Dissenters or Methodists, often with the tacit support of the local authorities—both religious and secular. Occasionally the scope of such

---

[15] Foster, *Class Struggle*, 130, 216–20.

activity was widened to include attacks on protesters against the secular Establishment, and the mobs, like the one which broke up a radical reform meeting at Royton in 1794, could be of considerable proportions.[16] This sort of spontaneous popular loyalism seems to have gone into a decline in the later 1790s and to have remained fairly dormant during the Reform era. It showed no signs of significant revival until the anti-Roman Catholic riots of the 1850s. The role of the churches in this later period is rather difficult to pin down. There is certainly no evidence of any direct instigation of anti-Catholic violence, which is more likely to have been a product of rising ethnic tensions than of straightforward religious feuding. On the other hand, it is clear that individual church-goers did play an important role in organizations like the Orange order and the Oldham Protestant Association which provided a focus for anti-Catholic loyalism and the reconstruction of a popular Protestant conservative identity. The same men may also have played a role in a wider resurgence of popular conservatism during the 1860s.[17]

The influence of churches and church-goers on political radicalism in Oldham and Saddleworth is rather more clear. Many historians have recognized that the churches provided both a model for working-class political organization and a rhetoric which could be used to challenge the existing order. Patrick Joyce has concluded that in urban Lancashire at least the 'institutions and ideas of religion supplied most of the form and vocabulary of popular politics'.[18] Some political organizations, like the Hampden clubs of Middleton in the early nineteenth century, mixed orthodox religion with radical politics quite freely, and in Oldham one or two churches, like the Unitarians described by Foster, became themselves virtual political organizations. Other churches assumed key political roles as the representatives of wider residential communities, like the Primitive Methodists among the colliery villages of Knott Lanes and almost all the churches provided a natural home for local radicals in their associational culture of rational recreation and self-improvement. The churches also provided political leaders. Some of these were men of the first rank, like John Fielden, the Unitarian MP, or J. R. Stephens, the Methodist agitator. More typical, however, were the home-grown leaders, who played crucial if less prominent roles in local organizations, like

---

[16] Rowbottom Diary, 4 Jan., 21 Apr. 1794.

[17] Foster, *Class Struggle*, 218–20; Joyce, *Work*, 249–62.

[18] Ibid. 242; McLeod, 'New Perspectives', 39. For an account of the symbiotic relationship between the churches and popular radicalism in Oldham see Winstanley, 'Oldham Radicalism', *passim*.

Henry Atherton of Lees, a devout member of his local Methodist church and a long-standing member of the Lees Political Union. In 1843 Thomas Lowe compiled a list of fifteen men arrested for 'speaking' during the disturbances of 1842. The list included thirteen men who had made reference to their religious affiliation. These comprised one 'infidel', one 'chartist former Methodist', one 'former Churchman', two Congregationalists, one Wesleyan Methodist, and two New Connexion, two Primitive, and two Independent Methodists. One of these men was a teacher, and no fewer than seven were local preachers.[19] Secularists were also well represented in local radical circles, but they were far less strong than the mainstream Christian radicals who advocated moral and spiritual as well as material and intellectual self-improvement. In 1834, for example, the radicals of Oldham passed a strong vote of confidence in the reliability of the scriptures, despite the advocacy of Richard Carlile on the other side. Secularism was in fact something of a distraction for local radicalism, endangering the united front of the working-class radicals and threatening the alliances with middle-class radicals facilitated by common church connections. The secularists never became a dominant factor in local radicalism, and the very readiness of Oldham's radicals to divide along lines of churchmanship is a testimony to the seriousness with which they took their religion.[20]

If the churches were influential in the political life of their communities, they were even more so in the field of education. Finding the traditional approach to catechism inappropriate in the new social conditions, local churchmen first successfully broadened its appeal by translating it into a more popular form, and then supplemented it with a series of vigorous educational initiatives. Building on the traditional links between religion and education, the churches by 1851 had grown to dominate the provision of schooling. Day schools directly operated by the main denominations or heavily influenced by them accounted for over 90 per cent of the scholars in the public day-school sector counted by the 1851 census of education. Ministers of religion probably also maintained their traditional interest in the private day-school sector which was responsible for about half the day scholars in Oldham and Saddleworth. The religious instruction provided in day schools began to play an increasingly important role, during the second half of the nineteenth century, in the religious

---

[19] R. Glen, *Urban Workers in the Early Industrial Revolution* (1984), 229; Foster, *Class Struggle*, 31–2; *MNM* 93 (1890), 3–4; *PMM* 48 (1867), 108–9; CC, file 1,443, Lowe to CBC, 1843.
[20] Butterworth Diary, Oct. 1834; Gadian, 'Class Formation', 54–5.

socialization of the young. However, even in 1851 the combined attendance at public and private day schools accounted for only 7,097 children or 25 per cent of the population aged between 5 and 19 in Oldham and 1,828 pupils or 32 per cent of the eligible population in Saddleworth.[21] Much more important during the whole of the period under consideration, therefore, were the Sunday schools. Sunday-school attendance in the area covered by the O'Neil survey of 1847 totalled 16,254, which was equivalent to more than 67 per cent of all 5–19 year olds. In Saddleworth 3,457 Sunday scholars—equivalent to 60 per cent of the population aged between 5 and 19—were counted by the rather less complete 1851 census survey.[22] The proportion of Sunday-school attenders in both Oldham and Saddleworth probably increased after 1847, indicating a continuing mass interest in institutions which, because of changes in their curriculum, were becoming more exclusively 'religious' in their orientation. Sunday schools taught the language of religion, inculcating a familiarity with evangelical concepts and idioms which helped to render the subsequent efforts of preachers, Bible readers, and evangelistic visitors intelligible to the majority of the population. They also promoted the general diffusion of Christian belief throughout the district. However, the schools were not important merely because they laid a foundation for future recruitment to the churches. They also maintained in their own right a vital religious culture among the 40 per cent of the population aged between 5 and 19. The Christianity of the Sunday schools may have played a particularly important role in interpreting a world characterized by relatively high child mortality rates and low life expectancy. The schools certainly provided communal and spiritual support for the sick and the dying, and teachers must often have spent as much time in the pastoral visitation of their charges as they did in evangelism and teaching. The schools also provided practical help and a comprehensive network of support structures, including sick and burial societies. It is also important to remember that the same schools offered their pupils an entrance into an associational world of leisure—of tea parties, treats, and outings and eventually of railway trips to the country and the seaside—events that, however hedged

[21] Cox, *English Churches*, 95; PP 1852–3, xc [1692]. The proportion of scholars aged over 15 was, according to the census, relatively small. However, any distortion produced by calculating the eligible population on the basis of the number of 5–19 year olds is counterbalanced by the presence of scholars aged less than 5.

[22] PP 1852–3, xc [1692]; O'Neil, *Sunday Schools*. The population figure for 1847 has been calculated on the assumption that the population grew evenly over the decade between 1841 and 1851.

about by the canons of respectability, were aimed at providing straightforward fun—a counterpoint to the seriousness of the message of the atonement and the earnest striving after improvement.[23]

The relationship between the churches and popular leisure in Oldham and Saddleworth was complex. Certainly, the relatively cordial relationship between the churches and the hard drinking, hard fighting, popular culture of leisure that had been characteristic of the earlier eighteenth century, especially among some Anglicans, deteriorated after 1780. Attitudes towards the more brutal aspects of popular amusements began to harden, especially among the middle-class supporters of the churches, and concern about the destructive potential of alcohol began to rise. As an alternative, the churches promoted a culture of 'rational recreation' offering education, mutual improvement, and escape from the most common causes of secondary poverty. It would be a mistake, however, to view this development as a simple product of middle-class influence. Many features of the alternative approach to recreation had their own resonances with popular culture and some were appropriated whole-heartedly by the workers and were transformed in the process. Sabbatarianism, for example, was often, as Callum Brown has pointed out, incorporated into proletarian culture as a day of freedom from work—a partial substitute for the lost St Monday. Temperance too, especially when pushed to its teetotal extreme, had considerable proletarian appeal. The temperance societies founded in the early 1830s in Oldham and Saddleworth continued to recruit strongly throughout the period. Some societies were denominationally based and operated with active clerical support; others were more clearly independent working-class institutions, like the society at Royton whose seventy members combined 'the principles of temperance with those of mutual instruction' and, according to the *Manchester Courier*, produced 'a marked moral influence in the neighbourhood'.[24] At the same time, the churches never entirely lost contact with traditional forms of popular leisure. Their own anniversary and special musical services continued to draw large crowds and to provide occasions for more general communal celebration. Churches and Sunday schools also provided

---

[23] SMC, Diary, 4 Apr. 1846, 2 May 1857; Foster, *Class Struggle*, 91–3; Laqueur, *Religion and Respectability*, 160–9; Bebbington, *Evangelicalism*, 124; Cox, *English Churches*, 95–7.

[24] *Manchester Courier*, 9 Oct. 1833, 11 Jan. 1834, 16 Mar. 1850; Foster, *Class Struggle*, 221; Brown, *The Social History of Religion in Scotland since 1730*, 106; J. Rule, 'Methodism, Popular Beliefs and Village Culture in Cornwall 1800–50', in Storch (ed.), *Popular Culture*, 50–60.

venues for public meetings, informal gatherings, and the distribution of welfare. They thus retained much of their traditional position as the focus of community life.[25]

The Meanings of Attendance and Non-Attendance

Why did people go to church, and why did they stay away? What were the meanings in both social and religious terms of these contrasting behaviours? If statistics of church attendance are difficult to compile, the answers to these questions are even more obscure. For some people church attendance may have represented participation in a community group, and their assent to a concomitant set of theological commitments may have been an entirely secondary consideration. However, as Hugh McLeod has pointed out, this is to beg the question of why it was specifically religious groups, rather than pubs or secularist societies, that met the need for community. It seems plausible to suggest that most people attended primarily 'religious' institutions for primarily 'religious' reasons, even if their reasons did not always precisely coincide with those approved by the churches. Moreover, most versions of Christianity have tended to place great emphasis on the importance of 'fellowship'. It would be a mistake, therefore, to assume that the desire to participate in a community group could not itself be an orthodox 'religious' motivation and one should beware of drawing too sharp a distinction between the social–communal and the 'religious' functions of the churches.[26] It is also possible that, for some people, church attendance may have been related to a desire to participate in a culture of respectability. This almost certainly had a particularly compelling effect on the middle classes, and both Foster and Kirk have suggested that the pull of respectability was also felt by the working class. It is, in fact, tempting to paint a picture of two distinct cultures in Oldham and Saddleworth—a respectable culture based on the social world of the church and Sunday school, and a rough culture based on the social world of the beer shop and the wrestling match. However, this simple dichotomy is misleading. The churches were not the only advocates of a respectable culture of mutual improvement, and in some communities they found themselves in direct competition with a similar version promoted by socialists or secularist radicals. Moreover, while it is true that church membership imparted a certain respectability, this

---

[25] Rycroft, 'Craven', 132, 269–71; Cox, *English Churches*, 5.

[26] McLeod, *Religion and the Working Class*, 22–4; G. Parsons, 'A Question of Meaning: Religion and Working-Class Life', in Parsons (ed.), *Religion in Victorian Britain*, ii. 77–9.

was not a monolithic phenomenon. It was compatible both with extreme wealth and with extreme poverty, and it would be a mistake to assume that the public ecclesiastical respectability which was virtually intrinsic to middle-class status had either the same content or the same function as the evangelical respectability which lent dignity to the lives of the Primitive Methodist miners of Knott Lanes. Furthermore, while there may have been some polarization between the rough and respectable members of small communities, especially as the more proletarian churches began with increasing enthusiasm to support teetotalism, it would be misleading to see these as discrete cultural alternatives. Many leisure activities, from wakes celebrations and mid-Lent visiting, to public tea meetings and special musical services, were equally accessible to all members of the community. It was perfectly possible for the same individual to be 'rough' in one context and 'respectable' in another, and those who had rejected the fellowship of the church in favour of the easy conviviality of the beer shop could nevertheless have been drawn back into the orbit of church-based activity. They would probably have sent their children to Sunday school and might themselves have attended camp meetings and anniversaries, especially when these became celebrations that embraced the whole community. Churches, too, could appear less than respectable in certain contexts. They might, as was the case with early Wesleyanism, cut across existing communal norms, invade families, and promote evangelistic and devotional activities which had much more in common with the spontaneous celebration associated with 'rough' popular culture than with the more restrained middle-class version of acceptable activity. In their influence on popular leisure and on rough and respectable culture, the churches managed to look both ways. On the one hand, they were clearly identified with the respectable culture of improvement—supporting temperance and education and providing a mass of lectures, magic lantern shows, and tea meetings as well as prestigious cultural and educational institutions like the Oldham Lyceum. At the same time, the churches retained links with an older more spontaneous culture of informal celebration, providing venues for its activities and a degree of official support. They thus established a foothold for organized religion in those informal institutions of leisure which are increasingly being recognized as central to the formation of 'traditional' working-class culture.[27]

[27] Kirk, 'Traditional Working-Class Culture'; R. McKibbin, *The Ideologies of Class: Social Relations in Britain, 1880–1950* (Oxford, 1990); H. McLeod, 'White Collar Values and the Role of Religion', in G. Crossick (ed.), *The Lower Middle Class in Britain* (1977), 61–88; Koditschek, *Class Formation*, 452.

Indifference, Infidelity, and Superstition

The implications of absence from church are also difficult to interpret. At one end of the scale were those who stayed away simply because church-going was a public activity in which they felt unable to participate be-cause of a lack of decent clothing. At the other extreme was a small group of local people who had consciously opted for 'infidelity'. Thomas Paine's *Age of Reason* was probably the first infidel publication to make an impact on the area at a popular level, and local clergymen expressed concern during the 1811 visitation about the emergence of infidelity in general and Paine's influence in particular.[28] However, clerical fears were to prove largely unfounded. Absenteeism from public worship continued to attract notice, but there was no upsurge of popular anti-clericalism in the local-ity, and most observers ascribed such absenteeism to indifference rather than hostility to the activities of organized religion. Sporadic infidel ac-tivity continued, but it left little in the way of permanent organization until the middle decades of the nineteenth century. A socialist Sunday school operated in Oldham in the early 1840s and there was a good reception among a section of the population for the more thoroughgoing secularism of Holyoake in the middle of the decade. In 1854 the Oldham secularists were sufficiently organized to send delegates to a general con-ference in Stockport, and by 1860 there was a regular secularist meeting in a room belonging to the local co-operative society. Nevertheless, though the secularists could usually muster a decent audience for their most famous lecturers, and Edward Royle can describe Oldham as one of the strongholds of Lancashire secularism, its popular appeal in the town was negligible. Consistent secularism demanded of its adherents a discipline analagous to that required by the evangelical churches, and very few people seem to have been willing to make such a commitment. Even in the 1860s, after several decades of strenuous effort, the total membership of the various secularist and socialist societies in Oldham was probably no more numerous or influential than that of the smallest of the non-conformist congregations.[29]

The world-view espoused by the majority of the local population, whether they were regularly in attendance in local churches or not, was—

[28] CVR 1811, 120, 183, 189; McLeod, *Religion and the Working Class*, 17–25; E. Royle, *Radical Politics 1790–1900: Religion and Unbelief* (1971), 17–25.

[29] E. Royle, *Victorian Infidels* (Manchester, 1974), 99, 142, 177, 212–40; *Oldham Standard*, 31 Mar. 1860.

at least at the beginning of the period—overwhelmingly supernaturalistic in character. Especially for those not integrated into church communities —those described by contemporary clerical observers as 'indifferent'— this popular supernaturalism extended far beyond the orthodox Christianity taught by the churches. Intermingled with the residue of more than a thousand years of various kinds of Christian witness in Oldham and Saddleworth could be found the elements of another religious world whose representatives were witches, wise women, and cunning men. There was a considerable demand in the locality for charms and potions, and for traditional medical advice, while fortune-tellers were asked for help in making important decisions and in finding lost objects or lost people. The most valuable commodity on offer in the occult market, however, was protection. Charms were prepared in order to ward off the curses of ill-disposed neighbours, and horseshoes were nailed on the doors of the shippons to protect cattle against disease. Cunning men and wise women might be able to interpret or even deflect the misfortune presaged by an encounter with a brocken-spectre on the moor and to allay the fears created by the activities of a malevolent boggart. These occult specialists consequently enjoyed a high status, especially in the villages of Saddleworth and Oldham's out-townships.[30] Popular superstition or 'traditional religion' was not systematic, however, and, along with what Alexander Murray has recently described as the debris or bric-à-brac of abandoned religious forms, there is much evidence of an eclectic borrowing from Christian tradition in local patterns of observance. In some cases barely a trace of Christian orthodoxy survived the popular appropriation of the tradition, and one or two Christian festivals, most notably, All-Hallows' eve and St John's eve, were virtually drained of all orthodox content and regarded simply as auspicious occasions for the practice of magic. Similarly Bible verses were frequently regarded not so much as vehicles of divine revelation, but as receptacles of a beneficent power to be written out on slips of paper and attached to the horns of cattle as charms against disease. In other cases the residue of orthodoxy—sometimes perhaps a pre-reformation orthodoxy—was more apparent. Thus dough and butter were marked with the sign of the cross to preserve them against the influence of evil, the power of the sacraments of the Church was widely recognized (and in the case of Holy Communion widely feared), and clergymen were

---

[30] A. Wrigley, *Saddleworth Superstitions and Folk Customs* (Oldham, 1909), 25–8; Bamford, *Walks*, 207–9, *Early Days*, 160–4.

frequently called in to lend their authority to the battle against the curse and the boggart.[31]

Little is known about the survival of this sort of popular supernaturalism after the first few decades of the nineteenth century, especially in the towns and cities. Obelkevich has suggested that the Victorian period saw a marked change in the nature of popular belief, as the rise of class society disrupted the many-stranded, face-to-face relationships within communities that had supported the traditional concept of the curse and the role of the witch and the cunning man. Koditschek and Cox have both detected a recession of conscious pagan belief in an urban environment into vaguer concepts of 'luck', and McLeod has noted a parallel shift in the focus of popular religion 'from magic to moralism' as a recessive paganism mixed with a recessive Christianity to produce an optimistic folk pelagianism.[32] Samuel Bamford certainly felt that superstition was already on the retreat in the early nineteenth century, and it is clear that by the end of the century the fear of boggarts had, even in the more remote farmsteads of Saddleworth, largely subsided into a form of rural entertainment.[33] However, both L. H. Lees and D. Clark have demonstrated the long-term survival capacity of popular superstition, and there is some evidence of its persistence in Oldham and Saddleworth. Bamford described Burnley-lane near Oldham in the early 1840s as a neighbourhood rife with cunning men; Butterworth, writing in the 1850s, noted that cunning men were still active in Oldham, and Ammon Wrigley described one famous Saddleworth practitioner being consulted well after 1865.[34]

Faced with this complex and shifting pattern of unorthodox Christianity, infidelity, superstition, and indifference to organized religion, the evangelical churches added to their activism two important ideological advantages. In the first place, the churches were in the vanguard of the modernizing forces of the late eighteenth century and early nineteenth century. Bebbington has pointed out the extent to which the evangelical revival acted as the bearer of an enlightenment rationality to its adherents, and Hilton has revealed the extent to which the churches provided a moral content for the new political economy and helped to mediate it to

[31] A. Murray, 'Missionaries and Magic in Dark-Age Europe', *Past and Present*, 136 (1992), 186–205; Wrigley, *Saddleworth Superstitions*, 27; Butterworth, *Oldham*, 106–7; Brierly, *History of Saddleworth*, 6–7.

[32] Obelkevich, *Religion and Rural Society*, 310–12; Koditschek, *Class Formation*, 54; Cox, *English Churches*, 95; McLeod, *Religion and the Working Class*, 26–35.

[33] Bamford, *Passages*, 99; Wrigley, *Saddleworth Superstitions*, *passim*.

[34] L. H. Lees, *Exiles of Erin* (1979); D. Clark, *Between Pulpit and Pew* (1982); Bamford, *Walks*, 207–9; Butterworth, *Oldham*, 107; Wrigley, *Saddleworth Superstitions*, 29.

the leaders of a maturing industrial society. Both Morris and Koditschek in their studies of Leeds and Bradford have concluded that the churches, and especially the evangelical churches, were fundamental to the formation of a cultural identity among the industrial bourgeoisie.[35] Callum Brown has suggested that evangelicalism dominated middle-class attitudes to urban civilization until the 1860s. It provided both an analysis of the problems of the new urban industrial environment and a programme of action. 'Church extension was only one part of a much wider evangelical social policy, providing an overarching moral and religious interpretation of the cities' social problems which, from the evangelical point of view, were all inter-related products of spiritual failure of the individual.'[36] Moral and spiritual failure at all levels of society were to be tackled both by extending the influence of the churches—by the personal justification and sanctification of thousands of individuals—and also by the most strenuous devotion to civic improvement.

In some towns evangelicals promoted ambitious housing improvement schemes and collaborated across party lines in local government to support all manner of municipal welfare programmes. They also, especially after the middle of the nineteenth century, began to develop a vast apparatus for philanthropic endeavour with a multitude of voluntary organizations tackling various problems of ignorance, disease, and poverty.[37] In Oldham and Saddleworth this commitment to an evangelical moral modernity was made manifest in the vast network of church-inspired initiatives for the promotion of temperance, sabbath observance, and child and adult education. It also underlay much of the political activity of the churches, especially their support for liberal and radical causes—both traditional evangelical enthusiasms like the abolition of slavery and more general political interests like parliamentary reform and corn-law repeal.[38] Some clergymen were particularly notable for their commitment to municipal reform. The funeral notice of Daniel Brammall, incumbent of Shaw, remarked on the close attention he paid to the public business of Crompton, and the biographer of Richard Durnford, the rector of Middleton, described a heavy involvement in local affairs, including measures to improve the

---

[35] Bebbington, *Evangelicalism*, 46–74; Hilton, *Atonement*, 7–35; Morris, *Class, Sect and Party*, 178–98, 321; Koditschek, *Class Formation*, 52. For the similar modernizing role played in Irish rural society by evangelical landlords, see D. Hempton and M. Hill, *Evangelical Protestantism in Ulster Society 1740–1890* (1992), 86–8.

[36] Brown, *Social History*, 136–43.

[37] Ibid. 131–2; Cox, *English Churches*, 89, 271.

[38] *Oldham Free Press*, 15 Apr. 1854; *Oldham Advertiser*, 26 Feb. 1853, 2 June, 29 Dec. 1855; *Manchester Guardian*, 15 Dec. 1832, 28 Jan. 1843; Butterworth, *Oldham*, 196–7.

paving, drainage, and water supply of the township.[39] More generally, local clergymen and leading evangelical laymen stood in the forefront of a wide variety of initiatives in civic improvement, from attempts to establish an infirmary and a new burial ground to the promotion of a Board of Health during the cholera scare of 1832 and a number of local government reforms culminating in the incorporation of the borough of Oldham in 1849.[40]

Commitment to moral and social improvement emphasized the relevance of evangelicalism as a means of understanding and dealing with the problems of the new industrial society and thus provided the churches with a useful ideological edge as well as an important point of contact with mainstream popular radicalism. It was complemented by a second ideological advantage—a thoroughgoing supernaturalism which provided an important point of contact with popular belief. The clergymen of South Lindsey seem, judging by Obelkevich's account, to have had a less supernaturalistic world-view than that of the labourers they served, but those of Oldham and Saddleworth were rather more prepared to enter the spiritual battleground on terms that were intelligible to the bulk of their parishioners. This proved to be particularly important in the context of the darker side of traditional religion. Samuel Bamford had vivid memories of the terror he experienced when as a child in the early nineteenth century he believed he had been confronted by a boggart, and Ammon Wrigley described a more general fear inspired by famous boggarts like 'Old Delph Will': 'Big strong men, who feared nothing human, scarcely dared to stir off their door stone at night.' One man from Saddleworth was alleged to have died of fright after an encounter with the Black Dog of Grange—a particularly terrifying spectre which was held to presage a death in the family. The fear of the curse and of witchcraft also persisted into the nineteenth century, while a slip in a complex pattern of observances might bring bad luck to an individual or an entire household. Evangelical Christianity may sometimes have engendered guilt as well as

---

[39] *Oldham Standard*, 2 Dec. 1865; Stephens, *Richard Durnford*, 99–101.

[40] *Manchester Mercury*, 17 Apr., 22 May 1792; *Manchester Courier*, 4 May 1832; *Oldham Free Press*, 21 Jan. 1854; Foster, *Class Struggle*, 201. There is insufficient evidence about the eschatological convictions of local evangelicals to allow a full discussion of Hilton's suggestion that support for interventionist policies was largely confined to evangelical 'extremists' who held premillenialist views. In the municipal context improvement proposals were supported by a wide range of evangelical opinion. However, support for infirmary schemes and the like was compatible with the economic individualism and moral paternalism associated by Hilton with moderate evangelical opinion as well as with premillenialist interventionism: Hilton, *Atonement, passim*; M. Berg, 'Progress and Providence in Early Nineteenth-Century Political Economy', *Social History*, 15 (1990), 365–75.

release; the world of folk belief seems to have offered only very uncertain protection against its own terrors.[41]

In the eighteenth century both Anglican clergymen, like the Evangelical John Buckley of Friarmere, and local Dissenting ministers seem to have regarded dealing with this fear as a routine part of their ministry. They lifted curses, laid ghosts, and dealt with witches, and perhaps most importantly they could be called upon to lay an angry boggart with prayer and psalm-singing.[42] In the nineteenth century, though aspects of evangelical theology—particularly the emphasis on special providences—continued to link the religion of the Established Church with the world of folk belief, the initiative in this area seems increasingly to have passed to the Methodists. For the men who proclaimed 'Jesus the name high over all, in hell or earth, or sky, Angels and men before it fall, and devils fear and fly', the world of traditional religion held few terrors, and this hymn was not infrequently used in the exorcism of boggarts—a widespread Methodist practice in Oldham and Saddleworth. The Methodists seem to have been particularly willing to accept the forms of traditional religion and to integrate them into a framework of orthodox demonology. Perhaps most importantly, however, the democratization of spirituality characteristic of Methodist activity extended also to the confrontation with the curse and the evil spirit. Victory as proclaimed by the Methodists was now available not just to those able to call on the services of a religious professional or an occult specialist, but to the ordinary believer in a cottage prayer meeting. John Rule has suggested that part of the reason for the popularity of Methodism in Cornwall was that it did not demand a rationalistic view of the world, but was willing to translate traditional folk-belief into its own religious idiom. Moreover, 'the starkness of many aspects of Methodist theology enabled it to be woven in existing folk-beliefs, the more especially since its regular interpreters were not the educated Wesleys but the local preachers and class leaders'. The willingness to take seriously, but not so much to baptize as to exorcize popular belief, seems to have been equally characteristic of Methodism in southeast Lancashire, and also to have persisted in a more or less attenuated form in other denominations.[43]

Janus-like, evangelicalism looked both forward to the world of urban

---

[41] Obelkevich, *Religion and Rural Society*, 278; Bamford, *Early Days*, ch. 13, 16; *Passages*, chs. 20–3; Butterworth, *Oldham*, 106–7; Wrigley, *Saddleworth Superstitions*, 15–26.

[42] Ibid. 16, 26.

[43] Hudson, 'Delph Methodism', 14; Bamford, *Early Days*, 163–4; Ward, *Religion and Society*, 79; Rule, 'Village Culture', 62–6.

industrial modernity and back to the world of traditional religion. The determination with which evangelicals sought to build the Jerusalem of municipal welfare and moral and social reformation from the elements of industrial society derived its fire from the same confident orthodox supernaturalism which lent conviction and intelligibility to the confrontation with popular superstition. The evangelical churches were thus well placed to extend their influence in Oldham and Saddleworth, and their efforts clearly had an effect on those commonly regarded as indifferent. In practice, those missionaries who took their Gospel outside consecrated buildings and into cottages or the open air often found non-church-goers far from indifferent. In 1859, for example, the *Oldham Standard*, reporting on the crowds attending Anglican open-air preaching, commented that they were 'a clear proof that the working classes of Oldham are not averse to the Gospel, but that they will listen to it whenever it is brought to and faithfully set before them'.[44] Even genuine indifference to the activities of organized religion did not always signify indifference to Christianity itself, and popular culture in any case was thoroughly permeated by a 'diffused Christianity' which prompted many non-church-goers to seek out the services of the churches at times of personal and communal celebration and crisis. Hence the prevalence of death-bed conversions and the large crowds attracted to musical services, anniversaries, and camp meetings. The influence of diffused Christianity almost certainly increased during the nineteenth century as religious education grew more pervasive and the efforts of tract and Bible distributors reached ever more people. In Waterhead in 1859, although 285 families regularly attended no church, only forty-five families were without a Bible, and much of the popular literature current in the district, especially the dialect poetry of the second half of the nineteenth century, was drenched in sentimental Christianity.[45]

Builders of Zion

As we noted at the outset, the difference between the 'optimistic' and 'pessimistic' schools of nineteenth-century church history is, to some extent, a matter of perspective. A number of recent writers have pointed out that the 1851 religious census, even without allowing for its inherent underestimation of attendance, is, when viewed as a measure of the

---

[44] *Oldham Standard*, 20 Oct. 1860.
[45] SMC, Diary, 27 Mar. 1838, 10 June 1845, 21 Feb. 1854; Holy Trinity, Waterhead, MS History; Bebbington, *Evangelicalism*, 114–15.

church-going population rather than of the number of absentees, a tribute to the strength of the churches.[46] However, there has been a tendency for historians to be mesmerized by the census, and an estimate of church attendance on a rainy Sunday in 1851 does not go far to illuminate the changing relationship between religion and industrial communities. We have detected little effective difference between the texture of life in the industrialized rural settlements of Saddleworth and the more urban settlements of Oldham. In neither sort of community did the churches have to overcome widespread 'anomie' or a notably 'secularized' popular worldview. However, they did have to cope with a mushrooming population, changing patterns of work that restricted leisure time, and increasing social tensions, all of which made life difficult for inclusive institutions that placed heavy demands on their members. Some churches faced difficulties in breaking into close communities that objected to their potentially disruptive influence. All churches faced communities that were to some extent alienated from regular weekly church attendance and had to compete for scarce working-class leisure time with an alternative associational culture based on the public house.

In response, the churches launched vigorous building programmes and strove to maintain high standards of pastoral and devotional activity. As the influence of evangelicalism became dominant, they also embarked on a continuous and increasingly co-operative programme of aggressive evangelism, determined not just to diffuse the Gospel, but also to proclaim it. As a consequence of their efforts, local communities began to support a variety of religious subcultures. There was a tight group of the 'godly', amounting to perhaps 10 per cent of the adult population in the middle of the nineteenth century, who supported the churches financially and participated in their sacramental life. There was also a much wider culture of regular weekly attendance in church and Sunday school, which extended to all social classes and all stages of the life cycle. This group grew in absolute size during the nineteenth century, and may have formed the majority in some communities by the later 1850s. Most of the remainder of the population formed a penumbra of occasional attenders. Some of these, like Samuel Bamford's father and uncle, may have separated from their church and yet remained orthodox and even theologically articulate Christians. Others, like the young Bamford himself, while being favourably disposed towards organized religion, may have found an incongruity between the sometimes stereotyped expectations of the

---

[46] Joyce, *Work*, 241; Cox, *English Churches*, 5.

churches and their own spiritual experience.[47] However, many more probably stayed away because they lacked decent clothing, and still more because they did not see regular weekly church-going as relevant to the Christianity that they themselves embraced.

It was part of the genius of the evangelicals that they discovered that this penumbra was not beyond their reach. Many people who would not come to church would attend meetings in the cottage next door. They would possess a Bible and a handful of tracts, they would send their children to Sunday school and entertain home visits, and they would also participate in occasional church festivities. As a consequence, the possibility of closer church involvement could be promoted, the density of reformed orthodoxy within diffused Christianity was increased, and the churches retained their position as a popular resort in moments of personal or communal crisis when preoccupation with temporal concerns receded. The churches also maintained a wider social significance. At various times the churches moved in the vanguard of reform and modernity and articulated the identity of entire social classes and residential communities. They provided institutions that communities could make their own and celebrations like small Sunday-school anniversaries and huge camp meetings which were fundamentally inclusive in character. They enriched and focused the cultural life of Oldham and Saddleworth and sometimes lent their discipline and intensity to its politics. Religion was not always a unifying force and communities sometimes felt threatened by aggressive evangelism. The churches themselves were far from uniform, and parish and circuit, and the contrasting rhythms of Anglican and nonconformist calendars, introduced competing versions of sacred space and time into the district. However, the overwhelming local influence of evangelicalism reduced the disruptive potential of this pluralism and produced a relentless commitment to growth that brought enormous dividends.

The various subcultures pictured above in terms of concentric rings had no firm boundaries. Individuals were constantly passing between them through gradual attraction, conversion, backsliding, or their changing place in the life cycle. The religious experience of the inhabitants of Oldham and Saddleworth, as well as its social meaning, would have varied considerably with their age, gender, and the nature of the religious group to which they were linked. However, it is clear that the churches had succeeded in preventing the development of a culture in which they

---

[47] Bamford, *Early Days*, 43, 113–14.

were marginalized. The proliferating industrial communities of the locality displayed resistance to regular weekly church-going, but not decisive indifference to the Gospel, especially when it came into their own homes and spoke to their own needs. The churches had sown and tended their crop with great diligence throughout the period, and, as the revival of the 1860s began to gather force, local evangelicals must have viewed the prospect of the harvest with growing confidence. To this extent at least we can answer Blake's famous question in the affirmative—Jerusalem was builded here, among these dark satanic mills.

Afterword

> If anyone asked me to name a town in which to study industrial life in England, I should unhesitatingly say Oldham.[1]

How far can one generalize from the experience of the churches in Oldham and Saddleworth? It would be implausible in a country with so many diverse regional cultures and distinct religious traditions to present any single area as a microcosm, and Oldham has, in the past, been regarded as exceptional. In particular, historians have singled it out among other towns of a comparable size and type as displaying an unusually low level of religious activity as reflected in church attendance.[2] This present study has demonstrated that this 'pessimistic' view of religion in Oldham and Saddleworth is misleading. Far from being ineffectual or marginalized, the local churches were extremely vigorous institutions, growing steadily in absolute size, commanding the active support of a substantial minority of the population, and exercising a considerable influence over most of the remainder. Should Oldham and Saddleworth then be regarded as atypical because of the exceptional *vitality* of their religious life?

It is clear that there were some special elements in the local situation. One might doubt, for example, that the effects of pluralism and non-residence were everywhere of quite so little consequence as they seem to have been in Oldham and Saddleworth—though the experience of the Established Church in these two districts does provide a corrective to the simplistic assumption that the irrationalities of the 'unreformed' ecclesiastical system were necessarily damaging to its pastoral effectiveness. Again, the unusual preponderance of Evangelicals among the local Anglican clergy, especially towards the middle of the nineteenth century, may have made the development and maintenance of good relations with evangelical nonconformity, and therefore of active co-operation in evangelism, exceptionally easy. However, the local pan-evangelical experience does open up the possibility that the application of the concepts of competition and co-operation may prove a more fruitful approach to understanding inter-church relationships from the later eighteenth to the

[1] A. Shadwell, *Industrial Efficiency* (1906).
[2] Joyce, *Work*, 244; Inglis, 'Patterns of Religious Worship', 74–86.

mid-nineteenth century than has the paradigm of conflict. Similarly, while special problems with the 1851 religious census in Oldham have led some scholars to underestimate church attendance in the town to a degree rarely paralleled in other industrial areas, the questions raised about the value of the census as an indicator of the influence of the churches in local society are almost certainly applicable on a much wider basis. Thus, even in the cases where Oldham and Saddleworth were exceptional, their particular experience allows us to see that there were possibilities open to the churches which have been obscured in other accounts.

Notwithstanding the peculiarities of the situation in Oldham and Saddleworth, it is also clear that a number of leading features of the experience of the local churches were common to other industrial areas. The vitality of the 'unreformed' Establishment as reflected in its rate of church-building and its general pastoral effectiveness was paralleled elsewhere in Lancashire and to some extent in the industrial district of Craven in Yorkshire. The ambiguous effects of centrally directed Church reform and its dependence on local initiative and effort has been traced at a diocesan level throughout the country by Arthur Burns, and was also matched at the parochial level elsewhere in the industrial north.[3] The important role played by nonconformist churches, their evangelistic and pastoral flexibility, and their predominantly working-class social composition have also been confirmed by a number of other studies.[4] Perhaps most important, however, has been the accumulation of evidence not merely for the vitality of the churches in industrialized areas, but also for the general success of their mission to the population at large. Statistical surveys by K. D. M. Snell and by Callum Brown have demonstrated that there is no clear relationship between urbanization and a decline in the strength of organized religion or the importance of religious belief. There is a growing consensus that the churches and their associated voluntary organizations played a crucial role in shaping the development of a middle-class identity in the new industrial towns, and Jeffrey Cox has illustrated the widespread influence exercised by the churches not only on middle-class, but also on working-class culture in the late Victorian period. Donald Lewis has shown that the influence of religion even extended to the unchurched working classes. They participated in church-organized

---

[3] Albers, 'Seeds of Contention'; Smith, 'Richard Podmore'; Rycroft, 'Craven'; Burns, 'Diocesan Revival'.

[4] Lovegrove, *Itinerancy*; C. G. Brown, 'Religion, Class and Church Growth', in W. H. Fraser and R. J. Morris (eds.), *People and Society in Scotland 1830–1914* (Edinburgh, 1990), 321.

social activities, welcomed the visits of evangelical domestic missionaries,
and espoused a popular religiosity which moved closer to an evangelical-
inspired christian orthodoxy during the course of the nineteenth century.[5] This view has received a degree of support from reviews of oral
evidence relating to the late nineteenth and early twentieth centuries
which have indicated that religion played a much greater part in the lives
of working people than was previously believed. According to Hugh
McLeod, few people developed a consistently secular approach to life,
and few were without contacts with organized religion. For Elizabeth
Roberts the most striking fact about religion in the late nineteenth century was the significant part it played in the lives of all but one of the
working-class families she studied in Barrow and Lancaster.[6]

The cumulative effect of these various studies has been to pose a
challenge to the 'pessimistic view' that presented nineteenth-century industrial society as an arena in which struggling churches fought a losing
battle to impose an essentially middle-class religiosity on a working-class
culture characterized by mass indifference. Instead, they have drawn
attention to the vitality of church life in an urban environment where the
predominantly voluntaristic nature of church affiliation seems to have
produced a particularly dynamic form of religious culture. The churches
and church-goers of Oldham and Saddleworth participated in this culture
in a consistently enthusiastic manner. To that extent they may fairly be
judged to be representative.

[5] K. D. M. Snell, *Church and Chapel in the North Midlands: Religious Observance in the
Nineteenth Century* (Leicester, 1991), 25–7; Brown, 'Urbanisation'; Koditschek, *Class Formation*, 52; Morris, *Class Power and Social Structure*, 178–98, 321; Cox, *English Churches*, 93–
109; Lewis, *Lighten their Darkness*, 138, 274–5.

[6] McLeod, 'Oral Evidence'; E. Roberts, *Working Class Barrow and Lancaster 1890 to 1930*
(Lancaster, 1976), 62.

APPENDIX I. *Anglican Evangelical Clergymen in Oldham and Saddleworth 1829*

St Chad's, Saddleworth: F. R. Raines.
St Thomas's, Friarmere: John Buckley.
St Peter's, Oldham: William Winter.
St John's, Hey: John Mattinson.
St James's, Oldham: W. F. Walker.

St Anne's, Lydgate: H. Alkin (possible).

Sources: Raines, 'Diary', 13 Aug. 1826, 29 July, 7 Aug. 1827, 29 Aug. 1829; OLIC, Minutes of Oldham Auxiliary to the BFBS, 1813–30; EA, *Conference Report* (1847); B. Nightingale, 'Independency a Century Ago', *Oldham Chronicle*, 2–9 Aug. 1919.

Anglican Ministers in Oldham and Saddleworth 1846

Holy Trinity, Dobcross: W. Simpson.
Churchmanship unknown.

St Michael's, Tonge: M. Lawler.
Trinity College, Dublin. Churchmanship uncertain.
Supported: SPCK, SPG, ACS, CMS.
Cultivated friendships with Dissenters.

St Anne's, Lydgate: G. Cowell.
St Bees' College. Possibly High Churchman.
Supported: CPAS.
Employed CPAS curate, introduced *Hymns Ancient and Modern*.

St Leonard's, Middleton: R. Durnford.
Magdalen College, Oxford. Moderate High Churchman.
Supported: CMS, ACS, SPG.

St Chad's, Saddleworth: R. Whitelock.
Lincoln College, Oxford. Moderate High Churchman.
Supported: CPAS, ACS, SPG.

St Thomas's, Friarmere: W. Grant.
St Bees' College. Evangelical.
Supported: BFBS.

St Mary's, Birch: H. P. Thomas.
St David's College, Lampeter. Evangelical.
Supported: CPAS.
Former curate at St Peter's, Oldham.

St Mary's, Oldham: T. Lowe.
St Catharine's College, Cambridge. Evangelical.
Supported: CMS.
Treasurer CPAS; former curate St Peter's, Oldham.

St Peter's, Oldham: W. Lees.
St John's College, Cambridge. Evangelical.
Supported: CMS, CPAS, BFBS, RTS.

St James's, Oldham: W. F. Walker.
Magdalen Hall, Oxford. Evangelical.
Supported: CMS, CPAS, BFBS, Jews' Society, EA.
Developed close friendships and co-operation with Dissenters.

St Margaret's, Hollinwood: R. Hill.
Corpus Christi College, Cambridge. Evangelical.
Supported: ACS, CMS, RTS, Jews' Society.
Former curate at St Peter's, Oldham.

St John's, Hey: G. D. Grundy.
Brasenose College, Oxford, Evangelical.
Supported: CMS, CPAS, Jews' Society.
Influenced by Hill of St Edmund Hall and Bulteel.

Holy Trinity, Shaw: D. Brammall.
University College, Oxford. Evangelical.
Supported: CMS, CPAS, RTS, Jews' Society.

Christ Church, Glodwick: S. G. Poole.
St Bees' College. Evangelical.
Supported: CMS, CPAS.
Accepted a lecturership at St Dunstan's, Stepney, in opposition to the High
Church incumbent.

Holy Trinity, Waterhead: P. Reynolds.
Trinity College, Dublin. Evangelical.
Supported: CMS, CPAS.
Employed CPAS lay-reader. Black Gown.

St Matthew's, Chadderton: J. R. Dunne.
Trinity College, Dublin. Evangelical.
Supported: SPCK, CMS, CPAS, BFBS.
Former curate at St Peter's, Oldham.

St James's, East Crompton: J. Littler.
St Bees' College. Evangelical.
Supported: CMS, CPAS.

St Thomas's, Leesfield: R. Whittaker.
St John's College, Cambridge. Evangelical.
Supported: CMS.
Opening sermon preached by W. Lees; Black Gown.

St John's, Chadderton: H Tull.
St Edmund Hall, Oxford. Evangelical.
Supported: CMS, CPAS.
Opening sermon preached by Hugh Stowell.

Holy Trinity, Coldhurst: J. Godson.
St Catharine's College, Cambridge. Evangelical.
Supported: CMS, CPAS, BFBS, RTS.
Opening sermon preached by Hugh Stowell.

St Thomas's, Werneth: T. Ireland.
Trinity College, Dublin. Evangelical.
Supported: CMS, CPAS, BFBS, RTS, Jews' Society.
Black Gown.

From 1850:
Christ Church, Friezland: T. Green.
Brasenose College, Oxford. Evangelical.
Supported: CMS, CPAS.
Specifically selected as an Evangelical by the patron.

Sources: MPL 09, St Chad's, Saddleworth, Parish Records; MPL L93, Box 9, Delph Branch Bible Society Minutes; RVR 1–62; Raines MSS; Butterworth Diary; Oldham BFBS Minutes; CC, file 45, 026, R. R. Whitehead to F. F. Whitehead, 12 Nov. 1844; Holy Trinity, Waterhead, MS History; St Michael's Tonge, MS History; Crockford *Clerical Directory* (1860); EA, *Annual Reports* (1847–61); CPAS, *Annual Reports* (1843–65); CMS, *Proceedings* (1846–65); *Manchester Guardian*, 6 Jan. 1844, 16 July 1845; *Manchester Courier*, 11 Feb. 1832; *Oldham Standard*, 24 Sept., 26 Nov. 1859, 4 May, 12 Oct. 1861; *Oldham Advertiser*, 3 Dec. 1853; Stephens, *Richard Durnford*; Grundy, 'G. D. Grundy'; Deem, *St Thomas*'; D. H. Price, *A Century of Church Life in Chadderton* (Oldham, 1957).

APPENDIX 3. *Occupational Classification*

    I. Industrial employer, manufacturer, banker, gentleman, master merchant. All group V and VI occupations linked with trade directories.

    II. Merchant, farmer, shopkeeper, publican, butcher, grocer, coal, corn, and waste dealer, master craftsman. All group IV occupations linked with trade directories.

    III. Minister, doctor, schoolmaster, book-keeper, postman, manager, surveyor, warehouseman.

    IV. Clogger, tailor, shoemaker, blacksmith, stonemason, iron and wood turner, shuttlemaker, spindle-maker, machine-maker, rope-maker, basket and brush-maker, brass and roller-filer, whitesmith, wheelwright, turner, sawyer, plasterer, joiner, slater, glazier, bricklayer, cordwainer, roller-turner, hairdresser, silk-weaver.

    V. Mechanic, engineer, moulder, spinner, overlooker, dresser, woolsorter, slubber, fireman, coalhewer, boiler-maker, cloth printer, finishers in the hat and wool trades.

    VI. Twiner, roller-twiner, foundryman, collier, weaver, forgeman, carder, reeler, spindle-stretcher, frame-tenter, tenter, stretcher, rover, clothier, dyer, fine-drawer, piecer, maker-up of twist, twister, stripper, roller coverer, woollen-cropper, warper, winder, cotton-feeder, sinker, hatter, polisher, banksman, delver, card-nailer, striper, limer.

    VII. Willower, breaker, labourer, navigator, carter, female servant, woman with no occupation.

Bibliography

I PRIMARY SOURCES

Manuscript

Chetham's College Library, Manchester
Raines MSS.
Raines Letter Collection.

Chester Record Office
Chester Diocesan Visitation Returns 1778, 1789, 1804, 1811, 1821, 1825.

Church of England Record Centre
Church Commissioners' Parish Files: Christ Church, Denshaw; Christ Church, Friezland; Christ Church, Glodwick; Holy Trinity, Coldhurst; Holy Trinity, Dobcross; Holy Trinity, Shaw; Holy Trinity, Waterhead; St Anne's, Lydgate; St Chad's, Saddleworth; St James's, Oldham; St James's, East Crompton; St John's, Chadderton; St John's, Hey; St Leonard's, Middleton; St Margaret's, Hollinwood; St Mary's, Birch; St Mary's, Oldham; St Matthew's, Chadderton; St Michael's, Tonge; St Paul's, Royton; St Peter's, Oldham; St Thomas's, Leesfield; St Thomas's, Werneth.
National Society School Files: Chadderton, St John; Hollinwood, St Margaret; Middleton, St Leonard; Oldham, Manchester St., Mumps, Primrose Bank, St Mary, St Peter, Werneth; Royton, St Paul; Saddleworth, Uppermill; Shaw, Holy Trinity.

John Rylands Library, Manchester
Rushton MSS.

Lambeth Palace Library
Incorporated Church Building Society Files: Christ Church, Glodwick; Holy Trinity, Coldhurst; Holy Trinity, Waterhead; St Chad's, Saddleworth; St James's, East Crompton; St John's, Chadderton; St John's, Hey; St Margaret's, Hollinwood; St Matthew's, Chadderton; St Paul's, Royton; St Thomas's, Leesfield; St Thomas's, Werneth.

Lancashire Record Office (Preston)
Lancashire Congregational Union Records.
Oldham Quaker Preparative Meeting Records.

Returns of the Numbers of Places of Worship not of the Church of England in Each Parish.

St Mary's Roman Catholic Church, Oldham, Baptism Register.

Microfilm: New Jerusalem Church, Wood Street, Middleton, Baptism Register; St Stephen's Countess of Huntingdon's Chapel, Baptism Register; Wesleyan Methodist Chapel, Middleton, Baptism Register; Wesleyan Methodist Chapel, Shaw, Baptism Register.

Manchester Public Library (Central)

Giles Shaw MSS.
Delph, Branch Bible Association Minutes.

Diary of Revd Henry Newcome, 1701–14.
Manchester Diocesan Registry Records.
Rushton Visitation Returns, vols. 1–62.
St Anne's, Lydgate, Parish Records.
St Chad's, Saddleworth, Parish Records.
St John's, Hey, Parish Records.
St Margaret's, Hollinwood, Parish Records.

Oldham, Methodist New Connexion Circuit Records.
Union Street, Methodist New Connexion Chapel Records.
Union Street, Methodist New Connexion Chapel Trust Treasurer's Accounts.
Werneth, Methodist New Connexion Chapel Records.
Bardsley, Primitive Methodist Chapel Records.
Henshaw Street, Primitive Methodist Chapel, Baptism Register.
Irk Street, Middleton, Primitive Methodist Chapel Records.
Lees Road, Primitive Methodist Chapel Records.
Oldham Primitive Methodist First Circuit Records.
Oldham Primitive Methodist Second Circuit Records.

Higginshaw, United Methodist Free Church, Sunday School Records.

Cowhill, Wesleyan Sunday School Records.
Delph, Wesleyan Chapel Records.
Greenacres, Wesleyan Methodist Chapel, Marriage Register.
Oldham Wesleyan Circuit Steward's Account Book.
Saddleworth, Wesleyan Circuit Records.
Uppermill, Wesleyan Chapel Records.

Methodist Archives and Research Centre

C. Hallam MS Circuit Book.
Derby Faith Secession Papers.
General Methodist Correspondence Collection.
MS Circuit Plans: Mr Farrar, 1798; J. Bunting, 1799.

Notes on the Early Days of Methodism in Oldham and District Compiled by Revd J. McOwan and sent to Revd J. Everett.
Primitive Methodist MS Conference Journals, 1827–69.
United Methodist Free Church MS Annual Assembly Minutes, 1857–66.
Wesleyan Association Annual Assembly Minutes, 1835–56.
Wesleyan Manchester District Meeting Minutes, 1825–66.

Oldham Local Interest Centre (now Oldham Local Studies Library)

Butterworth Diary, 1829–43.
Census Enumerator's Book, Royton 1821.
Gornall 'Secession to Rome', 1874.
Notes on Bellringing, 1808, 1819.
Notes on St James's, East Crompton.
Oldham British and Foreign Bible Society Auxiliary Minutes, 1813–53.
Rowbottom Diary, 1788–1830.
St Mary's, Oldham, Petition to the Bishop of Chester, 1840.
W. A. Westley, MS Notebook.

Microfilm: Population Census Enumerators' Books, Oldham and Saddleworth, 1841, 1851, 1861; Non-Parochial Registers; Parochial Registers; Subscription List, Delph Independent Chapel.

Public Record Office (Kew)

Religious Census MS Returns: Ashton-under-Lyne, Oldham, Saddleworth.

Uppermill Public Library (Saddleworth)

Hewkin MSS.

Collections of Parish Records were consulted at:

Christ Church, Friezland
Holy Trinity, Coldhurst
Holy Trinity, Shaw
Holy Trinity, Waterhead
St James's, East Crompton
St James's, Oldham
St Mary's, Oldham
St Michael's, Tonge
St Paul's, Royton
St Thomas's, Friarmere
St Thomas's, Leesfield

Collections of Non-Conformist Chapel Records were consulted at:

Bethesda Particular Baptist Church, Royton
Glodwick Baptist Church

King Street Baptist Church
Mills Hill Baptist Church, Chadderton

Delph Independent Church
Ebenezer Independent Church, Uppermill
Greenacres Independent Church
Providence Independent Church, Middleton

George Street Independent Methodist Church
Smith Street Independent Methodist Church

Salem Moravian Church

Parliamentary Papers

House of Lords

1818, xciii CP, Account of Benefices and Population, Churches, Chapels, and their Capacity; Number and Condition of Glebe Houses, and Income of all Benefices not exceeding £150 per annum.

House of Commons

1835, xxii (54), Report of the Commissioners appointed by His Majesty to Inquire into the Ecclesiastical Revenues of England and Wales.

1836, xliii (583), Return of all persons appointed to act as Justices of the Peace in each and every county in England and Wales.

1840, xli (484), Return of the names, addresses, and residences of Justices of the Peace, Ministers of the Established Church, now in the Commission of the Peace in the several counties in England and Wales.

1842, xvii [382], Appendix to the First Report of the Commissioners (Mines).

1842, xxii [31], Reports of the Inspectors of Factories for the half-year ending 31 December 1841.

1842, xxxiii (524), Return of all persons appointed to act as Justices of the Peace in each and every county in England and Wales since the 21 day of July 1836.

1849, xxi [1087], Appendix to the Ninth Annual Report of the Registrar General of Births, Deaths and Marriages in England.

1852–3, lxxxvi [1632], Census of Great Britain Population Tables.

1852–3, lxxxviii [1691–I], Census of Great Britain Population Tables.

1852–3, lxxxix [1690], Population (Great Britain) Religious Worship England and Wales.

1852–3, xc [1692], Census of Great Britain 1851, Education, England and Wales.

1863, xlviii (322), A Return of the number of Clergymen placed in the Commission of the Peace in the counties of England and Wales during the last twenty years.

1863, liii [3221], Population (England and Wales): Census of England and Wales (1861), Population Tables.

1864, xxii [3309], Reports of the Inspectors of Factories to Her Majesty's

Principal Secretary of State for the Home Department for the half-year ending 31 October 1863.

1872, lxvi [*c*.676–I], Census of England and Wales, 1871 Population Tables.

1873, liv (388), Nominal Return of all the Clerks in Holy Orders in the Commission of the Peace in any county in England or Wales.

Newspapers, Periodicals, and Other Serial Publications

Arminian Magazine
Baptist Magazine
British and Foreign Bible Society Proceedings
The Church Builder
Church Missionary Society Proceedings
Church Pastoral Aid Society Annual Reports
Church Pastoral Aid Society Quarterly Papers
Church Pastoral Aid Society Occasional Papers
Clergy List
Congregational Yearbook
Crockford's Clerical Directory
Evangelical Alliance Annual Conference Reports
Independent Methodist Conference Minutes
Independent Methodist Magazine
Lancashire and Cheshire Baptist Association Circular Letters
Lord Street Unitarian Chapel Calendar
Manchester Courier
Manchester Diocesan Directory
Manchester Guardian
Manchester Mercury
Methodist Magazine
Methodist New Connexion Conference Minutes
Methodist New Connexion Magazine
Middleton Parish Church Sunday School Annual Reports
Oldham Advertiser
Oldham Almanack and Yearbook
Oldham Chronicle
Oldham Free Press
Oldham Standard
Primitive Methodist Conference Minutes
Primitive Methodist Magazine
United Methodist Free Church Conference Minutes
United Methodist Free Church Magazine
Wesleyan Methodist Association Conference Minutes
Wesleyan Methodist Association Magazine
Wesleyan Methodist Conference Minutes

Wesleyan Methodist Magazine
Wheeler's Manchester Chronicle

Printed Primary Sources

[Place of publication is London unless otherwise stated.]

ALEXANDER, D. M., *Lay Co-operation in Oldham* (Oldham, 1863).

ANON., *Ashton Methodist New Connexion Circuit Plan* (Ashton-under-Lyne, 1832).

ANON., *George Street Independent Methodist Circuit Plan* (Oldham, 1860).

ANON., *George Street Independent Methodist Circuit Plan* (Oldham, 1861).

ANON., *Ninth Annual Report of Oldham Lycaeum* (Oldham, 1849).

ANON., *Oldham Church Rebuilding Accounts* (Oldham, 1834).

ANON., *Oldham Poll Book* (Oldham, 1835).

ANON., *Oldham Primitive Methodist Circuit Plan* (Oldham, 1852).

ANON., *Oldham United Methodist Free Church Circuit Plan* (Oldham, 1868).

ANON., *Oldham Wesleyan Methodist Association Circuit Plan* (Oldham, 1835).

ANON., *Oldham Wesleyan Methodist Circuit Plan* (Lees, 1819).

ANON., *Oldham Wesleyan Methodist Circuit Plan* (Ashton-under-Lyne, 1825).

ANON., *Oldham Wesleyan Methodist Circuit Plan* (Oldham, 1864).

ANON., *Parson Lo* (Oldham, n.d.).

ANON., *Preachers Plan Lord Street Oldham* (Oldham, 1835).

ANON., *Primitive Methodist Itinerant and Local Preachers Plan for the Oldham Circuit* (Oldham, 1852).

ANON., *Primitive Methodist Manchester Circuit Plan* (Bemersley, 1827).

ANON., *Primitive Methodist Sunday School Anniversary Service Sheet* (Oldham, 1844).

ANON., *Saddleworth Wesleyan Methodist Circuit Plan* (Uppermill, 1864).

AUTY, A., *Annie, Being a Faithful Account of the Life, Experience and Labours of Annie Auty, the Yorkshire and Lancashire Revivalist*, 4th edn. (1888).

BAINES, E., *History, Directory and Gazetteer of the County Palatine of Lancaster* (Liverpool, 1825).

BAMFORD, S., *Early Days* (1849).

——*Passages in the Life of a Radical* (Heywood, 1842).

——*Walks in South Lancashire* (1844; ed. J. D. Marshall, Hassocks, Sussex, 1972).

BENNETT, J. (ed.), *Lancashire Miscellany* (Oldham, 1980).

BLACKBURN, N., *Attachment to the World Lamented and a Throne of Grace Petitioned or the Distressed Saint Seeking Quickening Grace: A Sermon Preached in the Independent Chapel Delph* (Manchester, 1807).

BLOMFIELD, C. J., *A Charge Delivered to the Clergy of the Diocese of Chester at the Primary Visitation in August and September 1825* (1825).

BUMSTEAD, J., *Church Matters Past and Present in Oldham* (Oldham, 1853).

BUNN, H., *An Address to Communicants at the Lord's Table* (Kidderminster, 1848).

BUTTERWORTH, E., *Historical Notices of the Town and Parish of Middleton* (Middleton, 1840).

——*A Statistical Sketch of the County Palatine of Lancaster* (1841).

——*Historical Sketches of Oldham* (Oldham, 1856).

CHALMERS, T., 'Vindication of a Religious National Establishment, in Opposition to the Reasonings and Opinions of the Economists', in *Lectures on the Establishment and Extension of National Churches* (Glasgow, 1838).

CONGREGATIONAL UNION, *Religious Statistics of Eight Towns in South Lancashire* (Oldham, 1880).

DOW, L., *History of Cosmopolite: or, The Writings of Revd Lorenzo Dow: Containing his Experience and Travels in Europe and America* (Cincinatti, 1849).

EVANS, J., *Lancashire Authors and Orators* (Manchester, 1859).

GADSBY, J., *A Memoir of the Late Mr William Gadsby Compiled from Authentic Sources* (Manchester, 1844).

GRUNDY, G. D., *Episcopacy and the Three-fold Order of the Christian Ministry Proved to be both Apostolic and Primitive: A Lecture Given in St John's Schoolroom Hey* (1862).

HALBERT, C. E., *The Jubilee Celebration of the Charter of Incorporation* (Oldham, 1899).

Lancashire Congregational Union, *Annual Report* (Manchester, 1867).

LEE, J. P., *A Charge Delivered at his Second Visitation in December 1855 to the Clergy of the Diocese of Manchester* (1856).

LITTLER, J., *A Sermon Preached at the Opening of St James East Crompton* (Oldham, 1847).

NIELD, D., *Addresses to the Different Classes of Men in the Parish of Saddleworth* (1795; repr. Saddleworth, 1983).

OLIVER, A. C., *An Appeal to Christians in Oldham* (Oldham, 1852).

O'NEIL, C. A., *An Account of the Origin of Sunday Schools in Oldham and its Vicinity* (Oldham, 1848).

OWEN, E., *Jottings on the Rubrics for Morning and Evening Prayer* (Manchester, 1874).

PIGOT, J., AND SON *General, Classified and Street Directory of Manchester and Salford* (Manchester, 1838).

POPILIUS, *A Statement of Facts Relative to the Purchase of the Methodist Chapel at Middleton from the Old Connexion* (Manchester, 1806).

PORTEUS, B., *A Letter to the Clergy of the Diocese of Chester, Concerning Sunday Schools* (1786).

RAINES, F. R., 'Diary', *Oldham Chronicle*, 23 Jan.–27 Feb. 1926.

RANSOME, M. (ed.), *Wiltshire Returns to the Bishop's Visitation Queries 1783* (Devizes, 1972).

SHAW, G., *Local Notes and Gleanings*, ii (Oldham, 1888).

SLATER, I., *General and Classified Directory and Street Register of Manchester and Salford with their Vicinities* (Manchester, 1865).

STEPHENS, W. R. W., *A Memoir of Richard Durnford D.D.* (1899).

STEWART, A., and REVINGTON, G., *Memoir of the Life and Labours of the Revd Adam Averell* (1849).

STOWELL, H., and KEENE, A., *Two Sermons Preached in St John's Chadderton by A. Keene Together with a Biographical Sketch of the Author* (Oldham, 1863).

SUMNER, J. B., *A Charge Delivered to the Clergy of the Diocese of Chester at the Primary Visitation* (1829).

——*A Charge Delivered to the Clergy of the Diocese of Chester at the Triennial Visitation* (1832).

——*A Charge Delivered to the Clergy of the Diocese of Chester at the Triennial Visitation* (1835).

——*A Charge Delivered to the Clergy of the Diocese of Chester at the Triennial Visitation* (1838).

——*A Charge Delivered to the Clergy of the Diocese of Chester at the Visitation in 1841* (1841).

——*A Charge Delivered to the Clergy of the Diocese of Chester at the Triennial Visitation* (1844).

VENABLES, G., *St Patrick and the Church of Ireland: A Sermon Preached in Christ Church Friezland* (1866).

WADDINGTON, G. G., *A History of the Independent Church at Greenacres from its First Establishment down to the Present Date* (Manchester, 1854).

——*Historical and Biographical Notices* (Dewsbury, 1886).

WARD, W. R. (ed.), *The Early Correspondence of Jabez Bunting 1820–1829* (1972).

WHELLAN, W., *A New Alphabetical and Classified directory of Manchester and Salford* (Manchester, 1852).

WHITTAKER, R., *Sermon Preached at St Thomas' Leesfield* (Oldham, 1867).

——*Collected Sermons* (Oldham, 1868).

WRAY, J. J., *The Sabbath School Teacher: What he has to do and how to do it* (Oldham, 1857).

II CHURCH AND CHAPEL HISTORIES

[Place of Publication is Oldham unless otherwise stated.]

AIRNE, C. C. W., *St Anne's Lydgate: The Story of a Pennine Parish 1788–1988* (Saddleworth, 1988).

ALLEN, G., *Notes on Shaw Church in Byegone Days* (York, 1907).

ANDREW, S., *A History of Hey* (1905).

ANON., *Baptist Church and Sunday School Oldham Road Royton Jubilee Souvenir* (1911).

ANON., *Churches in Oldham* (volume of Newscuttings in OLIC).

ANON., *The Chapel in the Valley: The Centenary Handbook of Greenfield Methodist Church* (Uppermill, 1945).

ANON., *A Centenary History of King Street Independent Methodist Church Oldham* (n.p., 1954).

ANON., *Centenary History of Smith Street Sunday School* (1937).

ANON., *Centenary Souvenir of the Establishment of Independent Methodism in Oldham, 1816–1916* (1916).

ANON., *Friarmere Parish 1768–1968* (Uppermill, 1968).

ANON., *Historical Account of the Christian Brethren Chapel, Lees* (Lees, 1891).

ANON., 'Historical Sketch of Bethesda Baptist Chapel Royton', in *Handbook of the Church Bazaar* (1894).

ANON., *History of Failsworth Macedonia* (1825).

ANON., *History of Providence Congregational Church 1822–1972* (Middleton, 1972).

ANON., *History of St Stephen's Church, Middleton 1803–1938* (Middleton, 1938).

ANON., *Notes on the History of St Margaret's Church and Parish, Oldham* (1950).

ANON., *Our Lady of Mount Carmel and St Patrick, Oldham Centenary Souvenir* (Farnworth, 1958).

ANON., 'Queen Street Sunday School', in *Queen Street Sunday School Oldham Handbook of the Grand Bazaar and Fancy Fair* (1879).

ANON., 'Methodism in Oldham', in *Christian Journal*, 22 Apr. 1885.

ANON., 'St John's Methodist Church Hollins', in *Oldham Chronicle*, 27 May–2 June 1930.

ANON., *St Margaret's Church Hollinwood 1769–1969* (n.p., 1969).

ANON., *St Paul's Methodist Church Shaw* (Shaw, 1961).

ANON., *St Peter's, Middleton Centenary Souvenir* (Ashton-under-Lyne, 1967).

ANON., *These Fifty Years 1859–1909* (1909).

ANON., 'Wesley Chapel and Schools Greenacres Road Oldham Jubilee History', in *Souvenir of the Grand Springtime Bazaar* (1926).

ANON., *Wrigley Mill Wesleyan Chapel and Sunday School History and Jubilee Souvenir* (1914).

BALL, R. O., *One More Light: A History of Middleton Junction Methodist Church* (Wigan, 1951).

BATESON, H., *Early Days of Springhead Sunday School* (1930).

——*Providential Lives* (1957).

BESWICK, L. J., *History of the Village School Royton* (Royton, 1922).

BINTLEY, H., *A Brief History of Salem Moravian Church 1824–1974* (1974).

BRIDGE, A., and Lee, G., *Queen Street Congregational Church Oldham* (Bolton, 1921).

BUTTERWORTH, G. E., *Greenfield Methodist Church Jubilee Souvenir* (Manchester, 1932).

CHRISTIE, G. H., 'Werneth Church Oldham' *The Methodist Evangelist*, 1 Jan. 1898.

CLERWORTH, T. E., *A Sketch of the History of the Parish Church of St Leonard Middleton* (London, 1898).

CURLEY, T., *The Catholic History of Oldham* (Market Weighton, 1911).

DAVIES, R. M., 'History of Congregationalism in Oldham—Incidents in the History of Forty Years' Ministry', *Oldham Express*, 28 July 1883.

DEEM, S., *St Thomas' Church and Parish of Werneth 1844–1937* (1938).

E., *Historical Account of Providence Chapel* (Middleton, 1871).

FARNDALE, W. E., *The Story of Primitive Methodism in Lees* (1911).

FLETCHER, J., *Cowhill School 1849–1949* (Manchester, 1949).

GORE, G. P., *The Story of the Ancient Parochial Chapelry of St Mary's, Oldham* (1906).

GRUNDY, G. B., *Fifty-Five Years at Oxford An Unconventional Autobiography* (London, 1945).

GRUNDY, G. F., 'A Sketch of the Life of the Late Revd G. D. Grundy', in Andrew, S., *A History of Hey* (1905), 66–98.

HALL, W. H., *Delph Independent Sundy School Centennial Souvenir* (Delph, 1918).

HIGSON, C. E., 'Lees Chapel, otherwise Hey Chapel in Lees', *Transactions of the Lancashire and Cheshire Antiquarian Society*, 34 (1916), 179–200.

HIRST, L. W. M., *St Paul's Church Scouthead* (1967).

HOWCROFT, A. J., *The Chapelry and Church of Saddleworth and Quick* (1915).

——*Supplement to the History of the Chapelry and Church of Saddleworth* (1933).

HUDSON, E., 'History of Delph Methodism 1770–1850', *Oldham Chronicle*, Feb. 1902.

JONES, J., *A Century of Hope* (Perth, 1966).

JONES, P., *The Story of Hollinwood Congregational Church Oldham* (1951).

JONES, R., *A Short History of the Wesleyan Methodist Sunday-School Middleton* (Middleton, 1886).

LAWTON, J. J., *Ebenezer Congregational Church Uppermill: Church Memoirs* (Uppermill, 1923).

LEWIS, E., 'The Story of Dobcross Congregational Church', *Oldham Chronicle*, Aug. 1970.

MANSLEY, J. D., 'Queen Street Church Looks Back 100 Years', *Oldham Chronicle*, 22 Oct. 1955.

MARCROFT, A., *A Historical Account of the Unitarian Chapel Oldham* (1913).

MARRAT, J., *A Centenary Memorial or Brief Record of the Origins and Progress of the Wesleyan Sunday Schools in Oldham and the Neighbourhood* (1885).

MAXWELL, R. B., *A Brief History of the Royton Congregational Church* (Royton, 1961).

MOUNTFIELD, A., *A Short History of Independent Methodism* (Wigan, 1905).

N., 'A Century of Methodism at Hollins', *Oldham Chronicle*, 8–21 May 1937.

NIGHTINGALE, B., 'Independency a Century Ago', *Oldham Chronicle*, 2–9 Aug. 1919.

NORCROSS, J. J., *Brunswick Wesleyan Chapel* (1912).

OWEN, E., *A Brief History of the Church and Parish of St Peter's Oldham* (1868).

PACKER, I., *The Moravian Church Westwood 1865–1965* (Royton, 1965).

PRICE, D. H., *A Century of Church Life in Chadderton* (1957).

RICHARDSON, S., *On Zion's Hill* (Rochdale, 1965).

SELLERS, U., *A Short History of the Wesleyan Sunday School, Shaw* (Shaw, 1911).

SEVILLE, T., 'Historical Note', in *Official Handbook to the Grand Bazaar* (1896).

SMITH, F., and WILDE, J., *Springhead Congregational Chapel Centennial Souvenir 1807–1907* (1907).

SMITH, W. J., *A Brief History and Description of the Parish Church of St Leonard's Middleton* (Gloucester, 1970).

STOCKWELL, A. H., *The Baptist Churches of Lancashire* (London, 1910).

TAYLOR, W., *Jubilee Souvenir of the Oldham Friends First Day School* (1915).

UPRIGHT, W., *The Story of Primitive Methodism in Washbrook* (1916).

VERITY, J., *Primitive Methodist Chapel Bowlee Jubilee Souvenir and Historical Sketch* (Middleton, 1914).

WALKER, W., *Builders of Zion* (London, 1914).

WARD, J., *A Retrospect of the Oldham Meeting of the Society of Friends, its Schools and Kindred Societies* (1911).

WATKINS, J. P., 'A Brief History of Greenacres Chapel', in *Greenacres Tercentenary Yearbook* (1972).

WESTLEY, W. A., 'The Position Occupied by St Peter's Schools in the History of Education in Oldham', *Oldham Chronicle*, 1936.

——*A Brief History of St John's Chadderton* (1945).

WHITEHEAD, S., 'The Rise and Progress of Methodism in Glodwick', in *Handbook of the Grand Bazaar in the Town Hall Oldham* (1884).

WRIGGLESWORTH, M. (ed.), *There is Holy Ground: A History of Methodism in Middleton 1760–1850* (n.p., 1950).

III SECONDARY SOURCES (UNPUBLISHED)

ALBERS, J. M., 'Seeds of Contention: Society, Politics and the Church of England in Lancashire 1689–1790', Ph.D. thesis (Yale, 1988).

BARNES, B., 'The Upper Tame Valley', BA thesis (Manchester, 1957).

BURNS, R. A., 'The Diocesan Revival in the Church of England c.1825–1865', D.Phil. thesis (Oxford, 1990).

CHADWICK, R., 'Church and People in Bradford and District', D.Phil. thesis (Oxford, 1986).

CRAGOE, M., 'The Tory and Anglican Gap in Welsh Historiographical Perceptions: The Case of Carmarthenshire 1832–1886', D.Phil. thesis (Oxford, 1990).

FOSTER, J. O., 'Capitalism and Class Consciousness in Earlier Nineteenth Century Oldham', Ph.D. thesis (Cambridge, 1967).

LEBARBOUR, A. M. P., 'Victorian Baptists: A Study of Denominational Development', Ph.D. thesis (Maryland, 1977).

LEWIS, D. M., 'The Evangelical Mission to the British Working Class', D.Phil. thesis (Oxford, 1981).

MAYNARD, W. B., 'The Ecclesiastical Administration of the Archdeaconry of Durham 1774–1856', Ph.D. thesis (Durham, 1973).

NEWTON, D., 'Aspects of Historical Geography in the Saddleworth Area', BA thesis (Durham, 1971).

NOCKLES, P. B., 'Continuity and Change in Anglican High Churchmanship in Britain 1792–1850', D.Phil. thesis (Oxford, 1982).

PARRY, T. V., 'The Incorporated Church Building Society 1818–1851', M. Litt. thesis (Oxford, 1984).

ROBISON, O. C., 'The Particular Baptists in England 1760–1820', D.Phil. thesis (Oxford, 1963).

RYCROFT, P., 'Church, Chapel, and Community in Craven 1764–1851', D.Phil. thesis (Oxford, 1988).

SMITH, M. A., 'Religion in Industrial Society: The Case of Oldham and Saddleworth 1780–1865', D.Phil. thesis (Oxford, 1987).

WARD, C. E., 'Education as Social Control: Sunday Schools in Oldham 1780–1850', MA thesis (Lancaster, 1975).

WESTON, G. A., 'The Baptists of North-West England 1750–1850', Ph.D. thesis (Sheffield, 1969).

WOLFFE, J., 'Protestant Societies and Anti-Catholic Agitation in Great Britain 1829–1860', D.Phil. thesis (Oxford, 1984).

IV SECONDARY SOURCES (PUBLISHED)

[Place of Publication is London unless otherwise stated.]

ANDERSON, M., *Family Structure in Nineteenth Century Lancashire* (Cambridge, 1971).

ARCHBISHOP of CANTERBURY's COMMITTEE on URBAN PRIORITY AREAS, *Faith in the City: A Call for Action by Church and Nation* (1985).

BALLARD, E., *A Chronicle of Crompton* (Crompton, 1967).

BARNES, B., 'Early Woollen Mills in a Penine Parish: Saddleworth and the Upper Tame Valley', *Bulletin of the Saddleworth Historical Society*, 13 (1983), 24–56.

BARRY, J., 'The Parish in Civic Life: Bristol and its Churches 1640–1750', in Wright, S. J. (ed.), *Parish Church and People: Local Studies in Lay Religion 1350–1750* (1988), 152–178.

BATESON, H., *A History of Oldham* (Oldham, 1949).

BEBBINGTON, D., *Evangelicalism in Modern Britain* (1989).

BERG, M., *The Age of Manufactures* (1985).

BEST, G. F. A., *Temporal Pillars: Queen Anne's Bounty, the Ecclesiastical Commissioners, and the Church of England* (Cambridge, 1964).

BINFIELD, C., 'Thomas Binney and Congregationalism's Special Mission', *Transactions of the Congregational Historical Society*, 21 (1971), 1–10.

——*So Down to Prayers: Studies in English Nonconformity 1780–1920* (1977).

——'The Place of Family in a Felt Religion', *Journal of the United Reformed Church Historical Society*, 2 (1978), 2–9.

BRIERLEY, M., *Outlines of the History of Saddleworth* (Manchester, 1883).

BROSE, O. J., *Church and Parliament: The Reshaping of the Church of England 1828–1860* (1959).

BROWN, C. G., *The Social History of Religion in Scotland since 1730* (1987).

——'Did Urbanization secularize Britain?', *Urban History Yearbook* (1988), 1–14.

——'Religion, Class and Church Growth', in Fraser, W. H., and Morris, R. J. (eds.), *People and Society in Scotland* ii (Edinburgh, 1990) 310–35.

BROWN, K. D., *A Social History of the Nonconformist Ministry in England and Wales 1800–1930* (Oxford, 1988).

BROWN, R., *Church and State in Modern Britain 1700–1850* (1991).

BROWN, S. J., *Thomas Chalmers and the Godly Commonwealth in Scotland* (Oxford, 1982).

CALHOUN, C., *The Question of Class Struggle* (Oxford, 1982).

CARPENTER, S. C., *Eighteenth Century Church and People* (1959).

CARTER, H., *The Study of Urban Geography*, 3rd edn. (1981).

CARWARDINE, R., *Transatlantic Revivalism: Popular Evangelicalism in Britain and America 1790–1865* (Westport, Conn., 1978).

CHADWICK, W. O., *The Victorian Church*, 3rd edn., 2 vols. (1971).

—— *The Secularization of the European Mind in the Nineteenth Century* (Cambridge, 1975).

CHALKIN, C. W., 'The Financing of Church Building in the Provincial Towns of Eighteenth Century England', in P. Clark (ed.), *The Transformation of English Towns 1600–1800* (1984), 284–310.

CHRISTIE, I. R., *Stress and Stability in Late Eighteenth Century Britain* (1984).

CLARK, D., *Between Pulpit and Pew* (1982).

CLARKE, B. F. L., *The Building of the Eighteenth Century Church* (1963).

CONYBEARE, W. J., 'Church Parties', *Edinburgh Review*, 98 (1853), 273–343.

COX, J., *The English Churches in a Secular Society: Lambeth, 1870–1930* (Oxford, 1982).

CROSSICK, G., (ed.), *The Lower Middle Class in Britain* (1977).

CURRIE, R., *Methodism Divided* (1968).

——GILBERT, A., and HORSLEY, L., *Churches and Church-Goers* (Oxford, 1977).

DAVIES, R. E., and RUPP, E. G. (eds.), *A History of the Methodist Church in Great Britain*, i (1965).

——GEORGE, A. R., and RUPP, E. G. (eds.), *A History of the Methodist Church in Great Britain*, ii (1978).

DELL, R. J., 'Social and Economic Theories and Pastoral Concerns of a Victorian Archbishop', *Journal of Ecclesiastical History*, 16 (1965), 196–208.

DENNIS, R., 'Intercensal Mobility in a Victorian City', *Transactions of the Institute of British Geographers*, NS 2 (1977), 349–63.

—— *English Industrial Cities of the Nineteenth Century: A Social Geography* (Cambridge, 1984).

ELBOURNE, R., *Music and Tradition in Early Industrial Lancashire 1780–1840* (Woodbridge, 1980).

FARNIE, D. A., *The English Cotton Industry and the World Market 1815–1896* (Oxford, 1979).

—— 'The Emergence of Victorian Oldham as the Centre of the Cotton Spinning Industry', *Bulletin of the Saddleworth Historical Society*, 12 (1982), 41–53.

FOSTER, J. O., *Class Struggle and the Industrial Revolution Early Industrial Capitalism in Three English Towns* (1974).

GADIAN, D. S., 'Class Consciousness in Oldham and other North-West Industrial Towns 1830–1850', *Historical Journal*, 21 (1978), 161–72.

—— 'Class Formation and Class Action in North-West Industrial Towns, 1830–1850', in Morris, R. J. (ed.), *Class Power and Social Structure in British Nineteenth Century Towns* (Leicester, 1986), 23–66.

GASH, N., *Aristocracy and People: Britain 1815–1865* (1979).

GILBERT, A. D., *Religion and Society in Industrial England: Church, Chapel and Social Change 1740–1914* (1976).

——— *The Making of Post-Christian Britain* (1980).

GILL, R., *The Myth of the Empty Church* (1993).

GILLEY, S., 'Official Religion', in Thomas, T. (ed.), The British: Their Religious Beliefs and Practices, 1800–1986 (1988), 19–47.

GINSWICK, J. (ed.), *Labour and the Poor in England and Wales 1849–1851* (1983).

GLEN, R., *Urban Workers in the Early Industrial Revolution* (1984).

GOLDHAWK, N. P., 'The Methodist People in the Early Victorian Age: Spirituality and Worship', in Davies, R. E., George, A. R., and Rupp, E. G. (eds.), *A History of the Methodist Church in Great Britain*, ii (1965), 113–42.

GOWLAND, D. A., *Methodist Secessions: The Origins of Free Methodism in Three Lancashire Towns* (Manchester, 1979).

HAIG, A., *The Victorian Clergy* (1984).

HARRISON, J. F. C., *The Second Coming: Popular Millenarianism 1780–1850* (1979).

HEENEY, B., *A Different Kind of Gentleman* (Hamden, Conn., 1976).

HEMPTON, D., *Methodism and Politics in British Society 1750–1850* (1984).

——— 'Methodism in Irish Society 1770–1830', *Transactions of the Royal Historical Society*, 5th ser. 36 (1986), 117–42.

——— and HILL, M., *Evangelical Protestantism in Ulster Society 1740–1890* (1992).

HILTON, B., *The Age of Atonement* (Oxford, 1988).

HOWE, A., *The Cotton Masters 1830–1860* (Oxford, 1984).

HOWSE, E. M., *Saints in Politics* (1953).

HYLSON SMITH, K., *Evangelicals in the Church of England 1734–1984* (Edinburgh, 1989).

INGLIS, K. S., 'Patterns of Religious Worship in 1851', *Journal of Ecclesiastical History*, 11 (1960), 74–86.

——— *Churches and the Working Classes in Victorian England* (1963).

ISICHEI, E., *Victorian Quakers* (Oxford, 1970).

JEREMY, D. J. (ed.), *Dictionary of Business Biography*, iv (1985).

JONES, R. T., *Congregationalism in England 1662–1962* (1962).

JOYCE, P., *Work, Society and Politics* (Hassocks, Sussex, 1980).

——— 'Labour Capital and Compromise: A Response to Richard Price', *Social History*, 9 (1984), 67–76.

KENDALL, H. B., *The Origin and History of the Primitive Methodist Church*, ii (1906).

KENT, J., 'The Wesleyan Methodists to 1849', in Davies, R. E., George, A. R., and Rupp, E. G. (eds.), *A History of the Methodist Church in Great Britain*, ii (1978), 213–75.

KIRK, N., *The Growth of the Working-Class Reformation in Mid-Victorian England* (1985).

——— 'Traditional Working-Class Culture and the Rise of Labour: Some Preliminary Questions and Observations', *Social History*, 16 (1991), 203–16.

KODITSCHEK, T., *Class Formation and Urban-Industrial Society: Bradford 1750–1850* (Cambridge, 1990).

LANGFORD, P., *A Polite and Commercial People: England 1727–1783* (Oxford, 1989).

LAQUEUR, T. W., *Religion and Respectability: Sunday Schools and Working-Class Culture 1780–1850* (New Haven, Conn., 1976).

LEES, L. H., *Exiles of Erin* (1979).

LEWIS, D. M., *Lighten their Darkness; The Evangelical Mission to Working-Class London 1828–1860* (Westport, Conn., 1986).

LINEHAM, P., 'Restoring Man's Creative Power: The Theosophy of the Bible Christians of Salford', *Studies in Church History*, 19 (1982), 207–23.

LOVEGROVE, D. W., 'Particular Baptist Itinerant Preachers during the Late Eighteenth and Early Nineteenth Centuries', *Baptist Quarterly*, 28 (1979), 127–41.

——*Established Church, Sectarian People: Itinerancy and the Transformation of English Dissent 1780–1830* (Cambridge, 1988).

LUKER, D., 'Revivalism in Theory and Practice: The Case of Cornish Methodism', *Journal of Ecclesiastical History*, 37 (1986), 601–19.

MACHIN, G. I. T., *Politics and the Churches in Great Britain 1832–1868* (Oxford, 1977).

McKIBBIN, R., *The Ideologies of Class: Social Relations in Britain 1880–1950* (Oxford, 1990).

McLACHLAN, H., *The Methodist Unitarian Movement* (Manchester, 1919).

MACLAREN, A. A., *Religion and Social Class: The Disruption Years in Aberdeen* (1974).

McLEOD, H., *Class and Religion in the Late Victorian City* (1974).

——'White Collar Values and the Role of Religion', in Crossick, G., *The Lower Middle Class in Britain* (1977), 61–88.

——*Religion and the People of Western Europe* (Oxford, 1981).

——*Religion and the Working Class in Nineteenth-Century Britain* (1984).

——'New Perspectives on Victorian Working-Class Religion: The Oral Evidence', *Oral History Journal*, 14 (1986), 31–49.

—— 'The "Golden Age" of New York City Catholicism', in Garnett, J., and Matthew, C., *Revival and Religion Since 1700* (1993).

McPHILLIPS, K., *Oldham, the Formative Years* (Swinton, 1981).

MALCOLMSON, R. W., *Life and Labour in England 1700–1780* (1981).

MALMGREN, G., 'Domestic Discords: Women and the Family in East Cheshire Methodism 1750–1830', in Obelkevich, J., Roper, L., and Samuel, R. (eds.), *Disciplines of Faith* (1987), 55–70.

MARTIN, D., *The Religious and the Secular* (1969).

——*A General Theory of Secularization* (Oxford, 1978).

MARTIN, R. H., *Evangelicals United: Ecumenical Stirrings in Pre-Victorian Britain 1795–1830* (Metuchen, NJ, 1983).

MATHER, F. C., 'Georgian Churchmanship Reconsidered: Some Variations in Anglican Public Worship 1714–1830', *Journal of Ecclesiastical History*, 36 (1985), 255–82.

MAYFIELD, D., and THORNE, S., 'Social History and its Discontents: Gareth Stedman Jones and the Politics of Language', *Social History*, 17 (1992), 165–88.

MAYNARD, W. B., 'Pluralism and Non-Residence in the Archdeaconry of Durham

1774–1856: The Bishop and Chapter as Patrons', *Northern History*, 26 (1990), 103–30.

—— 'The Response of the Church of England to Economic and Demographic Change: The Archdeaconry of Durham, 1800–1851', *Journal of Ecclesiastical History*, 42 (1991), 437–62.

MEACHAM, S., 'The Church in the Victorian City, *Victorian Studies*, 11 (1967–8), 359–78.

MOORHOUSE, H. F., 'The Marxist Theory of the Labour Aristocracy', *Social History*, 3 (1978), 61–82.

MORRIS, J., 'Church and People Thirty-Three Years On: A Historical Critique', *Theology*, 94 (1991), 92–101.

—— *Religion and Urban Change: Croydon 1840–1914* (Woodbridge, 1992).

MORRIS, R. J., *Class and Class Consciousness in the Industrial Revolution 1780–1850* (1979).

—— *Class, Sect and Party: The Making of the British Middle Class, Leeds: 1820–50* (Manchester, 1990).

—— (ed.), *Class, Power and Social Structure in British Nineteenth-Century Towns* (Leicester, 1986).

MURRAY, A., 'Missionaries and Magic in Dark-Age Europe', *Past and Present*, 136 (1992), 186–205.

MUSSON, A. E., 'Class Struggle and the Labour Aristocracy 1830–1860', *Social History*, 1 (1976), 335–66.

NORMAN, E., *The English Catholic Church in the Nineteenth Century* (Oxford, 1984).

OBELKEVICH, J., *Religion and Rural Society: South Lindsey 1825–1875* (Oxford, 1976).

—— 'Music and Religion in the Nineteenth Century', in Obelkevich, J., Roper, L., and Samuel, R. (eds.), *Disciplines of Faith* (1987), 550–65.

O'DAY, R., 'The Clerical Renaissance in Victorian England and Wales', in Parsons, G. (ed.), *Religion in Victorian Britain* i (Manchester, 1988), 184–212.

PARSONS, G., 'From Dissenters to Free-Churchmen: The Transitions of Victorian Nonconformity' in Parsons, G. (ed.), *Religion in Victorian Britain* i (Manchester, 1988), 67–116.

—— 'Liberation and Church Defence: Victorian Church and Victorian Chapel', in Parsons, G. (ed.), *Religion in Victorian Britain* ii (Manchester, 1988), 147–65.

—— 'A Question of Meaning: Religion and Working-Class Life', in Parsons, G. (ed.), *Religion in Victorian Britain* ii (Manchester, 1988), 63–87.

—— 'Reform, Revival and Realignment: The Experience of Victorian Anglicanism', in Parsons, G. (ed.), *Religion in Victorian Britain* i (Manchester, 1988), 14–66.

—— 'Victorian Roman Catholicism: Emancipation, Expansion and Achievement', in Parsons, G. (ed.), *Religion in Victorian Britain* i (Manchester, 1988), 146–83.

PERKIN, H., *The Origins of Modern English Society 1780–1880* (1969).

PICKERING, W. S. F., 'The 1851 Religious Census—A Useless Experiment?', *British Journal of Sociology*, 18 (1967), 382–407.

POOLE, R., 'Oldham Wakes', in Walton, J. K., and Walvin, J. (eds.), *Leisure in Great Britain 1780–1939* (Manchester, 1983), 72–98.

POOLEY, C. G., 'Residential Mobility in the Victorian City', *Transactions of the Institute of British Geographers*, NS 4 (1979), 258–77.

PORT, M. H., *Six Hundred New Churches: The Church Building Commissioners, 1818–1856* (1961).

PROCHASKA, F. K., *Women and Philanthropy in Nineteenth Century England* (Oxford, 1980).

RACK, H. D., 'Domestic Visitations: A Chapter in Early Nineteenth Century Evangelism', *Journal of Ecclesiastical History*, 34 (1973), 357–76.

——*Reasonable Enthusiast* (1989).

ROBERTS, E., *Working-Class Barrow and Lancaster 1890 to 1930* (Lancaster, 1976).

ROBINSON, W. G., *A History of the Lancashire Congregational Union 1806–1956* (Liverpool, 1955).

ROYLE, E., *Radical Politics 1790–1900: Religion and Unbelief* (1971).

——*Victorian Infidels* (Manchester, 1974).

——*Modern Britain: A Social History 1750–1985* (1987).

RULE, J., 'Methodism, Popular Beliefs and Village Culture in Cornwall 1800–1850', in Storch, R. (ed.), *Popular Culture and Custom in Nineteenth Century England* (1982), 48–70.

——*The Labouring Classes in Early Industrial England 1750–1850* (1986).

RUSSELL, A., *The Clerical Profession* (1980).

SAMUEL, R. (ed.), *People's History and Socialist Theory* (1981).

SELLERS, I., *Nineteenth Century Nonconformity* (1977).

SEMMEL, B., *The Methodist Revolution* (1974).

SMITH, M. A., 'The Reception of Richard Podmore: Anglicanism in Saddleworth 1700–1830', in Walsh, J. D., Haydon, C., and Taylor, S. (eds.), *The Church of England c.1689–c.1833 From Toleration to Tractarianism*, 110–23.

SNELL, K. D. M., *Church and Chapel in the North Midlands: Religious Observance in the Nineteenth Century* (Leicester, 1991).

SPAETH, D. A., 'Common Prayer? Popular Observance of the Anglican Liturgy in Restoration Wiltshire', in Wright, S. J. (ed.), *Parish Church and People: Local Studies in Lay Religion 1350–1750* (1988), 125–51.

STEDMAN JONES, G., 'Class Struggle and the Industrial Revolution', *New Left Review*, 90 (1975), 35–69.

STORCH, R. (ed.), *Popular Culture and Custom in Nineteenth Century England* (1982).

SYKES, N., *Church and State in England in the Eighteenth Century* (Cambridge, 1934).

SYKES, R. A., 'Some Aspects of Working-Class Consciousness in Oldham 1830–1842', *Historical Journal*, 23 (1980), 167–79.

SWIFT, R., and GILLEY, S. (eds.), *The Irish in the Victorian City* (1985).

TAYLOR, J. H., 'The Bicentenary of 1662', *Transactions of the Congregational Historical Society*, 19 (1960), 18–25.

——'The Survival of the Church Meeting, 1691–1901', *Transactions of the Congregational Historical Society*, 21 (1971), 31–44.

THOMAS, T. (ed.), *The British: Their Religious Beliefs and Practices, 1800–1986* (1988).

THOMPSON, D., 'The Religious Census: Problems and Possibilities', *Victorian Studies*, 11 (1967), 87–97.

——(ed.), *Nonconformity in the Nineteenth Century* (1972).

THOMPSON, E. P., *The Making of the English Working Class*, 2nd edn. (1968).

THOMPSON, K. A., *Bureaucracy and Church Reform: The Organisational Response of the Church of England to Social Change, 1800–1965* (Oxford, 1970).

TOON, P., *The Emergence of Hyper-Calvinism in English Nonconformity, 1689–1765* (1967).

TURNER, C. B., 'Revivalism and Welsh Society in the Nineteenth Century', in Obelkevich, J., Roper, L., and Samuel, R. (eds.), *Disciplines of Faith* (1987), 311–22.

URDANK, A. M., *Religion and Society in a Cotswold Vale: Nailsworth, Gloucestershire 1780–1865* (Los Angeles, 1990).

VALENZE, D., *Prophetic Sons and Daughters* (Princeton, NJ, 1985).

VICKERS, J., *A History of Independent Methodism* (Bolton, 1920).

VIRGIN, P., *The Church in an Age of Negligence* (Cambridge, 1989).

WADSWORTH, A. P., and MANN, J. L., *The Cotton Trade and Industrial Lancashire 1600–1780* (Manchester, 1937).

WALKER, R. B., 'Religious Changes in Cheshire, 1750–1850', *Journal of Ecclesiastical History*, 17 (1966), 77–84.

WALSH, J. D., 'Methodism at the End of the Eighteenth Century', in Davies, R. E., and Rupp, E. G. (eds.), *A History of the Methodist Church in Great Britain*, i (1965), 275–315.

——'Methodism and the Mob in the Eighteenth Century', *Studies in Church History*, 8 (1972), 213–29.

——'The Anglican Evangelicals in the Eighteenth Century', in M. Simon (ed.), *Aspects de l'Anglicanisme* (Paris, 1974), 87–102.

——'Religious Societies: Methodist and Evangelical 1738–1800', *Studies in Church History*, 23 (1986), 279–302.

——HAYDON, C., and TAYLOR, S. (eds.), *The Church of England c.1689–c.1833* (Cambridge, 1993).

WALTON, J. K., and POOLE, R., 'The Lancashire Wakes in the Nineteenth Century', in Storch, R. (ed.), *Popular Culture and Custom in Nineteenth Century England* (1982), 100–24.

WALTON, J. K., and WALVIN, J. (eds.), *Leisure in Great Britain 1780–1939* (Manchester, 1983).

WALVIN, J., *English Urban Life 1776–1851* (1984).

WARD, W. R., 'The Cost of Establishment: Some Reflections on Church Building in Manchester', *Studies in Church History*, 3 (1966), 277–89.

——*Religion and Society in England 1790–1850* (1972).

——'Swedenborgianism: Heresy, Schism or Religious Protest', *Studies in Church History*, 9 (1972), 303–9.

—— 'The Baptists and the Transformation of the Church 1780–1830', *Baptist Quarterly*, NS 25 (1973), 167–84.

WARNE, A., *Church and Society in Eighteenth Century Devon* (Newton Abbott, 1969).

WATTS, M. R., *The Dissenters* (Oxford, 1978).

WEAVER, S. A., *John Fielden and the Politics of Popular Radicalism 1832–1847* (Oxford, 1987).

WERNER, J. S., *The Primitive Methodist Connexion* (Madison, Wis., 1984).

WHITELY, W. T., *The Baptists of North West England 1649–1913* (1913).

WICKHAM, E. R., *Church and People in an Industrial City* (1957).

WILD, M. T., 'The Saddleworth Parish Registers', *Textile History*, 1 (1969), 214–32.

WILLIAMS, V. O., 'The Platts of Oldham: A Chapter in the History of a Caernarvonshire Parish', *Transactions of the Caernarvonshire Historical Society*, 18 (1957), 75–88.

WILSON, B. R., 'Aspects of Secularization in the West', *Japanese Journal of Religious Studies*, 3/4 (1976), 259–81.

—— *Religion in Sociological Perspective* (Oxford, 1982).

WINSTANLEY, M. J., *The Shopkeeper's World 1830–1914* (Manchester, 1983).

—— 'Oldham Radicalism and the Origins of Popular Liberalism', *Historical Journal*, 36 (1993), 619–43.

WRIGHT, S. J., 'Confirmation, Catechism and Communion: The Role of the Young in the Post Reformation Church', in Wright, S. J. (ed.), *Parish, Church and People: Local Studies in Lay Religion 1350–1750* (1988), 203–28.

WRIGLEY, A., *Saddleworth Superstitions and Folk Customs* (Oldham, 1909).

WRIGLEY, J., *The Rise and Fall of the Victorian Sunday* (Manchester, 1980).

YATES, N., *Buildings, Faith and Worship* (Oxford, 1991).

Index